RELIGION IN VICTORIAN BRITAIN

VOLUME I
TRADITIONS

RELIGION IN VICTORIAN BRITAIN

VOLUME I
TRADITIONS

EDITED BY
GERALD PARSONS
AT THE
OPEN UNIVERSITY

MANCHESTER UNIVERSITY PRESS
MANCHESTER AND NEW YORK
IN ASSOCIATION WITH THE
OPEN UNIVERSITY
DISTRIBUTED EXCLUSIVELY IN THE USA AND CANADA
BY ST. MARTIN'S PRESS

Published by Manchester University Press
Oxford Road, Manchester M13 9NR, UK
and Room 400, 175 Fifth Avenue, New York, NY 10010, USA

Distributed exclusively in the USA by St. Martin's Press, Inc.,
175 Fifth Avenue, New York, NY 10010, USA

Reprinted 1991, 1995, 1997

British Library cataloguing in publication data
Religion in Victorian Britain.
Vol. 1: Traditions
I. Great Britain, Christian church, 1837–1901
I. Parsons, Gerald II. Open University 274.1'081

Library of Congress cataloging in publication data
Religion in Victorian Britain.
Includes bibliographies and index.
Contents: v. 1. Traditions — v. 2. Controversies —
v. 3 Sources — [etc.]
1. Great Britain — Church history — 19th century.
2. Great Britain — Religion. 3. Great Britain —
Religious life and customs. I. Parsons, Gerald.
BR759.R43 1988 274.1'081 88-12359

ISBN 0 7190 2511 7 *paperback*

This book forms part of an Open University course AA313 *Religion in Victorian Britain*. For information about this course please write to the Student Enquiries Office, The Open University, PO Box 71, Walton Hall, Milton Keynes, MK7 6AG, UK

Typesetting information
This book is set in 10 point Baskerville
Typeset in Hong Kong
Printed in Great Britain
by Biddles Ltd, Guildford and King's Lynn

CONTENTS

PREFACE

This book is one of a five-volume series entitled *Religion in Victorian Britain*, published by Manchester University Press in association with the Open University. The five volumes form the nucleus of an Open University Course. Volumes I and II, *Traditions* and *Controversies* (edited by Gerald Parsons, 1988), consist of sets of specially written essays covering the major religious denominations and groups of the Victorian period and the issues and controversies between and within them. Volume III, *Sources* (edited by James R. Moore, 1988), is a collection of primary source material from the period, while Volume IV, *Interpretations* (edited by Gerald Parsons, 1988), is a collection of recent essays and articles in the field by other writers. Volume V, *Culture and Empire* (edited by John Wolffe, 1997), provides a new and important expansion of the first four volumes. It contains both specially written essays and primary source material, and explores the wider context of religion in Victorian Britain.

References to other volumes in the series are made in the following style:

RVB, II, 4 (*Religion in Victorian Britain*, Volume II, *Controversies*, chapter 4), or

RVB, III, 1.2 (*Religion in Victorian Britain*, Volume III, *Sources*, item 1.2)

The authors wish to acknowledge the essential contribution made to the production of these volumes by a number of other members of Open University staff: Gillian Kay, Staff Tutor in History, for her comment and criticism, Barbara Humphreys and Wendy Clarke (secretaries), Jenny Cook (course manager), Tony Coulson (Library), Pam Higgins (Design Studio), and Jonathan Hunt (Publishing).

The authors would also like to thank Professor John Kent of the University of Bristol for his careful and constructive comments on first drafts of their essays. Each of the authors has benefited from Professor Kent's criticism and observations: needless to say, any questionable judgements which remain are the responsibility of the authors alone.

The authors are all members of staff of the Faculty of Arts at the Open University:

Michael Bartholomew, Staff Tutor in the History of Science and Technology

David Englander, Lecturer in European Humanities

Antony Lentin, Reader in History

James R. Moore, Lecturer in the History of Science and Technology

Gerald Parsons, Lecturer in Religious Studies

Rosemary O'Day, Senior Lecturer in History

Terence Thomas, Staff Tutor in Religious Studies

Recommended Further Reading

Books and articles particularly recommended for further reading are marked with an asterisk in the bibliographies at the end of each chapter.

Illustration Sources

The sources for the illustrations reproduced in this book are as follows: front cover, *Punch* 17.9.92; Introduction, *Punch* 24.2.66; Ch. 1, *Punch* 10.5.79; Ch. 2, *Punch* 20.5.72; Ch. 3, *Punch* 13.5.80; Ch. 4, *Punch* 25.10.62; Ch. 5, *Punch* 9.11.95; Ch. 6, *Punch* 24.10.68; Ch. 7, *Illustrated London News* 1.2.1900; Ch. 8, *The Freethinker* 28.5.82 and 9.7.82.

Acknowledgement

The authors gratefully acknowledge their thanks to the British Library of Political and Economic Science at the London School of Economics for permision to reproduce material in the Booth Collection in Chapter 7.

INTRODUCTION

THE BATTLE OF THE RUBRIC.

ARCHBISHOP OF CANTERBURY. "MY FRIENDS! MY FRIENDS! YOU'LL DESTROY THAT GOOD OLD BOOK OF-PRAYER BETWEEN YOU."

VICTORIAN RELIGION: PARADOX AND VARIETY

THE essays in this book comprise the first of a set of four volumes which together make a self-standing series on *Religion in Victorian Britain*. The present volume focuses, as its title indicates, on major religious *Traditions* in Victorian Britain.

The authors also recognize, of course, the inevitable interaction and interrelationship between the various traditions. The inclusion of two essays (one on the varieties of Victorian revivalism and the other on the clergy of various denominations) which deliberately deal with several traditions at once, and also the presence of cross-references to other essays, make such interdependence clear. Nevertheless, the principal concern of this volume is the history and development of particular religious and, indeed, anti-religious groups and denominations in Victorian Britain.

The second volume in the series, sub-titled *Controversies*, also consists of a collection of individual essays. The focus, however, is rather different in that volume, where each essay addresses a particular issue or controversy in Victorian religious life and approaches it from a perspective which encompasses the viewpoints and experiences of a variety of traditions, denominations and groups.

The third and fourth volumes in the series, entitled *Sources* and *Interpretations*, provide, respectively, a collection of primary sources for the study of religion in Victorian Britain and a selection of recent studies of aspects of Victorian religion by historians other than those responsible for the writing and compilation of the present series.

The initial and principal aim of the authors of these collections of original essays and the compilers of the anthologies of primary and secondary sources has been the provision of a coherent and integrated body of material for use by Open University students studying a course on *Religion in Victorian Britain*. The two volumes of original essays are thus designed primarily as text-books, for the use of Honours level undergraduates. The volumes of primary and secondary sources are, accordingly, designed to support that enterprise by supplying a representative variety of contemporary Victorian documents and historical evidence, and a number of examples of scholarly articles and essays characteristic of recent developments in the academic study of the role and significance of religion in Victorian Britain.

Although thus originally designed with a quite specific purpose in mind, however, it is also intended that both the four-volume series and, in particular, the first two volumes of original essays, will possess a much wider appeal and relevance. On the one hand, it is hoped that the series as a whole will provide a core of essential material for the study and teaching of the history of religion in Victorian Britain in institutions other than the Open University. On the other hand, the authors of the first two volumes of essays have also attempted to provide not only a pedagogically orientated body of information concerning religion in Victorian Britain, but also an interpretation and overview of the subject itself.

With this in mind the various authors have written as individuals, each adopting and presenting his or her own particular standpoint and approach both to the subject as a whole and to the specific topic of any given essay. At the same time, however, all the authors have written with certain agreed aims and objectives in mind. Thus, each author has sought to supply simultaneously, an introduction to the specific topic of each essay, a survey and assessment of the principal developments within the given topic during the Victorian period, and an interpretation of the significance of the subject of the essay in relation to Victorian religious life as a whole. In so doing, each author has also attempted both to engage with and synthesize the results of recent and current research and scholarship in the field concerned.

The authors have also sought to avoid *both* a narrow and conventional concentration on 'church history' or the portrayal of Victorian religion as essentially a matter of ecclesiastical institutions and theological ideas, *and* the alternative of an over-reaction and consequent over-concentration on the social history of Victorian religion to the exclusion of the still relevant and essential denominational, institutional, and theological aspects of the subject. The essays therefore reflect the conviction that an adequate understanding of the history and significance of religion in Victorian Britain requires a combination of both the insights and perspectives of 'conventional' denominational, institutional and theological history, and those of the more recent trend towards the study of Victorian religion primarily through its social, cultural, intellectual and political context. In short, there is an underlying assumption that if churches, theologies and religious beliefs cannot properly be understood apart from their social and cultural context, neither can they or their context properly be understood without taking the churches, theologies, and beliefs seriously in their own right.

The present volume on *Traditions* reflects rather more of the traditional, institutional, approach. The second volume on *Controversies*, on the other hand, tends more towards the social and cultural history of Victorian religion. That said, the distinction in question is relative, not absolute, and elements of both approaches will be found in each volume.

Each individual essay is a complete and integral unit in itself, designed to address a particular topic and supply a self-standing statement and interpretation of its subject. At the same time, since the same themes and issues occur in several different essays, inevitably and quite properly, individual essays frequently refer to other essays in the two volumes. Similarly, particular topics are dealt with directly in more than one essay — but are thus addressed from significantly different perspectives. Thus, for example, in the present volume the role of the courts in the conflicts between various factions within the Victorian Church of England is discussed briefly as part of the overall history and development of the Church of England in the Victorian period, whilst in the second volume the same topic is discussed in more detail as part of an examination of the changing relationship between the state and religion in Victorian Britain. Similarly, the Disruption of the Church of Scotland in 1843 appears in this volume as an aspect of the history of Scottish Presbyterianism, and in the second volume as a further case study in church-state relations. Or again, the controversies in various churches over the rise of biblical criticism are mentioned in several of the essays in the present volume and are then the subject of an essay in their own right in the second volume. Thus, whilst each volume and each essay is an entity in itself, the overall value and impact of each will be greater if read in the context of the larger project of which they are a part.

The example of Scottish Presbyterianism and the Disruption of 1843 highlights another common objective. The authors have been conscious of the tendency for accounts of Victorian religion to be, in practice, accounts of religion in Victorian England — with the history of religion in Victorian Scotland, Ireland and Wales receiving at best no more than occasional attention. The present collection of essays on major religious traditions in Victorian Britain, together with its companion volume on controversies, and the supporting anthology of primary sources, seeks to avoid an exclusively English focus and convey, instead, a genuinely British perspective on Victorian religious life and thought.

There is no attempt to supply a neatly uniform interpretation of Victorian religion and its place, role and significance in Victorian society. The essays reflect a number of different interpretative standpoints and methodological perspectives. Nevertheless, it is possible to identify, from the evidence presented, a number of common themes and notable similarities between different traditions within Victorian religious life. It is also, however, inescapably clear that there are notable exceptions to virtually any given similarity or common theme thus identified. This should hardly cause surprise. Not the least of the virtues of historical study in general is its capacity to confound the convenient tidinesses of over-neat interpretation by demonstrating the stubborn intractability of the surviving evidence of the behaviour and significance of equally intractable, stubborn, and unique human beings. It is a not uncommon theme in the essays in the first two volumes of this series that received wisdom — both scholarly and 'popular' — concerning the history of religion in Victorian Britain frequently fails to take account of the intriguing (and sometimes baffling and inconvenient) diversity in Victorian religious life.

II

How far, then, is it possible to identify common themes and important similarities and differences between the various religious traditions examined in the present volume of essays? The observations which follow below do not constitute an exhaustive list of such themes, similarities and differences. They are, rather, an attempt to identify the more significant of such, and to set the collection of essays within an overall context.

The over-arching theme which most readily suggests itself is that of paradox. Victorian religion at once presents us with a profoundly and fundamentally paradoxical and ambiguous combination of crisis and confidence, faith and doubt, revival and decline.

That Victorian Britain was, indeed, a society remarkable for the extent and intensity of its religious life is barely open to question. Any serious doubt in the matter may be removed not only by consideration of the vitality and diversity of religious activity among the Victorians themselves, but also by comparison with the centuries which preceded and succeeded their era.

The intensity of the Evangelical and Methodist revivals notwithstanding, the eighteenth century was, religiously speaking, a less passionate, more restrained era than its nineteenth-century — and especially Victorian — successor. The predominance of the Moderate party in the Church of Scotland, the genteel and gentle piety of the *Garden of the Soul* tradition in English Catholicism, the undemonstrative piety of eighteenth-century Anglicanism, and the gently declining ethos of the Old Dissenting tradition prior to the Evangelical Revival, were characteristic of the essentially 'cool' religious outlook of the majority in the eighteenth century. The significance of the eighteenth-century Evangelical and Methodist revivals is so great precisely because they represented such a marked contrast to the predominant religious style and ethos.

Similarly, although historians and sociologists may debate the precise degree and meaning of the secularity or the residual religiousness of twentieth-century Britain (and a good case can be made for religion remaining more significant than many commentators customarily assume), no-one would seriously consider describing twentieth-century Britain as a notably religious society.

Viewed within the context of the contrasting centuries before and after it, the religious confidence and vitality of the Victorian age stand out. In absolute terms numbers of churchgoers continued to rise throughout the period, although relative to the growth of the population most churches had begun to lose ground by about 1880. It is true, of course, that such increases reflected the rapid growth of the population itself, but they also represented a remarkable effort and vitality on the part of the churches in bringing so many of an expanding population within the orbit of their activities and in providing facilities and pastoral oversight for them: for the increases in the number of church and chapel buildings and in the number of clergy were no less striking.

For example, between the mid-1830s and 1901 the Church of England built over 5,500 new churches and increased the number of its parish clergy by 11,000. In Scotland the combined efforts of the Church of Scotland and the Free Church between 1843 and 1901 resulted in over 1,800 new churches and 1,700 more ministers. The Primitive Methodists increased the number of their ministers by 500 and the Wesleyans by 1,200 between the 1830s and 1900. The Congregationalists built 1,500 new churches between 1856 and 1900.[1] To such figures must then be added the building of mission halls and of schools. The scale of increase of both buildings and professionals in its turn reflected the extent to which the various churches had developed increasingly efficient and sophisticated denominational structures, administrations and bureaucracies.

Alongside the churches and their full-time ministries, Victorian religious life also produced and sustained a rich and at times bewildering diversity of voluntary societies and agencies. Temperance societies such as the United Kingdom Alliance, the Band of Hope Movement, or the Church of England Temperance Society; Home and Overseas Missionary Societies; societies for the distribution of religious literature such as the Religious Tract Society or the S.P.C.K.; the Lord's Day Observance Society; the Girls' Friendly Society; the Y.M.C.A.; the Saint Vincent de Paul Society; societies for church defence such as the English Church Union or the Church Defence Institution; societies for the promotion of dissenters' rights such as the Liberation Society; societies such as the Church Association or the Protestant Truth Society for the defence of Protestantism and the organization of opposition to both Anglo- and Roman Catholicism: a simple list could be extended for several pages.

Such societies and agencies were a reflection of the vitality and passion of Victorian religious life. On the one hand they reflected, quite simply, the missionary zeal of the age: the mission to the 'heathen' overseas was matched by the mission to the 'unchurched masses' of the urban environment at home. And the mission to the unchurched urban masses was itself comprised of two distinct but related parts: there was, of course, the straightforward mission to convert, but alongside it there was the mission to 'civilize' and 'improve' by providing avenues for education, self help and 'respectable' recreation.

On the other hand, many of the societies reflected the combativeness, aggression, and militancy of much of Victorian religious life. Not only was Victorian religion militant and assertive in its attacks upon disbelief, 'infidelity' and indifference to religion — whether in the form of middle-class intellectual doubt and criticism of orthodox Christianity, articulate working-class radicalism and atheism, or the general working-class absence

[1] The figures quoted in this paragraph are taken from Currie, Gilbert and Horsley, 1977.

from organized religion — it was also militant and combative in its internal life and relations. Evangelical Protestants campaigned against both Roman Catholics and Anglo-Catholics (whom they saw as papists in Anglican guise); Dissenters fought for their rights against an establishment which fought to retain its privileges; orthodox Christian believers (evangelical and catholic, high church and low) fought liberal believers as they sought to adjust their theology to the moral, historical and scientific insights of the age. In a twentieth century accustomed to the ecumenical orthodoxy that strength is to be found in co-operation, it is sometimes difficult to appreciate the extent to which the vigorous and sometimes bitter conflicts between Victorian Christians were in some respects an indication of the vitality of Victorian Christianity rather than the reverse.

That vitality was also reflected in the sheer quantity and variety of religious literature produced by the various churches and religious societies of Victorian Britain. The scale of such publishing was remarkable. The Religious Tract Society, for example, produced as many as 33 million items a year during the 1860s; and in 1841 the Wesleyan Methodist Book Room issued 1,300,000 items (Scott, 1973, p. 217). Or, again, it has been pointed out that whereas in 1770 there were only a handful of religious magazines, by 1870 religious periodicals and newspapers could be numbered in hundreds. By 1870, the same author observes, most influential religious groups had their own penny weekly press (Billington, 1986, pp. 113 and 131).

The nature of the religious life fostered and sustained by all these structures, organizations and activities was also notable for its broadly, and often intensely, subjective and experiential quality. All the major Christian traditions — evangelical, catholic and liberal, Anglican, Protestant Nonconformist, Roman Catholic and Scots Presbyterian — increasingly emphasized the experiential element of their religious life. Worship generally became more liturgical and more participatory, more colourful, more musical and more aesthetically developed. Hymns became central to the worship and piety of every major tradition. Organ accompaniment became equally common.

The forms of personal piety fostered by the various traditions also encouraged an experiential, subjective style of religion. Even where doctrine remained 'orthodox' — as in revivalist Protestantism or Ultramontanist Catholicism — there was a distinct tendency to base the maintenance of orthodoxy upon an intensity of experience and emotion rather than upon an intellectual apprehension of a doctrinal system. Liberals and Broad Churchmen also shared — if less dramatically — in the emphasis on the subjective and experiential. The tendency, both among contemporaries and among historians, to concentrate upon their intellectual objections to orthodoxy often obscures the extent to which they protested against orthodoxy, not only because they found it irrational or at odds with modern knowledge, but also because they considered it an arid objectification of a religion which was essentially a matter of feeling, relationship and experience. The concept of the 'religion of the heart' was not the exclusive property of evangelicals: though differently conceived, it was equally the property of a variety of theological liberals.

Similarly, in Victorian Judaism there was the intense devotionalism and piety of the *chevroth* founded by East European immigrants, for whom the devotional options on offer in the existing Anglo-Jewish establishment were not sufficient. Even in Victorian secularism and agnosticism the experiential element was important. The religious forms adopted by secularism — its use of hymns and its formation of secular societies sometimes resembling nonconformist chapels in style and ethos — and the moral, even religious, intensity with which many freethinkers, atheists and agnostics espoused their cause suggest a more than merely intellectual commitment.

Victorian Britain was, therefore, a profoundly religious society. On the other hand, however, no account or characterization of Victorian religion would be adequate which failed to attach *equal* significance to the various manifestations of crisis and decline in the religious life and institutions of the nation.

At the intellectual level Victorian Christianity faced a combination of distinct yet interrelated moral, historical and scientific challenges. The moral critics of traditional Christian doctrine asked whether hell, substitutionary atonement, or many of the Old Testament stories were suggestive of a genuinely moral deity. Growing awareness of critical historical methods posed questions concerning the nature and status of the biblical text. The discoveries and theories of scientists, especially in the fields of geology and natural history, posed challenges to traditional understandings of the Bible, to notions of miracle, and to the whole concept of a creation designed and superintended by a benevolent and purposive creator.

Such intellectual challenges were not merely posed to the churches by critics from without. Indeed, the sharpest and most traumatic aspect of such criticisms and questions was the fact that, from mid-century onwards, the questions and challenges came from within as much as from without. As would-be loyal and committed church members — and often prominently placed clergy — themselves began to ask whether traditional Christian doctrine was either fully credible or tolerably moral, every major tradition experienced tensions and went through crises in respect of the relationship of traditional belief to modern knowledge and contemporary perceptions of morality.

Controversies over belief were by no means the only signs of crisis in the religious life of Victorian Britain, however. The failure of the churches to convert, in large numbers, the urban unchurched, on whom they expended so much missionary energy and effort, haunted Victorian Christianity. By 1900, moreover, concern was beginning to grow that even the churchgoing middle classes were becoming more lukewarm in their religious observance and belief, and increasingly prone to regarding involvement in church or chapel not as the central commitment in life but rather as one of a number of 'leisure' activities.

If religion was thus beginning to occupy a less central place in the lives even of the churchgoing middle classes, it also occupied, by the end of the Queen's reign, a less central place in the political and social life of the nation. Between, roughly, 1828 and 1880 religion and politics had been intimately related in British political life, and throughout the Victorian period the churches' commitment to the 'civilizing mission' had made them the principal source of social welfare provision. After 1880, however, it began to become clear that religion was no longer so central in national political life: many of the religious issues which had dominated mid-century politics had either been resolved or had lost their urgency, whilst issues of class and society were becoming increasingly central in national politics. And by the end of the first decade of the twentieth century the combination of state provision of education, increasing local government responsibility for local public welfare, and the welfare reforms of the 1906 Liberal government had signalled the coming end of the churches' predominance over the provision of social welfare. The beginning of the age of professional and secular social service, though not yet fully operational, was at hand.[2]

III

How is the essential paradox of Victorian religious life as at once vital yet insecure, confident yet in crisis, reflected in the essays which follow? Whilst the essays (for the most part) deal with particular religious traditions or denominations, it is instructive to note the extent to which significant similarities and differences between traditions begin to emerge. Three broad themes illustrate the process.

At the level of structures and institutions it is striking that in every one of the essays which follow some reference is made to the importance of the reform, revival or establishment of adequate administrative and organizational structures in the life of the various groups dealt with. Bishop Blom-

[2] The speed and extent of the transition in social welfare provision must not be exaggerated. As Brian Harrison has observed, the decline of the 'traditional' Victorian philanthropic ideal should not be either over-stated or ante-dated: voluntary philanthropy remained (and still remains) an important social phenomenon. But, as Harrison also notes, by 1900 philanthropy was losing its plausibility as an overall solution to national social problems, whilst much of the philanthropy which remained was becoming more secular. (Harrison, 1982, pp. 237–8 and 256–9). Both developments tended to undermine the churches' existing self-understanding of their social role.

field and the Ecclesiastical Commission in the Church of England; the emergence and consolidation of Nonconformist denominational structures and the role of organizational leaders such as Bunting, Wells and Hinton; the organizational genius of Thomas Chalmers in both the Church of Scotland and the Free Church; the administrative and organizational talents of Roman Catholic cardinals such as Wiseman, Manning, Cullen and Eyre; the rise of the professional revivalist and the systematic organization of missions and revivals; the development of effective institutional expressions of clerical opinion; the centralizing role of both Nathan and Hermann Adler in the Anglo-Jewish community; and the organizing talents of Holyoake and Bradlaugh in the development of Victorian Secularism: all of these illustrate the institutional vitality characteristic of Victorian religious life and, incidentally, demonstrate the continuing importance of the study of Victorian religious institutions.

The essays also reflect both the turn to the experiential and the subjective, and the internal crises over doctrine and orthodoxy noted above. Here, however, the essays reveal significant differences as well as similarities. As far as similarities are concerned, two are characteristic of all the broad traditions dealt with. First, each in one way or other, as suggested above, was characterized by a deeply experiential dimension. Second, all of the essays which follow illustrate very clearly that the essential variety and diversity of Victorian religion was not only a matter of competing denominations: the variety and diversity was internal to each tradition as well. Each major tradition was made up of a variety of internal traditions: High, Low and Broad church Anglicans; Baptist, Congregationalist and Methodist Nonconformists (and further divisions among them); Evangelical and Moderate Scots Presbyterians; traditional English, Scottish and Irish Catholics and new-style Ultramontanists; assimilated middle-class Jewry and fiercely traditional working-class immigrant Jewry; radical and aggressive freethought and atheism, and genteel, tentative, agnosticism.

Thirdly, the essays which follow also illustrate a further paradox of Victorian religious life, namely, that whilst missionary zeal, religious vitality and theological controversy led some groups to sharpen their doctrinal identities, the same combination of zeal, vitality and controversy caused some entire denominations to retreat from theologically specific positions and accept the existence of a *de facto* doctrinal pluralism within their ranks.

Thus, whereas in both England and Ireland in the eighteenth and early nineteenth centuries Catholic-Protestant relations were not generally hostile and were sometimes even positively co-operative, the rival zeal of Evangelical Protestants and Ultramontane Catholics in the Victorian period put an end to such peaceful co-existence. Similarly, in the Church of England, Tractarian-Evangelical rivalry put an end to genuine doctrinal consensus, and then orthodox-liberal controversy further fragmented Anglicanism, just as it created parties within most Nonconformist denominations and in the various branches of Scottish Presbyterianism. Only in Roman Catholicism was there a fully determined resistance to the development of such internal doctrinal pluralism. The doctrinal stance of late Victorian Roman Catholicism remained traditional, conservative and clear. The doctrinal stances of most other major denominations, on the other hand (taken as a whole, as opposed to doctrinally specific parties within them), were by then generally on the way to becoming matters of studied ambiguity. Ecclesiastical pragmatism and the need to preserve denominational unity made such imprecision a necessity.

IV

If Victorian religious life was thus characterized so strongly by *both* confidence *and* crisis, *both* vitality *and* decline, why in the twentieth century have crisis and decline so predominated and confidence and vitality been in such short supply?[3]

In a discussion of the decline of organized religion in post-Victorian Britain which is refreshing for its steady insistence that such decline was not inevitable, Jeffrey Cox has observed that, by 1900, 'A century of intellectual disarray had been accompanied by the growth of liberal theology and by a massive institutional revival' (Cox, 1982, p. 273). Cox's own detailed interpretation of the causes of twentieth-century decline in British religious life remains, as yet, a hypothesis awaiting further testing. His juxtaposition of 'intellectual turmoil' and 'institutional revival' is, however, a perceptive one, and one, moreover, which bears directly upon the essays in this volume. The accounts of major traditions in Victorian religious life which follow do indeed suggest the prevalence of precisely such a combination of massive institutional revival alongside a deep and ongoing theological turmoil.

Quite how far and how precisely the rank and file of any church at any time actually believe specifically what their church's doctrinal statements say they should believe is a pertinent if difficult question. What seems clear, in the Victorian context, however, is that most of the churches themselves became (or were obliged to become) less precise and less specific in their interpretation of their own doctrinal standards. The intellectual challenges of the age, and the development by some believers of a liberal theological response to those challenges, had made the preservation of doctrinal and theological precision impossible, or possible only at the cost of institutional schism or theological repression of a kind and on a scale which most

[3] Many of the themes and issues identified, briefly, in the following paragraphs are dealt with in more detail in essays in *RVB*, II.

denominations were unwilling to contemplate.

The result was a tendency to broader and more permissive interpretations of the limits of acceptable belief within a given church — plus the occasional furore when a particular liberal statement went too far or was expressed too clearly and therefore excited the protests of the still orthodox. Three quarters of a century later the sense of intellectual turmoil has become somewhat greater, the bounds of belief have been stretched somewhat further, and occasional flurries of controversy continue to occur. The basic pattern, however, has changed barely at all. That it has not suggests something of the complexity of the problem which the Victorian churches faced.

In intellectual and theological life, then, the Victorian churches experienced profound challenge and ongoing turmoil and passed on both to their twentieth-century successors. What then of the institutional revival? By 1900 it, too, was beginning to encounter a crisis of identity not unlike the theological crisis of identity which was already long established.

The urban working classes, to whom so much of the effort and energy of the institutional revival had been directed, were not persuaded to adopt the habit of regular churchgoing and denominational commitment. Much of the middle-class churchgoing backbone of Victorian Christianity also began to adopt a more relaxed attitude towards religion. The social welfare role which had been so prominent in Victorian church life began to be addressed by secular agencies. The controversies between establishment and dissent which had lent passion to the religious-political struggles of mid-century were largely over — Nonconformists, especially, found that the passing of such controversies removed something of their Dissenting rationale. Similarly, as freethought became respectable and prosecution for blasphemy less likely, organized secularism declined, its passion reduced by the liberty granted to its opinions.

Increasingly aware that regular churchgoing (despite three-quarters of a century of home missionary zeal and institutional revival) remained the activity of a minority of the population; conscious that secular agencies and the state were increasingly beginning to provide social welfare and education; and faced with the fact that religion was no longer firmly at the centre of either the nation's political agenda or the lifestyle of the middle classes, the churches entered the twentieth century on the verge of a period of profound soul-searching as to their role in society.

Such soul-searching, like the theological turmoil with which the churches were already familiar, remains on the agenda some eighty-odd years later. To understand the condition of the churches and the nature of the religious life of contemporary Britain, one of the prerequisites is to understand something of the Victorian origins from which both spring. The chapters which follow are essays towards such an understanding.

BIBLIOGRAPHY

L. Billington (1986) 'The religious periodical and newspaper press, 1770–1870' in M. Harris and A. Leigh (eds.) *The Press in English Society from the Seventeenth to the Nineteenth Centuries*, pp. 113–32, Madison (NJ), Fairleigh Dickinson University Press.

J. Cox (1982) *The English Churches in a Secular Society: Lambeth, 1870–1930*, Oxford, Oxford University Press.

R. Currie, A. Gilbert and L. Horsley (1977) *Churches and Churchgoers: Patterns of Church Growth in the British Isles Since 1700*, Oxford, Oxford University Press.

B. Harrison (1982) 'Philanthropy and the Victorians' in *Peacable Kingdom: Stability and Change in Modern Britain*, pp. 217–59, Oxford, Oxford University Press.

P. Scott (1973) 'The business of belief: the emergence of "religious" publishing' in D. Baker (ed.) *Sanctity and Secularity: The Church and the World*, pp. 213–24, Oxford, Blackwell.

CHAPTER 1

HEDGING.

RECTOR. "AND WHAT ARE YOUR VIEWS?"
CANDIDATE FOR CURACY. "WELL, SIR, I'M AN EVANGELICAL HIGH CHURCHMAN OF LIBERAL OPINIONS."

REFORM, REVIVAL AND REALIGNMENT: THE EXPERIENCE OF VICTORIAN ANGLICANISM

In late 1832 informed observers of contemporary British political and religious events seriously contemplated the possibility that the Church of England was in imminent danger of ceasing to be the established church of the English, Irish and Welsh nations and that its administrative, pastoral and financial arrangements might be subjected to far-reaching reform by a Parliament composed of political and religious radicals opposed to the privileged position of the Church of England in national life and indeed to its very status as a National Church. Such thoughts of disestablishment were not wholly implausible.

In 1828 the Test and Corporation Acts had been repealed. The Acts, dating from the reign of Charles II, had obliged holders of public offices to be members of the Church of England. In practice, Nonconformists had long been enabled to hold public office by virtue of Indemnity Acts setting aside, but not repealing, the penalties involved in the Test and Corporation Acts. The repeal thus made little practical impact, but it was a powerful symbol of both the growing influence of Nonconformity and a changing attitude towards religious establishment. A year later in 1829 the Roman Catholic Relief Act was passed and Roman Catholics were placed on the same legal and civil footing as Nonconformists after the 1828 repeal. In the Catholic case the act involved practical as well as symbolic change, but the most significant aspect of the two Acts together was the clear signal that, in the emerging urban, industrial society of nineteenth-century Britain, the relationship between religion and public life was changing. Private religion was not to be a bar to public office. Personal belief was not to determine political and social rights. In such a context the nature and meaning of an established church must also be brought into question: the established relationship of church and state might still remain in place but could not remain unchanged.

To this was added, in 1830, the fall of a Tory Government (the Tories being the traditional allies of the churchmen and upholders of the established position of the Church of England) and the accession to power of a Whig Government (the Whigs being the traditional allies of the Dissenters and Nonconformists). Moreover, between 1830 and 1832 political attention focused upon the struggle to pass a Parliamentary Reform Act which would much increase the power of the Whig-Dissenting-Nonconformist tradition. The passing of the Reform Act in 1832 thus brought with it the possibility that a radical and reforming Parliament might be returned in which Dissenters and Nonconformists would have a major voice, and in which a highly Utilitarian spirit would prevail. Such a Parliament would bode ill for an established church whose administrative, pastoral and financial arrangements were known to be at best inefficient, at worst chaotic and riddled with abuses and injustices. Thus, Richard Whately, newly appointed Archbishop of Dublin, ventured the opinion that whatever turn events took there was nothing that would bode well for the church establishment; its days, he feared, were numbered. Thomas Arnold, headmaster of Rugby School, observed that 'the church as it now stands no human power can save'; and *The Times*, in an editorial, spoke of the establishment of the Church of England being in serious peril, a peril which became hourly more imminent (References in Chadwick, 1971, p. 47).

By the end of the nineteenth century, however, the prospects of the Church of England had taken on an altogether healthier appearance. Mandell Creighton, eminent historian and bishop successively of Peterborough and London, could reflect at the close of the century upon the position of the Church of England in the heyday of empire and observe that 'the Church of England has before it the conquest of the world. We can only succeed if we gird up our loins with the assurance that the future is ours'. The Church of England, Creighton maintained, had unique and unparalleled opportunities as a missionary agency and the relationship between church and state was 'fruitful of great promise for the future' (quoted in Bowen, 1968, p. vii).

The prospect of the end of establishment itself, so clearly perceived in 1832, had indeed disappeared. True, in 1869 the Church of Ireland had been disestablished, and the disestablishment of the Church in Wales was soon to come. But in England, despite some fifty years of militant Nonconformist pressure between 1832 and 1880, the issue of disestablishment had ceased to be practical politics. By the 1880s even the Liberation Society, the chief organ of Nonconformist pressure on the establishment between 1844 and 1880, was a spent force.

The contrast, then, is a striking one. It can, of course, be overstated. By 1840 it was already clear that the more apocalyptic visions of 1832 were unfounded. The reformed Parliament had not swept away the religious establishment and a steady process of reform had changed the Church of England from within. Equally, however, serene optimism such as Creighton's was not unchallenged; the Church of England at the beginning of the twentieth century faced turbulent controversy from within and a variety of challenges from without.

Allowing such qualification, however, the contrast remains and is central to the history of the Victorian Church of England. The Church of England of 1832 was a church in danger, under threat and quite unequipped for ministry to an emerging urban, industrial society. The Church of England of 1900 was under no threat from the state, had made immense (if still inadequate) progress in reforming its life to address the conditions of modern British society and was, thanks largely to the growth of empire, the centre of an increasingly world-wide communion.

The conventional view of this contrast is that the history of the Victorian Church of England is essentially a history of revival and that the roots of the revival are to be found preeminently in the Oxford Movement and the steady rediscovery of the Catholic heritage of the Church of England. Indeed, as Nigel Yates has recently observed, in older histories of the Oxford Movement the impression was often given that every reform in the Victorian Church of England, and every pastoral or theological advance, was the result of the Oxford Movement and its legacy (Yates, 1983, p. 36). This, as Yates himself adds, is absolute nonsense. But it is nonsense with an extraordinarily tenacious and persistent influence. Accounts of the Victorian Church of England remain remarkably attached to an interpretation which is centred on the notion of revival and the crucial role of the Oxford Movement in that revival. That revival and the importance of the Oxford Movement are essential elements in the history of the Victorian Church of England can hardly be denied. To give them undue priority, however, is to neglect the importance of other equally fundamental trends. It is also to miss the complexity of the transformation which occurred not only in the fortunes but also in the nature of the Church of England between 1830 and 1900.

The present essay seeks to achieve both a balance and a sense of this complexity by exploring the thesis that the transition which occurred between 1830 and 1900 was simultaneously a process of reform, revival, and re-alignment: reform of the structure, organization and administration of the Church of England; revival of its spiritual, theological, pastoral and liturgical life; and re-alignment of both its internal structure and its relationship to (and place within) national life and the religious community of the nation as a whole. The essay will argue that in each of four broad areas of its life — the administrative-pastoral, the doctrinal-theological, the liturgical-ceremonial, and the national-constitutional — the Victorian Church of England experienced a fundamental change amounting to a minor revolution.

I THE ADMINISTRATIVE AND PASTORAL REVOLUTION

Churchmen had good cause in 1832 to fear that a radical and reforming Parliament might impose sweeping reforms upon the Church of England. Such reforms were long overdue. As Olive Brose observed in a classic study of the relationship between Church and Parliament between 1828 and 1860, the need for internal reform of the established church was analogous to the need for parliamentary reform (Brose, 1959, p. 7). The analogy is apposite. Parliament had ceased to be even remotely representative of the political realities of early nineteenth-century Britain. The unreformed parliamentary system was not only grossly inequitable in its exclusion from political power of the new urban, industrial middle class, but was also subject to appalling abuses and to simple inefficiency — many parliamentary seats, for example, representing underpopulated (or even depopulated) areas of the country whilst new centres of population remained wholly unrepresented in Parliament.

The Church of England in 1832 bore a striking resemblance to this state of affairs. Most obviously, the Church of England of 1832 paralleled the unreformed Parliament in the mismatch between the geographical location of its human, financial and physical resources, and the growing centres of population in early nineteenth-century Britain. The diocesan and parochial system had remained virtually unchanged for over 500 years. During that period the population had not only expanded but had concentrated in greatly enlarged, and in some cases new, urban centres. The diocesan and parochial arrangements of the church took no account of such demographic changes, however, and thus new or vastly expanded towns and cities existed without remotely adequate pastoral oversight or church accommodation.[1] The financial arrangements of the Church of England reflected the same problem: the wealth, or poverty, of a diocese bore no relation to its size and population. The classic case was Chester, where one of the largest and poorest dioceses included within its boundaries both Liverpool and Manchester. Some dioceses were also impossibly large and administratively unwieldy, which invited, and frequently resulted in, chaotic, lax or infrequent arrangements in such matters as the conduct of confirmations and visitations.[2]

Close behind the problem of the location of resources came the problem of abuses and inequalities. The inequalities noted above were not only absurdly inappropriate and unsuited to the needs of a changing, increasingly urban, industrial society, but were also unjust in themselves and thus bred abuses. At the diocesan level episcopal incomes varied immensely: the ten wealthiest sees had an average annual income of £11,634 and the wealthiest of all an income of £22,305; but the average income of the remaining sixteen sees was less than £3,000. They varied no less strikingly at the parochial level: whilst the richest of livings were worth over £1,000 a year, there were, c.1830, over 3,500 worth less than £150 a year: curates received even less, of course. The consequences of such anomalies for the

[1]For example, in 1824 it was revealed in Parliament that Manchester had church accommodation for 22,468 and a population of 187,000; Birmingham had accommodation for 16,000 and a population of 100,000; Leeds had accommodation for 10,000 and a population of 84,000 (Bowen, 1968, p. 22).

[2] Partly owing to laxity and partly to sheer size, pre-Victorian confirmations were often triennial or quadrennial and of huge size, in centres far removed from most confirmation candidates' parishes. This was not conducive to effective confirmation instruction or a sense of the importance of the occasion. Changed ideas of episcopal vocation and practice, more bishops and the coming of the railways were to make Victorian confirmations steadily more frequent and local.

quality of pastoral care ranged from the disturbing to the appalling. There were too many cases of pluralism, absenteeism and non-residence even where economic hardship did not make them inevitable. On top of such outright abuses, there were many cases where clergy necessarily held plural benefices in order to secure an adequate income at all; even some bishops found themselves in such a position. The educational level of the clergy and the amount of training they received was a further cause of concern.

Last, but not least, just as parliamentary reform included the issue of the adequacy of representation, so also the internal government of the Church of England in 1832 lacked adequate representation — indeed it lacked even a working existence. The Convocations of Canterbury and York, which might in theory have provided a forum in which the church, or at least its clergy, could have formulated policies to overcome the various administrative, financial and organizational difficulties which it faced, had not met since 1717 (and were in fact, not to do so again until 1852). The machinery for adequate self-government and self-instituted reform thus simply did not exist within the Church of England in 1832.[3]

This is not to say that prior to 1832 churchmen were not themselves concerned about the state of the church and the need for reform. Nor is it to say that the contrast between the late eighteenth and early nineteenth-century Church of England and the Church of England of the Victorian era is simply one of pre-Victorian darkness and Victorian light. Such over-sharp contrasts are part of that older tradition of Anglican historiography which saw the Victorian period too straightforwardly in terms of early crisis and steady revival. For some fifty years now, ever since the publication of Norman Sykes' *Church and State in England in the Eighteenth Century*, the eighteenth-century Church of England has been gradually cleared of the charge of pervasive slackness and abuses, and revealed, rather, as an essentially practical, rational, moderate church, with a low regard for mystery and emotion, a dislike of extremes, and an avoidance of organized churchmanship. In respect of slackness and abuses the appropriate charge is not one of pervasive failure (which is untrue) but of failure to reform energetically (which is more just). The point is one of balance. The pre-Victorian Church of England was not void of dedicated pastors at both parochial and episcopal level. Nor was it without would-be reformers well aware of the deficiencies of the existing system. Indeed, by the early 1830s most dioceses had been at least moderately affected by the pressure for reform (Best, 1964, p. 239). Prior to 1832, however, the reformers within the church had to contend with an ethos and an ecclesiastical machinery ill-suited to their initiatives.

[3] At the beginning of each Parliament, Convocation met formally, thus preserving the name and memory, but was prorogued without discussion.

Within the episcopacy prior to 1832, men such as Charles James Blomfield and John Bird Sumner stand out as examples of bishops who sought reform in such matters as diocesan administration and the training of clergy. Blomfield first brought his reforming zeal and efficiency to the unwieldy and neglected diocese of Chester between 1824 and 1828. He was then translated to London and brought his considerable talents to bear on the problem of the metropolis. In London, one of his major achievements was the Metropolis Churches' Fund, which enabled a major programme of Church Extension to be undertaken, funded by philanthropic subscription. It was an approach subsequently followed in other urban dioceses which lacked adequate church accommodation. Sumner, who succeeded Blomfield at Chester, continued his predecessor's reforming work in the diocese before himself becoming Archbishop of Canterbury in 1848.

There were also national initiatives for the building of new churches and the creation of new parishes: in 1818 Parliament voted a million pounds for the building of Anglican churches in industrial areas. In 1824 it voted a further half million, and the Church Building Commission set to work. But such efforts were fatally hampered by legal restrictions: most crucially, until 1843 it was not possible to create a new parish without an Act of Parliament. Progress was necessarily slow.

By 1832, however, genuinely radical and innovative proposals for reform had begun to emerge even from within the Church of England itself. The most famous were those of Lord Henley and Thomas Arnold. Henley's *Plan of Church Reform* advocated greater clerical discipline, a radical redistribution of ecclesiastical wealth, the revival of Convocation and the removal of the bishops from the House of Lords. Arnold's *Principles of Church Reform* went even further and advocated that the Church of England broaden itself sufficiently to incorporate dissenters within it: it would thus become the church of the great majority of the English people.

Despite all such concern within the church, however, by 1832 the fundamental inability of the church to reform itself effectively from within had led to the initiative passing to the state and to the likely reform of the church from without. Hence the sense of impending crisis which arose with the passing of the 1832 Reform Act and the probable return of a radical and generally reforming Whig government. In the event there occurred no sudden, radical, state-imposed revolution, but rather a steady, if also in its way dramatic, transformation of the pastoral and administrative arrangements of the Victorian Church of England. In its totality the transformation did in fact amount to a minor revolution, but in practice it was made up of a series of piecemeal initiatives and overlapping, sometimes conflicting, reforms and developments.

One strand of the process was the result of direct intervention by Parliament, but it proved to be a moderate initiative in which churchmen themselves played a leading role. In June 1832 an Ecclesiastical Revenues Commission was set up to investigate the financial state of the Church of England. It was slow in its work and achieved little. In 1835 a new Commission was set up to 'consider the state of the Established Church', and in 1836 was renamed and made permanent under the title of the Ecclesiastical Commission. The Commission was originally envisaged as an instrument for the reform and improvement of diocesan and episcopal finances and revenues, but the very complexity of the financial organization of the church, and the fact that Blomfield (who had been a member of the Commission in each of the stages of its evolution from 1832 onwards) seized the opportunity to exploit the Commission as a forum for his reforming zeal and formidable administrative talents, meant that the Ecclesiastical Commission in practice took a very broad view of its role and became the centre of organizational, administrative and financial reform of the church as a whole. The government recognized this development in the Commission's role and in 1840 enlarged its membership, strengthened its powers to implement its policies, and gave it the comprehensive task of making 'better provision for the cure of souls'.

In enlarging the membership, Parliament also sought to allay the worst fears of those churchmen — especially High Churchmen — who saw the Commission as simply one more example of the interference of secular authority in the affairs of the church, and thus a threat to the rights and privileges of the Church of England. Even in 1836 the worst fears of conservative churchmen should have been somewhat allayed: the original Ecclesiastical Commission was appointed with a membership of thirteen, including five bishops, one of whom, Blomfield, took the lead from the start. Despite this, however, the Commission remained a cause of alarm and opposition. In particular, its small size and the fact that members could be dismissed at Parliament's behest meant that many churchmen remained opposed to it. Accordingly in 1840 it was enlarged in membership to forty-nine and all the diocesan bishops were made *ex officio* members, thus ending the possibility of an individual's removal at the request of government. Many High Churchmen still remained suspicious of the Commission, seeing it as a blatantly Erastian phenomenon, but the larger membership after 1840 much reduced the general level of disquiet.

The Commission's principal approach was to take into its own hands revenues from endowments which were notably wealthy. In particular, by the Dean and Chapter Act (1840), it abolished a number of cathedral offices and took over their revenues, a move which ensured the continued hostility of High Churchmen. The Commission then redistributed this wealth, either by augmenting the revenues of very poor parishes or by creating completely new parishes (especially in the poor, urban industrial areas). Between 1840 and 1853 the Commission augmented and endowed

5300 such parishes from the revenues arising from the abolition of cathedral offices alone.

Other achievements were the passing of a Church Building Act in 1843 (which established a straightforward procedure for sub-dividing parishes, in place of the hopelessly cumbersome requirement of a separate Act of Parliament for each such sub-division); the re-adjustment of episcopal salaries by the Established Church Act of 1836, so that the glaring inequalities were removed (and the scramble for translation to wealthier sees thus averted); and the creation of new dioceses to serve new populous urban areas and alleviate the absurd size of some old dioceses.

The previous barrier to new dioceses had been the automatic increase which would have resulted in the number of bishops in the House of Lords. This was now resolved by the simple expedients of, first, in 1836, uniting the dioceses of Bristol and Gloucester in order to create a vacancy in the Lords for the newly-created Bishop of Ripon; and second, in 1841, adopting the procedure that the junior bishops would not sit in the Lords, the bench being limited henceforth to the twenty-four senior bishops. This opened the way for the creation of the diocese of Manchester in 1847 and, later, the creation of Truro and St Albans in 1877, Liverpool in 1880, Newcastle in 1882, Southwell in 1884 and Wakefield in 1888. A further achievement was the curtailment of pluralism and non-residence by the Pluralities Act of 1838. Severe limits were placed on the number of benefices that could be held, the distance between them, their population, and their value. They could only be held plurally by archiepiscopal dispensation and the bishop could require two services per Sunday.

The key to the success of the Ecclesiastical Commissioners was the severely pragmatic nature of their approach. In this, Blomfield set the pattern of their subsequent development. Blomfield was a dedicated practitioner of the art of the possible and apt to be impatient with the abstract and theoretical arguments of High Churchmen whose stance, in his view, left no hope of achieving effective and creative reform for the church's own good. The route to effective practical reform, Blomfield held, was the moderate and pragmatic co-operation of church and state. In this political pragmatism Blomfield was undoubtedly correct: he established a mode of operations and approach for the Ecclesiastical Commission which continued after his own retirement from its work and enabled it to consolidate its achievements in the second half of the century. The Ecclesiastical Commission was thus a moderate, not a revolutionary, affair. And yet in the five years between 1836 and 1840 three crucial reforming Acts were passed which paved the way for a thoroughgoing reform of the church's pastoral administration in ensuing decades, as the augmentation and endowment of the 5300 parishes between 1840 and 1855 and the creation of new dioceses amply demonstrated.

Inevitably, however, given its basically pragmatic approach, the Commission remained a severely bureaucratic affair, not a vehicle for the reform of pastoral ideals or principles. The potentially one-sided bureaucratic style of reform which could have thereby resulted was in practice averted by the presence of a second strand in the administrative and pastoral transformation of the Victorian Church of England, namely a revival of the pastoral ideal. Here, too, it is possible to over-emphasize the extent and the nature of the change which occurred. The caricature of the universally slack and lethargic eighteenth-century Church of England includes a portrayal of the eighteenth-century clergy as everywhere pastorally lax, worldly, and void of a sense of vocation and pastoral dedication. In point of fact there were many devoted pastors in the eighteenth-century Church of England, possessed of a definite understanding of their priestly vocation. Indeed, when, in the nineteenth century, the issue of the vocation and profession of the clergy became a prominent topic of debate, the Victorian ideal of the clerical profession which emerged owed as much to eighteenth-century (and earlier) concepts of priestly vocation as it did to nineteenth-century concepts of 'professionalization' among the secular professions.[4] Allowing such caveats, however, it remains the case that alongside the pragmatic reform of the pastoral administration of the Church of England there was also a revival of pastoral discipline and ideals, which occurred at the level of both diocese and parish, episcopacy and clergy, and also affected methods of, and provision for, clergy training.

At the level of the diocese and the episcopacy, Victorian bishops became both more diocesan and more pastoral in the focus of their interests and their understanding of their role. They spent more time in their dioceses and more time travelling around their dioceses. In part this was a product of the railways, which enabled Victorian bishops to travel around often large dioceses as their predecessors could never have done, but it was also a change of style and self-understanding. Speaking in Parliament in 1861, Lord Ebury observed that the clergy 'wanted Bishops who would be nearer to themselves, and not Prince bishops' (quoted in Crowther, 1970, p. 140). If that was what they wanted, it was also what they got. The bishops of the Victorian Church of England became, increasingly, men of their dioceses, known by their clergy and laity, active pastors to their diocesan flocks rather than prince-bishops whose main concerns were political and national affairs.

The shift from prince-bishop to pastor can be seen clearly in the contrast between William Howley, Archbishop of Canterbury from 1828 to 1848, and his successor John Bird Sumner, who was Archbishop from 1848 to 1862. Howley was a representative of the old order, not corrupt or unpopu-

[4] For a more detailed discussion of this point, see *RVB*, I, 5.

lar (he was quite admired, in fact), but simply opposed to reform in general; he naturally assumed an aristocratic life-style. Sumner, by contrast, was a reforming bishop, a pious Evangelical; he, equally naturally, assumed the style of a country gentleman, but no more. Over the century the change became general. Among the hallmarks of the change were such things as frequent and locally held confirmation services, the public institution of new incumbents, personal care of ordinands, greater solemnity at ordinations, public leadership of the diocese, and the development of a knowledge of and pastoral relationship with the clergy. The Victorian bishops progressively worked harder and were closer to their clergy and laity than their predecessors had been: a fact reflected in the growth of the call for more bishops — both in the form of new dioceses and through the creation of suffragan bishops and the use of ex-colonial bishops as assistants. The bishops, as a group, also succeeded in increasing their influence over the patronage of the benefices under their jurisdiction, thereby further extending episcopal control and oversight of the dioceses (Roberts, 1981).

Analogous changes were wrought at the parochial level. As Owen Chadwick has put it, 'No one doubted in 1860, and few will doubt now, that the clergy of 1860 were more zealous than the clergy of 1830, conducted worship more reverently, knew their people better, understood a little more theology, said more prayers, celebrated sacraments more frequently, studied more Bible' (Chadwick, 1971, p. 127). Contemporary observation reached a similar conclusion. In 1854, G. A. Selwyn, colonial Bishop of New Zealand, returned to England after a thirteen-year absence. He spoke of 'a great and visible change' in the Church of England since his departure for New Zealand in 1841. 'It is now a very rare thing to see a careless clergyman, a neglected parish or a desecrated church', he observed. There was, as A. D. Gilbert has remarked, no single explanation for this change (Gilbert, 1976, p. 132). The Ecclesiastical Commissioners helped provide a context. The Church Pluralities Act of 1838 made a major impact on the problem of non-residence. The Church Discipline Act of 1840 sought to further limit the possibilities of clerical excess, abuse or laxity.

In addition there was the impact of both the Evangelical and Oxford Movements. Although they differed in so much, and not least in their understanding of the sacramental nature and status of the ordained ministry, both Evangelicals and Tractarians held the pastoral role of the parish clergyman in high regard. The years between, roughly, 1833 and 1860 were, as we shall see shortly, a period of intense controversy between the Evangelical and Catholic wings of the Anglican tradition. Out of that controversy came much sharpened Evangelical and Catholic identities, yet, as Nigel Yates has observed, in many respects the parochial ministry of Tractarians and Evangelicals was very similar: 'both placed a strong emphasis on pastoral visiting, more frequent services, experimental forms of worship, and parochial organisations, particularly those of a social character' (Yates, 1983, p. 25). Both movements were also fired by a deep concern for holiness and personal piety. The pastoral ministry and the life of the parishes of the Victorian Church of England reflected these influences, whilst societies such as the Evangelical Church Pastoral Aid Society (founded in 1836) and the High Church Additional Curates Society (founded in 1837) worked to provide funds for more clergy to embody them.

Nor was the revival of the pastoral ideal and pastoral practice only the product of Evangelical and Tractarian devotional and pastoral idealism. The Broad Church tradition within Victorian Anglicanism also worked out a pastoral ideal, perhaps the most outstanding example of which was the Curates Clerical Club in London between 1856 and 1906. Led by Harry Jones, Broad Church Vicar of St Luke's, Berwick Street and then of St George's in the East, the Club articulated a Broad Church pastoral commitment that combined a liberal understanding of theology with devoted parochial work, especially among the London poor (Heeney, 1978). The laity were also involved in the effort to develop parochial life and activity: district visiting societies (through which selected lay people sought to establish personal contacts, distribute religious literature, and encourage Sunday School attendance and membership of savings or benefit schemes) became a feature of many parishes. In Chester diocese in the 1830s Sumner sought to organize such a scheme on a diocesan scale (Rack, 1973).

The increase in church building,[5] the emphasis on clerical residence, and the trend towards the use of additional curates in parishes, required an increase in the number of clergy. The number of Anglican clergy increased throughout the Victorian period. In 1841 there were just over fourteen and a half thousand clergy in the Church of England. By 1891 this figure had risen to just over twenty-four thousand. Over the same period the educational background of the clergy and their training underwent important changes. In 1841 eighty-six per cent of the candidates for ordination came from Oxford and Cambridge, seven per cent from Trinity College Dublin and Durham University and seven per cent from other sources, such as St David's College, Lampeter, King's College, London, or the earliest of the specifically theological colleges such as St Bee's or St Aidan's. By the 1860s these proportions had changed, Oxford and Cambridge providing sixty-five per cent of candidates, Dublin and Durham nine per cent and other sources twenty-six per cent. This trend continued, as did the trend towards the foundation of theological colleges either for the training of non-graduate ordinands or for the vocational training of graduates: by 1877 the list included colleges at Chichester, Wells, Cuddesdon, Salisbury, Exeter,

[5] Church building, repair and restoration were, it has been observed, of the essence of the revival of the Anglican church in the nineteenth century (Jones, 1984, p. 216). From 1801–30 447 churches were built or rebuilt; and from 1851–75 a further 2,438 (Gilbert, 1976, p. 130).

Gloucester, Leeds, Truro, Lichfield, Ely and Lincoln, and by the end of the century there were also colleges for graduates at Oxford and Cambridge. The emergence of such theological colleges in the Victorian Church of England was in part the result of a desire to improve the educational standards and pastoral training of ordination candidates, in part the result of the simple need for more places in which to train men for the ministry of the Church of England, and in part the result of episcopal concern that without training in sufficiently 'orthodox' theological environments, ordinands would fall prey to the 'wrong kind' of theological ideas: depending on the college concerned, the 'wrong kind' of ideas might be Evangelical, Tractarian or Broad Church.

Just as Blomfield occupied a special place in the bureaucratic and administrative reform of the church, so particular individuals occupied important places in the reform of the pastoral ideal. At the episcopal level, Samuel Wilberforce, Bishop of Oxford from 1845 to 1869 and Bishop of Winchester from 1869 to his death in 1873, was the equivalent, in terms of the reform of the pastoral ideal, of Blomfield in his influence on the organization and revenues of the church. Wilberforce is better remembered for his famous — or infamous — opposition to both theological liberalism in the *Essays and Reviews* controversy of 1860–65 and to Darwin and Huxley in the equally controversial debates over the *Origin of Species* in 1859–60. In fact his greatest achievement was not in the field of controversy or theology but in the administration of the diocese of Oxford and the demonstration of what a conscientious and pastoral bishop might achieve. Wilberforce was, one might say, the mature mid-Victorian expression of the reformed espiscopal ideal hinted at in the work of Blomfield and Sumner at Chester. He was tireless in travelling about his diocese and imposing a new discipline on the life of the church. During his episcopate at Oxford he secured the building of 106 new churches, the restoration of 250 and the rebuilding of 15, and increased the number of livings in the diocese from 356 to 630. He founded a teachers' college at Culham and a theological college at Cuddesdon. He also wished the bishops to be national leaders and represent the Church in national life. He thus took his role in the House of Lords seriously and entered into public controversy fearlessly — even recklessly. He also appreciated the need within the church for a coherent forum of debate and policy making and therefore supported, in the 1850s and 1860s, first the revival of Convocation and then the development of diocesan synods and Church Congresses.

At the parochial level the example of W. F. Hook became the equivalent of Samuel Wilberforce at the episcopal level. Hook became Vicar of Leeds in 1837. His parish consisted of the whole of Leeds, with a population variously estimated as between 125,000 and 150,000 and although there were seventeen other churches in the city they were all chapels of ease of the parish church, poorly attended and without endowment. Hook sacrificed a third of his income to create new parishes and endow them and in all had twenty-one new churches built in Leeds as well as rebuilding the parish church and making it a focus for the style of choral and sacramental worship which became characteristic of Victorian Anglicanism. His motive was simple: to advance the cause of the evangelization and pastoral oversight of the urban poor in Leeds. It was Hook's misfortune to be involved in one of the first major controversies over Ritualism when the clergy of St Saviour's — one of the new parishes created by Hook — adopted an extremely Catholic style of ritual and ministry, including confession. Between 1846 and 1851 a bitter dispute raged at St Saviour's until the more extreme clergy joined the Roman Catholic Church. As with Wilberforce and the relative importance of his diocesan leadership and his role as a controversialist, however, the disputes at St Saviour's should not be allowed to detract from the scale of Hook's overall achievement at Leeds.

Alongside the administrative pragmatism of the Ecclesiastical Commissioners, therefore, the Victorian Church of England experienced a wide-ranging revival of the ideal of the ordained pastoral ministry. As Brian Heeney demonstrated, pastoral theologians of all parties came to assert two fundamental principles in respect of the pastoral ideal: first, that the ordained ministry was a unique religious vocation, not a mere analogue of secular professions; and second, that it therefore demanded distinctive qualities and standards of character and behaviour — pre-eminent among which were pastoral sympathy and self-discipline (Heeney, 1974).

The Anglican pastoral revival was also intimately connected with the Victorian Church of England's deeply-felt sense of mission to the poor, and especially the urban poor. The particular rationale of the mission to the poor could take a variety of forms, from the early Victorian Evangelical concern for religion as an essential element in the ordering of life and disciplining for self-improvement of the poor (a view held, for example, by J. B. Sumner), to the more general sense of a civilizing mission bringing literacy, charity, morality and education to the poor, to the liberal individualism and local self-help of a Harry Jones, the moderate Christian Socialism of the Christian Social Union or the Settlement Movement in the 1880s and 1890s, or the full-blooded Christian Socialism of many late Victorian Anglo-Catholic slum priests such as Arthur Stanton, Stewart Headlam or Thomas Hancock. What all these approaches shared, however, was the recognition that successful mission to the urban poor required pastoral discipline and devotion of the highest order.

A third strand to the administrative and pastoral revival of the Church of England, one lying somewhere between the pragmatic reform of the Ecclesiastical Commissioners and the revival of the pastoral ideal, was the revival and development of the church's corporate institutional life.

First, in the 1840s and 1850s, came pressure to revive Convocation so that the Church of England, or at least the bishops and clergy, might have a proper forum in which to debate and formulate policy. Initially the archbishops, many of the clergy and most of the laity resisted the idea, fearing it would prove a focus of partisan feeling and potential schism: Evangelicals and Liberals especially feared that Tractarians and High Churchmen would seek to use revived Convocations to narrow the range of opinion in the Church of England. But with the leadership of Gladstone in the House of Commons, Henry Hoare, a prominent layman, outside Parliament and Samuel Wilberforce in the Lords, the campaign gathered momentum. Eventually, in 1852, the Convocation of Canterbury met to conduct meaningful business for the first time since 1717. The Convocation of York did not meet unitl 1861 because of the opposition of the Archbishop of York to its revival. After 1861, however, both Convocations met regularly and became important arenas for the conduct of the Church of England's business, although their role remained one of debate and the formulation of policy, not the enactment of new measures which would have required the sanction of Parliament.

In the 1850s and 1860s pressure developed for the creation of diocesan synods or conferences. In 1866 the first diocesan conference met at Ely. By 1882 all but three dioceses had such conferences. They divided into houses for voting, both clergy and laity being represented. In the 1860s and 1870s another important development occurred with the invention of the Church Congresses. The meetings were annual, public, and chaired by the bishop of the diocese in which the Congress was being held. Clergy and laity attended and participated. The Church Congresses quickly became a barometer of opinion in the Church of England and, until the 1890s at least, were an important element in the continuing revival of the church's institutional life. In the 1890s their significance declined, not least because the laity were by then admitted to Convocations, the Convocation of Canterbury accepting a House of Laity for the first time in 1886, and that of York following the example in 1892. As the laity were brought into the affairs of the church via Convocation so the unique role of the Church Congress as a meeting ground of clergy and laity declined.

The causes of this series of institutional developments were mixed. In part the revival of Convocation and the institution of diocesan conferences and Church Congresses were the product of increased clerical concern and identity: the product of a desire to assert the revived sense of clerical and episcopal authority and self-understanding. In part they grew out of 'church defence': the sense that the Church of England after 1832 faced serious threats from Parliamentary interference, from Dissenting and Nonconformist efforts to remove the privileges of the church, and from the unchecked growth of theologically heterodox opinions within the church. And in part they were the product of lay pressure for a place and a voice in the affairs and government of the Church of England. These causes frequently conflicted in their aims and directions, but the one common factor was their mutual testimony to a revived vitality and energy in the established church.

Taken together, this network of movements and reforms, although not always harmonious and certainly never neat, constituted an impressive reform and revival of Anglican organization and pastoral provision. Looking back on the late Victorian and Edwardian Church of England, Cosmo Gordon Lang once observed that he considered the years 1890 to 1914 to be the Golden Age of parochial work in the Church of England (quoted in Bowen, 1968, p. vii). That may well be an exaggeration and the product of nostalgia prompted by the new problems of a new age. But it is striking nevertheless. Even if it was a nostalgic exaggeration, it was not patently absurd when said of the 1890s — which it would have been if applied to the conditions of 1830, so great was the transformation of the Church of England's pastoral and institutional life in the intervening Victorian years.

II THE DOCTRINAL AND THEOLOGICAL REVOLUTION

The administrative and pastoral transformation of the Victorian Church of England, as we have seen, eventually brought within its scope all the parties within the church: High, Low and Broad; Catholic, Evangelical and Liberal (even if their involvement was also often bound up with advancing party interests). In the early 1830s, however, far from commanding a shared (if competitive) allegiance from all parties in the Church of England, the movement for administrative reform was itself the immediate cause of perhaps the most fundamental and far-reaching assertion of party identity ever seen in the church.

The immediate cause of the Oxford Movement was the attempt of the Whig Government in 1833 to rationalize, by means of an Irish Church Temporalities Act, the situation of the established Church of Ireland. The measure was not particularly radical. In a country which was predominantly Catholic, yet which had no less than twenty-two Anglican dioceses, ten dioceses were to be suppressed, boundaries being adjusted so as to amalgamate them with other dioceses, and the revenue thus saved was to go to augment the many very poor livings in the Irish Church. To the Whigs this was merely a sensible and efficient reform. To many High Churchmen, however, it appeared as an act of gross and dangerous Erastianism: the state, in the shape of a reformed Parliament which included much Radical and Dissenting opinion, was interfering with the ministry, property and administration of the established church. It was grossly Erastian because it was to be imposed by Parliament upon the Irish Church. It was dangerously Erastian because it established a precedent in Ireland for what might subsequently be done in England also.[6]

The clash of perceptions was brought sharply into focus in July 1833 by John Keble. Keble was one of a group of Oxford dons, Fellows of Oriel College, whose informal discussions had turned the Oriel senior common room of the 1820s into a centre of High Church opinion. The four principal members of the circle had been Keble himself, Edward Bouverie Pusey, John Henry Newman and Richard Hurrell Froude. By 1833 Keble was Professor of Poetry at Oxford, having published in 1827 an immensely popular collection of poems entitled *The Christian Year*, in which he supplied poems for the Sundays and Holy Days of the Christian calendar. The tone of the volume was unambiguously and uncompromisingly Catholic.

In 1833 Keble was invited to preach the annual assize sermon before the University of Oxford. Keble's theme was 'National Apostasy' and the apostasy in question was the, to him, sacrilegious interference of the state in the affairs of the Irish Church. The sermon struck a chord among High Churchmen concerned about the changing relationship between church and state which had been developing since 1828 and of which the Irish Church Temporalities Bill seemed merely the latest example. By striking such a chord the sermon also came to be seen as the beginning of the 'Oxford Movement'.

In the months which followed, leadership of the Movement gradually coalesced around the Oxford trio of Keble, Pusey and Newman. It made its initial impact through a programme of *Tracts for the Times*. Beginning with Newman's first Tract, 'Thoughts on the Ministerial Commission of the Clergy' in 1833, and culminating with Newman's Tract 90 in 1841, the *Tracts for the Times* progressed from an initially brief, indeed 'tractarian', format to substantial works in theology and theological history. They were, above all, Catholic and clerical in orientation and intention. Addressed to the clergy, Tract 1 on the 'Ministerial Commission' set the tone in its recall of the clergy, and thus the church, to 'our apostolical descent'. The process reached its end in Tract 90, 'Remarks on Certain Passages in the Thirty-Nine Articles', which sought to show the compatibility of the formularies of the Church of England with a thoroughly Catholic understanding of doctrine. Between Tract 1 and Tract 90 came a series of pamphlets and monographs which emphasized the place, role and importance of liturgy,

[6] For the consequences of the Act for the Church in Ireland, see the essay on Irish Disestablishment in *RVB*, II, 6.

sacraments, priesthood, apostolic descent and continuity, and the authority of clergy and bishops within the Church of England.

Initially sparked by an issue of church-state politics and centred on Oxford University, Tractarianism was, however, much more than merely an Oxford or a University phenomenon, and in time made an impact on every dimension of the life, worship and belief of the Church of England. The explanation of this immense impact lies in the way in which the Tractarians set out to challenge the doctrinal and theological consensus which then prevailed within the Church of England and to argue that the true identity of the Church of England was essentially Catholic, not Protestant.

Prior to the impact of the Oxford Movement there existed a basic doctrinal consensus within the Church of England. Certainly there were, even then, parties within the church. On the one hand there was a Low Church tradition which stressed the sole authority of scripture, which was strongly Protestant in its emphasis on personal devotion and piety (and correspondingly cautious about the priestly role of the clergy) and was much influenced by the Evangelical revival of the eighteenth century. In the early nineteenth century it produced, from it own ranks, the 'Clapham Sect' of earnest Anglican Evangelicals, whose combination of Evangelical personal piety, commitment to mission — both abroad and in the urban centres of Britain — and work for social reform became a byword for Evangelical Anglicanism.

On the other hand there was a High Church tradition which also gave a high place to scripture and the Book of Common Prayer but in addition gave more emphasis to the role and authority of the church in interpreting them. This group was also much more concerned about the organization, ministry and ministerial functions of the church and its traditional sacramental and pastoral provision. It too had developed a concern for the revival of personal devotion and charity, known, in contrast to the Evangelical Clapham Sect, as the 'Clapton Sect'.

Both of these groups also shared a commitment to the eighteenth-century Anglican tradition of 'evidential theology' as exemplified in the works of Joseph Butler and William Paley. Butler in his *Analogy of Religion* (1736) had argued that Christianity was not incredible, because the supernatural revelation it claimed was, in fact, no more improbable than the natural religion that the eighteenth-century Deist critics proposed: both were a matter of probability. Paley in his *Natural Theology* (1802) and *Evidences of Christianity* (1794) had argued that the evidence of design, of miracles, and of fulfilled prophecies demonstrated not merely the probability but the proof of Christian revelation. This variety of 'evidential' theology, with its essentially rational appeal and method of argument, underlay much of Victorian Anglican theology until at least the last quarter of the nineteenth century.

There was also a third group within the pre-Oxford Movement Church of England which was even less sharply defined than the High and Low church 'parties'. This third group of 'Broad Churchmen' was characterized by a commitment to tolerance of a breadth of theological opinions and to the idea of the essential comprehensiveness of the church. In a representative such as Thomas Arnold they even saw comprehensiveness extending to the inclusion of Dissenters within the established church. The Broad Churchmen were also, as a group, much indebted to the theological thinking of Samuel Taylor Coleridge and, in consequence, stressed the importance of religious experience, feeling, and intuition over against the claims of essentially rational and evidential theology.

Prior to the Oxford Movement, however, such 'parties' existed within a consensus which, as Paul Avis has recently suggested, may be likened to a series of mutually overlapping circles. The consensus, as Avis persuasively argues, consisted of an unquestioned tacit acceptance of the essentially Protestant nature of the Church of England (albeit allowing that the Protestantism concerned incorporated a significant number of Catholic emphases). This essentially Protestant nature was exhibited especially in the doctrine of justification by faith, the paramount authority of scripture, a high regard for the Reformers, and an unambiguously Protestant understanding of the Thirty-Nine Articles and the Book of Common Prayer (Avis, 1986, p. 16; Crowther, 1970, pp. 18–19).

This consensus the Tractarians set out, consciously and deliberately, to undermine. They sought to deny the essentially Protestant nature, character and identity of the Church of England and asserted instead its Catholic roots, traditions and identity. They stressed the authority of the church, of the priesthood, of the sacramental system, and of the early Christian Fathers. They sought to downgrade, and even to denigrate, the Reformers. And they sought to give a consistently Catholic interpretation of the Thirty-Nine Articles and the Book of Common Prayer.

Tracts for the Times was only one of the means by which the Tractarians set out to emphasize the Catholic nature of the Church of England. They also set about their task through sermons, through scholarly lectures and monographs, and through poetry and devotional literature. They sought to establish their continuity with earlier Anglican High Churchmen, and, in turn, the continuity of such earlier High Churchmen with the early Christian Fathers. To this end, some of the Tracts were little more than collections of extracts from the Fathers or the writings of seventeenth and eighteenth-century High Churchmen (eighteen of the ninety Tracts were in fact of this kind). In addition they undertook ambitious projects to republish editions of the Christian Fathers and the seventeenth and eighteenth-century Anglican High Churchmen. The *Library of the Fathers* was begun in 1838 with an edition of St Augustine's *Confessions* edited by Pusey, and between 1841 and 1863 the *Library of Anglo-Catholic Theology* reprinted eighty-eight volumes of post-Reformation High Church writings.

The Tractarians were also active in matters of church architecture and liturgy. In 1839 John Mason Neale and Benjamin Webb formed the Cambridge Camden Society, renamed in 1846 the Ecclesiological Society. Its avowed aim was the building of new churches and the restoration of old and existing ones in a manner which was more Catholic and in the style of fourteenth-century Gothic — which the Ecclesiologists believed to be a style free of 'late medieval corruptions'. They sought to reverse the trend towards Anglican churches being essentially pulpit-dominated preaching houses. Instead they advocated cleared chancels and proper sanctuaries with raised and clearly visible altars, pulpits and lecterns moved to the sides of the chancel and — later in their campaign — they advocated such things as choir stalls, robed choirs, lighted candles, altar frontals, side-chapels, representational stained glass, and organ chambers located off the chancel. These views they urged between 1841 and 1868 in the pages of their journal *The Ecclesiologist*. It was, as we shall see in due course, only a short way from such architectural matters to liturgical ones, and indeed the combined architectural and liturgical dimension of the Oxford Movement was an essential element in the Tractarian assault upon the Protestantism of the pre-Victorian Church of England. John Mason Neale was also active in the translation of hymns of the ancient Eastern churches and in the re-establishment of religious communities in the Church of England. In the 1840s and 1850s a number of sisterhoods were founded, amidst considerable Protestant opposition. Religious orders for men were not founded until the 1860s, but then became firmly established.[7]

Last, but not least, the Tractarians, as Bernard Reardon has indicated, sought to catholicize the Church of England by using language alien to the Protestant ethos of pre-Oxford Movement Anglicanism. Simply by asserting the vocabulary of 'apostolic succession', 'priesthood', 'eucharistic sacrifice', 'real presence' and 'absolution', the Tractarians pressed their Catholic challenge upon contemporaries (Reardon, 1980, p. 105).

The challenge was accepted. Even some old-fashioned High Churchmen resisted the Tractarian attempt to actually 'unprotestantize' the Church of

[7] Among the early sisterhoods the most successful were those founded at Wantage (1848), Plymouth and Devonport (1848) and East Grinstead (1855). The first successful men's orders were the Anglican Benedictines founded in 1862 by Fr. Ignatius Lyne and the Society of St John the Evangelist founded in 1865 by R. M. Benson.

England and in so doing gave rise to the term 'Evangelical High Churchman'. Some Evangelicals and Broad Churchmen also made a pragmatic partnership in opposition to the Tractarians. They found a range of common ground on which to oppose the Tractarian position: they both opposed notions of salvation through infused sacramental grace; they both defended scripture against tradition; they both defended the Reformation as a breakthrough for conscience, personal judgement and toleration; they both urged an essentially simple (though crucially different) gospel. On such grounds Evangelicals and Broad Churchmen jointly opposed Tractarians, until other theological issues such as biblical criticism and the moral critique of orthodoxy moved to the centre of the theological stage and made such an Evangelical-Broad Church alliance unthinkable (Avis, 1986, pp. 15–16). From within the Broad Church camp Thomas Arnold launched one of the bitterest early attacks on the Tractarians in an essay, written in 1836 and published in the Edinburgh Review, entitled 'The Oxford Malignants'.

The most crucial response to the challenge, however, was that of the Evangelicals. It was the most crucial because it resulted in a decisive sharpening of the identity of Anglican Evangelicalism itself. As Peter Toon has observed, from the vantage point of the late twentieth century, what is likely to strike us most is the large area of agreement between Tractarians and Evangelicals in the 1830s, 40s and 50s (Toon, 1979, p. 203). Both Evangelicals and Tractarians espoused the quest for holiness of living (although they conceived such holiness rather differently), both agreed on the divine inspiration of scripture, both agreed on the essentiality of the doctrines of divine judgement and eternal punishment, both held uncompromisingly supernaturalist views of Christianity, and both firmly believed in miracles, revelation and the literal fulfilment of prophecy. But these issues were not yet the storm-centre of Victorian theology, as they were to become in the 50s, 60s and 70s. In the 30s, 40s and 50s, the issues of tradition and scripture, the authority of the ministry and the nature of the sacraments were the centre of Anglican theological debate. On these issues Evangelicals and Tractarians were in conflict, and as a result, by the time the focus of theological controversy had shifted to matters of historical and moral criticism of orthodox Christian doctrine, the Evangelicals, just as much as the Tractarians, were a distinct and organized party within the Church of England. The creation of that distinct and more defined identity was in large part the result of the controversies with Tractarianism in the years between 1833 and, roughly, the mid 1850s.

In those controversies the Evangelicals, no less than the Tractarians, deployed a variety of means to publicize and pursue their aims. Individual Evangelical theologians published responses to and criticism of aspects of Tractarianism — although only one Evangelical, William Goode the younger, seems to have set out to reply systematically to Tractarian theology as a whole. Evangelicals also sought to re-assert the theology of the Reformers and the Protestant tradition and to that end published an edition of Fox's *Acts and Monuments*, erected a memorial to the Protestant martyrs of the Reformation at Oxford, formed the Parker Society in 1840 to republish the works of the English Reformers, and the Calvin Translation Society in 1843 to publish the works of John Calvin. Local Protestant Committees were also formed to defend Protestantism and keep watch on the activities of local Tractarian clergy. As they defended and publicized their views they also defined them increasingly precisely.

The period between 1833 and the mid 1850s is itself divided into two by the secession of the Tractarian leaders Newman, Faber and Ward to Rome in 1845. As Yates has recently cautioned, it is important not to overestimate the significance of Newman's secession. The older tendency to see the 'Oxford Movement' proper as a phenomenon of the twelve years between 1833 and 1845, and the later development of 'Anglo-Catholicism' and 'Ritualism' as related yet distinct phenomena simply will not do. Newman's secession was only one — albeit a psychologically crucial one — in an ongoing series of crises in the development of Tractarianism, and the emergence of later Anglo-Catholicism and Ritualism out of Tractarianism is a process entirely consonant with the early development of Tractarian views on theology, liturgy, architecture and church order (Yates, 1983, pp. 21–3).

The secession of Newman nevertheless remains an important watershed. Until 1845 Tractarianism was indeed predominantly, though even then not exclusively, an Oxford movement. Certainly, most of the significant crises in the movement between 1833 and 1845 arose out of events at, or the works of persons at, Oxford University. The first major crisis occurred with the publication, in 1838–9, of the literary *Remains* of Hurrell Froude who had died in 1836. Froude had hated the Reformation and described it as a limb badly set which must be broken again in order to be righted. Protestantism he described as odious. These remarks, confided to his private journal, now appeared in published form and excited an entirely predictable Protestant fury. In 1841 came Tract 90, in which Newman sought to give a Catholic account of the Thirty-Nine Articles and to demonstrate that the literal and grammatical sense of the Articles did not in fact condemn many Roman Catholic practices and doctrines which it was commonly supposed they did condemn. Such argument caused suspicion. The Tractarians were, in any case, thought by many to be simply Romanizers — and Jesuitical Romanizers at that. In 1838 Isaac Williams had published 'On Reserve in Communicating Religious Knowledge' as Tract 80. Williams was a devoted pastor and a man of retiring character with a deep sense of the sacredness of Christian doctrine: he wished to protest against the coarseness and crudity of much Evangelical preaching. But 'Reserve' seemed to suggest withholding of truth, and doubts about the honesty of the

Tractarians were further fuelled. When Newman in Tract 90, arguing from the literal meaning of the Articles, suggested, for example, that condemnation of the 'sacrifice of masses' was not to condemn the 'sacrifice of the mass,' the impression of evasiveness and deviousness was increased rather than dispelled. At once condemned by the heads of most of the Oxford Colleges, Tract 90 led the Bishop of Oxford to request the cessation of *Tracts for the Times*. Newman agreed, but also retired to his retreat at Littlemore outside Oxford and began to withdraw from leadership of the Oxford Movement.

In 1843 Pusey preached a University sermon at Oxford on 'The Holy Eucharist a Comfort to the Penitent'. In it he strongly espoused a version of the doctrine of the Real Presence and was consequently condemned by two of his professorial colleagues and suspended for two years from preaching. Finally, in 1844, two of the more extreme members of the movement pressed matters to crisis point. F. W. Faber published a *Life of St Wilfred* which was blatantly pro-Roman Catholic, and W. G. Ward published *The Ideal of a Christian Church*, in which he claimed to accept all Roman Catholic doctrine whilst remaining an (uncensured) Anglican. Thus challenged, the heads of the Oxford Colleges called a special meeting of the Convocation of Oxford University in February 1845 to condemn both Ward's book and, retrospectively, Newman's Tract 90. Ward's book was duly condemned. Newman's Tract 90 was saved from probable condemnation by the veto of one of Newman's supporters who, as proctor, could *non placet* the proceedings. Newman, Faber and Ward duly entered the Roman Catholic church.

After Newman's departure to Rome, Tractarianism was less markedly an Oxford movement, certainly it was no longer centred there, but rather possessed a number of parochial and regional centres around the country. London, Leeds and Brighton were prominent among the early centres of such extra-Oxford Tractarianism, but also important were the many individual parishes across the country which provided an early home for Tractarian ideas. Also, by the late 1840s there were signs of a rejoining of forces between the Tractarians and some of the older High Churchmen. As early as 1836 they had made common cause (but so, then, had many Evangelicals) in opposing the appointment of a Broad Churchman, R. D. Hampden, to the Regius Professorship of Divinity at Oxford. (Hampden had led those at Oxford who wished to end subscription to the Thirty-Nine Articles as a condition of taking a degree, and thereby admit Dissenters to degrees.) They had also been brought into an alliance of disquiet over the establishment of a joint Anglican-Lutheran bishopric in Jerusalem in 1841: the appointment (which was a curious confusion of Anglican-Lutheran co-operation and Anglo-Prussian foreign policies) split both High Church and Tractarian opinion, but in so doing brought some traditional High Churchmen and some Tractarians into common cause. In 1847, Hampden again brought old High Churchman and new Tractarian into alliance when he was appointed Bishop of Hereford — in the event their fears over his unorthodoxy were unfounded and Hampden proved surprisingly orthodox and even anti-liberal in his subsequent episcopal pronouncements.

The dispersed, extra-Oxford dimension, and the re-alliance of Tractarians and old-style High Churchmen were both reflected in two important clashes between Tractarians and Evangelicals between 1846 and 1858. The Gorham and Denison cases were similar in that both were simple in outline and ferociously complex in their detail.

The Gorham case was the more famous. In 1847 the High Church Bishop of Exeter, Henry Phillpotts, refused to institute the Rev. George Gorham to a living in his diocese on the grounds that Gorham, as a professed Calvinist, held views concerning baptism which were inconsistent with the doctrine of the Church of England. Gorham took the case to the ecclesiastical Court of Arches, where the decision of the bishop was upheld. Gorham then appealed to the Judicial Committee of the Privy Council, which, in 1850, found in his favour: not on the grounds that it claimed the right to settle what the faith of the Church of England ought to be, but on the grounds that the role of the Judicial Committee was to determine what the formularies of the Church of England established the church's doctrine to be. They concluded in this case that Gorham's views were not ruled out by the Church of England's formularies. The case dismayed Tractarians and High Churchmen, who saw it as a clear defeat for their high doctrine of the sacraments, and a defeat, moreover, from a secular court. For some it was proof that Newman, Faber and Ward had been right and that Rome was now the only option:[8] Evangelicals, on the other hand, rejoiced.

In the Denison case the theological allegiances of prosecuted and prosecutor were reversed. George Anthony Denison was Archdeacon of Taunton and a leader of Tractarian opinion in the Lower House of the Convocation of Canterbury. Denison was a peculiarly inflexible and contentious man who positively relished controversy and prosecution. Between 1854 and 1858 his views on the eucharist became the subject of legal actions. He held a particularly high view (which Evangelicals held to be Roman Catholic) of the nature of the real presence in the eucharist. When he preached this in Wells Cathedral and subsequently published the sermons, an Evangelical clergyman brought charges against him in the Ecclesiastical Courts and eventually forced the Archbishop of Canterbury to prosecute Denison. Denison was found guilty and was deprived of his living. He then appealed to the Court of Arches, which refused to hear the appeal. Denison

[8] Among them were Archdeacon Henry Manning, who, in 1865, was to succeed Nicholas Wiseman as Roman Catholic Archbishop of Westminster, and Archdeacon Robert Wilberforce, the brother of Bishop Samuel Wilberforce.

then used the secular courts to compel the Court of Arches to hear the appeal. It dismissed the case on a legal technicality, whereupon Denison's opponent appealed to the Judicial Committee of the Privy Council, which upheld the decision of the Court of Arches. Denison the Tractarian had thus had recourse to the secular courts in order to compel the Ecclesiastical Court of Arches to hear the case. (He was also disappointed eventually to have escaped only through a legal loophole.)

The Gorham and Denison cases illustrate three important trends. First, the role of the courts (including, crucially, the secular courts) was central to the controversies and, as similar events unfolded in relation to matters of theological liberalism and the legitimate limits of Anglican doctrine in the 1860s, this aspect of the controversies was to become an issue in itself. Second, the sharpened identity of the Evangelicals in their disputes with the Tractarians had forced them into taking positions on sacramental theology which pressed traditional High Churchmen into alliance with Tractarians: given the positions being contested over baptismal theology in the Gorham case and eucharistic theology in the Denison case, the briefly held ideal of the Evangelical High Churchmen became almost impossible. The various publications on baptism and the eucharist which these controversies prompted from both Tractarian and Evangelical hands had defined matters with new precision and had obliged men to take sides. Out of such taking of sides emerged also first local and then national Societies, Associations, and Unions for 'Church Defence' (in the case of Tractarians and Anglo-Catholics) and for 'Protestant Protection' (in the case of Evangelicals).

Third, such controversies illustrate the way in which both Tractarian and Evangelical identities had been sharpened to the point where not only was the traditional doctrinal consensus broken, but in fact the Evangelical and Tractarian traditions began to appear not merely as parties but rather as competing sects within a single ecclesiastical framework. And sects, moreover, which were ready to use the courts — including the secular courts — to advance their own perceptions of the appropriate future development of the Church of England.

By the end of the 1850s, however, the focus of theological and doctrinal conflict within the Church of England was about to shift sharply away from the Tractarian-Evangelical issue (which would henceforth be pursued in the realm of liturgy and worship) and towards the issue of theological liberalism: the pre-Oxford Movement Anglican consensus, already shattered, was about to experience further fragmentation.

As early as the 1830s and 40s morally sensitive spirits had begun to doubt the moral propriety of a creator who sentenced many of his creatures to eternal punishment and who required an innocent victim's suffering to appease his wrath: in short, the traditional doctrines of hell and substitutionary atonement were themselves under moral judgement and were becoming the cause of loss of faith. The classic cases were those of George Eliot, Francis Newman (John Henry's brother) and James Anthony Froude (Hurrell's brother) (Murphy, 1955).

Many of those who came to have moral doubts over specific Christian doctrines also became both morally and intellectually worried by the apparent conflict between traditional belief concerning the Bible on the one hand and the implications of historical criticism of the Bible and the discoveries of geologists, astronomers and natural scientists on the other. Both historical study and scientific discovery seemed to render intellectually untenable traditional views of the Bible as inerrant. But if such views were intellectually untenable, then to continue to hold them whilst simultaneously holding other, contradictory, views would be dishonest and immoral. Such a moral, ethical and intellectual web lay at the heart of the personal crises of faith which affected so many Victorian intellectuals, and also challenged each of the churches as clergymen, especially, sought to face such moral and intellectual questions and remain within both their church and its ordained ministry.

The specifically Anglican version of the crisis of faith was played out, for the most part, in the 1850s and 60s. Naturally it had a pre-history: Thomas Arnold, for example, had been urging a broader, more critical, less dogmatic approach to theology in the 1830s; Connop Thirlwall, Bishop of St David's, was familiar with German biblical criticism and had translated Schleiermacher's critical study of Luke's Gospel as early as 1825; and in 1840 Samuel Taylor Coleridge's *Confessions of an Inquiring Spirit* was posthumously published, revealing Coleridge's very liberal understanding of biblical inspiration. All these early ventures in theological liberalism, important though they were, remained essentially isolated, individual affairs, however. By the 1850s the issues had become more pressing and a number of Anglican theologians began tentatively to work towards a more systematically liberal standpoint. Three cases in the 1850s and 60s illustrate particularly well the nature of the Anglican version of the crisis of faith.

In 1853 F. D. Maurice, Professor of Theology at King's College London, published a collection entitled *Theological Essays*. Maurice was never a clear writer and *Theological Essays* (dedicated to Tennyson and addressed to Unitarians) were even more tortuously constructed than usual. But on at least two points Maurice made himself sufficiently clear to bring orthodox condemnation upon himself. He rejected both the traditional substitutionary view of the Atonement and also the notion of eternal punishment. In respect of each he insisted that there were alternative interpretations of scripture which were both morally and theologically of greater soundness. His views on the Atonement brought condemnation from Evangelicals in particular, whilst his criticism of the traditional view of eternal punishment and his suggestion that 'eternal' punishment might not mean 'everlasting' punishment (but that 'eternal' might refer to quality of life, not endless time) aroused the wrath of many orthodox critics and also the Council of King's College, which condemned the volume of essays and dismissed Maurice from his post. Maurice's dismissal brought sympathy from many Broad Church theologians and also from many of the public — Chadwick has suggested that some leading laymen believed a majority of laymen agreed with Maurice in rejecting the doctrine of eternal punishment (Chadwick, 1971, p. 548). But Maurice was also undeniably a victim of his own obscurity: he lost sympathy because he appeared to play games with words.

During the 1850s other Broad Church theologians published works which espoused views similar to those of Maurice. In 1855 A. P. Stanley and Benjamin Jowett published commentaries on the Pauline epistles: Stanley's on Corinthians was unexceptional; Jowett's on Thessalonians, Galatians and Romans was both impressive and controversial, being critical, pleading for a simple non-dogmatic faith, and revolting against traditional substitutionary atonement. Between 1855 and 1859 Baden Powell, Professor of Geometry at Oxford but also a very able theologian, published three collections of essays in which he asserted that nature obeyed the laws of God, but did so in an orderly, uniform manner (therefore miracles did not happen) and also that the Bible must be read in the light of such knowledge. Science, he argued, revealed God and was an ally to theology if both were critically approached. All these essays in theological liberalism, however, were either too academic or too isolated to attract the full force of condemnation or controversy. The publication of *Essays and Reviews* in February 1860 was quite another matter.

The publication of *Essays and Reviews* initiated what was arguably the greatest theological and religious controversy of the Victorian era. *Essays and Reviews* consisted of seven essays, each by a different author. All the authors were Anglican, one a layman and the other six clergymen. Frederick Temple argued that mankind had become sufficiently adult to study the Bible in a way which accepted scientific and literary criticism. Rowland Williams reviewed the work and implications of German critical scholarship on the Bible. Baden Powell concentrated on the theme of science, religion and the idea of the miraculous. Henry Wilson on 'The National Church' discussed the nature of an established church, its limits and its comprehensiveness, stressing the moral quality of Christian life rather than doctrinal orthodoxy. Charles Goodwin, the one layman, wrote on the 'Mosaic Cosmogony' discussing the relationship between geology and the accounts of the creation in Genesis. Mark Pattison wrote on 'Tendencies of Religious Thought in England 1688–1750', and the final essay, by Benjamin Jowett, discussed the appropriate interpretative approach to the biblical text and was entitled 'On the Interpretation of Scripture'.

The book caused an enormous furore. In five years it went into thirteen editions, and over four hundred books, pamphlets and articles were written in reply to it. It was condemned by the bishops in 1861 and two of the authors, Williams and Wilson, were charged with heresy and found guilty by the Court of Arches in 1862 (though both were subsequently acquitted on appeal to the Judicial Committee of the Privy Council in 1864). The entire book was also 'synodically condemned' by the Convocation of Canterbury and made the subject of a declaration, affirming all that it questioned, which was signed by 10,906 Anglican clergy in England, Wales and Ireland — just under half the Anglican clergy in those provinces of the church.

The furore was so great because, taken as a whole, *Essays and Reviews* called for a thoroughly historical and critical approach to the Bible, for recognition of the moral and spiritual worth of religious traditions outside the Bible, and for acceptance of the findings of science concerning both the age of the earth and its geological history, and the possibility (or impossibility) of miracles. It also argued that the moral demands of the Christian life had a priority over dogma and doctrinal formulae.

Essays and Reviews also contained more specific criticisms of traditional Christian beliefs. Williams, for example, argued that historical study of the Bible made it clear that the first five books of the Bible, traditionally held to have been written by Moses, were in fact a complex compilation from many sources and by many authors. He also argued that the Book of Isaiah contained the work of more than one prophet; that the Book of Daniel was not contemporary history but belonged to the second, not the sixth century B.C.; and that prophecy in the Old Testament generally had a moral, not a predictive, role: it was, he argued, meant to recall people to the moral life, not to predict the future.

Wilson similarly challenged specific doctrines by arguing that the word of God might be found in the Bible, but was not to be identified with the words of the Bible, and by suggesting that the idea of hell and eternal punishment was morally dubious and that the Christian hope was better understood in terms of universal salvation. Jowett, meanwhile, in perhaps the single most notorious sentence in the book, directly challenged traditional views of scriptural authority by asserting that the only way in which the interpretation of scripture could meet the demands of critical historical understanding was to 'interpret the Bible like any other book'.

Such views were not new. Four factors now combined, however, to create a major controversy. First, the essayists were commonly held to have written with a self-consciously unified and critical aim. The writers denied this in their preface, claiming that each writer was responsible only for his own contribution. Public opinion saw otherwise, and the denial of joint responsibility for the whole volume only led to accusations of conspiracy on the part of the authors. Second, the tone of the book was held to be unduly destructive and provocative: the authors, it was said, merely presented negative criticism, offering no positive substitute for that which they attacked. Third, the book appeared to be addressed to the public rather than merely the academic community, as many of the authors' earlier expressions of such views had been. The public and popular aim of the essayists increased the concern of their opponents perhaps more than anything else. Fourth, and critically, the essayists were challenging traditional doctrines that were common to both Evangelicals and Tractarians. For all their disputes of the previous twenty-odd years, and for all their ongoing disputes over ritual in worship, Tractarians and Evangelicals remained agreed on the necessity of a traditional view of biblical authority and inspiration, a conservative view of the status of doctrine and dogma, the place of miracle and supernatural intervention, and the necessity of hell and eternal punishment. The essayists also threatened the dependence upon the eighteenth-century Anglican evidential theology of Butler and Paley which underlay both Evangelical and Tractarian theology: the rejection of miracle and predictive prophecy undermined the 'evidence' of the evidential approach, and Pattison's essay placed its development squarely within a particular historical context.

The essayists' work thus produced an unholy alliance of Evangelicals and Tractarians: the declaration of the clergy, for example, was organized by the Tractarian Pusey, the High Church Wilberforce and the Evangelical Shaftesbury. The network of unholy alliances in fact went even further. The furore over *Essays and Reviews* only really took off after two articles were published, by Frederic Harrison in the *Westminster Review* and by Samuel Wilberforce in the *Quarterly Review*. Harrison, an Oxford man turned fervent non-believer, approved of the essayists' criticisms of orthodoxy but urged them to follow their arguments to their logical conclusion and cease to be Christian believers at all. Wilberforce picked up this point: he too thought the essayists should either believe much more or much less: 'They believe too much not to believe more, and they disbelieve too much not to disbelieve everything' he observed. It was an interesting irony: conservative bishop and radical positivist could both agree that in Christian belief it was either/or, all or nothing — a critical liberalism was both intellectually and morally untenable.

The climax of the affair was the trial of Williams and Wilson for heresy (the former for denying the inspiration of scripture, the latter for that and also for denying the doctrine of everlasting punishment) and their acquittal on appeal to the Privy Council after being found guilty by the ecclesiastical courts. As in the Gorham Judgement, the judgement of the Privy Council was based not upon the issue of what the Church's doctrine should be, but upon the question of whether the views of the accused were consonant with the Thirty-Nine Articles of the Church of England. The Privy Council concluded that the views of Williams and Wilson were consonant with the Articles. Making no comment on the theological merit or otherwise of their opinions, it acquitted them on the grounds of being legally within the bounds of the Church of England.

That was in 1864. Two years later another Broad Churchman, this time a bishop, also became the recipient of a legal acquittal and an ecclesiastical condemnation. Bishop John William Colenso, sometime scholar and teacher of mathematics, had become Bishop of Natal in 1853. In 1861 he published a *Commentary on the Epistle to the Romans* in which he added his voice to those who doubted the moral soundness of substitutionary atonement and everlasting punishment. In 1862–3 he followed this with the first two volumes of a study of *The Pentateuch and Book of Joshua Critically Examined*, in which he drew attention to the critical difficulties involved in such matters as ascribing the entire Pentateuch to Mosaic authorship. He also brought his mathematical interests to bear upon some of the figures and measurements detailed in these books of the Bible: many of the statistics given, he pointed out, were quite incredible. For both the English bishops and the South African Archbishop, Robert Gray, this combination of moral and mathematical misgivings amounted to heresy. The English bishops condemned Colenso's books and advised him to resign. Gray, when Colenso refused, tried him for heresy, found him guilty, deposed him and appointed a new Bishop of Natal. Colenso, however, appealed to the Privy Council, which in 1866 found on legal grounds that Gray had not the right to depose Colenso. Until 1883, when Colenso died, there were two Bishops of Natal.

Where, then, did *Essays and Reviews* and Colenso leave the doctrine and theology of the Church of England? The position was at best ambiguous, at worst, a downright muddle. The verdict of the church, in the form of bishops, archbishops and Convocation, and in the form of the overwhelming majority of the pamphlets and other responses to *Essays and Reviews* and Colenso, was condemnation and rejection. But in the courts the legal right of Broad Churchmen to hold views such as those of Williams and Wilson, and of Colenso to remain in his see, had been established. The conservatives had learned painfully that the law would not support their attempts to restrict the legitimate range of theological opinion within the Church of England. The liberals had learned, equally painfully, that although the law might give them the right to their views within the Church of England, the majority of their clerical brethren, and not a few of the laity, rejected and condemned them. Alongside the Tractarian-Evangelical dissolution of the Anglican doctrinal consensus there was now another clear division between theological liberals and conservatives. Not a few Victorian commentators on the position of the Broad Churchmen — men such as Leslie Stephen, sympathetic to their aims but doubtful of the viability of their stance — felt that morally the Broad Churchmen were left in an impossible position by the combination of legal acquittal and ecclesiastical condemnation: the honourable, intellectually ethical, course would be to leave the Church.[9]

In fact, nothing so clear-cut occurred. Altholz has suggested that the controversy over *Essays and Reviews* marked the exhaustion of both the Broad Church and of Anglican orthodoxy (Altholz, 1982, p. 187). If the remark is taken literally it is overstated. On the Broad Church side there remained in the 1870s and 1880s exponents of the kind of theology advocated by the essayists of 1860. Matthew Arnold, for example, attempted in the 1870s to set out a version of Christianity which eschewed both miracle — 'miracles do not happen' he asserted — and formal dogma, and emphasized instead experience, morality and conscience. But Arnold's version of Christianity, as presented in *St Paul and Protestantism* (1870), *Literature and Dogma* (1873), *God and the Bible* (1875) and *Last Essays on Church and Religion* (1877), was the work of a layman and thus capable of being quietly ignored, for as such it had no official ecclesiastical status.

Another example of the continued spirit of the mid-century Broad Churchmen was the work of Edwin Hatch. In the 1880s, Hatch's researches on the history of the early Christian church won him an international reputation. His work on the influence of Greek ideas upon the development of Christianity led him to the conclusion that the gospel was originally a way of life, centred on the ethics of the Sermon on the Mount, and was turned, by Greek influences, into a system of doctrine. For all his reputation abroad, he remained, however, a marginal figure in British theological life.

By the end of the century the issues raised by the Broad Churchmen of the 50s and 60s were again being determinedly raised by a new generation of theologically liberal clergy. The new generation of liberal churchmen, centred in the 1890s around the figure of Hastings Rashdall, formed, in 1898, the 'Churchmen's (later Modern Churchmen's) Union for the Advancement of Religious Thought' with the avowed aim 'to unite Churchmen who consider that dogma is capable of re-interpretation and restatement in accordance with the clearer perception of truth attained by discovery and research'.

On the orthodox side, meanwhile, a full-blooded orthodoxy continued to have its advocates and supporters. Evangelicals such as J. C. Ryle, the first Bishop of the new diocese of Liverpool, and C. J. Ellicott, Bishop of Gloucester, and Anglo-Catholics such as H. P. Liddon or G. A. Denison, continued to present versions of Christian belief which were traditionally orthodox, thoroughly supernatural and highly conservative. The mid-century Anglican orthodoxy which opposed *Essays and Reviews* was certainly

[9] On which see *RVB*, II, 9.

The contrast between the situation in the 1890s, with *Lux Mundi* and the Churchmen's Union for the advancement of Liberal Thought co-existing with strongly conservative Anglo-Catholicism and Evangelicalism, and that of 1830, is striking indeed. The tacit and overarching doctrinal and theological consensus of 1830 (in which parties reflected different shades of an essentially shared theological and doctrinal identity) had been subjected in the intervening decades to overwhelming pressure from two theological revolutions. Under the impact of first, the Tractarian attempt to re-catholicize the Church of England, and then the Liberal-Broad Church attempt to address the implications of historical criticism, natural science and moral critiques of orthodoxy, the consensus was progressively fragmented, so that by 1900 the Anglican situation was one of doctrinal and theological pluralism. The parties of 1900 no longer reflected shades of an agreed position (were no longer, in Avis' analogy, overlapping circles) but now held logically and theologically incompatible doctrinal attitudes, co-existing and competing within a single ecclesiastical body.

III THE LITURGICAL AND CEREMONIAL REVOLUTION

If the keynotes of the administrative and pastoral experience of the Victorian Church of England were 'reform' and 'revival', and that of the doctrinal and theological experience was 're-alignment', then the keynote of the experience of the liturgical life of the Victorian Church of England was a combination of revival and re-alignment.

The revival manifested itself in a widespread concern to revitalize and improve the spirit, forms and quality of the observance of public worship in the Church of England. Public worship in the Church of England in 1830 remained a comparatively dull, plain and unceremonious event. The principal Sunday services were Matins and Evensong and the Holy Communion was, in general, celebrated only once a quarter. The Daily Offices were, for the most part, not performed, and even the Sunday services of Matins and Evensong were still dominated by the sermon and the saying, not singing, of the responses and the psalms, not infrequently in the form of a dialogue between priest and parish clerk, the congregation merely listening and participating only when hymns were sung. Anglican liturgy and worship were, in fact, in a similar position to Anglican doctrine and theology on the eve of the Victorian period. Although 'parties' existed (there were, for example, Evangelicals who urged greater use of hymns and congregational chanting of psalms, and High Churchmen who urged more frequent celebration of communion), there was a general 'diffusion of a moderate ecclesiastical conservatism throughout the church' which was reflected in liturgy and worship as much as in doctrine and theology (Mather, 1986, p. 282).

By 1900, however, weekly communion was common, daily performance

of the offices frequent, robed choirs, organs, and choral services had become the new norm, and hymns had become an integral part of the worship. The congregation was immensely more involved in the worship. The modern observer of, or participant in, Anglican worship would have little difficulty in recognizing the ethos of the typical service of 1900, whereas that of 1830 would be severely alien. The change was the result of the efforts in the intervening years of both High and Low Churchmen, Evangelicals and Anglo-Catholics, who had worked in different and sometimes (but not always) competing and conflicting ways to revive and improve Anglican worship.

Alongside such revival, however, there was also drastic re-alignment. In 1906 a Royal Commission appointed to examine the state of worship and of ecclesiastical discipline in the Church of England concluded that the law of public worship in the Church of England was too narrow and needlessly condemned many liturgical practices which a large section of the most devoted members of the church highly valued. The revival of spiritual life and activity of the recent past — the Commission argued — had created new conditions for which existing regulations governing public worship were unsuitable. The Church of England should, therefore, be given the power to adjust its regulations on public worship so as to accommodate the new breadth in its liturgical and devotional life.

The conclusion of the report is important precisely for the way in which it acknowledges — and indeed commends — the emergence of a greater diversity in the worship of the Church of England. The Commission was the culmination of a long series of conflicts, reports, legislation and legal cases concerning the legitimate limits of liturgical practice in the Church of England. Those reports, conflicts and legal cases in turn arose from the attempts of the Tractarians, Anglo-Catholics and Ritualists to catholicize not only the doctrine but also the worship and the spirituality of the Church of England.

The two strands, of revival and re-alignment, were, of course, in practice inextricably intertwined, but for clarity we may consider revival first. In the 1830s both High and Low Churchmen, Evangelicals and Tractarians, were deeply concerned about the state of worship in the Church of England and were actively seeking both to improve the quality and also to change the nature of that worship. Their common ground eventually proved to be concern over the musical dimension of parochial worship — but in the 1830s, and for some time after, even the music of parish worship seemed to present the prospect of conflict between High and Low Church aims.

Even before 1830 Evangelicals had been urging a more active involvement of the congregation in parochial worship. Hymns were an essential part of this, but Evangelicals were also anxious to involve the congregation in the saying of the prose canticles and psalms. They were concerned that

the congregation should participate and not become an audience observing the 'performance' of a service by others. To this end they were prepared to advocate greater use of secular styles of tune for hymns, the use of emotion in hymn tunes, and the widespread introduction of the organ. For other reformers, especially High Churchmen, but also some traditional Low Churchmen of a less Evangelical kind, the major concern in the 1830s was not congregational participation, but the need for greater musical quality in worship. For High Churchmen, especially, the cathedral style of service, with a robed choir and choral setting of the services (pioneered so successfully by Hook at Leeds) became the ideal for parish worship also.

These two reforming ideals — on the one hand greater congregational participation and on the other greater musical quality — were not, as Nicholas Temperley has observed, easy to reconcile (Temperley, 1979, p. 243). That they *were* eventually reconciled was due not least to the Tractarian contribution to attitudes to Victorian church music. Just as they sought to recover older traditions of church architecture, so also the Tractarians sought to rediscover and re-introduce the older Catholic traditions (or what they took to be the older Catholic traditions) of church music, chanting and hymnody. Despite the fear of some older High Churchmen that hymns were unduly Evangelical or Dissenting, there had been High Churchmen even before the Oxford Movement who recognized the power of popular hymnody and set out to exploit it. Thus Reginald Heber in the first two decades of the nineteenth century had compiled a collection of hymns which followed the Christian year and had attempted to get the collection adopted by the church authorities. In the latter project he failed, though in 1827 his widow published the collection, adapted to each weekly church service of the year. To this early experiment in High Church hymnody the Tractarians in due course added their enthusiasm for the Latin hymns of the mediaeval church, the hymns of the Eastern church, and the chants and music of earlier ages. Hymnody, in short, offered the Tractarians a way to present their own highly liturgical view of the church and its calendar, the opportunity of writing new devotional hymns for this purpose, and of presenting to the modern Anglican worshipper Catholic hymns and devotions of the past. It also offered a further opportunity for congregational participation of which Tractarians, no less than Evangelicals, thoroughly approved. In hymnody, therefore, Evangelical and Tractarian concerns met. Moreover, both Tractarians and Evangelicals also shared a concern for the holiness, seriousness and hence the quality, of worship. Out of these two shared concerns emerged the parochial choral service of central Anglican churchmanship, which was to become — and largely remains — the characteristic Anglican mode of worship.

The choral service, with congregation led by choir in chanted psalms and canticles and with congregational hymns liberally interspersed, was the most fundamental Anglican liturgical development of the Victorian period. As Temperley has pointed out, at one level it was a fusion of Tractarian and Evangelical ideals for worship: hymns appealed to both Tractarians and Evangelicals; the choral setting also appealed to both, not least as a means of raising the quality, dignity and devotional seriousness of the services; and the attempts of the ecclesiologists to reform, restore and generally improve the condition and appearance of churches also facilitated this end.

At another level, however, the choral service of central churchmanship developed a life of its own and existed alongside specifically Tractarian and Evangelical modes of worship. Tractarians and Evangelicals fought bitterly over issues of worship, ritual and liturgy. But the controversies were the pre-occupation of highly committed minorities, not the product of a division down the centre of the church. Rather, in the centre, there emerged a majority Anglicanism whose characteristics were the choral service, moderate and dignified ceremony (more elaborate than the pre-Victorian norm, but less elaborate than the Ritualist ideal), and the centrality — in terms of the focus of congregational spirituality — of the hymn. The growing centrality of hymns in Anglican worship in the Victorian period was crucial. Hymnody became increasingly prevalent in all Victorian denominations and each gradually produced its own official or semi-official hymn book. The period between 1850 and 1900 has indeed been described by Temperley as that of 'the deluge of hymns'. And Anglicanism provides the paradigm for the process in the publication in 1861 of *Hymns Ancient and Modern*: out of the plethora of Anglican hymn books available in the 1850s and 1860s, this emerged as one of the most popular hymn books of all time (Temperley, 1979, ch. 9).

This whole line of development was of immense significance for the future of Anglicanism in general and the Church of England in particular. On the one hand this 'central' tradition of choral service and hymn-centred devotion provided a solid and unifying base in a church which was growing increasingly (and often increasingly bitterly) fragmented and pluralistic. Even the ends of the Anglican theological spectrum agreed on the desirability of choral services and hymns *per se* — although quite how you conducted the services and which collection of hymns you used remained matters of sharp controversy. On the other hand (and in the longer perspective even more significantly), the combination of choral service and hymns was one peculiarly well suited to the kind of religious commitment which was becoming increasingly prevalent in late nineteenth and early twentieth century Britain. The emerging pattern was one in which active participation and commitment in church life became increasingly the preserve of minorities of religiously-inclined people, whilst for a growing majority of the population (and even the majority of actual church-goers) religious commitment became an increasingly residual, lukewarm, and passive phenomenon: more an affair of undogmatic feeling and emotion; less an affair of articulate belief and clearly-held doctrine. Choral services and hymns are peculiarly suited to such a religious outlook: hymns (even when doctrinally written) are notoriously matters of the heart, not the head, moving rather than rational, loved for their tunes as much as their words, emotional rather than dogmatic; and the choral service is a near perfect vehicle for the religiously lukewarm and passive — it is familiar, ordered, comfortable, offers the opportunity to join in, yet has the choir to lead and instigate. Not a little of the Church of England's relative success in retaining at least some hold over a lukewarm and declining popular religious commitment in the twentieth century (the retention of what one recent commentator (Moyser, 1985, p. 6) has called a 'unique saliency' within English religious life) may be related to this development.

It would be an interesting, though difficult, exercise to explore in detail the possibility that the devotional life and theological assumptions of many lay Anglicans of central choral churchmanship were more in line with the undogmatic religion of hymns and the lay liberalism of Matthew Arnold than with any of the more developed theological and devotional strands of Victorian Anglicanism.[11]

If hymns and the music of parochial worship proved a meeting ground for Evangelicals and Tractarians, however, other areas proved just the opposite. Many of the early Tractarians had been moderate, even conservative, in their attitude towards ritual. The characteristic devotional concern of the early Tractarians was not the ritual but the frequency of the celebration of Holy Communion. During the 1830s, 40s and 50s, both the frequency of Holy Communion and the saying of the Daily Offices increased as a result of Tractarian influence and the general revival of the church's pastoral life. Moreover, the simple fact that from the late 1830s onwards Tractarian parish priests began to say and even sing Morning and Evening prayer publicly every day, and to celebrate Communion every Sunday and Saint's Day, was not of itself a cause of controversy. Controversy arose over the way in which such services were conducted.

[11] It would probably be equally revealing to explore the relationship between such hymn-centred and Arnoldian theological-cum-devotional styles and the immensely popular mid and late Victorian 'Lives of Jesus', of which Dean Farrar's *Life of Christ* (1874) was pre-eminent. Such 'Lives', whilst heavily romantic, sentimental, speculative (and therefore far short of fully scholarly biblical criticism) nevertheless made use of critical methods, emphasized the life and humanity of Jesus (rather than doctrine about him) and sought to place him in a first-century Palestinian context. In this sense they were 'critical' and 'liberal', but because of their overtly devotional aim and emotional appeal they 'domesticated' a variety of biblical criticism and provided an approach to Jesus which was 'popular', not 'academic', perceived to be constructive and an aid to faith, but also in fact far removed from and even antithetical to traditional Christian doctrine. (On the Victorian 'Lives of Jesus' see Pals, 1982 and Ellis, 1986.)

What caused the furore was the enthusiasm among some of the early Tractarians, and many of their second and third generation Ritualist successors, for highly Catholic forms of ritual and ceremony. As we have already noted, the development of Ritualism out of early Tractarian and ecclesiological concern over the sacramental life and the architecture of the church was entirely logical, even inevitable: that did not make it any less controversial, however.

In the 1840s Tractarian ceremony and ritual remained relatively modest: services were intoned, lighted candles were placed on the altar, robed choirs were introduced and surplices were worn for preaching. Even these actions offended some by their Catholicity, were regarded as popish, and brought forth not merely protests but on occasion riots (for example at Exeter in 1845 and 1848, at East Grinstead in 1848 and 1857, and at two London churches, St Barnabas', Pimlico in 1850–1 and St George's in the East in 1859–60). During the 1850s, however, some clergy moved much further and laid the basis of the advanced Ritualism of the 1860s and 1870s. In 1858 the Vicar of St James', Brighton, the Rev. John Purchas, published the *Directorium Anglicanum*, in which directions were given for supplementing the Book of Common Prayer with ceremonial practices of the western Catholic Church. By the 1860s the more advanced Anglo-Catholic or Ritualist churches were identifiable by their observation of the 'six points': use of the eastward position by the celebrant at the eucharist, use of full eucharistic vestments, use of lighted candles on the altar, use of unleavened wafer bread, use of incense and the mixing of water and wine in the chalice. It was noted in the 1860s that advanced Ritualism of this kind was particularly favoured by the younger generation of Anglo-Catholic priests. Around the 'six points' many other liturgical and ceremonial practices were also experimented with, but it was the six points themselves which formed the core of Ritualist liturgical practice and the focus of liturgical controversy. The other practices included such matters as coloured altar frontals, altar crosses, crucifixes, holy water, elevation of the elements, statues and credence tables.

Moreover, alongside the controversies over ritual and liturgical practice, there was suspicion of and opposition to the Ritualists' enthusiasm for the revival of the religious life in the Church of England and to their enthusiastic encouragement of private confession. Confession had never completely died out in the Church of England and, indeed, the Book of Common Prayer made provision for it. Equally, however, it had not enjoyed a prominent place within Anglican devotional and spiritual life. The Tractarians and Ritualists set out to change this and succeeded to the extent that they established confession as a definite option for ordinary Anglicans and incorporated it firmly into their own theory of pastoral and spiritual counselling. On the other hand it remained very much a minority choice with the laity, even in Ritualist parishes, and beyond such parishes aroused the opposition, suspicion and anti-Catholic prejudices of Protestants in general and Evangelicals in particular.

Inevitably, as with theological and doctrinal controversy, so with liturgical conflict: the issues became the subject of prosecutions and court cases. In 1854, as Denison was being prosecuted for heresy over eucharistic doctrine, the Hon. Robert Liddell, Vicar of St Paul's, Knightsbridge, was prosecuted for alleged liturgical illegalities — including use of altar cross and candles, coloured altar frontal and credence table. Initially found guilty, he was upheld on appeal on the grounds that the ornaments in question were acceptable under the Book of Common Prayer rubric that such matters should be consistent with the usage sanctioned 'by the authority of Parliament in the second year of the reign of King Edward VI'. The meaning and limits of that phrase — and the historical facts of the practice in 1542 — became the focus of a whole series of prosecutions and court cases. The process of prosecution and defence was in turn the cause of the formation of rival church societies. In 1855 the Society of the Holy Cross and in 1859–60 the English Church Union were formed for 'Church Defence' — that is to say, the defence of Ritualist clergy. In 1865 the Church Association was formed to protest against what it saw as Romanizing tendencies in the Church of England. It was an extreme Evangelical society and the main instigator of anti-Ritualist prosecutions: by 1869 it had over 7000 members.

Between 1867 and 1871 the Church Association brought prosecutions against A. H. Mackonochie, Curate of St Alban's, Holborn, and John Purchas, Vicar of St James', Brighton. After lengthy proceedings in the ecclesiastical courts and in the Judicial Committee of the Privy Council, a number of ritual practices were ruled illegal. In the Purchas case a total of thirty-three points were found illegal, including such matters as the wearing of birettas. Crucially, however, four of the six points were ruled illegal (namely vestments, the eastward position, wafer bread and the mixed chalice). During the same period as these two prosecutions, a Royal Commission on Ritual, set up in 1867, delivered four reports, the last of them in 1870. The Royal Commission was critical of liturgical innovation and was almost unanimous in wishing vestments banned. On other matters, however, there was wider disagreement. The Ritualists, for their part, would not accept the decisions of the courts, or for that matter comply with the requests, or obey the directions, of their bishops. Their defiance and continuance of ritual practice was prompted in part by their deep conviction that the defence of such Catholic practice was essential to the defence of the Catholic nature of the Church of England, in part by their rejection of the authority of secular courts in such matters, and in part by the fact that many of the Ritualist clergy were, in personality, a remarkable combination of devoted pastors and pugnacious controversialists. Contrary to the image which some opponents sought to foster of the Ritualist as essentially effete and effeminate (Hilliard, 1982), Ritualist clergy tended to be strong characters whose strength of character issued in remarkable lives of pastoral devotion and equally remarkable campaigns of provocation and confrontation: Ritualism and Ritualists alike, it has been observed, thrived on conflict (Yates, 1983, p. 415).

Public reaction to the Ritualists is difficult to gauge accurately. *Punch* thought it knew the views of Protestant Englishmen and ridiculed the Ritualists in a whole series of cartoons and satires, just as it had ridiculed the earlier Tractarians. The riots at leading Ritualist churches also suggested popular opposition. On the other hand, *Punch* was not synonymous with public opinion and the riots were often the result of agitation by militantly Evangelical extremists. Many of the Ritualists, and even some of the bishops, held that among the non-Evangelical laity Ritualism was popular. Episcopal reaction was mixed, the bishops themselves being divided on the issue. They had dioceses to keep in good order and Ritualists not only stirred up Protestant protests but were also remarkably intransigent and uncompromising in their own behaviour. It was thus understandable that the bishops were, generally, irritated by Ritualist priests; but on the other hand many of the Ritualists were excellent pastors and it did the bishops little credit that they rarely openly supported Ritualists, on such pastoral grounds, against Evangelical protests.

Out of the prosecutions, Royal Commission reports, and controversies of 1867–71 there emerged the Public Worship Regulation Act of 1874. Deliberately designed to curb Ritualism, it received overwhelming support in Parliament and also attracted much public enthusiasm. The bishops were more cautious and insisted, successfully, upon the inclusion of a clause which allowed diocesan bishops to veto prosecutions under the Act. The Act set up a new court, with a lay judge appointed by the archbishops to adjudicate in ritual cases. The Church Association at once began a new series of prosecutions. The first such, against C. J. Ridsdale, Vicar of St Peter's, Folkestone, resulted in Ridsdale's conviction and his compliance with the judgement.[12] It was to be the only such compliance. In five further cases, Ritualist priests refused to accept the jurisdiction of the court and complainants then cited the priests concerned for contempt of court. This resulted in the imprisonment of the priests. In four cases the imprisonment was of short duration. In one case, however, that of S. F. Green, Rector of

[12] Ridsdale appealed, lost and asked Tait, his archbishop, for a dispensation from the rubric in the Book of Common Prayer that Ridsdale believed required him to perform ritual acts which the court now forbad him to do. Tait granted the dispensation; Ridsdale remained Vicar of St Peter's.

St John's, Miles Platting, Manchester, the imprisonment lasted nineteen months.

The Act did not work: at least not as an effective means of curbing Ritualism, since the Ritualists carried on and were prepared to go to prison rather than accept the authority of the court. This in turn caused public revulsion: the imprisonment of priests of known pastoral devotion on the grounds that they had conscientious objections to obeying a secular court in matters of religious ritual was sufficiently unedifying to cause public opinion to change sides. It also made the Church of England look simultaneously silly and vindictive.

The bishops, therefore, vetoed prosecutions under the Act (all except the Evangelical J. C. Ryle of Liverpool, a former Church Association member, who insisted as late as 1885 in allowing to proceed a case against James Bell Cox, Vicar of St. Margaret's, Toxteth Park: Cox was jailed for contempt in May 1887 but released after only sixteen days when his sentence was quashed on a technicality). The Act was reduced to a dead letter. By 1881 the 1874 Public Worship Regulation Act was widely acknowledged by churchmen to be an embarrassing and unedifying failure. A Royal Commission on ecclesiastical jurisdiction was set up which proposed the repeal of the 1874 Act and new courts which separated ritual and doctrinal cases from ones concerning clerical misconduct. The Commission proved insufficiently unanimous to enable Parliament to proceed confidently. The Public Worship Regulation Act remained and the bishops continued to veto it, Ryle apart. For their part, the Ritualist clergy took advantage of the veto to press their ritual practice further: by the turn of the century there were almost 400 churches in England using incense and over 70 practising perpetual reservation of the sacrament.

The Church Association now tried a different approach. In 1888 it prosecuted a bishop for using altar lights, mixed chalice, eastward position, ceremonial ablutions, the sign of the cross and the Agnus Dei. Unfortunately for the Church Association, it chose to prosecute Edward King, Bishop of Lincoln, whose pastoral devotion and personal saintliness were well known and much admired. A trial ensued in which the Archbishop of Canterbury, Benson, sought to concede as much as he could to King. King was upheld by Benson on everything but the sign of the cross and the fact that the mixing of the chalice, if done, should have been completed before the service. King complied with the judgement. The prosecutors not only lost but lost credibility by their persecution of a pastorally devoted and much-loved bishop.

The trial of King still did not end controversy, however. Anti-Ritualist publications were produced, such as the *Ritualistic Clergy List* (published by the Church Association), which claimed to identify practitioners of Ritualism. *The Secret History of the Oxford Movement* (1897) by Walter Walsh purported to reveal the real superstition and extremism of Anglo-Catholicism. It was, in fact, an outburst of 'no popery' in Anglican guise. Extreme Evangelicals meanwhile formed the Protestant Truth Society, led by John Kensit, and made themselves an unpleasant nuisance by demonstrating and disrupting services at Ritualist churches. Bishops opposed to Ritualism continued diocesan campaigns against Ritualist clergy, and between 1899 and 1902 no less than six anti-Ritualist bills were brought before the House of Commons.[13] They all failed, but their existence at all pointed to the continuing problem, and in 1904 Parliament set up a Royal Commission on Ecclesiastical Discipline. The Commission reported in 1906 and concluded, as we noted earlier, not only that ecclesiastical discipline in matters of liturgy and ritual had broken down hopelessly, but also that existing limitations on ritual were too narrow and should be broadened to officially accommodate the greater range of spiritualities and devotional styles which, *de facto*, now flourished within the Church of England.

The practical effect of the 1906 Royal Commission report was the initiation of the long process of revision of the Book of Common Prayer, which, in various stages, has occupied the Church of England throughout the twentieth century. The report was also, however, in effect an official recognition that in worship and spirituality, as well as in doctrine and theology, the Victorian Church of England had developed an internal pluralism.

IV THE NATIONAL AND CONSTITUTIONAL REVOLUTION

At the beginning of this essay, it was noted that in the early 1830s churchmen genuinely feared for the preservation of the established status of the Church of England. The repeal of the Test and Corporation Acts in 1828 and the enactment of Catholic emancipation in 1829 clearly signalled a changing understanding of establishment. As Richard Helmstadter has observed of the 1828 repeal, 'it conferred constitutional confirmation upon the movement towards religious pluralism in English society' (Helmstadter, 1979, p. 145). The change, as we have seen, was moderate, not extreme, and did not run to disestablishment — at least not in England. In Scotland the Anglican tradition had never been the established church: Presbyterianism fulfilled that role and experienced its own Victorian tensions in consequence. By 1900 Irish Anglicanism was also non-established: Irish disestablishment having occurred in 1869. Wales was also well on the way to disestablishment. Welsh disestablishment did not finally arrive until 1920, but the fact that it would eventually do so was already clear by the

[13] For detail on the Public Worship Regulation Act, its aftermath and the resurgence of anti-Ritualism in the 1890s, see Bentley, 1978 and Machin, 1982.

1880s. In neither case was the transition a surprise, especially when placed in the context of the repeals and emancipations of 1828–9 and the constitutional recognition of religious pluralism. As Owen Chadwick has observed, 'an established church could marry with democracy only if it was not a grievance to an important minority in the nation' (Chadwick, 1972, p. 427). In point of fact, the established nature of the Anglican Church in both Ireland and Wales was an offence not merely to an important minority but to an actual majority of the population.

In Ireland an overwhelmingly Catholic majority and a large Presbyterian presence among the remaining Protestants made Anglicans a minority indeed. In Wales, Nonconformity, the Welsh language, and Welsh nationalism combined to provide an overwhelmingly Welsh Nonconformist majority over against an Anglicanism which was widely perceived to be English and alien. As the franchise was successively extended during the Victorian period, disestablishment in Ireland and Wales became practical, even inevitable. In England itself establishment survived, but arguably only because of a radical change in its nature whereby many of its own privileges and the concomitant disabilities of dissenters were removed in a process tantamount to 'gradual disestablishment'. The 'establishment' which remained was in reality stripped of the greater part of the power it had enjoyed in 1830 and was relatively weak.

In the present context the Irish case is striking, mainly for the calmness with which the majority of English churchmen eventually accepted it.[14] In 1833 the Irish Church Temporalities Act, with its very modest proposals for the reform of the Irish dioceses, had occasioned Keble's Assize Sermon and kindled the furore which issued in the Oxford Movement. In 1869 no comparable furore occurred and the Anglican church in Ireland was disestablished with relative calm. Certainly for some High Churchmen, such as G. A. Denison, it was the final straw. Following on the judgements of the Privy Council in the Gorham, *Essays and Reviews* and Colenso cases, Irish disestablishment seemed to Denison the end of establishment altogether. He wrote a pamphlet entitled 'The Church of England in 1869: Review of the Position' in which he argued that, after the 'revolution' of 1869, the Church of England must also now seek disestablishment in order to escape the tyranny and interference of a hopelessly Erastian Parliament. It was a reaction experienced also by a number of Ritualist clergy in the 1870s and 1880s, who, after the passing of the Public Worship Regulation Act, came to believe that disestablishment was the only way to preserve the Church's Catholicity and freedom.

But Denison was atypical in 1869, just as the Ritualists who favoured disestablishment were atypical later. The prevalent reaction was one of

[14] For Irish disestablishment and its effects see *RVB*, II, 6.

pragmatic resignation. Churchmen generally did not like the disestablishment of the Irish Church and most opposed it — sixteen bishops voted against it, only one voted for it. But once passed it was accepted — the Denisons aside — with equanimity. The Irish Church got on with the job of constructing a new identity and the Church of England discovered that disestablishment in Ireland did not presage disestablishment in England. Some English churchmen, including Frederick Temple and many Broad Churchmen, but also including Tractarians like R. W. Church and W. F. Hook, actually approved, and Gladstone, who had led the project and drafted the bill, was himself a High Churchman. In one sense, of course, Denison was right and there had been a revolution when the Irish Church Act was passed. For the first time, part of Great Britain had no established church. But in another sense it was no revolution at all, but merely one more stage in the Victorian constitutional adjustment to the realities of religious pluralism.

The position in Wales was less dramatic, the interrelationship of religion and nationalism less passionate, and the injustice of establishment less glaring than in Ireland. Nevertheless the pressure for Welsh disestablishment also mounted. Despite the efforts of notable individuals, such as Bishop Copleston of Llandaff and Bishop Thirlwall of St David's, the Anglican church in Wales was widely perceived as an essentially English, alien and gentry-dominated church, unsympathetic to Welsh language and culture. By mid-century — as the 1851 Census of Religious Worship clearly showed — the overwhelming majority in Wales was Nonconformist. From mid-century onwards the new Welsh-speaking press and leaders of Welsh national opinion were also all Nonconformist. The campaign for Welsh disestablishment began in earnest in the 1880s. It passed through a bitter tithe war from 1888 to 1890, during which Nonconformists refused to pay tithes to the established church, many clergy suffered severe poverty and not a few Nonconformists suffered imprisonment. Liberal MPs in Wales made disestablishment central to their platform. In 1895 the Commons passed a severely disendowing disestablishment bill through a second reading, but the government fell. The Welsh church was finally disestablished in 1914 and the first Archbishop of Wales enthroned in 1920: the delay was caused by inadequate drafting of the bill (which was amended by an Act of 1919), and by the First World War.

The position in England was different again. The fears of 1832 did not materialize. Over the next fifty years a long series of reforms and repeals radically changed the nature of establishment, but did not end it. By 1880 the state had become more nearly neutral in religion, the privileges of the established church had been much curtailed, the disabilities of dissenters and non-believers much reduced, and their rights much increased. That the Church of England remained securely established was due largely to the fact that the more offensive aspects of establishment had been removed and its continuing power much reduced. Between 1832 and 1880 a whole series of reforms and repeals were passed. Civil registration of births was made possible, thus removing the necessity to register births in the register of the parish church (1836); marriages could be solemnized outside the parish church (1836); the need to subscribe to the Thirty-Nine Articles to take a degree at Oxford or Cambridge was abolished (1854 and 1856); access to Grammar Schools was opened for Dissenters (1860); the necessity of religious oaths for public offices was abolished (1866);[15] compulsory church rate on all parishioners for the upkeep of the parish church was abolished (1868); the Irish Church was disestablished (1869); the higher degrees, fellowships and offices of Oxford, Cambridge and Durham Universities were opened to those of any religion or none (1871); non-Anglican services were permitted at burials in parish graveyards (1880). In the same period the laws governing divorce were liberalized and their religious dimension much reduced; the laws on blasphemy were steadily interpreted in a liberal manner by the courts so that prosecution for blasphemy became increasingly ineffective; and the need for an oath as a Christian in order to take a seat in Parliament was removed first for Jews and then for non-believers.

The radically altered nature of establishment is, in one sense, best illustrated by the history of its chief opponent, the Liberation Society. Formed in 1844 by a Congregational minister outraged at the imprisonment of a member of his church for refusal to pay church rates, the aim of the Liberation Society was the removal of the privileges of the established church and the disabilities of Nonconformists, and ultimately the disestablishment of the Church of England. Between 1850 and 1880 it was the major focus of Nonconformist agitation for reform. After 1880 the Liberation Society ceased to be the centre of Nonconformist politics and the issue of disestablishment *per se* became increasingly peripheral, so great had been the 'gradual' or 'piecemeal' disestablishment of the preceding half-century.

In one area only did the conflict between established church and Nonconformity remain passionate and bitter in the closing years of the century — elementary education. In 1833, for the first time, the state had provided funds for education. These amounted to £20,000 a year, were to assist in the building of schools, and were administered as a grant to the two major societies for building and maintaining schools: the British and Foreign Schools Society, which favoured education in religion but not in the principles of any specific denomination; and the National Society, which held that religious education should be in the principles of the established

[15] Although an oath upon the Christian faith remained essential to take a seat in Parliament until 1886 and gave rise to controversy in the Bradlaugh case between 1880 and 1886, on which see *RVB*, I, 8 and *RVB*, II, 4.

church. Nonconformists, not unnaturally, favoured the British and Foreign Society. They also noted and resented the fact that, since the annual grant was awarded proportionately according to the amounts raised by the societies themselves, and the National Society raised more, the conditions of state aid favoured the established church. Although admirably scriptural, the policy that to those who had, more would be given, offended Nonconformist feelings.

In 1839–40 it was proposed to increase the annual grant but also introduce compulsory inspection, the inspectors to be under the control of a non-denominational committee. The Church of England successfully resisted the latter part of the proposal, securing agreement that the archbishops should have the right of veto and of dismissal of inspectors of National Schools. The first concerted attempt at a religious but non-denominational system was thus frustrated by Anglican resistance. The National Society gained progressively more of a progressively increased annual grant: Nonconformists started to found societies of their own.

In 1843 it was the turn of Nonconformity to defeat an education proposal. Sir James Graham's factory bill included a requirement that children between the ages of eight and thirteen working in factories must receive three hours' education a day. The teacher was to be an Anglican and the syllabus and trustees of the school were also to be heavily Anglican in constitution. Although modest conscience clauses were included (for withdrawal of children from the most overtly Anglican teaching), Nonconformists were appalled and opposed the bill: even Wesleyan Methodism, which normally held itself aloof from Nonconformist attacks upon the established church, joined in this particular confrontation. The education clauses of the bill were dropped. In 1843 the government also conceded to the British and Foreign Schools Society the same rights of veto of its inspectorate as the National Society had secured in 1840. Between 1843 and 1870 a running battle continued between the government's Committee of Education (as set up in 1839) and the Church of England — or at least large parts of it. The Committee sought to secure conscience clauses from the management committees of National Society schools — so that in areas where only National Schools existed Nonconformists might be spared the choice of excluding their child from education altogether or submitting it to Anglican religious teaching. By the 1860s about half the Anglican clergy were accepting such clauses: but there remained the other half who would not.

In 1870 the Forster Education Act made the first concerted attempt to provide a nation-wide system of elementary education. Where there were no voluntary church schools or insufficiently large ones, School Boards were to be elected to provide Board Schools at public cost. School Boards were also empowered to pay from the rates for poor children to attend church schools. School Boards were not obliged to provide religious education in Board Schools (although in fact most did), but if they did choose to provide religious education it had to be in accordance with the Cowper-Temple clause of the 1870 Act, which insisted that Board School religious teaching must be non-denominational, and that all denominational schools must have an effective conscience clause. If a school board chose not to include religious education it must nevertheless include moral teaching on the syllabus — although relatively few people could then envisage what moral education apart from religious education would be. In 1876 elementary education was made compulsory and in 1893 it was made free.

The Cross Commission of Enquiry of 1886–8 found that standards were rising in all schools, but also found that denominational schools were finding it increasingly difficult to keep pace with the additional costs of rising standards. The Commission recommended modest aid from the rates for church schools, a measure which was enacted in 1897. In 1902 a new education act provided for rate support for all schools: in return the local authority was to be represented on school management boards and only a head teacher might be appointed on grounds of religious opinion. Nonconformists found the 1870 and 1902 Acts unsatisfactory: the latter especially. In 1870 the principle of rate support for pupils in voluntary schools had been established and in 1902 it had become available to all voluntary schools. In both cases this meant, by definition, much greater benefit for Anglicans than for Nonconformists, since there were more Anglican schools in existence to benefit. Also, the Anglicans, despite rising costs, were still able to build more schools and thus reap more benefit (as did the Roman Catholics, despite the poverty of much of the Catholic community), whilst Nonconformists found the expense beyond them, schools closed and their share of rate support declined yet further. In 1902 this produced the last great church and chapel confrontation; the last great campaign of Nonconformist civil disobedience, in the form of refusal to pay rates; and the last example of the classic Victorian alliances of Tory Party and established church, and Liberal Party and Nonconformity. But it was also, precisely because of the way a church-chapel controversy became so central in national politics, an anomaly, a survival into the post-Victorian era of an essentially early and mid-Victorian set of alliances. By the second decade of the twentieth century both the nature of British politics and the nature of religion in Britain had entered decisively upon a new phase.

In both education, therefore, and in the gradual disestablishment of the privileges of the Church of England by 1880, the relationship between the state and religion became less intimate and more neutral during the Victorian period. Where the state was perceived still to favour one religious tradition above another — as in the 1870 and 1902 Education Acts — a furore occurred. But the furore itself made more evident the overall trend towards the neutrality of the state in the matter of religious belief, and the increasing location of belief in the sphere of private choice. Even when, in elementary education, there was difficulty in grasping how morality might be taught apart from religion, in practice the religion that was desired was a biblical, non-denominational ethic — as far as the state was concerned it mattered that children should learn to be good, not that they should learn to believe in particular religious doctrines. The Church of England thus became a part of a broader, less well-defined national religious tradition, and the state, in the shape of the courts, took the same view of its role within the established church as it did of its role in relation to different religious traditions in society at large. In a series of cases — Gorham, Denison, Williams and Wilson, Colenso — the courts refused to judge matters of doctrine *per se* and maintained that their role was to interpret the legal limits of the Church of England in the broadest way possible. And on the one occasion that the state sought to assist the Church of England in maintaining a narrow conception of the breadth of its ritual and doctrine, it faced defeat by virtue of the stubbornness of individual clerical consciences: the Public Worship Regulation Act was rendered unworkable and the Royal Commission of 1906 gave its seal of approval to the *de facto* pluralism of early twentieth-century Anglicanism. The 1906 report gave official recognition to the way in which the national and constitutional position of the Church of England had been radically altered over the seventy years since 1832. It remained an established church, but only because the nature of its establishment had been modified and broadened. It was no longer a glaringly privileged religious institution with relatively clear limits. It had become, rather, an internally pluralistic established church in a religiously pluralist state.

V CONCLUSIONS

What, then, were the essential characteristics of the experience of the Victorian Church of England? Without doubt, the Church of England of 1900 was a more complicated, more complex church than that of 1830. In 1830 it was possible to ask, with some hope of a reasonably clear and succinct answer, 'What do Anglicans believe?' The answer would have been along the lines of Paul Avis's analogy of overlapping circles: the Church of England was Protestant — though possessed of High, Low and Latitudinarian versions of Protestantism, and the Church of England was the national church, with privileges to match. By 1900, the question 'What do Anglicans believe?' had become, in any straightforward sense, impossible. The answer would have to begin by asking 'Which Anglicans?' In theology and in worship there had been an assertion of the fundamentally Catholic nature of the Church of England, and in theology and doctrine there had also been a painful process of controversy and conflict, establishing the legal right of clergymen to hold liberal theological views and remain ordained members of the Church of England.[16] In 1830 the 'parties' of the Church of England were only loosely defined. By 1900 the 'parties' were more clearly distinct and more combatively committed to the defence and propagation of their particular standpoints: the Protestant Truth Society, the English Church Union, the Churchmen's Union — these and similar societies competed to shape the future character and development of the Church of England.

Such competition and complexity was also a sign of vitality. The Church of England of 1900 was a more passionate, active, energetic church than the Church of England of 1830. Theological debate was more intense, the administration of the church more efficient, the pastoral work of the church more consistently dedicated and professional, and the worship of the church both more varied and more deeply devotional. But alongside such reform and revival in the life of the Church of England there was also dramatic re-alignment. Both the reform and revival were also part of a changing identity, both internally and in national life. Internally the Church of England experienced fragmentation and became not merely broad but pluralist. In national life the Church of England lost privileges, other churches gained in both rights and stature, and in the process the Church of England became more like one denomination among others.

And yet, as it became one more denomination among others it also retained a special status (in England anyway). With that special status came also a relatively greater ability to withstand the decline of the twentieth century — certainly a greater ability than that of the Nonconformists who had grown so spectacularly and achieved so striking a rise in status in the same period. The special status which the Church of England retained is not easy to define. It had to do with becoming both an expression and a location of an emerging national religious ethos. As Antony Lentin has observed, 'in a moral, social and aesthetic sense, the Church remained, if not altogether a national Church, at least a national institution' (*RVB*, II, 4). It remained also a national institution in a religious sense. Its own internal pluralism — in which committed Anglo-Catholics, Evangelicals and Liberals were obliged to co-exist, and in which the majority, especially of the laity, occupied a variety of less passionately held theological opinions somewhere near one or other of these 'parties' but often eclectically

[16] It did not mean that any theological views were acceptable; in 1862 the Judicial Committee of the Privy Council removed from office the Vicar of Brading in the Isle of Wight, on grounds of heresy in published sermons: and in 1871 it similarly removed Charles Voysey, Vicar of Heaulaugh, for expressing (in his book *The Sling and the Stone*) unorthodox views which pressed beyond the Broad Churchmanship of *Essays and Reviews*. But after *Essays and Reviews* and Colenso it was clear that the Broad Churchmanship of a Jowett, Wilson, or Williams was legally legitimate within the Church of England.

borrowing from each — mirrored the religious pluralism of modern British, and especially English, society. No-one would seriously have questioned that Britain remained, in some sense, a Christian society — but rather fewer would have cared to define that sense too closely.

Similarly, the Church of England had become a very broad church — but not in the way the mid-century Broad Churchmen had in mind. For many of the Broad Churchmen of mid-century — F. D. Maurice for example, or H. B. Wilson — the ideal Church of England was one in which greater breadth and comprehensiveness would be embraced as a matter of conviction. In the event, the Victorian Church of England accepted breadth and comprehensiveness not from conviction but out of pragmatism: the courts insisted on the right of Liberals, Catholics and Evangelicals to interpret the formularies of the Church of England in a variety of ways; and the conscientious stubbornness of Ritualist priests demonstrated the impossibility of restraining the liturgical diversity of the church. Such breadth and internal pluralism gave the Church of England a broader basis of appeal in the twentieth-century than that of more narrowly-defined denominations — even if, in practice, the price was an ecclesiastical institution which was no longer genuinely unified and within which various factions frequently themselves behaved more and more like undeclared sects in national religious life.

BIBLIOGRAPHY

J. L. Altholz (1982) 'The mind of Victorian orthodoxy: Anglican responses to "Essays and Reviews", 1860–1864', *Church History*, Vol. 51, pp. 186–97.

P. Avis (1986) 'The Tractarian challenge to consensus and the identity of Anglicanism', *King's Theological Review*, Vol. 9, pp. 14–17.

*J. Bentley (1978) *Ritualism and Politics in Victorian Britain: The Attempt to Legislate for Belief*, Oxford, Oxford University Press.

G. F. A. Best (1964) *Temporal Pillars: Queen Anne's Bounty, the Ecclesiastical Commissioners and the Church of England*, Cambridge, Cambridge University Press.

D. Bowen (1968) *The Idea of the Victorian Church: A Study of the Church of England 1833–1889*, Montreal, McGill University Press.

O. J. Brose (1959) *Church and Parliament: The Reshaping of the Church of England 1828–1860*, Stanford (CA), Stanford University Press.

O. Chadwick (1971) *The Victorian Church*, Part I, A. & C. Black.

O. Chadwick (1972) *The Victorian Church*, Part II, A. & C. Black.

*M. A. Crowther (1970) *Church Embattled: Religious Controversy in Mid-Victorian England*, Newton Abbot, David and Charles.

I. Ellis (1986) 'Dean Farrar and the quest for the historical Jesus', *Theology*, Vol. 89, pp. 108–15.

A. D. Gilbert (1976) *Religion and Society in Industrial England: Church, Chapel and Social Change 1740–1914*, Longman.

B. Heeney (1974) 'The theory of pastoral ministry in the mid-Victorian Church of England', *Historical Magazine of the Protestant Episcopal Church*, Vol. 42, pp. 215–30.

B. Heeney (1978) 'Harry Jones and the Broad Church pastoral tradition in London' in P. T. Phillips (ed.) *The View from the Pulpit: Victorian Ministers and Society*, pp. 67–86, Toronto, Macmillan of Canada.

R. J. Helmstadter (1979) 'The Nonconformist conscience' in P. Marsh (ed.) *The Conscience of the Victorian State*, pp. 135–72, Brighton, Harvester.

D. Hilliard (1982) 'Un-English and unmanly: Anglo-Catholicism and homosexuality', *Victorian Studies*, Vol. 25, pp. 181–210.

P. Hinchcliff (1984) 'Jowett and Gore: two Balliol essayists', *Theology*, Vol. 87, pp. 251–59.

I. G. Jones (1984) 'Ecclesiastical economy: aspects of church building in Victorian Wales' in R. Davies, R. Griffiths, I. Jones and K. Morgan (eds.) *Welsh Society and Nationhood*, pp. 216–31, Cardiff, University of Wales Press.

G. I. T. Machin (1982) 'The last Victorian anti-Ritualist campaign, 1895–1906', *Victorian Studies*, Vol. 25, pp. 277–302.

F. C. Mather (1986) 'Georgian churchmanship reconsidered: some variations in Anglican public worship 1714–1830', *Journal of Ecclesiastical History*, Vol. 36, pp. 255–83.

G. Moyser (ed.) (1985) *Church and Politics Today: The Role of the Church of England in Contemporary Politics*, Edinburgh, T. & T. Clark.

H. R. Murphy (1955) 'The ethical revolt against Christian orthodoxy in early Victorian England', *American Historical Review*, Vol. 40, pp. 800–17.

D. L. Pals (1982) *The Victorian Lives of Jesus*, San Antonio (TX), Trinity University Press.

H. D. Rack (1973) 'Domestic visitation: a chapter in early nineteenth century evangelism', *Journal of Ecclesiastical History*, Vol. 24, pp. 357–76.

B. M. G. Reardon (1980) *Religious Thought in the Victorian Age: A Survey from Coleridge to Gore*, Longman.

M. J. D. Roberts (1981) 'Private patronage and the Church of England 1800–1900', *Journal of Ecclesiastical History*, Vol. 32, pp. 199–223.

N. Sykes (1934) *Church and State in England in the Eighteenth Century*, Cambridge, Cambridge University Press.

N. Temperley (1979) *The Music of the English Parish Church*, Vol. 1, Cambridge, Cambridge University Press.

*P. Toon (1979) *Evangelical Theology 1833–1856: A Response to Tractarianism*, Basingstoke, Marshall, Morgan and Scott.

*D. G. Wigmore-Beddoes (1971) *Yesterday's Radicals: A Study of the Affinity between Unitarianism and Broad Church Anglicanism in the Nineteenth Century*, Cambridge, James Clarke.

W. N. Yates (1978) '"The only true friend": Ritualist concepts of priestly vocation' in D. Baker (ed.) *Religious Motivation: Biographical and Sociological Problems for the Church Historian*, pp. 407–15, Oxford, Blackwell.

*W. N. Yates (1983) *The Oxford Movement and Anglican Ritualism*, The Historical Association.

CHAPTER 2

SOUNDINGS!

The Living down at our Village falling vacant, LORD PAVONDALE *left it to the Parish to choose the new Rector.*

Influential Parishioner. "THEN AM I TO UNDERSTAND, MR. MANIPLE, THAT YOU OBJECT TO BURY A DISSENTER?"

The Rev. Mr. Maniple (one of the Competitors). "O, DEAR ME, NO, MR. JINKS; QUITE THE CONTRARY!!"

FROM DISSENTERS TO FREE CHURCHMEN: THE TRANSITIONS OF VICTORIAN NONCONFORMITY

IN any period it is a mistake to treat Protestant Nonconformity in England as though it were uniform. There have always been important differences within and between the various denominations.

(David Thompson (ed.) (1972) *Nonconformity in the Nineteenth Century*, p. 1)

I OLD DISSENT, NEW DISSENT, AND THE STRENGTH OF NONCONFORMITY

In Victorian England, Protestant Nonconformity enjoyed a degree of prominence in national life which it had not previously experienced and from which, in the twentieth century, it has steadily declined. This prominence was never tranquil or untroubled and never free from ambiguity: far from it. The public prominence of Victorian Protestant Nonconformity was turbulent and full of controversy, both within the Nonconformist community itself and in the relationship between Nonconformity as a whole and the rest of the social, political and religious culture of Victorian Britain. But, in sheer numbers, in religious vitality, in its centrality to political debate, and in its contribution to the social, cultural and ethical *mores* of the era, Victorian Nonconformity was an integral and inescapable ingredient in national life. To begin to understand something of the identity and character of this phenomenon, however, one must recognize not only the sheer size and influence of Victorian Protestant Nonconformity, but also its essential diversity and variety. Both the extent and the diversity were in fact revealed with particular clarity by the 1851 Census of Religious Worship.

When, in January 1854, Horace Mann presented the results of the 1851 Census of Religious Worship, reaction focused predominantly upon two of the findings. One was the discovery that, in Mann's much quoted phrase, it was 'apparent that a sadly formidable portion of the English people are habitual neglecters of the public ordinances of religion'. The other was the apparent strength of Nonconformity. Neither finding was particularly original. In respect of the 'habitual neglecters' of public worship — of whom, Mann noted with concern, the majority were to be found among 'the labouring myriads' of the large towns and cities — Mann himself acknowledged that the problem had been recognized for some time. Programmes and campaigns of 'Church Extension' were already well established features of the religious landscape by the 1830s and 40s and Mann remarked especially on the rapid progress of the Church of England in the twenty years since 1830, the building of new churches being a regular phenomenon. Nor, he added, was the church's effort limited to the provision of new buildings. There were also a great many new voluntary societies and associations whose precise aim was the evangelization of the poor. Although

Mann remarked specifically on the example of the Church of England, Nonconformity was also involved in this activity well before the 1850s. The Congregationalist Home Missionary Society, for example, was founded in 1819, and the Baptist Home Missionary Society had been founded as early as 1797. Moreover, the efforts of the two societies had shifted significantly towards urban areas during the 1820s, 1830s and 1840s, whereas previously their efforts had been predominantly rural (Carwardine 1980, pp. 211–12; Rack, 1973, p. 366). Similarly, there were those before 1854 who were well aware that Nonconformity was a numerically significant force. One of the most famous examples was that of W. F. Hook, who, newly appointed as Vicar of Leeds, had observed in 1837 that 'the *de facto* established religion [of the area] is Methodism'. His was a much quoted recognition of Nonconformist strength, but it was not unique.

What was so startling about the 1851 Census of Religious Worship was not its reiteration of the *fact* of working-class non-attendance at public worship or its discovery of the *fact* that Nonconformity was strong. It was the *extent* of each which came as a shock. In respect of the figures for non-attendance, both the established church and Nonconformity found them a cause for serious concern. In respect of the relative figures for those attending worship in the established church and those attending one or other variety of Nonconformist worship on Census Sunday, there was cause for Nonconformist delight and Church of England despondency.

The Census revealed that, after the Church of England, the most numerous religious bodies were the Methodists, the Congregationalists and the Baptists. It also revealed that, although it varied in strength from area to area, Nonconformity was a force to be reckoned with throughout the country. Nowhere was Nonconformity statistically insignificant: the worst figure for Nonconformist church accommodation, relative to Anglican provision, was in Herefordshire, and even that was twenty-eight per cent. Nor was its strength exclusively, or even predominantly, urban, despite a widespread assumption that Nonconformists were essentially northern, provincial and urban creatures. The strength of rural Nonconformity came as a pleasant surprise to some Nonconformists themselves: the Rev. John Kennedy, for example, examined the census on behalf of the Congregational Union and observed in the Congregational Year Book of 1855 that, 'It does not appear so true as we thought, that the strength of Dissent is to be found in our great cities and large towns'.

There were areas of England, both urban and rural, in which Nonconformity was the religious majority — this included twenty out of the twenty-nine towns designated by the Census as the chief manufacturing districts. Nonconformity was also overwhelmingly the majority in the whole of Wales. Different Nonconformist traditions flourished in different areas. Such regional variations, however, were not the main point of interest about Nonconformist strength as revealed by the Census. The real surprise was that the attendances at public worship recorded on Census Sunday indicated that, taken *overall*, Anglicans and Nonconformists were roughly equal, or indeed that Anglican attendances may actually have been outnumbered by Nonconformists when the figures for all Protestant Nonconformist traditions were added together. Even some Nonconformists were taken aback by this discovery, although the Liberation Society still protested that the Census had continued to underestimate the strength of Nonconformity. Anglicans were at best shocked (though some Anglican commentators on the Census were ready to acknowledge its accuracy); at worst they were horrified and disbelieving. Samuel Wilberforce, never slow to enter into vigorous controversy, helped lead the assault on the accuracy of the Census from the episcopal benches of the House of Lords. Although the statistical methods of the Census were unreliable in detail, such protests were, however, quite unable to undermine confidence in the Census on the scale required to cast doubt on the underlying strength of Nonconformity which it revealed.[1]

The Census thus finally laid to rest any possibility of basing the claims of the established church upon the assumption that the Church of England was, in any active sense, the church of even a passable majority of the English people. At best it was the church of less than half those who actually chose to attend *any* public worship on Census Sunday; to say nothing of those other millions (Mann thought about five and a quarter million) who went nowhere at all. If establishment were still to be defended, it would have to be on grounds other than that of the Church of England being the majority religious choice. Conversely, the very size of the Nonconformist constituency lent weight to the arguments of those who protested that the existing situation in respect of the civil rights of dissenters from the established church represented an intolerable injustice. In 1851 there remained among the civil disabilities of dissenters the obligation to pay church rates for the upkeep of the parish church; virtual exclusion from the benefits of Oxford and Cambridge Universities; denial of the right of burial by their own ministers and of using their own rites in parish churchyards; and exclusion from many endowed schools and grammar schools, or admittance only at the cost of religious instruction in the tradition of the established church. As Owen Chadwick has observed, one of the fundamental questions facing the Victorians in respect of religion, was 'whether representative government was compatible with an established church, that is, how religious inequality could be married to political equality' (Chadwick, 1971, p. 6). The question had been pressing inexor-

[1] The accuracy of the Census has also been the subject of lively debate among historians. For a careful discussion of the issues see Thompson (1979).

ably since the late 1820s and the repeal of the Test and Corporation Acts in 1828, followed in 1829 by Catholic emancipation. The results of the Religious Census rendered it inescapable.

The 1851 Religious Census also made clear the diversity of Victorian Nonconformity. It revealed a Nonconformity that was genuinely nationwide, but also internally diverse and complex. It revealed in fact no less than thirty separate Nonconformist traditions. Some of these were outposts of foreign Protestant churches (Lutherans and French Reformed Protestants for example). But the majority were either descendants of the Wesleyan Methodist tradition (which the Census listed in seven separate groups, the largest of whom were the Wesleyan Methodist Connexion and the Primitive Methodists); Congregationalists; Baptists (split into six groups according to the Census); Calvinistic Methodists (split into two groups); Presbyterians; Unitarians; Quakers; or finally, 'isolated Congregations', who owned no allegiance to any organized branch of Nonconformity but together comprised a significant Nonconformist sub-culture of non-denominational local chapels, mission halls and city missions — Mann estimated that some 63,000 worshippers attended such 'isolated Congregations' on Census Sunday.

Such Nonconformist variety reflected differing historical origins, differing theological emphases, and differing convictions concerning church government. One important underlying contrast was the difference between the 'Old Dissent' and the 'New Dissent'. The Old Dissent consisted of four groups, the Congregationalists, the majority of the Baptists, the Presbyterians and the Quakers. These groups all had their origins in the religious debates and controversies of the mid-seventeenth century. The New Dissent consisted of the Methodists, Calvinistic Methodists and a minority of the Baptists (specifically the General Baptists of the New Connection) and was a product of the Evangelical Revival of the eighteenth century.

Within the Old Dissent the theological position was predominantly Calvinist. The Congregationalists, the Presbyterians, and the majority of the Baptists continued to describe themselves as 'Calvinist', even though in practice the majority in each of these traditions had quietly replaced the old 'high Calvinist' doctrine that only the elect would be saved by a more moderate, effectively Arminian, belief in the possibility of salvation for all. The largest groups within the Old Dissent — the Congregationalists and Baptists — also shared a congregational view of church government: each local congregation was autonomous and self-regulating. The eighteenth century had been, for the most part, a period of stagnation and decline for all branches of the Old Dissent. For English Presbyterianism the decline had been exacerbated by schisms in which many of the more educated English Presbyterians had rejected belief in the Trinity and become Unitarian. The New Dissent, even when calling itself Calvinist, as in the case of

Welsh Calvinistic Methodism, was in practice Arminian and evangelically motivated from the outset. All branches of the New Dissent were born out of the experience of revival and rapid growth, and all were centred upon the evangelistic task of taking the gospel *to* the people and beyond the confines of the community of the saved.

In point of fact, by the early nineteenth century all branches of the Dissenting tradition, Old and New, had been touched and influenced by the Evangelical Revival and its legacy. In many respects the Evangelical Revival proved the salvation of the Old Dissent as well as the origin of the New: the declining and increasingly stagnant Dissent of the mid-eighteenth century was re-invigorated and remotivated by the rise of Methodism in particular and the Evangelical Revival in general. The decline of the old high Calvinism (which, because of its fierce doctrine of election, had not generally inspired evangelism) and the formation of home and overseas missionary societies were specific examples of the impact of the evangelical revival upon the Old Dissent. In addition, by the early nineteenth century a broadly-based and broadly-defined evangelicalism was beginning to exercise a pervasive influence throughout the overwhelming majority of the Dissenting traditions, both Old and New. Old theological distinctions between Arminians and Calvinists, or between varieties of Calvinism, became progressively less central and less decisive in shaping the pattern of nineteenth-century Nonconformity.

On the eve of the Victorian era this trend received striking expression in the founding constitutions of both the Baptist and Congregational Unions. In 1832 the Baptist Union (first formed in 1813) revised its constitution. As a result the Union was able to accommodate both Particular Baptists (who were Calvinists) and General Baptists (who were Arminians) within its ranks. The key phrase which enabled it to do so occurred in the first object of the Union as defined by its revised constitution. This object was declared to be, 'To extend brotherly love and union among the Baptist ministers and churches who agree in *the sentiments usually denominated evangelical*' (Italics added). The move implied by the use of the phrase italicised above, without any further amplification or explanation, was, as David Thompson observes, 'a paradigm of the theological changes of the century' (Thompson, 1972, p. 7).

The same year, the formation of the Congregational Union furnished another example of the paradigm at work. The first object of the Congregational Union was simply 'to promote Evangelical Religion, in connection with the Congregational Denomination'. The Congregational case is less striking than that of the Baptists in that a year later, in 1833, the newly-formed Congregational Union also adopted a much fuller statement of faith. The 'Declaration of the Faith, Church Order and Discipline of the Congregational, or Independent Dissenters' presented an explicitly Calvinist position. But the Declaration took care to state that it was not 'a standard to which assent should be required' but rather a statement 'for general information, of what is commonly believed among them, reserving to everyone the most perfect liberty of conscience', and the Calvinism which it espoused was, in the words of the Committee of the Union, 'moderate'. In his centenary history of the Congregational Union, Albert Peel described it as diluted Calvinism, 'popular rather than scholastic, the product of preachers rather than theologians' (Peel, 1931, p. 75).

For an indication of the theological content of such 'sentiments usually denominated evangelical' one can conveniently turn to the doctrinal basis adopted by the Evangelical Alliance in 1846.[2] The Alliance, which was of individual Christians, not denominations, included Anglican Evangelicals as well as Nonconformists: its doctrinal basis was therefore required to encompass an even wider spectrum of denominational and theological traditions than the Baptist or Congregational Union constitutions. The result was a nine-point doctrinal statement that carefully avoided committing itself to theologically specific formulations. The members of the Alliance were to be 'such persons only as hold and maintain what are usually understood to be Evangelical views in regard to the matters of doctrine understated'. Then came the following nine points:

1. The Divine Inspiration, Authority, and Sufficiency of the Holy Scriptures.
2. The Unity of the Godhead, and the Trinity of Persons therein.
3. The utter Depravity of human nature in consequence of the Fall.
4. The Incarnation of the Son of God, His work of Atonement for sinners of mankind, and His Mediatorial Intercession and Reign.
5. The Justification of the sinner by Faith alone.
6. The work of the Holy Spirit in the Conversion and Sanctification of the sinner.
7. The right and duty of Private Judgement in the interpretation of the Holy Scriptures.
8. The Divine Institution of the Christian Ministry, and the authority and perpetuity of the ordinances of Baptism and the Lord's Supper.

[2] The foundation of the Alliance in 1846 was a reflection of, on the one hand, a desire among many evangelicals for greater unity across denominational boundaries; and, on the other hand, an anti-Catholicism made particularly aggressive by the decision of Peel's government in 1845 to increase the annual government grant to the Irish Roman Catholic seminary at Maynooth. The Scottish Disruption and the creation of the Free Church was also an important factor, the Free Church leaders being keen to promote the Alliance and thus gain support and sympathy for their own cause (Wolffe, 1986).

9. The Immortality of the Soul, the Resurrection of the Body, the Judgement of the world by our Lord Jesus Christ, with the Eternal Blessedness of the righteous, and the Eternal Punishment of the wicked.

It was a basis which could encompass all but the most theologically conservative or liberal branches of Nonconformity, and also Anglican Evangelicals. What, in practice, limited Anglican involvement was not the theological basis of the Alliance but its involvement in dissenting politics and the campaign for disestablishment. Within Nonconformity it was only members of groups with particularly liberal, heterodox theology (such as the Unitarians), and the minority of still firmly conservative Calvinists (such as the Strict and Particular Baptists) who were unable to ally themselves to such a generally defined evangelicalism.

The fact that by the 1830s there was a clear convergence within all the main traditions of both the Old and New Dissent towards a theology centred on 'the sentiments usually denominated evangelical' does not mean that the distinction between the Old and New Dissent had lost all significance by the Victorian period. The distinction remained important in at least two ways. First, the difference between the Old and New Dissent went far towards explaining the underlying pattern of geographical distribution of the various Nonconformist traditions. The 1851 Census of Religious Worship had shown the regional variations in strength and uneven distribution of the Nonconformist denominations. Recent studies of the Religious Census have shown that virtually any generalization about denominational distribution or regional strength will require qualification and caveat at the local level, and that adequate explanations of local or regional variations in denominational strength or religious allegiance will almost always require careful recognition of specifically local factors (McLeod, 1973; Thompson, 1979). That said, one of the few generally applicable explanations of regional variations in the strength of different Nonconformist denominations remains the distinction between Old and New Dissent. The New Dissent was generally strong where the Old Dissent was weak: conversely where the Old Dissent was well established and of long standing, the New Dissent made less headway.

Second, the distinction between Old and New Dissent also remained important because of the ambivalent position of Methodism in general and Wesleyan Methodism in particular. It was not merely that Methodism, in all its varieties, was the most determinedly connexional of the Victorian Nonconformist traditions. This was certainly the case, in contrast to the locally autonomous, independent, congregational polity characteristic of the majority of the Victorian Dissenting community. But connexionalism was not the sum of Methodist ambivalence. Nor was the instinctively Tory orientation of Wesleyan Methodism, in contrast to the instinctive Liberalism of most of the rest of Victorian Nonconformity, the sum of the matter. Both the connexionalism and the Tory political instincts were a reflection of a more deep-rooted ambiguity. The ambiguity is captured neatly by John Briggs and Ian Sellers in their observation that, 'if in the eighteenth century the Wesleyans had had slowly to learn the impossibility of existence as a society within the Church of England, it took the whole of the nineteenth century for them to reconcile themselves to the fraternity of Dissent' (Briggs and Sellers, 1973, p. 3). The ambivalent stance of Methodism, and especially Wesleyan Methodism, towards the rest of the Dissenting tradition was the more significant because of the relative size of Methodism and the other Nonconformist denominations during the nineteenth century. Membership figures for nineteenth-century Methodism are well preserved and reliable, those for other denominations are much less so. The following figures, however, give a suitable indication of the order of Methodist growth and the size of Methodism in relation to other Nonconformist denominations in nineteenth-century England.[3]

	Wesleyan Methodism	Primitive Methodism	All Methodist Groups	Congregationalists	Baptists
1800	88,334	N/A	93,793	c. 35,000	c. 27,403
1850	334,458	102,222	489,286	c. 165,000	c. 140,277
1900	410,000	186,466	728,289	257,435	239,114

The figures are the more significant in that the Congregationalists and Baptists were the next largest Nonconformist groups. Thus the denomination in English Nonconformity in the Victorian period which was most profoundly ambiguous about its own Nonconformist status and identity was also by far the largest Nonconformist denomination of the day. To better understand this paradox we must look more closely at the denominational variety of early Victorian Nonconformity and beyond the general agreement around the 'sentiments usually denominated evangelical'.

II THE VARIETIES OF VICTORIAN NONCONFORMITY

It is appropriate to begin with the largest of the branches of the Old Dissent. The Independents, or Congregationalists, owed their origins to one branch of sixteenth and seventeenth-century Puritanism. The two names by which they were known — and by which they described themselves — reflected the two convictions concerning church order which gave them

[3] These figures are adapted from Currie, Gilbert and Horsley, 1977, pp. 139–42, 147–9.

their identity. They were Independent congregations. Each chapel was self-governing and self-regulating. They financed themselves and they appointed their own ministers. They were also Congregational: absolute authority was not given to any individual officer of the congregation, including the minister: it was the congregation as a whole which governed, and all participated. Their independence notwithstanding, during the eighteenth century Congregationalists had formed County Unions and County Associations for mutual support. The County Associations were often a response to the influence of the Evangelical Revival and by the end of the eighteenth century, Congregationalism, like the other main branches of the Old Dissent, was emerging from a relatively moribund period and showing new signs of vitality. There was an increase in the number of Congregational chapels: many 'independent' chapels were established in the wake of the Evangelical Revival, had no formal denominational loyalty or identity and in due course drifted into Congregationalism. The decline and schism which occurred within eighteenth-century English Presbyterianism also brought more chapels, once Presbyterian, now too isolated for effective Presbyterianism to function, within the orbit of Congregationalism.

The new vitality, the increased number of chapels, an increasing desire to campaign against Dissenting disabilities, and the desire to further expand and evangelize produced new initiatives for central organizations. In 1795 the London Missionary Society had been formed to organize overseas missionary work: officially non-denominational, in practice it was overwhelmingly Congregational. In 1818, as we have already noted, a Home Missionary Society was formed. In 1806 and 1816 there were also attempts to found a union of County and District Associations, but they eventually came to nothing. In 1831 another attempt was made and it was resolved to present proposals for a union to the County Associations and note their response. In 1832 twenty-six of the thirty-four County Associations formed the Congregational Union and a year later adopted their moderately Calvinist Declaration of the Faith. The Union struggled during the 1830s, but in the 1840s further County Associations joined. The decade from the mid-40s to the mid-50s proved controversial and precarious, both in respect of organization (was it becoming too central, too unifying, too far removed from the essential independence of Independency?) and also in theological matters.

As ever in the life of churches and chapels, clashing personalities became involved in disputes over matters of principle. But the Union survived and by 1860 was well established, not least because of the managerial and diplomatic skills of Algernon Wells (who acted as secretary of the Union from 1837 until his death in 1850) and the financial security which came from the proceeds of sales of the phenomenally successful *Congregational Hymn Book* (published in 1836) and the denomination's newspapers. The paradox of a Union of Independent Congregationalists was reflected in the foundation document of the Union which stated that the Union was founded on the distinctive principle of 'the scriptural right of every separate church to maintain perfect independence in the government and administration of its own particular affairs; and therefore, that the Union shall not in any case assume legislative authority or become a court of appeal'.

The denomination thus united in independency was characteristically, though not exclusively, well educated, possessed of a generally learned ministry (which was paid at an average level well above that of the poorest dissenting ministries) and securely middle class. The classic expression of this ethos was found in a remark of Thomas Binney, for forty years minister at the King's Weigh House Church, Mayfair, in an address to the Congregational Union, in 1848: 'Our special mission is neither to the very rich nor to the very poor. We have a work to do upon the thinking, active influential classes . . .'. Binney's remark was not unique. In 1861 the lay secretary of the Congregational Home Missionary Society, Joshua Wilson, addressed the Congregational Union Assembly and proposed the building of at least one hundred new chapels. He conceded that Congregationalism should seek to pay more attention to the task of rural evangelism and to the provision of adequate free accommodation for the poor in urban Congregational chapels. But he also observed that 'it is unquestionable fact, that our strength as a denomination lies in the large cities and towns, as our special vocation is to the middle classes of the people, who form the chief portion of their inhabitants'. And in 1891 R. W. Dale could reflect in a similar manner that, 'the special mission of Congregationalism was to discipline to the highest intellectual and ethical perfection those never likely to be reached by such organisations as the Salvation Army' (quoted in Peel, 1931, p. 21). Congregationalist preaching reflected such self-understanding: it was, characteristically, theologically and intellectually demanding rather than emotional.

The Baptists, like the Congregationalists, were products of the seventeenth century and were predominantly congregational in their system of church government. They differed from Congregationalism, however, in their rejection of infant baptism and their adherence to believers' baptism. (This did not, however, preclude close relationships between Baptists and Congregationalists: there were cases of Baptists and Congregationalists sharing the same chapel and there were even some among the founders of the Congregational Union in 1831–2 who had wished to include Baptists within the one organization.) From as early as the mid-seventeenth century, Baptists were divided into General Baptists (who were Arminian in theology) and Particular Baptists (who were moderate Calvinists). In the eighteenth century this division doubled. The original General Baptists declined (often into Unitarianism) but did not disappear entirely, leaving the Particular Baptists as the majority of the Baptist community. In 1770, however, the General Baptists of the New Connexion were formed and preserved the Arminian theological tradition from within the Baptist fold. Lastly there were the Strict and Particular Baptists who held on to a high Calvinism which was anything but moderate.

Like the Congregationalists, the Baptists had long had County Associations and in the eighteenth century the General Baptists had even formed a General Assembly, thus enjoying something of a compromise between a purely congregational polity and a connexional one. They had formed a Missionary Society in 1792 and a Home Missionary Society in 1797. Again, like the Congregationalists, they had first formed a General Union in 1813 in response to much the same pressures: missionary and evangelical aims, the financial support of ministers and of poor chapels, expansion of the denomination, and the training of pastors. The Union of 1813 proved ineffective however, and was therefore re-organized in 1832, in the process providing the paradigmatic phrase 'the sentiments usually denominated evangelical'. The General Union of 1813 was of Particular Baptists, but the revised Baptist Union of 1832 gradually came to include General Baptists as well, a General Baptist presiding at the annual meeting of the Union in 1842.

Like the Congregational Union, the Baptist Union had a less than wholly secure existence for some twenty or thirty years and was troubled by controversies, most notably over whether the communion of the Lord's Supper should be closed or open, administered only to those who had received (adult) believer's baptism, or open to all those of evangelical belief, whether or not baptized as adults. But, again like the Congregational Union, the Baptist Union survived (J. H. Hinton acting as secretary from 1841 to 1866 and performing much the same role for the Baptists as Wells did for the Congregationalists) and by the early 1860s, although much less well established than its Congregational parallel, it occupied a strategic place in the expanding network of Baptist societies and voluntary agencies. In both the Baptist and Congregational cases the general evangelicalism which formed the basis of their denominational Unions also disposed them to give strong support to the Evangelical Alliance after its formation in 1846.

Among the varieties of Baptists, the Particular Baptists were not only the most numerous but also generally the most learned. Taken overall, however, the Baptists, both people and ministers, were less well educated, more conservative and rigid in doctrine, and less securely middle class than the Congregationalists. Baptist chapels were more likely to be distinctively lower middle class or upper working class in membership. That said, it was also noticeable that between the 1830s and the 1850s the ethos among Baptists shifted significantly towards a more middle-class style, especially in the towns. For Baptists as well as Congregationalists the second quarter of the nineteenth century saw, in Chadwick's neat characterization, a process in which 'the barn-chapel of the side-streets was becoming the church of the market square' (Chadwick, 1971, p. 409).

The Presbyterian position in England in the early decades of Victoria's reign was quite different from that of the Baptists and Congregationalists. Presbyterianism was also a product of the sixteenth and seventeenth centuries, but whereas the eighteenth-century experience of the Congregationalists and Baptists was one of initial decline followed by renewed vigour, the eighteenth-century experience of English Presbyterians was one of doctrinal dispute issuing in schism and the virtual disappearance of English Presbyterianism by the beginning of the nineteenth century. The doctrinal dispute and schism had occurred in 1719 and concerned the doctrine of the Trinity. A majority of the then Presbyterian ministers refused to subscribe to a doctrinal formula which included the Trinity. During the rest of the eighteenth century an increasing number of individual chapels became Unitarian in belief, Trinitarian members either seceding to found new chapels or joining Congregational chapels. The remaining Trinitarian Presbyterian chapels either clung tenaciously to a Presbyterian church order made nigh on impossible by the geographically scattered nature of the remaining chapels, or moved quietly into Congregationalism. The Unitarians proceeded quietly on their way and operated without any significant denominational structure whilst remaining definitely within the Dissenting community.

By the 1830s the continuing English Presbyterian tradition clung to its Presbyterian identity largely through looking to Scotland for inspiration and occasional moral support. As Scottish immigrants established communities in England during the nineteenth century, so new Presbyterian congregations formed. Eventually (though it took some fifty years from the idea first being raised to its realization) in 1876 the surviving English Presbyterianism and the newer Scots immigrant Presbyterianism joined to form the Presbyterian Church of England.

The Unitarians, meanwhile, in 1825 formed The British and Foreign Unitarian Association. Unlike other dissenting Unions, however, it failed to establish itself as an effective focus of denominational life. Moreover, the Unitarians found themselves increasingly pushed towards the periphery of the Dissenting community. After legal cases concerning the ownership of the property and endowments of Unitarian congregations established before 1813, the Unitarians formally separated from their previous alliance with the Dissenting community as a whole. (To be precise, they withdrew from the Nonconformist political pressure group of the eighteenth and early nineteenth centuries known as the Protestant Dissenting Deputies.)

The process of withdrawal was not, however, total. Unitarians and other

Dissenters could and still did co-operate. In the great centres of urban Nonconformity in Birmingham and Manchester, and also in Liverpool, Unitarians played a vital part in the Nonconformist dominance of these cities, in the evolution of a provincial urban culture dominated by Nonconformist wealth and values and, especially, in the evolution and implementation of the concept of the civic gospel. For the most part, however, the rest of the Dissenting community was content to see Unitarianism and its unorthodox, liberal theology move to, or even beyond, the borders of mainstream Nonconformity. The Unitarians themselves, moreover, were not an expanding denomination. Comprised of two theologically incompatible strands (one Bible-based, orthodox and distinguished from the rest of evangelical dissent only by its conviction that the doctrine of the Trinity was unscriptural; the other heir to the rationalism and deism of the Enlightenment and possessed of a calm and intellectual rather than fervent and emotional faith) and strongly intellectual in ethos, Unitarianism was always destined to be firmly middle class. It was never remotely likely to possess widespread appeal or to have much impact on the mass of working-class 'habitual neglecters of religion' discovered by Mann in his review of the 1851 Religious Census returns — although the Unitarian Domestic Mission movement demonstrated Unitarian concern over, and commitment to, the mission to the urban poor.

The achievements of Unitarianism were of a different kind. Unitarianism provided a spiritual home for many who were troubled by doubts and could no longer accept evangelical orthodoxy, but who nevertheless wished to retain religious belief of a more rational kind: Francis Newman, John Sterling and Arthur Clough were leading examples of the type. It also nurtured and sustained a tradition of provincial politicians, mayors and leaders of provincial civic life whose socially reforming contribution to Victorian society gave Unitarianism an importance out of all proportion to its actual size.

Last, but not least, in James Martineau Unitarianism produced a theologian whose liberal divinity, inspired by both a deep devotionalism and a critical intellect aware of the challenges of philosophical, historical and scientific thought, was well able to confront the Victorian intellectual crisis of faith and present a viable theological alternative to orthodoxy or disbelief. Like the Anglican Broad Churchmen, Martineau sought a theology which was intellectually critical and rigorous, morally sensitive, and experientially profound: he was equally opposed to both uncritical supernaturalism and cold rationalism. It says something about the continuing influence of the mainstream Christian denominations over the writing of religious history that Martineau remains, even now, a relatively neglected theologian.

The last of the branches of the Old Dissent, the Quakers, were in important respects similar to the Unitarians. The Quakers, in the 1830s, were more distinctive, more apart, than any other major Nonconformist group. Their own commitment to peculiarity of dress, speech, custom, and behaviour ensured their separateness. This separateness, despite their remarkable level of involvement in social reform and welfare projects, extended as far as doubting the propriety of involvement in politics (even non-partisan, reforming politics) and the holding of public office. The separateness of Quakerism also meant that, alone of Victorian Nonconformist bodies, they declined in numbers — at least until the 1860s. The decline in numbers prompted debate among Quakers. Those who advocated a less peculiar style, a more relaxed discipline, a more open and involved stance towards the world, prevailed. After 1865 Quakerism became much more open and experienced a modest growth in numbers.

Wherein, then, were the similarities with Unitarianism? Four factors justify the claim of similarity. Theologically, Quakerism was also outside the mainstream of evangelical dissent and tended towards a quietistic heterodoxy which stressed the inward religion of the heart rather than doctrinal orthodoxy. Like Unitarianism it was markedly middle class and commercial in social composition. Again, like Unitarianism, it did not share the predominant experience of Victorian Nonconformity and develop a fully centralized denominational structure. Most of all, however, it shared with Unitarianism a provincial, social and political influence out of all proportion to its numerical strength — Birmingham alone had seven Quaker mayors before 1892.

Of the Old Dissent, then, the Congregationalists and Baptists were the mainstream, and markedly so. Presbyterianism in England was too reduced in size for the greater part of the Victorian era to represent a significant force. The Unitarians and Quakers both exercised influence out of all proportion to their size but were, in different ways, on the fringes of Victorian Nonconformity, not at its centre. All of the branches of the Old Dissent, however, tended, despite their developing denominationalism, to an independent congregational polity and a reforming Whig-Liberal stance in politics, the latter born largely of the fact that such liberty as they enjoyed Dissenters owed to the Whig tradition in politics, whilst the Tory party and the established church were old and determined allies in opposing Nonconformity.

The New Dissent, and especially Wesleyan Methodism, was strikingly different. The Evangelical Revival was much more than Methodism alone, but Methodism was its largest element, and the roots of the difference between Methodism and the Old Dissent lay in the origin of Methodism as a movement within the eighteenth-century Church of England. Wesley had lived and died an Anglican — and a Tory High Church Anglican at that. He had never desired a separation from the established church and had been a vociferously loyal supporter of the monarchy and the government — sometimes almost extravagantly so. For all Wesley's desire not to separate from the Church of England and found a new denomination, however, that was precisely what eventually occurred. The definitive moment arrived in 1795, four years after John Wesley's death, when the Methodist Conference ruled that preachers should be allowed to administer Holy Communion if a majority of local lay leaders, and also the Conference itself, agreed. The Plan of Pacification, as this Conference decision was called, effectively marked the recognition that Methodism was a denomination separate from the established church. It did not, however, automatically make Methodism a branch of Dissent, rather it left Methodism in an ambiguous position somewhere between the Church of England, of which it was no longer a part (though many Methodists wished it was) and the Dissenting community, of which it was not yet a part (for which many Methodists were grateful). This ambiguity had important implications for Victorian Nonconformity as a whole, for it meant that Wesleyan Methodism — which was by far the largest Nonconformist denomination — did not lead the Nonconformist community. In particular, Wesleyan Methodism never committed itself to the cause of disestablishment. Wesleyan involvement in the Liberation Society was correspondingly limited.

At the beginning of the nineteenth century Methodism differed from the Old Dissent in many ways, but the distinctiveness can usefully be summarized under three broad headings. First, unlike the Old Dissent, Methodism was not a tradition re-emerging from a period of decline and stagnation. Possessed of an Arminian theology, an ebullient, emotional style of preaching and a passionate spirituality, it was a new movement still in the process of rapid expansion, and with an appeal especially to a lower middle-class and artisan constituency. Second, it was not associated with a radical stance in politics: Wesley's own political conservatism was reflected in the conservatism of the Methodist Conference and many of the individual leaders of the denomination. Third, Methodism did not need to introduce a national structure, a union of hitherto fiercely independent local societies. On the contrary, Methodism eschewed congregational independence and possessed instead a disciplined hierarchy extending from the 'class meeting', to 'the society' (i.e. local chapel), to the 'circuit' of local societies, to 'district committees', and finally to 'the Conference'. The Conference was ministerial as well as hierarchical. Its members were all ministers of at least fourteen years' service. The Conference which governed the connexion of local societies was thus effectively a conference of senior clergy. Yet, since ministers were itinerant, the regular life of the societies was in lay hands. The contrast between central clerical authority and local lay responsibility was one pregnant with constitutional tensions and conflicts which Methodism could not avoid in the first half of the nineteenth century (Bowmer, 1975, pp. 249–52).

The distinctiveness of Methodism within the varieties of Dissent continued in the 1830s and 1840s. Politically, for example, whilst the Old Dissent saw in the coming of Parliamentary Reform in 1832 the prospect of new opportunities and new scope, the Annual Address of the Wesleyan Methodist Conference in 1831 exhorted:

> Let not worldly politics engross too much of your time and attention. Avoid all undue eagerness and anxiety on subjects which, however much their importance might be magnified by the men of the world, are only of moment in the estimation of the Christian, as far as they can be rendered subservient to the best interests of mankind.

Only towards the end of the century — under the influence of leaders such as Hugh Price Hughes and John Scott Lidgett — did Wesleyan Methodism move decisively towards the Liberal Party in political allegiance, and even then Wesleyan Methodism tended to lend support to the Liberal Imperialist wing of the late Victorian Liberal party.

In one respect Wesleyan Methodism did reflect a common experience with the Old Dissenting traditions in these years. Despite its strongly Connexional polity, Methodism still lacked efficient internal organization of finance, property, missions, and ministerial training: in short the administrative facilities necessary for it to function effectively as the nationwide denomination which it aspired to be. One of its achievements in the first half of the nineteenth century was the establishment of such a denominational bureaucracy. But such organization was not achieved without cost. Whereas the Congregationalists and Baptists moved slowly but relatively smoothly towards greater national denominational unity, Wesleyan Methodism suffered a series of splits, secessions and schisms in the period from 1827 to 1849. There had been a secession as early as 1797, when a group led by Alexander Kilham, desiring more power for local chapels, broke away to found the Methodist New Connexion. In 1811 occurred the split that led to the emergence of Primitive Methodism, which in due course became by far the largest of the non-Wesleyan Methodist groups and a fully-fledged denomination in its own right. But these divisions had not seriously threatened the denomination as a whole or even restricted its growth. The divisions of the 1820s, 1830s and, especially, the 1840s did, however, threaten the very fabric of Wesleyan Methodism and for a time stopped expansion altogether.

In the present context the details of each particular schism are less important than the underlying and unresolved tensions which they revealed at the heart of Wesleyan Methodism.[4] The controversies, schisms, secessions and expulsions — though mightily compounded by personal rivalries — characteristically centred upon the tension between Conference policy and decisions on the one hand, and local preferences and desires on the other. Secession tended to follow the insistence of Conference on imposing its will upon the local society. Behind this, however, there lay a deeper contradiction. Wesley himself had been both an emotional and fervent revivalist and a clerical autocrat. He passed on that inner contradiction to the movement which he founded so that in Methodism 'there has always been an uneasy symbiosis of churchman and revivalist' (Turner, 1985, p. 60). In the second, third and fourth decades of the nineteenth century the Conference seemed to many to be progressively retreating from the revivalist strain and developing the clerical one, and in so doing making Wesleyan Methodism more sedately middle class. Those who resisted such trends appealed to the revivalist tradition and stressed the role of the laity.

The tension was heightened in the 1840s by two factors. On the one hand there was the conflict which arose over the role of Jabez Bunting. Bunting was the dominant figure in Wesleyan Methodism in the first half of the nineteenth century. He became assistant secretary of the Conference in 1806 and (annually re-elected) secretary in 1814. He was also in control of the Stationing Committee which placed ministers in local circuits. He was very much the heir of Wesley in his political conservatism, his clerical and autocratic manner, and his attitude towards the rest of the Dissenting community. He once observed that, 'If I went from the Methodists I would go to the church rather than Dissent. One of its first principles is — Every man shall choose his own minister. Can we be friendly to that?' (quoted in Turner, 1985, p. 131). At one level Bunting was to the Wesleyan Methodists what Algernon Wells was to the Congregationalists and J. H. Hinton was to the Baptists. He forged a denominational structure and organization for Wesleyan Methodism. But forged is the operative word. Whereas Wells and Hinton characteristically worked by diplomacy, Bunting was autocratic and pressed ahead in spite of controversy. Opposition reached its height in the 'Fly Sheets' controversy of the 1840s, when a series of pamphlets (anonymous, but probably written by James Everett) was circulated criticizing Bunting's domination of Wesleyan Methodism. In 1849 three ministers, Everett himself, together with William Griffith and Samuel Dunn, were expelled for refusing to answer questions concerning the Fly Sheets. The resultant schism, which produced the Wesleyan Methodist Reformers,

[4] The most significant secessions were those of the Leeds Protestant Methodists in 1827–8, Wesleyan Methodist Association in 1834–7 and the Wesleyan Reformers in 1849. These three groups then formed the United Methodist Free Churches in 1857. For the secessions see Bowmer 1975, pp. 103–60.

was the worst ever experienced by the Wesleyan tradition, caused expansion virtually to halt for some years, and may have caused the loss of up to 100,000 members.

The situation in the 1840s was also exacerbated by the presence in Britain of James Caughey, an American professional Revivalist, who divided many local circuits by his presence and style of evangelism. The opponents of Bunting and his clerical style supported Caughey and his revivalism. In 1847 Caughey was banned by Conference from using Methodist premises. The case of Caughey and the secessions and expulsions of 1849 are a good illustration of the complexity of the contradiction within Methodism: local revivalist enthusiasm clashed with central, clerical discipline. The seceders characteristically saw themselves as Reformers, restoring a lost purity. The mainstream saw themselves as preserving the balance which made Methodism not quite Dissent. Wesleyan Methodism did, however, survive, though its growth was never again so dramatic. The loss of many of the more radical members left the remaining Wesleyan Methodists even more securely middle class and even more securely connexional.

By far the largest of the non-Wesleyan Methodist groups was the Primitive Methodists. Formed in 1811, after the expulsion from Wesleyanism of Hugh Bourne and William Clowes for holding open-air revivalist meetings, by 1851 they were almost a third as large as Wesleyan Methodism and five times larger than any other Methodist seceders. If Wesleyan Methodism developed the clerical and disciplined aspect of Wesley's legacy and neglected the revivalist one, Primitive Methodism did just the opposite. In consequence it also remained more working class and indeed was the one large Victorian Nonconformist denomination which was predominantly working class in complexion. Its strength was predominantly rural, though in the Durham coalfields and the Staffordshire Potteries it also established an urban working-class strength. Its style was revivalist, emotional, fervent and unrestrained: sufficiently so for members to be described and ridiculed as 'Ranters'. The Primitive Methodists were also connexional and Conference led: but theirs was a more democratic and less clerical Conference with two laymen for every minister. They did not entirely avoid the constitutional tensions of centre and locality, or the drift towards a more middle-class style, but the presence of laymen in Conference and the essentially working-class membership prevented a simple repetition of the Wesleyan experience.

Of the remaining denominational products of the Evangelical Revival, two require brief mention. Alongside Wesley and his Arminian theology, the eighteenth century also produced Calvinistic Methodism, led by George Whitefield in England and Howell Harris in Wales. In England relatively little need be said of Calvinistic Methodism. Organizationally centred from

1770 upon the Countess of Huntingdon's Connexion, in the nineteenth century the Connexion declined and broke up; the majority of the chapels either joining mainstream Methodism or becoming independent chapels. In Wales the position was different. In England the 1851 Religious Census had revealed roughly equal attendances at Church of England and Nonconformist services. In Wales only nine per cent attended Anglican worship and eighty-seven per cent attended one or other Nonconformist chapel. Of these the Welsh Calvinistic Methodists were particularly significant for the way in which they developed an indigenous Methodism, based on a moderately Presbyterian form of government and retaining much of the ethos of early Methodism in England. Significantly, whilst the Old Dissent (especially the Baptists and Congregationalists) and Wesleyan Methodism were strong in Wales, Primitive Methodism was not, Calvinistic Methodism providing a sufficiently revivalist and 'primitive' presence (Jones, 1981, pp. 227–30; Lambert, 1976, p.4).

Last but not least, there must be mention of the Bible Christians. Almost entirely confined to Devon and Cornwall, they were founded in 1806, independently of Methodism but in imitation of it, and sought membership of the Wesleyan Methodist Conference. Denied membership because of the uncompromisingly individual style of their leader William O'Bryan, they formed their own Connexion and functioned rather as a local West Country version of Primitive Methodism. By 1900 they numbered some 17,000.

III 1830–1880: A HALF-CENTURY OF SYNTHESIS?

To its critics the complex variety of Victorian Nonconformity and its sub-groups and divisions was evidence of its narrowness: 'the habit of Dissent' created a frame of mind which tended to intolerance, disputation and jealousy. The classic expression of such a view was Matthew Arnold's attack on Nonconformity in *Culture and Anarchy* in 1869. 'Look at the life imaged in such a newspaper as the *Nonconformist*', he urged, 'a life of jealousy of the Establishment, disputes, tea-meetings, openings of chapels, sermons; and then think of it as an ideal of a human life completing itself on all sides, and aspiring with all its organs after sweetness, light, and perfection!' Such a life was, Arnold asserted, unlovely, unattractive, incomplete and narrow.

Nonconformists were well able to reply to such criticism, coming from a member of the Church of England. On the one hand they could point to the dispute-ridden ethos of an established church in which a range of beliefs from ultra-Protestant evangelicalism through Broad Churchmanship to Anglo-Catholic Ritualism managed to co-exist only at the cost of ongoing controversy, narrow party spirit and frequent recourse to litigation. Thus R. W. Dale replied to Arnold's attacks in an article, in the *Contemporary*

Review of July 1870, in which he pointed out that the language of Anglican controversy and prosecutions for heresy and liturgical innovation were not suggestive of mildness and reasonableness, and that when Anglican Evangelicals and Ritualists went out of their own parishes to worship in others more suited to their theological tastes they displayed a disputatiousness equal to anything in Nonconformity.

Eight years earlier, in 1862, both Dale and the Baptist Alexander McLaren had drawn attention to the disunity within the Church of England in lectures given to celebrate the 200th anniversary of the ejection of Nonconformist ministers from the Church of England in 1662. On that occasion both Dale (in a lecture on 'Nonconformity in 1662 and 1862') and McLaren (in a lecture entitled 'Fidelity to Conscience') made much of the disunity and disarray revealed in the controversy over *Essays and Reviews*, which was then at its height. McLaren also made an important point about the unity of Nonconformity: the Church of England, he urged, could not, on the basis of its claim to comprehensiveness, reconcile the rights of the individual and the power of society, the claims of free thought and the claims of dogmatic truth. Nonconformists, however, could 'In opposition to all impossible dreams of uniformity, ... proclaim the higher truth of a diverse unity'. In such ways, Victorian Nonconformists claimed underlying unity, a shared identity which transcended the many individual expressions of Nonconformity. Modern interpreters have also recognised this aspect of Victorian Nonconformity. In one of the more stimulating and ambitious of recent attempts to provide an overarching interpretation of Victorian Nonconformity, Richard Helmstadter has argued that, between roughly 1830 and 1880, it was precisely the cohesive and coherent *unity* of Nonconformity which explains its prominence and importance in Victorian public life (Helmstadter, 1979).

Helmstadter's thesis is worth summarizing in some detail. Between the early 1830s and the mid 1880s, he argues, Victorian Nonconformity achieved a coherent synthesis of religious, political and social attitudes. During this fifty-year period, Nonconformist theology, politics, social leadership, church organization and attitudes to social reform all reinforced one another. At the heart of this synthesis was a commitment to individualism. In each of these areas of Nonconformist life and belief the individual conscience was paramount. Thus, paradoxically, commitment to the moral priority of the individual conscience gave early and mid-Victorian Nonconformity a unity of purpose and an essentially common identity and standpoint.

Helmstadter examines the effect of this conscientious individualism in five areas of life and belief which he identifies as basic elements of the unifying synthesis of early and mid-Victorian Nonconformity. Religiously and theologically it was expressed in the overwhelmingly predominant evangelicalism which, by the 1830s, had influenced all the Nonconformist denominations and become characteristic of most of them. Subjective and experiential, the evangelical religion of the heart was above all the religion of the converted, redeemed and saved individual. Bible-based (on a pre-critical reading of the biblical text) and focused upon the atoning death of Christ on behalf of individual sinners and the necessity of each individual's personal acceptance of that atoning death, its classic expression was John Angell James' immensely popular tract *The Anxious Inquirer after Salvation.* Even when it continued to describe itself as Calvinist (as did the Congregationalists and Baptists) Victorian Nonconformity, in all but a few of its most extreme exceptions, proclaimed an evangelical gospel which maintained the *possibility* of salvation for every individual and centred upon the redemption of the individual soul rather than the community of the saved.

Politically, early and mid-Victorian Nonconformity took its stance firmly upon the liberty of the individual. The political stance and allegiance of early and mid-Victorian Nonconformity are explained by the dual commitment to the right of individuals to decide for themselves in matters of worship and belief, and to the concomitant right to freedom from civil disabilities because of such free decisions of the individual conscience. The repeal of the Test and Corporation Acts in 1828 was a decisive landmark in the constitutional recognition of the growth of religious pluralism in Britain, but far from marking an end to the Nonconformist search for religious liberty, it marked, rather, the beginning of a further intense phase of that struggle. For the next fifty years the political expression of early and mid-Victorian Nonconformist individualism was to be found in the successive struggles over church rates, marriages, civil registration of births and deaths, access to the Universities of Oxford and Cambridge, burial in consecrated ground by their own ministers and according to their own rites, education, and even the very continuation of an established church. The political stance of Nonconformity between 1830 and 1880 was thus peculiarly open to an alliance with Gladstonian Liberalism: an alliance which duly flourished, especially in the 1850s, 60s and 70s.

The position of the early and mid-Victorian Nonconformist social élite also reflected this liberal individualist ethos. Even if the statistical majority of Nonconformist members were from the lower middle class and upper working class, the ethos and leadership of Nonconformity were uncompromisingly middle class. The wealth of Nonconformity was urban, provincial and upper middle class: it was based upon a network of Nonconformist banking, manufacturing and professional families committed to the ideals of mid-Victorian free trade and *laissez-faire* individualism. These same middle-class Nonconformist leaders were also often leaders of local and provincial government, enthusiastically expressing their individualism in an assertion of local autonomy. Such local individualism, moreover, found its theological analogue in an independent, congregational theory of church order. Even as denominational structures and organizations developed and increased — perhaps because they did — Nonconformists jealously guarded their ecclesiastical tradition of independent self-governing congregations, hiring and firing ministers, self-financing, and responsible for their own rules and regulations.

Last but not least, the underlying individualism of the early and mid-Victorian Nonconformist synthesis was apparent in its view of poverty and social reform. Individual and independent responsibility for self-help and self-improvement, and individual responsibility for the overcoming of laziness, drunkenness and poverty were characteristic themes of Nonconformist social values and Nonconformist advice to the poor. The religious conversion of the individual from sin to righteousness was to be paralleled by the conversion of the individual from sloth, drunkenness and improvidence to industry, temperance and thrift: self-improvement and eternal salvation alike were responsibilities of the individual conscience.

Such, according to Helmstadter, was the nature of the synthesis which provided Nonconformity with both unity and effectiveness in the middle quarters of the nineteenth century. In the final two decades of the Victorian era, however, that synthesis, according to Helmstadter, collapsed under a series of pressures from a series of causes which emerged from the mid-1880s onwards. Theologically the evangelical synthesis was undermined by the spread of biblical criticism and by doubts concerning traditional evangelical teaching on eternal punishment and the atoning death of Christ. Biblical criticism undermined the pre-critical aspects of the biblical foundation of evangelicalism. Moral sensitivity cast doubt upon the character of a loving God who would sentence his creatures to eternal punishment and who required the vicarious suffering of an innocent victim to atone for the sins of others. Such moral doubts tended to issue in a shift of emphasis from the death of Christ to the life of Christ — from a theology centred on the Atonement to one centred on the Incarnation — and a shift from the wrath and judgement of God to the love and Fatherhood of God.

Socially and culturally, the identity of late Victorian Nonconformity became less distinct and more diverse. As civil disabilities were removed, Nonconformity became more fully integrated within the upper middle-class *milieu* of public school and Oxbridge. The temptation to dilute the distinctive features of Nonconformity and assimilate the characteristics of the prevailing culture proved attractive to many, irresistible for some. Recreational pursuits such as concert and theatre-going, previously eschewed as frivolous and evangelically unacceptable, became acceptable and even popular. After 1880 the political leadership of Nonconformity moved away from the Liberation Society and towards the emerging Free Church Congresses which led to the formation of the National Council of Free Churches in 1896: the very contrast of names being significant. The 'Liberation Society' was named after the fifty-year struggle to free Nonconformists from the constraints of civil disability and the intrusion of the established church. 'The National Council of Free Churches' reflected not only the achievement of 'freedom', but also the awareness of the need for co-operation between individual churches faced with the indifference to religion of an increasing number of the population. The call for such co-operation even extended to co-operation between Nonconformists and the Church of England.

Finally, in questions of social reform the earlier consensus on the unambiguous priority of individual responsibility and self-help was replaced by an awareness, especially among the more progressive ministerial leaders of Nonconformity, that the complexities of urban, industrial society and questions of social justice were not susceptible to such individualist solutions. Yet such progressive ministers could not carry their congregations with them into a clearly defined alternative social and political programme, because their congregations characteristically remained more conservative in social attitudes, and in any case the newer style of incarnational theology did not provide a clear basis for a political stance. The only issues on which a united Nonconformist political-moral stance remained possible were education and questions of personal morality: drink, gambling and prostitution. Thus, concludes Helmstadter, the great era of the 'Nonconformist Conscience' proved, paradoxically, to be the point at which the previous conscience-based synthesis of Nonconformist theology, politics, church order and social attitudes collapsed. It was replaced by a public political-moral stance which, however loudly proclaimed as the expression of a 'Nonconformist Conscience', was in practice a narrowly-based amalgam of conservative stances on issues of personal morality, owing its apparent political and social influence largely to the power and effectiveness of increasingly extensive and centralized denominational organizations.

IV THE PERSISTENCE OF VARIETY

Helmstadter's thesis is not only stimulating and ambitious; it is also constructive and illuminating. It provides an interpretation of Victorian Nonconformity as a whole which counterbalances the danger, inherent in accounts which emphasize its variety and diversity, of a collapse into an interpretative chaos in which no significant pattern can be discerned. Helmstadter offers an ordered, coherent view of the varieties of Victorian Nonconformity and identifies a basic Nonconformity which can be discussed above and beyond its individual expressions. He also offers an explanation of both the early and mid-Victorian prominence of Nonconformity, and its late Victorian and Edwardian crisis and incipient decline.

There is much in this interpretation and explanation to prompt the agreement even of those who wish to challenge important aspects of the overarching argument and conclusions. Thus, for example, the period from the early 1830s to the mid 1880s was indeed a distinctive era of Nonconformist history, and a peculiarly successful one. Marked at its beginning by the repeal of the Test and Corporation Acts in 1828, the passage of the Reform Act in 1832, and the Municipal Corporations Act in 1835, these fifty years saw first the opening up of opportunities for Nonconformists in public life and then the progressive exploitation of those opportunities, not least in the successive repeals of legislation limiting the rights of Nonconformists in public and civil life. So successful was this process of 'liberation' from civil disabilities that it has been described as amounting to a process of 'gradual disestablishment' (Mackintosh, 1972, p. xvi; Gilbert, 1976, p. 163).[5] Similarly, the end of the fifty-year period was indeed marked by the decline of the Liberation Society — which had so symbolized the militant stance of the Nonconformity of the previous half-century — the growth of a sense of self-doubt and uncertainty as to the nature of Nonconformist identity, and a growing public fragmentation of the Nonconformist political position. Thus far Helmstadter's chronology is real enough: a point recognized by other historians and reflected in, for example, David Thompson's characterization of the period following the repeal of the Test and Corporation Acts as one of 'growing confidence', and the period from 1862 to 1886 as 'the golden age' — whilst the period after 1886 he characterizes as 'the ebb tide' (Thompson, 1972).

Equally, it is appropriate to portray the Nonconformity of 1830 to 1880 as *predominantly* middle class in ethos and values, aspirations and aims. The centre of gravity of early and mid-Victorian Nonconformity was, certainly, firmly middle class, and the individualism of that middle-class Nonconformity, especially in its social values and political opinions, was unquestionably closely in tune with the values of Victorian Liberalism and the mid Victorian Liberal party. The values of free trade and the non-interference of the state, of self-help and the necessity of personal responsibility, were uniquely well attuned to the theological and moral pre-suppositions of evangelicalism. It was hardly surprising that Nonconformity proved to be one of the vital formative influences in the emergence of the Gladstonian Liberal party, or that the growing crisis of identity in Nonconformity after the mid-1880s should have coincided with the decisive split of the Liberal Party over Irish Home Rule in 1886. Helmstadter's chronology and charac-

[5] The most significant reforms were: civil registration of births and solemnization of marriage in 1836; degrees of Oxford and Cambridge without subscription to the Thirty-Nine Articles in 1854 and 1856; access to Grammar Schools in 1860; abolition of church rate in 1868; burial by Nonconformist rites and ministers in 1880.

terization of Victorian Nonconformity are thus a faithful reflection of major features of that tradition and its Victorian experience. He also consistently seeks to integrate the specifically religious dimensions of Victorian Nonconformity within a social, political and economic context.

There are, however, also limitations and shortcomings in Helmstadter's interpretation of Victorian Nonconformity. The clarity and boldness of his approach are a weakness as well as a strength. The synthesis he portrays is in some respects too uniform. The chronology he proposes is in important respects too neat. This, in turn, makes his explanation of the collapse of the early and mid-Victorian Nonconformist synthesis and the onset of decline too narow, and too exclusively the result of social and secular influences: too little the product of changing — and indeed ongoing — religious and theological developments in the life and thought of Victorian Nonconformity.

In fairness to Helmstadter it must be said that at various points in his essay he acknowledges that there were exceptions to the synthesis which he proposes. But equally it must be said that, although acknowledged, such exceptions tend to remain muted and merely marginal. This, however, is unsatisfactory. Not only are some of the exceptions noted more central to the history of Victorian Nonconformity than Helmstadter's presentation of the case allows (most notably, the ambiguity of Wesleyan Methodism and the distinctiveness of Primitive Methodism are *integral*, not exceptional, aspects of Victorian Nonconformity) but, in addition, a closer examination of important aspects of Nonconformist politics, attitudes to church order and organization, theology, and changing attitudes to social and recreational activities, casts more general doubt upon the degree of prevalence and uniformity of the fifty-year synthesis proposed by Helmstadter.

Politically, Helmstadter's fifty-year synthesis rests not only upon the role of the Liberation Society[6] but also upon an attitude to personal morality and social improvement centred upon self-help, temperance and hard work (an attitude exemplified for Helmstadter by Charles Haddon Spurgeon's advice to the poor in *John Ploughman's Talk* and *John Ploughman's Pictures*). As depicted by Helmstadter, the latter aspect of this political synthesis is certainly too monolithic.

Long before the emergence of late Victorian Nonconformist versions of the 'social gospel' and 'Christian Socialism' in the preaching and writing of leaders such as Hugh Price Hughes, John Clifford and John Scott Lidgett (what Helmstadter dismisses as a vague humanitarianism encouraged by

[6] Which in any case was not an exclusively unifying influence: there were Nonconformists who, though opposed to establishment, remained aloof from the Society because they felt it too political; and Wesleyan Methodist participation was, predictably, very limited (Thompson, 1974 pp. 227–32). See also *RVB*, II, 7.

a vague theology), there were Nonconformist voices clearly arguing that problems of poverty and social conditions were not merely matters of personal responsibility and self-help, that adequate social improvement also required government action, and that the moral imperatives of the gospel could legitimately support (even inspire) working-class political activism and were not simply a basis and justification for social deference and political passivity.[7]

Two examples will serve to illustrate the point. Although it was by no means exclusively a creation of Nonconformity, the mid and late Victorian 'Civic Gospel' was deeply indebted to Nonconformity — in this instance to the provincial, urban middle-class élite of Nonconformist ministers and businessmen of whom George Dawson, H. W. Crosskey, R. W. Dale, John Johns and Edward Baines were leading examples. Mid-Victorian Birmingham was the classic example of the Civic Gospel at work, and in its heyday in the 1870s and 1880s it found its foremost Nonconformist spokesman and exponent in R. W. Dale. In 1884 Dale gave a succinct summary of the ideals of the civic gospel in a sermon on 'Political and Municipal Duty'. Municipalities, he said, might do more for people than Parliament: health, morality, relief of poverty, and intellectual and cultural improvement, might all be advanced by municipal action. 'Medicine and not the gospel only', 'municipal action, and not the gospel only' were needed, he urged, to cure the sick and improve the homes of the poor.

Certainly, this is far from political radicalism, but it is also a far cry from the insistence upon the absolute priority of self-help and purely individual responsibility. Moreover, although Dale's sermon dates from the 1880s, it was the mature summation of a consistent Nonconformist commitment to the civic gospel in Birmingham which dated back to the 1840s, 50s and 60s and owed much to the ministries of the Baptist-turned-Unitarian George Dawson, Dawson's Baptist successor Charles Vince, and the Unitarian H. W. Crosskey. Similarly, in Liverpool the Unitarian Domestic Missioner John Johns was urging as early as the 1840s in his annual reports and articles in *The Christian Teacher* that personal service to the poor was not enough: municipal action was also essential.

Thus representatives of middle-class, urban Nonconformity — and, especially in the cases noted here, Congregational and Unitarian Nonconformity — were advocating a variety of interventionist and reforming social and political policies some three or more decades before the date Helmstadter proposes for the breakdown of the mid-Victorian synthesis and the emergence of a 'social gospel' in Victorian Nonconformity. As David Thompson has argued, the 1880s were a watershed not because Noncon-

[7] For the place of the social gospel of Hughes, Clifford and Scott Lidgett within the development of Victorian Christian social attitudes in general, see *RVB*, II, 2.

formists suddenly became concerned about social issues or changed the content of their social comment, but because the general prominence of concern over housing, social issues and industrial relations (symbolized especially by Andrew Mearns' pamphlet *The Bitter Cry of Outcast London* (1883), the London Match Girls' Strike (1888) and the London Dockers' Strike (1889), for example) meant that more notice was taken of the kind of things Nonconformists had been saying for some time (Thompson, 1986, p. 200).

It was not only urban middle-class Nonconformity which offered an alternative to the individualistic social morality characteristic of Nonconformists such as Spurgeon, however. There was also the alternative of active involvement in working-class politics and, especially, trade unionism. Here the contribution of Methodism, and especially Primitive Methodism, was important. The role of Methodism in relation to politics in general and working-class politics in particular during the nineteenth century has been the subject of a number of wide-ranging theses and generalizations, both scholarly and popular. Thus, for example, much debate has focused upon whether Methodism made the working classes more radical (by offering opportunities, education, and experience of organization and leadership) or more conservative (by diverting them from radical politics, inducing acceptance of worldly deprivation, and endorsing political conservatism). Also, there have been those who, keen to show that the Victorian churches were not always arrayed against the working classes, have sought to emphasize the extent of the Methodist contribution to trade unionism, in the process bequeathing to popular historical consciousness the conventional wisdom that 'the British labour movement owes more to Methodism than to Marx'. The recurrent weakness of such generalizations is their failure to give sufficient attention to local circumstances and to recognize that Methodism, like Nonconformity as a whole, was not one thing but many. As David Hempton has observed, 'The much described "chapel culture" was scarcely the same thing in rural Lincolnshire as it was in suburban Manchester. Similarly, the sermons of Conference dignitaries had little in common with those of Cornish folk preachers, and the political aspirations of Lancastrian manufacturers were poles apart from those of Durham trade unionists' (Hempton, 1984, p. 11).

Bearing such caution in mind, however, there remains, in the present context, an important general point to be made about Methodist, and especially Primitive Methodist, involvement in working-class politics and trade unionism. Even if assertions that the British labour movement as a whole owes more to Methodism than to Marx themselves owe more to Methodist historical apologetics and romanticism than to sober analysis, yet in certain geographical areas and in certain occupational groups Primitive Methodism did provide a vital element in the emergence of a strong and active trade unionism.

The numerical strength of Primitive Methodism lay in rural and industrial villages and the denomination was the one consistently working-class branch of Nonconformity. Recent studies have shown how the ethos, discipline, values and opportunities afforded by the life of the Primitive Methodist chapel were frequently an avenue into active participation by Primitive Methodists in trade union life. The agricultural trade unionism of Suffolk, Norfolk, Lincolnshire, Oxfordshire and Warwickshire was heavily influenced by Primitive Methodism — both in terms of leadership and membership in chapel and union and in respect of the forms and ethos of the organization and activities of the Agricultural Workers Union (Scotland, 1981; Howkins, 1985). Similarly the ethos and membership of the miners' unions in Derbyshire, Nottinghamshire and, especially, Durham and Northumberland were heavily influenced by Primitive Methodism (Colls, 1977; Moore, 1974; Hempton, 1984, pp. 214–16). The role and significance of the Primitive Methodist *milieu* in such trade union circles has been well described by Robert Colls, speaking of the situation in the mining villages of the northeast: 'The chapel had taken these men out of the mainstream of village life and nurtured civic abilities in them: some vision of Man's significance, some rhetoric of justice, some reading and a lot of speaking. Most importantly, Methodism had been a cocoon of seriousness in a pub and coursing-path world of careless enjoyment and self-mockery. The cocoon provided its own reason and reward for self-improvement so dearly won by the miner' (Colls, 1977, p. 100). Alun Howkins endorses this view from the very different setting of rural Norfolk. The chapel, Howkins observes, was an environment with an ease of language and an emotional freedom which were profoundly democratic. In such an environment, and with a high degree of lay participation, the Bible could easily become a politically radical, prophetic text. Howkins also points out that the emotion and sentiments of the revivalist hymnody adopted within Primitive Methodism were as relevant to an embattled and campaigning political minority as they were to an embattled and evangelical religious minority. Although in origin products of American revivalism and originally made popular in Britain by the visits of Sankey and Moody, hymns such as 'Hold the Fort' and 'Dare to be a Daniel', once placed in a Primitive Methodist and trade union setting, conveyed a rhetoric of heroism, persecution, purpose and defiance which was as applicable to trade union experience as it was to chapel membership (Howkins, 1985, ch. 3; see also Scotland, 1981). Moreover, such hymnody at once combined the individual

Dare to be a Daniel,
Dare to stand alone
Dare to have a purpose true,
Dare to make it known.

with the communal

Ho my comrades! see the signal
Waving in the sky,
Reinforcements now appearing,
Victory is nigh.

The mixture of rugged individualism and support from one's fellow companions in Daniel's band was a powerful one. The politically radical potential of such a Primitive Methodist environment is well illustrated by the autobiographical statement of George Edwards, a Norfolk farm labourer who became a Primitive Methodist local preacher in 1872: 'With my study of theology, I soon began to realise that the social conditions of the people were not as God intended them to be ... Many a time did I vow I would do something to better the conditions of my class' (quoted in Howkins, p. 50). Edwards went on to become a Labour Member of Parliament.

In the present context the significance of such examples lies in the variety which they once more indicate within Nonconformist social thought in the period *before* 1880. To be sure, there are important points of contact here with Spurgeon's thrifty, respectable, hard-working, individualism — as J. Munsey Turner has observed, 'Primitive Methodism in the last analysis produced the sober, hard working, thrifty "labour aristocrat" who would fight indeed for his place in the sun, but who would be a conciliator rather than a revolutionary ... and who would be as opposed to the working-class "ne'er-do-well" as he would be to the hard-line Marxist' (Turner, 1982, p. 7). But for all the points of contact there is also a radical political activism at work here, which contrasts sharply with the essentially apolitical individualism that Helmstadter argues epitomizes the attitude to poverty of the Nonconformist 'synthesis' prior to 1880. Moreover, Primitive Methodism may have been a minority within Nonconformity as a whole, but it was an important minority and one which existed within the mainstream of Victorian Nonconformist life, not on its periphery.

Middle-class Congregational and Unitarian involvement in the civic gospel and Primitive Methodist participation in trade unionism were thus significant and prominent alternatives to the individualism which Helmstadter presents as the characteristic position of Nonconformity on social morality and social reform in the middle decades of the nineteenth century. Similarly, mid-century developments in Nonconformist views of church order, denominational organization, worship, and the nature of the church pose equally important questions concerning the adequacy of Helmstadter's contention that local, individualistic congregationalism remained predominant in Nonconformist attitudes to the nature of the church between 1830 and 1880. For Helmstadter, local congregationalism and independency continued to flourish until late in the century, despite — or even because of — greater centralization. The shift to *effective*, centralized denominational structures and organizations he sees as a feature of the post-1880 era: part of the decline of the authentic Nonconformist synthesis and the move towards Free Church Unity (or even re-union with the established church), which in turn Helmstadter attributes to a loss of nerve in the face of the still unchurched masses and the increasing secularity of society. Such a chronology — with its sharp break in the 1880s — and such an explanation in terms of loss of nerve under secular pressures neglects the changes both in Nonconformist attitudes to worship and to the nature of the church, and also underestimates the extent of the developments in denominational consciousness and organization, all of which had been in progress since at least the 1830s.

These latter developments were already well under way by mid-century. We noted earlier that, after periods of opposition or uncertainty, the Baptist and Congregational Unions and the Wesleyan Methodist Conference emerged by roughly 1860 as central features of their traditions. They had, as Clyde Binfield puts it, 'become established voices of established denominations' (Binfield, 1977, p. 12). But it was not only the two Unions and the Wesleyan Conference which signalled the development of structured, centralized and effective denominational identities. Alongside and around the Unions and the Conference there were also networks of agencies and societies for home and overseas missions, for chapel building, and for such matters as tract distribution, Sunday Schools, and education. Add to these the emergence of theological and ministerial training colleges, the establishment of book rooms, the use of denominational service books and hymn books, and the publication of denominational yearbooks and magazines, and a definite pattern of structured, increasingly centralized identity is visible well before the 1880s.

If the period from 1880 to 1914 was one of peculiar power for the Nonconformist organizations and presses it was because much of the preceding fifty years had been spent preparing the way, establishing the means, and removing the civil and public obstacles to the exercise of such influence. Even Primitive Methodism, the most radical, revivalist, and working-class of the major Nonconformist denominations, possessed, by 1885, not only an increasingly centralized conference, a book room, a hymn book, magazines and a theological college, but also two public schools (Turner, 1982, p. 87).

Such developments must qualify both the prevalence and the significance of the individualistic congregationalism which Helmstadter proposes as the predominant style of Nonconformist church order and organization from 1830 to 1880. Moreover, such developments were not merely a matter of administrative bureaucratic organization, and the need to respond to the scale and pressures of an increasingly complex urban industrial society. They were also a constitutional and administrative expression of a changing theological and ecclesiastical self-understanding among many Nonconformists. We noted earlier Chadwick's observation that, in the 1840s and 1850s, the barn chapel of the side streets was becoming the church of the market square. That change was also reflected in a higher, more 'catholic' understanding of the doctrine of the church, in changes in liturgy and worship, and in the architecture of new chapels. Two retrospective reviews of Nonconformity — one from 1869, the other from 1902 — illustrate the point.

In 1869 Thomas Binney preached a farewell sermon at the end of his forty years as minister of the King's Weigh House Chapel. The sermon was entitled 'A Forty Years' Review' and reflected upon religious developments in the four decades during which he had been minister at the chapel. It included the observation that 'Meeting Houses' and 'Chapels' had become 'Churches' and that Nonconformist buildings and worship now extended to spires, transepts, chancels, painted windows, chants and anthems. Some thirty years later an article in the Anglican *Church Quarterly Review* in 1902 on 'Some Tendencies of Modern Nonconformity' observed that 'chapel' was now regarded as an insulting designation, that the corporate aspect of dissent was predominant, that urban Nonconformity had gone Gothic in its architecture, and that liturgical worship was increasingly encouraged.

The process of change identified by these observers was one leading from self-understanding as 'Dissenter', via self-understanding as 'Nonconformist', to self-understanding as 'Free Churchman'. The process is central to the history of nineteenth-century Nonconformity and one to which we must return in the conclusion of this essay. Of particular significance here, however, is the emergence of a more 'churchly', more 'catholic', aspect to the identity and style of nineteenth-century Nonconformity. The administrative, organizational developments were a constitutional expression of the rise of denominational self-consciousness. The theological and devotional expressions of growing denominational identity were to be found in changes in liturgy, in worship, and in architecture — and, as Binney's retrospective sermon demonstrates, the changes were already well under way by 1869.

Concern for the quality of Christian worship and the contemporary recovery and utilization of the liturgical and devotional riches of the church's past were not an exclusive prerogative of Tractarians and Anglo-Catholics. There was a lively movement towards liturgical renewal in Victorian Nonconformity as well as within Victorian Anglicanism, and in Scotland the Presbyterian tradition experienced a renascence in its worship through the efforts of a series of liturgical reform movements. These included the formation of a Church Service Society and Ecclesiological

Societies in Aberdeen and Glasgow, and court cases over liturgical practices which were somewhat similar, albeit in a Presbyterian context, to the English Anglican experience. The 'High Church' party in Scottish Presbyterianism, like the Anglo-Catholics in the Church of England, achieved an impact and influence on the conduct of worship and the design of church buildings out of all proportion to their relatively small numbers.[8] Nor was English Nonconformist liturgical renewal merely a reaction or response to Tractarianism or Scottish Presbyterian liturgical renewal. Wesleyan Methodism was, in any case, familiar with a liturgical style of worship, and in the older Dissenting traditions the origins of the renewal of interest in liturgical matters lay in a work published some two decades before the emergence of Tractarianism.

In 1812 a group of Dissenting ministers, concerned at what they saw as the improprieties of contemporary Dissenting worship, published *A New Directory for Nonconformist Churches Containing Remarks on Their Mode of Public Worship, and a Plan for the Improvement of It*. This review was the first attempt at a comprehensive assessment of the state of Dissenting worship for over 150 years. It proved to be both thorough and influential and set the pattern of liturgical development in English Nonconformity for the greater part of the nineteenth century. The *New Directory* noted with concern that Nonconformist services were unduly didactic in tone and content, lacking in adequate opportunity for congregational participation, and dominated by extempore prayer which was often of poor quality and conducted by ministers without any gift for it. The *New Directory* also noted that because some ministers were themselves aware of such deficiencies in Nonconformist worship they had already begun to adopt liturgies for their congregations, commit prayers to memory, or read prayers they had previously prepared. The *New Directory* advocated a balance between the traditional practice of extempore prayer and the use of a more formal and liturgical form of service. There was even a suggested Order of Worship in which the extempore prayer was divided into several parts and the suggestion made that some of the prayers should be printed to facilitate congregational participation.

The trend set by the *New Directory* was steadily developed during the Victorian period. The greater use of printed orders of service by individual congregations was gradually followed by the compilation of orders of service, service books and hymn books for whole denominations — the increasing organization of the denominations facilitating the production and dissemination of such measures. As well as the greater use of official service books (increasingly making use of responsive prayers) and hymn books,

[8] For the 'renascence' in Scottish Presbyterian worship, see *RVB*, I, 3.

there was also an increasing appreciation of the Communion Service and a trend towards its more frequent celebration, greater note taken of the festivals of the Christian Year, and increasing use of organs and choirs to accompany and assist in the singing of the congregation. Such liturgical developments had their opponents and could give rise to controversy: but by the end of the century, Nonconformist worship in general was more liturgical, more participatory and less didactic, more musical and more aesthetically self-conscious, than the norm observed by the *New Directory* in 1812. Services were also shorter, as were sermons, although the sermon remained the central feature of Nonconformist worship: the developments in congregational prayer and praise were an exercise in bringing balance to the structure of the service — by preventing the complete dominance of the sermon — not an attempt to diminish the importance of the sermon as such. Increasingly, also, the traditional pattern of morning and afternoon services gave way to a new pattern of morning and evening worship.

Such changes in Nonconformist worship were paralleled by changes in Nonconformist church and chapel architecture. The most striking change, visually and in its liturgical and theological implications, was the rise of Nonconformist Gothic. A writer in the Congregational Year Book of 1847 expressed the hope that 'the religion of barns was passing away'. His hopes were, taken all in all, fulfilled. Particularly in the cities and larger towns the main Nonconformist denominations experimented with varieties of Nonconformist Gothic, of which the most ambitious amounted to a type of Nonconformist cathedral. Inside such buildings the pulpit remained central, but increasingly the communion table occupied a more prominent place than hitherto, and the inclusion of stained glass and even choirs, chancels, transepts and side aisles became not uncommon. The change from 'barns', 'meeting houses' and 'chapels' to 'churches' was not total. In the countryside and small towns the barn and meeting house lasted much longer — not least for lack of funds for anything more grand. But generally, and particularly in the leading centres of the main denominations, a more 'churchly' architecture combined with more liturgical forms of service to produce a Nonconformist style of worship which increasingly saw prayer and praise as more than a prelude and postlude to preaching.

It is easy to dismiss such developments — and especially the development of Nonconformist Gothic — as a mere grasping after respectability, an imitation of Anglicanism by a religious tradition anxious to assert its equality with the establishment and its possession of a cultured lifestyle in refutation of the Arnoldian slur of provincial philistinism. Such dismissals are too glib, however. Certainly the demonstration of respectability and culture and the assertion of equality with Anglicanism were a part of this process, but there were theological and religious motives at work too. In 1850 F. J. Jobson, the apologist for Wesleyan Methodist Gothic, defended the propriety of Gothic architecture for chapels on the grounds that such architecture proclaimed a church to be a church — it could not be mistaken for a barn or warehouse, a concert hall or mere meeting room. The same point was made in 1878 by the Congregationalist J. A. Clapham: older, classical-style Congregational churches could be mistaken for town halls or railway stations: not so the newer Gothic ones (Davies, 1962, pp. 54–60).

Nonconformist Gothic was the product of *both* changing social status *and* changing theological self-understanding. Increasing Nonconformist wealth and, especially in the towns and cities, increasing Nonconformist prominence and influence in civic life, joined an increasingly 'churchly' theological self-understanding and a growing appreciation of the value of liturgical worship and moderate ceremony. Such Nonconformist Gothic also exhibited great flexibility and inventiveness in achieving the careful integration within church buildings of ancillary rooms for Sunday Schools, youth clubs, week-night meetings and the host of other activities which the mid and late Victorian Nonconformist chapel characteristically supported and sustained.

Developments such as these in liturgy, worship and chapel architecture, as well as recognition of the increasing secularity of the surrounding culture and society, caused many Nonconformists to seek greater unity among Free Churchmen. The desire for such unity began to take an organized form in the 1890s: a Free Church Congress met for the first time in 1892; in 1894 the Congress of that year invited local councils of Free Churches to send representatives formally to it; and in 1896 the name was changed to the National Council of the Evangelical Free Churches. There were at least four clearly identifiable influences behind the movement. First, there was the growing experience of local Free Church councils and initiatives. Second, there was indeed a growing recognition of the gulf which separated all the Nonconformist churches from the unchurched majority and which, it was felt, could only adequately be confronted by the co-ordinated missionary enterprise of co-operating Free Churches. Third, there was a need, in Nonconformist eyes, to present a united and effective alternative to the clericalism and Romanizing (as they saw it) of the Anglo-Catholics and Ritualists: they sought to present an alternative 'catholicism' which was 'catholic' but not 'Romanizing'. And last, but not least, there was the desire to express a growing sense of the positive nature of Nonconformity, rather than its negative 'Dissenting' aspect.

As David Bebbington has shown, the heyday of the Free Church Council was brief. It made rapid progress in the 1890s and, in the last great church-versus-chapel confrontation over the 1902 Education Act, provided the basis for a remarkably successful Nonconformist political campaign. But the very politicizing of the Council contributed to its relatively rapid decline: by the Edwardian era it was becoming more political than religious in orientation and in consequence many Nonconformists began to question its role and priorities. Its brief heyday and rapid transition to a highly political role should not, however, obscure its genuinely religious and theological origins, for as Bebbington also makes clear, the origins of the movement lay in local initiatives which were genuinely led from below, not imposed by central organization, and which were frequently inspired by pastoral and evangelistic ideals such as the co-ordination of local visitations. From the mid-90s onwards, the leaders of the movement went on to emphasize the theological point that they were 'Free Churchmen', advocating positive principles, not 'Dissenters' or 'Nonconformists' based essentially on negative protest. Here, it was said, was a 'scriptural Catholicism', as opposed to the unscriptural Catholicisms of Rome and the Church of England (Bebbington, 1982, ch. 4).

On the other hand, the mid and late Victorian era also saw a continuing expression of the inherent diversity of nineteenth-century Nonconformity. Even as the mainstream Nonconformist denominations explored a more 'catholic', more unified, dimension to their life, other groups within Nonconformity continued to assert essentially Protestant aspects of their identity. Groups such as the Brethren, the Churches of Christ and the Salvation Army remained aloof from the increasingly established denominational pattern. They advocated either a version of primitive New Testament Christianity, or, in the case of William Booth and the Salvation Army, a version of Christianity that aimed to attract the urban working classes by rejecting traditional Christian styles of worship and organization and substituting instead an emotional mixture of evangelical Protestant theology, military organization and symbols, and proletarian music and milieu. The architecture of Salvation Army citadels was aggressively non-liturgical just as their worship was non-sacramental.[9] There was also a large growth in the number of local, non-denominational mission halls, gospel halls, temperance halls, railway missions and the like. In 1851 Mann had estimated that 'independent congregations' accounted for some 63,000 worshippers on Census Sunday. Working from the figures collected in the *Daily News* survey of religious life in London in 1903, John Kent has estimated that by 1903 some 97,000 people in London alone were attending services in large independent evangelical missions or in small temperance or gospel missions. There were more such small halls and missions than there were Congregational or Wesleyan churches in London. The Baptists had more churches than there were mission halls, but only just (Kent, 1978, pp. 299–301).

[9] The continuing diversity was reflected in the Free Church Council Movement itself; the movement appealed to the Methodists, Congregationalists, Baptists and Presbyterians; the Salvation Army and Plymouth Brethren were excluded as insufficiently 'churchly', the Unitarians as theologically heterodox.

The religious sub-culture of such non-denominational Protestant Nonconformity remains largely uncharted and unexplored, but its significance in mediating a version of Christianity to the lower-middle and working classes (not least through its Sunday Schools and youth groups) in late nineteenth and early twentieth-century Britain can hardly be doubted. Nevertheless, to return to the main theme in the present context, when all such exceptions are noted, it remains the case that the movement towards Free Church unity and self-identity as Free Churchmen was religiously and theologically, as well as politically and strategically, motivated.

A similar point must be made about the pace and motives of theological change within Nonconformity. For Helmstadter the adoption of a liberal and incarnational theology by many leading Nonconformists in the 1880s is a sign of capitulation to secular intellectual pressures and a collapse out of a previously unified and strong theology into a vague theology and concomitant vague humanitarianism. Neither the proposed earlier unity nor the pejorative evaluation of the later developments do justice to the variety in mid and late nineteenth-century Nonconformist theology.

To begin with, the contrast with the pre-1880 situation was not so marked. In 1871 James Baldwin Brown, a prominent Congregational minister of distinctly liberal theological opinions, marked the removal of a large part of the congregation of his Lambeth chapel to a new and larger church in Brixton by delivering a series of lectures. Brown had been their minister for some twenty-four years. He therefore addressed his congregation on 'The Revolution of the Last Quarter Century' and in so doing remarked upon 'the theological revolution' of those years. Thoughtful observers, he argued, must note that the hold of traditional evangelicalism was severely shaken, and the key to the theological transformation which had been taking place was the insistence upon the priority of the notion of God as father, not king. Brown's remarks were themselves a part of the very pressure for change which he claimed to describe, but they were, nonetheless, well made, and indicate clearly that the emergence of alternatives to traditional evangelicalism — and especially alternatives sensitive to the morality of the theology and concept of God involved — was an important feature of the period prior to 1880 (indeed prior to 1870), not a sudden development of the last twenty years of the century.

In fact, in the 1850s, 60s and 70s, sometimes with considerable drama, but more usually with much less controversy than in the contemporary Church of England, Nonconformists (and especially Congregationalists and Unitarians) explored various liberal and critical versions of theology. Two of the more controversial incidents occurred in Congregationalism in the 1850s. In 1855 Thomas Lynch published a collection of religious poems entitled *Hymns for Heart and Voice: The Rivulet*. Conservative members of the Congregational Union attacked *The Rivulet* for being pantheistic in its celebration of nature. It was also urged that the collection was pervaded by the influence of rationalizing German theology. More theologically liberal members of the Union, among them Thomas Binney and James Baldwin Brown, defended Lynch and *The Rivulet*. The controversy which ensued between 1855 and 1857 was complicated by becoming involved in a dispute over control of the various Congregational magazines then published. It was sharp and bitter. The liberal members of the Congregational Union who supported Lynch were, it has been remarked, characterized by 'an unreadiness to assert the unique inspiration of the Bible and a positive desire to assert the Fatherhood of God rather than eternal torment' (Tudor Jones, 1962, p. 253).

The inspiration of the Bible and fears of German rationalism were also to the fore in the second Congregational theological controversy of the 1850s. Samuel Davidson had been a lecturer at Lancashire Independent College (a college for the training of Congregational ministers) since 1842. In 1856 he published a book entitled *The Text of the Old Testament Considered* in which he espoused a moderate biblical criticism (including, for example, the rejection of Mosaic authorship of the entire Pentateuch) and argued that the general inspiration of the Bible did not entail total infallibility but merely extended to infallibility on moral and religious matters. The position was a moderate one, but already too radical for the conservative wing of Congregationalism and the committee of Lancashire College. After investigation of Davidson's views during 1856 and 1857 the committee voted for Davidson's suspension pending revision of the offending parts of his book. Davidson duly resigned and continued to write his biblical criticism, but in increasing isolation from Congregationalism.

At first sight the Davidson controversy was simply a defeat for theological liberalism and evidence of the correctness of Helmstadter's contention that the period prior to 1880 was one of theological conservatism in Nonconformity. A closer examination, however, reveals a more subtle picture. For example, the vote for Davidson's suspension was only by a majority of eighteen to sixteen: it was thus by no means overwhelming and there were many who strongly supported Davidson. They may have been a minority, but they were an important and increasingly influential minority. Nor was support limited to Congregationalists: in 1860 Thomas Nicholas, Professor of Biblical Literature at Carmarthen Presbyterian College, published a spirited defence of Davidson which argued that his work was not only intellectually but also religiously more healthy and more truly faithful than the 'debilitated spiritual habit' of the majority of the clergy for whom 'forms of words exercise a regal sway' and in whom there is 'a dread of all enterprise in thought — a phenomenon in our day confined to theology alone'.

Moreover, although it was not until the 1870s that Congregational scholars generally abandoned the doctrine of inerrancy, and not until the 1880s and 1890s that a significant number of ministers became public about their acceptance of biblical criticism, between 1860 and 1880 the leadership of the Congregational Union was often in the hands of ministers who urged acceptance of the views for which Davidson was suspended. Thus in 1864 Henry Allon, as chairman of the Union, argued that since the dogma of verbal inspiration had produced a revolt among thousands of religious men it could not be defensible. Again, in 1868 the chairman of the Union, Alexander Raleigh, spoke of errors and mistakes in the Bible considered as a human book, and R. W. Dale, who was chairman in 1869, maintained that controversy should centre on the authority of Christ, not the threatened 'demonstration of the historical untrustworthiness of a few chapters here and there in the Old Testament'. By the late 1870s the change of mood was already so great that Henry Allon told William Robertson Smith that he would be welcome at an English Congregational college if his own Free Church of Scotland deprived him of his chair at their college in Aberdeen (which in fact they did) because of his acceptance of biblical criticism (Tudor Jones, 1962, pp. 256–7).

Just as biblical criticism, although remaining the position of a minority, gained ground in Congregationalism in the 1850s, 60s and 70s, especially among the leadership of the denomination, alternatives to the traditional doctrines of eternal punishment and substitutionary Atonement also gained ground in the same period and among the same group of liberal ministers. As early as the 1840s Thomas Binney was rejecting belief in eternal torment, and in 1846 Edward White expounded the view that immortality was found only in Christ and that the ungodly would not suffer eternal punishment but would be destroyed. White at this stage suffered exclusion from many pulpits and much ostracism, even fearing he had no future in the Congregational ministry, but in 1887 he eventually became chairman of the Union. In the 1870s the question of eternal punishment was again prominent: White reissued his 1846 book on the subject and R. W. Dale indicated his support for White's position. Others, among them Baldwin Brown, pressed further and advocated universalism and the eventual salvation of all.

Baldwin Brown was also prominent in discussion of the Atonement. In 1859 he published *The Divine Life in Man* in which he made the Fatherhood of God central and the Incarnation rather than the Atonement the vital Christian doctrine: faith was the apprehension of the work of Christ and established a union between believer and Redeemer, and that work was the revelation of God's compassion, not a transaction to remove guilt by the appeasement of divine wrath. A year earlier, J. H. Godwin had pursued a similar line of argument, urging that faith in Christ meant trust *in* him, not belief in doctrines *about* him. Baldwin Brown, like Edward White, went on, despite his liberalism, to become chairman of the Union in 1878. R. W. Dale also addressed the subject of the Atonement in one of his weightiest books. He too sought to reject any notion of Atonement as a transaction between Father and Son and shifted the emphasis to the realm of moral and spiritual relationship (Tudor Jones, 1962, pp. 265–8).

Thus Congregationalism, in particular, had moved, especially among many of its most able leaders, towards a more liberal theology well before the 1880s. Nor was Congregationalism unique, although it was somewhat ahead of the other major Nonconformist denominations. J. M. Turner has observed of the *Wesleyan Methodist Magazine* that, by the 1870s, 'hell has moved off the scene' (Turner, 1985, p. 61) and even among the generally more conservative Baptists there was Samuel Cox, who in 1877 published *Salvator Mundi*, in which he explored the possibility of some kind of further hope, after death, of the opportunity of eventual redemption even for the wicked. The implacably conservative C. H. Spurgeon was already worried by increasing liberalism among Baptists concerning hell as early as the 1870s.

And always in the background, quite apart from the example of the Church of England with its controversies over F. D. Maurice, *Essays and Reviews* and Colenso, there were also the experiences of the Unitarians and the Scottish Presbyterians to be observed. Leading Unitarians such as Martineau were consistently liberal in their theology and had many affinities with the more pronounced of the Anglican Broad Churchmen on issues as varied as biblical criticism, miracles, providence, atonement and eternal punishment (Wigmore-Beddoes, 1971). The Scottish Presbyterians, meanwhile, from the 1840s onwards, provided a whole series of debates and controversies over the legitimacy of theologically liberal opinions concerning the Bible, the Atonement and the status of doctrine.[10]

Given such precedents, the public opening up of Nonconformity to more liberal theological ideas in the 1880s does not appear so sudden. Whether or not it was a capitulation to secular pressures depends on one's view of theological development and the nature of theology itself: if theology is *defined* as supernatural in orientation and essentially opposed to accommodation to secular knowledge, then any liberal theological adjustment will be 'capitulation'; but if theology is defined more broadly, judgements as to whether or not a particular response to secular knowledge constitutes 'capitulation' will be more complex. Nor, however, was the change so complete as the idea of the crumbling or collapse of an earlier theological synthesis would suggest.

[10] On which see *RVB*, I, 3.

In the 1870s, 80s and 90s Nonconformity also had ardent exponents of a traditional and conservative evangelical theological position. Charles Haddon Spurgeon's secession from the Baptist Union in 1887 over the 'Downgrade Controversy' was probably the most dramatic example of the conservative reaction against more liberal theology. In 1887, Spurgeon, who was by far the most famous and influential preacher the Baptists had, used his magazine *The Sword and Trowel* to charge contemporary Nonconformity with a betrayal of evangelical orthodoxy. Doctrine was being downgraded, he maintained, especially that relating to atonement, scripture, sin and hell. Within the Baptist Union controversy over Spurgeon's charges occupied much of 1887 and 1888. The Baptist Union adopted a Declaratory Statement in 1888 which was very similar to the 1846 doctrinal basis of the Evangelical Alliance. Spurgeon, however, had wanted a more specific, and more specifically conservative, statement to be adopted by the Union. When it was not, he resigned from the Union. A decade earlier the Congregational Union had experienced a similar but much less bitter and intense controversy. At the meeting of the Congregational Union at Leicester in 1877 a fringe meeting of young ministers had espoused a number of liberal ideas including 'the principle that religious communion is not dependent on agreement in theological, critical or historical opinion'. The Congregational Union appointed a committee to review this group and its opinions and the meeting of the Congregational Union in May 1878 reaffirmed the allegiance of the Union to the Declaration of Faith of 1833. But it did no more than that. There was no question of expulsions and the chairman of the Union in 1878, Baldwin Brown, actually spoke against the reaffirmation. Moreover, alongside such conservative protests within the denominations there was also the development of the Salvation Army, the enthusiasm for revivalism of the Sankey and Moody type, and the phenomenal growth of non-denominational evangelical protestantism noted above — all of which were expressions and exponents of a doctrinally conservative evangelicalism (although the Salvation Army was also in other respects unorthodox, as for example in its rejection of an ordained ministry and all sacramentalism).[11]

What we see in Nonconformity in the 1880s and 90s is not, therefore, the collapse of a hitherto firm theology, but rather the *public* diversification of a theology that had been steadily broadening for several decades. In a process common to other denominations as well — and one which would

[11] There was also, as Jeffrey Cox has pointed out, an important distinction to be made by the end of the century between the 'liberal Nonconformity' of the middle class and ministerial élite, and the 'plebeian Nonconformity' of the lower middle-class and working-class chapels within the various denominations. Although the theological differences between them were by no means rigid or absolute, it is clear that the liberal/liturgical strand within late Victorian Nonconformity was predominantly a phenomenon of the élite, whilst the 'plebeian' chapels preserved more theologically conservative versions of their faith (Cox, 1982, pp. 136–51).

become increasingly pronounced in the twentieth century — a new theological division arose which cut across traditional denominations. The new division was between those who were essentially liberal in theology and those who were essentially conservative. When denominations chose, like the Congregationalists in 1878, or like the Baptists in response to the Downgrade Controversy ten years later, to reaffirm declarations but not to formally exclude liberal theology or adopt more conservative positions, they chose to live with internal pluralism in theology (Spurgeon withdrew — he was not ejected) and leave more explicit theological statements to individuals. The contrast between this situation and that of the 1830s is neatly summarized in John Briggs' observation that at the beginning of the Victorian era a Nonconformist evangelicalism centred simply on the Atonement and a personal conversion experience was predominant. Thus, to be an evangelical was the norm and not to be an evangelical required one actively to opt out. By contrast, at the end of the Victorian era an 'evangelical' allegiance was one which required explicit definition and to which one opted in (Briggs, 1986, p. 223).

One further aspect of Helmstadter's generally pejorative view of post-1880 Nonconformity calls for questioning. For Helmstadter the new openness of Nonconformity to recreation, culture and entertainment and the attempt, in the form of the institutional church, to attract large numbers through an array of social, recreational and educational clubs was a further sign of decline: a selling short of old-style distinctiveness in an unseemly obsession with size and numbers. There is some truth in such a view. Late Victorian and Edwardian Nonconformists were seduced by questions of size. Along with the Anglicans they set themselves impossible targets — the conversion of (all) the urban masses for example, or the wholesale alleviation of poverty, slum housing or drunkenness, and then suffered crises of confidence when the impossible could not be achieved. Also, it must be acknowledged that the institutional church was, at best, a two-edged sword. Among its more notable dangers were the financial burden of maintaining the buildings required for all the various chapel agencies of an institutional church; the risk of the agencies and sub-groups (the cricket or football or cycling clubs, Christian Endeavour Group, YMCA or YWCA, Band of Hope, Boys' Brigade, Young Peoples' Guild, Pleasant Sunday Afternoon, Women's Group or whatever) becoming ends in themselves and parasitic upon the best talents and energies of the church they were supposed to be but a small part of; and the problem of distinguishing membership of one of the recreational or educational clubs from commitment to and membership of the church itself (Sellers, 1977, pp. 49–50).

But there was also a positive side to the institutional church and the changed Nonconformist attitude to recreation. It can also be seen as an attempt by late Victorian Nonconformity to meet the growing challenge of the secular and materialist entertainment culture which increasingly emerged from the 1880s onwards. Placed in this context, the institutional church can be seen either as the attempt to take the integrated and rich world of the chapel culture beyond the confines of the chapel community and into the community at large in a bold act of confidence, simply competing with the world of secular entertainment. Or it can be seen as a determined attempt on the part of Nonconformity to confront the emerging culture of entertainment and recreation by providing an alternative world of entertainment for those within the orbit of the church, but under the auspices and influence of the chapel tradition. One might still judge either strategy to be both ill advised and doomed to failure, but it would be a failure (as indeed it was in the long term) based on mistaken confidence, not mere capitulation to secularity.

V CONCLUSIONS

Dissent to Nonconformity to Free Churchmanship: the changing self-consciousness reflected in that sequence is central to the history explored in this essay and to the debate between Helmstadter's interpretation and evaluation of Nonconformity and the alternative interpretation and evaluation presented here. In both interpretations it is 'Nonconformity' or 'Free Churchmanship', not 'Dissent', that occupies the centre of the stage. That is hardly surprising. By the 1830s the 'Dissenting tradition' was already becoming a group of Nonconformist denominations which together made up a Nonconformist community. It is one of the strengths of Helmstadter's analysis that he identifies this larger Nonconformist community so clearly. At the end of the Victorian period, after a fifty-year sequence of reforms which removed the majority of the remaining Nonconformist disabilities, and a parallel series of developments within the theological life of Nonconformity which made it, as a whole, more churchly, the notion of the main Nonconformist denominations being 'Free Churchmen' — *Free* as opposed to *Established*, but *Churchmen* nonetheless — had taken root. The late Victorian and Edwardian era was also one in which Nonconformist social and political status reached new heights; it was, to borrow a phrase from Clyde Binfield, the great era of Nonconformist mayors and MPs. The 1906 general election returned no less than 157 Nonconformist MPs (Binfield, 1977, p. 18).

In the twentieth century, however, Nonconformity was to experience a serious and steady decline. Local censuses of religious worship in 1881 had revealed that although church attendances had increased overall since 1851, the increase had not kept pace with the growth in the population.

The more astute among late Victorian Nonconformists recognized that the new century would pose severe problems. At the Congregational Union in 1895 one speaker noted that agricultural depression threatened rural chapels, whilst the drift out of the cities by many of the middle classes deprived city churches of their income, and the rise of the suburbs called for new churches. These were perceptive remarks which foresaw much that was to become central to the experience of the Nonconformist churches in the twentieth century. But it is doubtful whether the extent of the decline which ensued was foreseen by many. How may such decline be accounted for?

For Helmstadter the explanation lies in the crumbling of the fifty-year synthesis of politics, social morality and evangelical theology which gave Nonconformity its identity and effectiveness between 1830 and 1880: vague theology, vague humanitarianism and a loss of nerve in the face of the growing secularity of British life and society replaced a confident, coherent and clear synthesis of values and beliefs. Yet such an interpretation, it has been argued here, overstates the degree of synthesis between 1830 and 1880 and misses the degree to which the move away from the theology, politics and social values of 1830–80 was merely the late Victorian expression of a theological, social and political diversity which was always present in Victorian Nonconformity. It neglects also the extent to which late Victorian Nonconformist stances — in politics, theology and churchmanship — were a continuation of ideas and attitudes already present in mid-Victorian Nonconformity. Helmstadter's thesis also has the unfortunate consequence of both equating strong, coherent and effective Nonconformity with a pre-critical evangelical theology and of isolating the post-1880 Nonconformist 'crisis' from the more general crisis of confidence which began to occur in most denominations during the 1880s.[12] There is, however, an alternative explanation, and one, moreover, which locates the crisis and decline of Nonconformity firmly within the crisis and decline of late nineteenth-

[12] When Helmstadter states that evangelicalism was a religion of strength which encouraged democracy through equal opportunity, whilst 'incarnationism' was a religion of weakness which encouraged democracy through welfare for the unsuccessful (p. 160), he uncritically adopts the self-assessment of the old evangelicalism itself. His proof is the failure of 'incarnationism' to sustain an alternative political-theological synthesis after 1880. But this neglects the changed context. A relatively uniform synthesis was possible between c. 1830–80 because both Nonconformist theology and the wider social, intellectual and political context facilitated one. By the 1880s the mid-Victorian political and intellectual milieu was itself fragmenting and giving way to new alignments. Anglicans and Scottish Presbyterians also found their earlier 'syntheses' and 'consensuses' giving way, and also found it impossible to construct equally 'coherent' or unified new ones (see *RVB*, I, 1 and 3). The significant question is whether, in the changed circumstances — intellectual, social and political — of the post-1880 era, any theological stance could have supplied Nonconformity with a new synthesis which was simultaneously politically effective and genuinely unifying: it seems doubtful.

century British Christianity as a whole, whilst still accounting for the particularly drastic decline which has befallen Nonconformity in the twentieth century.

Victorian Nonconformity and Victorian Anglicanism shared at least three fundamental experiences. They both experienced the intellectual pressure of modernity upon traditional theology: science, historical criticism and changing notions of morality applied to traditional doctrine caused both Anglicans and Nonconformists to modify traditional beliefs — especially ones concerning the nature of the biblical text, the nature and significance of the Atonement and the propriety of eternal punishment. For some in both traditions — for a Spurgeon or a Denison, for example — the answer was to hold fast to traditional doctrine. For others, varying degrees of adjustment, change or development were required. Despite the attempts of the Spurgeons and the Denisons (and even the efforts of the clergy, bishops and church courts over *Essays and Reviews* and Colenso), by 1900 both Anglicanism and most of the major Nonconformist denominations were doctrinally pluralist. Theological liberals and theological conservatives co-existed, often uneasily, within the same denominations — not infrequently having more in common with fellow liberals or conservatives in other churches than with their theological opposites within their own denomination. A similar political pluralism emerged within the churches: the passing of the age of Nonconformist disabilities and the passing of the age of Church/Tory Party-Chapel/Liberal Party alliance gave way to a plurality of political allegiances within both 'Church' and 'Chapel'. Both are patterns which have continued in this century.

The second common experience of Nonconformity and Anglicanism was the challenge of the unchurched masses. Faced with the scale of unbelief apparently laid bare in 1851, the churches — Anglican and Nonconformist — threw themselves into the attempt to convert the masses. The effort involved not merely church building and evangelism but also philanthropy and social commitment, education, settlements, and a vast church and chapel-sponsored network of agencies for self-help, education and social advancement. It was an initiative which has been aptly described as the 'civilizing mission', and one which reached its height in the years between 1870 and 1914.

Within these two shared experiences there lurked a number of difficulties. First, and most simply, the civilizing mission could never hope to achieve the ends it aimed for. Only the state could hope to achieve such ends in the context of a modern society and only the state possessed the resources for the task. Accordingly, as the caring professions emerged and the social welfare provision of the state increased, the churches lost their role as the principal sustainers of the civilizing mission. For Nonconformity and Anglicanism alike, the growing commitment to a social gospel was overtaken by the growing intervention of the state in matters of social welfare: but once involved the churches could neither keep pace with the resources needed for such work nor bring themselves to give it up. As for theology, a cruel dilemma began to emerge. Popular education presented the unchurched with access to popularized science and criticism of the Bible, and with popularized moral objections to traditional doctrine, so that an unequivocal theological conservatism, though capable of producing converts in useful numbers, was not likely to command mass support. But equally, liberal theology, although it might appeal to those who were inclined to religious belief but found orthodoxy unacceptable, was too complex an intellectual system for successful mass evangelism. This too was a dilemma common to both Nonconformity and Anglicanism and a common (and still quite unresolved) factor in their mutual twentieth-century decline.

The third experience common to both Nonconformity and Anglicanism was the impact upon their *own* members of internal theological pluralism and the rise of a secular, entertainment culture. It was not only the unchurched for whom neither traditional conservative theology nor new liberal theology possessed an appeal. The rise of internal pluralism did not involve a simple division of a denomination into two wings, one conservative, the other liberal (or, in the Anglican case, Anglo-Catholic, Evangelical and Modernist). Rather, it involved the emergence of articulate conservative and liberal groups *within* each denomination and left between such groups a large number (probably a large minority on the way to becoming a majority) who knew they were Christian and that they were Nonconformist, not Anglican (or vice versa) and that they were not only Nonconformist but Methodist, or Baptist, or whatever, but whose belief, beyond that, was not systematic or defined. They did not believe in evangelical orthodoxy or Anglo-Catholic orthodoxy or liberal heterodoxy, but occupied a denominational and theological middle ground, nurtured by the fellowship and liturgy and traditions of their denomination (and increasingly by a cross-denominational tradition of hymns), and happily unspecific about the detail of their faith. When R. W. Dale spoke of aspects of evangelical orthodoxy being 'silently relegated, with or without very serious consideration, to that province of the intellect which is the house of beliefs which have not been rejected, but which we are willing to forget', he might have been describing such believers. A generation later, in 1918, Archbishop Randall Davidson observed in a private letter, 'It is to me amazing to find how many good Christian people emasculate Christianity into a sort of sentimental good nature' (quoted in, respectively, Gilbert, 1976, p. 183, and Lentin, 1984, p. 90).

For such 'good Christian people' — Anglican or Nonconformist — belief still mattered but had to co-exist with a steadily widening range of leisure and recreational pursuits: religion, Anglican and Nonconformist, was becoming, for many, one leisure activity among others. Only in the Roman Catholic church, among the major denominations, was there a concerted effort to prevent the emergence of such internal pluralism and maintain a precise commitment at both individual and communal level to life wholly within the orbit of the church. Late Victorian Roman Catholicism provided a more disciplined *milieu* than its Nonconformist or Anglican counterparts; it also resisted decline and continued to expand effectively in the first half of this century.[13]

Thus, for Nonconformity, the achievement of 'liberation' from civil disabilities, the achievement of a social status sufficient to produce 157 Members of Parliament, and the emergence of the self-confidence and theological inclination to replace the negative sounding 'Dissent' and 'Nonconformity' by the confident self-designation 'Free Church' all coincided with the point at which the Victorian tension between religious revival and crisis of faith gave way to the pattern of twentieth-century denominational decline. But for Nonconformity there was a further difficulty. In 1897 the Congregationalist theologian A. M. Fairbairn observed that,

> It is perhaps harder to be a Nonconformist today than it has ever been in the history of England. The very decay of the disabilities from which our fathers suffered has made it harder for us than it was for them to dissent.

It was a perceptive remark. To the extent that Nonconformity gained its identity through dissent against the encroachments of established religion upon the beliefs, practices and liberties of non-Anglicans, the achievement of 'gradual dis-establishment' removed an important part of the rationale of Nonconformity. As British society became more secular and pluralist and religious allegiance less precise, so religious Nonconformity lost much of its apparent meaning. To that extent becoming 'Free Church' instead of 'Dissenting Chapel' was a decidedly ambiguous development.

Moreover, quite apart from a loosening of theological precision within the churches, historians of religion in late nineteenth and early twentieth-century Britain have noted the emergence of a widespread 'diffusive Christianity', a vague religiousness, clearly derived from orthodox Christianity but lukewarm towards, and but loosely attached to, *any* regular religious practice or institution. Such a marginal, nominal, religious allegiance is best suited to a religious tradition in which participation and commitment may easily be minimal and anonymity preserved. The Church of England is

[13] For the theme of religion and leisure, see *RVB*, II, Introduction. For Roman Catholicism, see *RVB*, I, 4.

such a religious environment.[14] By contrast, as David Thompson has observed, it is virtually impossible to be an uncommitted or casual Nonconformist, and certainly it was so in the nineteenth century. The Chapel culture, in all its varieties, nurtured a discipline and commitment which were part of the nature of 'Dissent' and 'Nonconformity' (Thompson, 1972, p. 17).

Thus there is a poignancy about the dilemma of late Victorian Nonconformity. It shared fully in the theological dilemmas and loss of social role which contributed to the decline of all the major denominations in the twentieth century. But to these shared pressures, it added its own ironic causes of decline, born of its very success. Free of the need to dissent, but characterized by a chapel culture of commitment and participation, Nonconformity in process of becoming Free Churchmanship was not well adapted to the increasingly optional, lukewarm religious ethos of twentieth-century Britain.

BIBLIOGRAPHY

D. W. Bebbington (1982) *The Nonconformist Conscience: Chapel and Politics 1870–1914*, George Allen and Unwin.

C. Binfield (1977) *So Down to Prayers: Studies in English Nonconformity 1790–1920*, Dent.

J. C. Bowmer (1975) *Pastor and People: A Study of Church and Ministry in Wesleyan Methodism*, Epworth.

J. H. Y. Briggs and I. Sellers (1973) *Victorian Nonconformity*, Arnold.

J. H. Y. Briggs (1986) 'Charles Haddon Spurgeon and the Baptist Denomination in nineteenth-century Britain', *The Baptist Quarterly*, Vol. 31, pp. 218–40.

R. Carwardine (1980) 'The evangelist system: Charles Roe, Thomas Pulford and the Baptist Missionary Society' *The Baptist Quarterly*, New Series, Vol. 28, pp. 209–25.

O. Chadwick (1971) *The Victorian Church*, Part I, A. & C. Black.

R. Colls (1977) *The Collier's Rant*, Croom Helm.

* J. Cox (1982) *The English Churches in a Secular Society: Lambeth, 1870–1930,* Oxford, Oxford University Press.

[14] Compare Cox's perceptive observation that 'The Church of England was the traditional path out of Dissent for wealthy Nonconformists, and as affluence and social standing spread further down the social scale, the local parish church must have seemed a sensible choice for the young Nonconformist who wished only to attend an attractive service occasionally' (Cox, 1982, p. 253). Nonconformist parents, Cox notes, would sometimes justify their non-objection to such religious choice by their children on the grounds that they liked their children to think for themselves: a version of Nonconformist principle which both invites respect and demonstrates the costly vulnerability of Dissent when it both possessed liberty and eschewed narrowness.

R. Currie, A. Gilbert, and L. Horsley (1977) *Churches and Churchgoers: Patterns of Church Growth in the British Isles since 1700*, Oxford, Oxford University Press.

H. Davies (1962) *Worship and Theology in England: From Newman to Martineau, 1850–1900*, Oxford, Oxford University Press.

*A. D. Gilbert (1976) *Religion and Society in Industrial England: Church, Chapel and Social Change 1740–1914*, Longman.

*R. J. Helmstadter (1979) 'The Nonconformist conscience' in P. Marsh (ed.) *The Conscience of the Victorian State*, pp. 135–72, Brighton, Harvester.

D. Hempton (1984) *Methodism and Politics in British Society 1750–1850*, Hutchinson.

A. Howkins (1985) *Poor Labouring Men: Rural Radicalism in Norfolk 1870–1923*, Routledge and Kegan Paul.

I. G. Jones (1981) 'Religion and society' in *Explorations and Explanations: Essays in the Social History of Victorian Wales*, pp. 217–35, Llandysul, Gomer Press.

*J. Kent (1978) *Holding the Fort: Studies in Victorian Revivalism*, Epworth.

W. R. Lambert (1976) 'Some working-class attitudes towards organised religion in nineteenth century Wales', *Llafur*, Vol. 2, pp. 4–17.

A. Lentin (1984) *Lloyd George, Woodrow Wilson and the Guilt of Germany*, Leicester, Leicester University Press.

W. H. Mackintosh (1972) *Disestablishment and Liberation: The Movement for the Separation of the Anglican Church from State Control*, Epworth.

H. McLeod (1973) 'Class, community and region: the religious geography of nineteenth-century England', in M. Hill (ed.) *A Sociological Yearbook of Religion*, pp. 29–72, S.C.M. Press.

R. Moore (1974) *Pit-men, Preachers and Politics: The Effects of Methodism in a Durham Mining Community*, Cambridge, Cambridge University Press.

E. A. Payne (1958) *The Baptist Union: A Short History*, Welwyn, Carey Kingsgate Press.

A. Peel (1931) *These Hundred Years: A History of the Congregational Union of England and Wales 1831–1931*, Independent Press.

H. D. Rack (1973) 'Domestic Visitation: a chapter in early nineteenth century evangelism', *Journal of Ecclesiastical History*, Vol. 24, pp. 357–76.

N. G. A. Scotland (1981) *Methodism and the Revolt of the Field*, Gloucester, Alan Sutton.

*I. Sellers (1977) *Nineteenth Century Nonconformity*, Arnold.

*D. M. Thompson (ed.) (1972) *Nonconformity in the Nineteenth Century*, Routledge and Kegan Paul.

D. M. Thompson (1974) 'The Liberation Society 1844–1868', in P. Hollis (ed.) *Pressure from Without in Early Victorian England*, pp. 210–38, Arnold.

D. M. Thompson (1979) 'The Religious Census of 1851', in R. Lawton (ed.) *The Census and Social Structure*, pp. 241–86, Frank Cass.

D. M. Thompson (1986) 'John Clifford's Social Gospel', *The Baptist Quarterly*, Vol. 31, pp. 199–217.

R. Tudor Jones (1962) *Congregationalism in England 1662–1962*, Independent Press.

J. M. Turner (1982) 'Primitive Methodism from Mow Cop to Peake's Commentary', in *From Mow Cop to Peake 1807–1932*, pp. 1–13, Wesley Historical Society, Yorkshire Branch.

*J. M. Turner (1985) *Conflict and Reconciliation: Studies in Methodism and Ecumenism in England 1740–1982*, Epworth.

*D. G. Wigmore-Beddoes (1971) *Yesterday's Radicals: A Study of the Affinity between Unitarianism and Broad Church Anglicanism in the Nineteenth Century*, Cambridge, James Clarke.

J. Wolffe (1986) 'The Evangelical Alliance in the 1840s: an attempt to institutionalise Christian unity', in W. J. Sheils and D. Wood (eds.) *Voluntary Religion*, pp. 333–46, Oxford, Blackwell.

CHAPTER 3

"AVAUNT!"

Free-Kirk Divine (of advanced opinions, who has recently introduced an Organ into his Chapel). "I'M SORRY TO HEAR, MRS. MCGRAWLY, THAT YOU ARE BY NO MEANS SO REGULAR IN YOUR ATTENDANCE AT CHURCH AS YOU USED TO BE."

Fair Beggite (indignant at the Pastor's latest iniquity). "KIRK, INDEED! WUD YE LUURRE ME TAE ROME WI' THE REST O' THEM, WI' YOUR ORGINS AN' ANTHUMS AN' SICH LIKE ABOMINATIONS? NA, NA, UNTIL YE GIE ME TH' AULD HUNDER' AGAIN WITHOUT THE WHUSTLES, I'LL TAK' MA' SPEERITUAL COMFORT AT HAME!"

VICTORIAN BRITAIN'S OTHER ESTABLISHMENT: THE TRANSFORMATIONS OF SCOTTISH PRESBYTERIANISM

VICTORIAN Britain possessed two established churches, one Anglican and predominantly English,[1] the other Presbyterian and definitely Scottish. Each established church also had sister churches, of the same theological and ecclesiastical tradition, but not of established status, in the other national regions of Britain. Thus the Anglican establishment also had a non-established episcopal sister church in Scotland and, after Irish disestablishment in 1869, another in Ireland; and the Presbyterian establishment in Scotland had sister churches in England (a small community for much of the century, much dependent upon Scottish support), in Wales (where it was known as Calvinistic Methodism), and in Ireland (most especially in the north).

Arising from different historical circumstances, existing in different social and cultural contexts, and embodying different theological traditions, comparisons between the two religious establishments of Victorian Britain require caution. Nevertheless, there remain good reasons for attempting such comparisons. Their intrinsic potential is one reason: the possibility that by identifying both common features and differences we may enhance our understanding of the place of religion in Victorian Britain as a whole. Another is the possibility of genuinely incorporating the history of religion in Victorian Scotland within the history of religion in Victorian Britain in general, for it remains the case that accounts of 'Victorian religion' remain predominantly accounts of religion in Victorian England. Relatively few studies seek to integrate English, Scottish, Irish and Welsh dimensions into a genuinely 'British' account of Victorian religion. The present essay begins to explore the potential of such comparison and integration, first by examining the major developments in Scottish Presbyterianism in the Victorian period, and second by seeking to compare briefly the experiences of the Presbyterian and Anglican establishments, thereby placing both Scottish Presbyterianism and English Anglicanism within a broader and more genuinely British context.

I SCOTTISH PRESBYTERIANISM IN THE EARLY VICTORIAN AGE

At no point in the Victorian age was Scottish Presbyterianism fully unified, but in 1837, at Victoria's accession, the established church, the Church of Scotland, was overwhelmingly predominant: in relation to it the other Presbyterian churches (dating from various controversies and secessions in the

[1] 'Predominantly' English because although established in Ireland and Wales also, by 1869 it was disestablished in Ireland and by 1900 well on the way to disestablishment in Wales too. See *RVB*, I, 1 and *RVB*, II, 5 and 6.

preceding century) were statistically small. By 1837, however, the Church of Scotland was already internally divided and in the midst of a ten-year long struggle between two 'parties' within it (known as the Moderates and the Evangelicals), and in 1843 the division between them issued in the Disruption which left an established Church of Scotland and a new 'Free Church'.

In 1847 the two largest groups from the earlier eighteenth-century secessions from the Church of Scotland (the United Secession Church and the Relief Church) combined to form the United Presbyterian Church, thus creating three main branches within Victorian Scottish Presbyterianism. During the latter half of the century the Free Church made increasingly common cause with the United Presbyterian Church in seeking the disestablishment of the Church of Scotland and, although the disestablishment campaign itself failed, such co-operation led them to seek union. In 1900 they combined to form the United Free Church, although not without giving rise to a new secession in which congregations of the staunchly conservative Highland region of the Free Church withdrew to form a continuing Free Church, popularly known as the 'Wee Frees'.[2]

Such controversies, schisms and reunions, however, all existed within the context of another much more fundamental process of transformation that to a greater or lesser extent affected all the various Presbyterian churches of Victorian Scotland. A. C. Cheyne has suggested that this latter process amounted to a 'religious revolution', the four main aspects of which were the transformation of traditional Presbyterian views on the Bible, the Westminster Confession and its doctrinal implications, the appropriate style of worship, and the implications of Presbyterianism for the social attitudes and the life-styles of both individuals and communities (Cheyne, 1983, pp. 1–3). To appreciate the extent of this transformation amounting to a revolution, however, it is essential to consider first the nature and ethos of Scottish Presbyterianism prior to its occurrence.

At least until the Disruption of 1843 the Church of Scotland remained unambiguously the national church. It not only possessed the status of the established religion of the country but also retained a nationwide parochial structure and an intimate role in the system of poor relief and moral discipline. The ecclesiastical structure led from parochial kirk sessions to area presbyteries and then to the General Assembly.[3] The local kirk session was

[2] There was also a similar secession by conservative north-western congregations of the Free Church in 1892, on that occasion because of the adoption by the Free Church of a more liberal form of doctrinal assent.

[3] The Free Church and United Presbyterians repeated this structure, though the latter called their assembly a Synod.

also the main source of poor relief, local educational provision, and moral oversight of the community. The network of religious, moral and social values thus embodied was distinctly and emphatically Calvinist and 'Puritan' in ethos. In social ethics it fostered an insistence upon the virtues of self-help and the conviction that the general root of poverty was moral laxity and the root of such moral deficiency irreligion: resolve the irreligion and from this would flow both moral and economic improvement. As for life-style, both personal and communal, the early nineteenth-century Presbyterian ethos was severe, scriptural, morally ascetic and highly disciplined. It was also an essentially communal ideal, an attempt to construct and maintain a 'godly community'. One of the classic expressions of the ethos was the scrupulous observance of the Sabbath.

Early nineteenth-century Scottish Presbyterianism was equally thoroughly Puritan and Calvinist in its theology and worship. It maintained the supreme authority of scripture and, as yet, did not appreciably doubt that the scriptures were not only divinely inspired but also infallible. The other doctrinal basis of Scottish Presbyterianism was the Westminster Confession. Despite some late eighteenth and early nineteenth-century debates concerning the status and interpretation of certain chapters of the Confession, its status remained essentially intact and included the doctrine of predestination: God had eternally predestined the elect (and only the elect) to salvation and Christ's atonement was for them, not for all. The spirituality nurtured by this severely scriptural and doctrinally precise theology was characteristically intellectual and rational (but not 'critical') rather than emotional or experiential. The emphasis lay upon hearing, understanding and doing God's will, not on exploring and experiencing God's presence: it has been described as the application of (theological) logic to mystery.

The worship of early Victorian Scottish Presbyterianism reflected this theological orientation. It was formal, plain, heavily didactic and unemotional. The order was psalm, long prayer, exposition of a passage of scripture, psalm, short prayer, sermon, prayer, psalm or paraphrase and benediction. Congregational participation was limited to the psalms and these were sung unaccompanied. Sermons were long and the 'long prayers' might equal them in length. Communion services were infrequent and also extremely protracted. Marriages and baptisms were usually conducted in homes.

By the 1830s, however, the Church of Scotland was experiencing increasing pressure from three directions. Within the church the long rivalry of the 'Moderate' and 'Evangelical' parties entered a new and more urgent phase. The Moderates had been the leaders of the eighteenth and early nineteenth-century Church of Scotland. Rational and unemotional in their style of faith, they sought to soften the harsher aspects of traditional Calvinism. They also believed in the value of lay patronage as a safeguard against local congregational whims and a means of ensuring an 'enlightened élitism' in the leadership of the church. The Evangelicals, meanwhile, whilst remaining firmly orthodox Calvinist in doctrine added to this orthodoxy a zeal, fervency and militancy which was energetic in its pastoral commitment, jealous of the rights of the church within the church-state relationship and therefore opposed to unrestricted lay patronage. Led by Thomas Chalmers, the outstanding Presbyterian personality of the first half of the nineteenth century, the Evangelicals went from strength to strength in the first third of the century. They founded flourishing Sunday schools, Bible societies and missionary societies; made the need for a personal sense of conversion an integral part of their version of Presbyterianism; and, from the early 1830s, combined this with a successful reassertion of strict adherence to the Westminster Confession. By 1834 they had also achieved a majority in the General Assembly of the Church of Scotland — although Chalmers had in fact already been Moderator two years earlier in 1832.

The coming of the Evangelical majority in the General Assembly also began a conflict over patronage in the Church of Scotland which continued over ten years and culminated in the Disruption in 1843. The issue of patronage, and the further issue of church-state relations which it raised, constituted the first major area of challenge which confronted the Church of Scotland in the early Victorian years. In 1834 the Evangelical majority in the General Assembly passed a Veto Act which asserted the right of the parishioners (or at least the male heads of families in communion with the local church) to reject a minister nominated by the patron of the living. A series of complex cases ensued, the general pattern of which was that Evangelical parishes rejected the patron's nominees, whereupon the Moderates took the matter to the civil courts and, in most cases, succeeded in getting the patron's nominee upheld: the Scottish civil courts and eventually the House of Lords ruling the Assembly's Act unlawful. The Evangelicals sought to persuade the government to introduce legislation which would establish the right of parishioners to reject a patron's nominee. Although the matter was discussed in Parliament and some modest attempts at compromise legislation were explored, no legislation in fact materialized. By 1842–3 it was clear that the opponents of patrons' rights were not going to obtain reform and preparations were made for secession. At the General Assembly of 1843 Chalmers led over a third of the ministers (454 in number) out of the Assembly. The 454 ministers founded the Free Church of Scotland, whilst the remaining 752 ministers remained in the established church. The Free Church, in an exceptional display of energy, set about providing an alternative nation-wide organization. It succeeded, despite losing all access to the funds of the established church and having to raise voluntary funds for churches, manses, ministers and schools, in building 700 churches and 500 schools within four years. In 1850 the Free Church opened its first theological college in Edinburgh. The Disruption thus resulted in two churches both genuinely national (although the Free Church was particularly strong in the Highlands, and the Church of Scotland in the south), both Presbyterian, but only one established. The theological legacy of the Disruption was also significant. On the one hand there was no rigid division of Evangelicals in the Free Church and Moderates remaining in the Church of Scotland: theological differences, it has been observed, ran through, rather than between, the post-Disruption churches (Drummond and Bulloch, 1975, p. 16). On the other hand more of the Evangelicals (and more of the extreme Evangelicals) did go to the Free Church, whilst more of the Moderates remained in the Church of Scotland. The temper of the two churches was accordingly different.[4]

The conflict between Evangelicals and Moderates (focused on the issue of patronage but also involving 'conservative' or 'liberal' approaches to Presbyterianism as a whole) thus came to a head at an early stage. The other two pressures faced by early Victorian Scottish Presbyterianism did not issue in such dramatic events as the Disruption but, rather, foreshadowed the shape of controversies and problems which were to continue to confront the various branches of Scottish Presbyterianism — and to confront them with increasing urgency — throughout the Victorian period.

The problems of rapid urban expansion and the consequent breakdown of the parochial system (or at least its drastic and inevitable inability to cope adequately with urban industrial conditions, having been 'designed', like its English counterpart, for a rural situation) confronted the Presbyterian Church of Scotland just as it confronted the Anglican Church of England. Thomas Chalmers was again the central figure. From 1815 to 1823 Chalmers had served as a parish minister in Glasgow. He was appalled to discover the degree of working-class absence from the worship and life of the kirk. Moreover, not only were the working classes largely absent: if they wished to attend, or if effective appeals were made to them to attend, there would not in any case be church accommodation for them. Chalmers was not alone in recognizing the problem, but he was outstanding in his efforts to address it.

The threat posed by the effective breakdown of the parochial system and the widespread absence of the urban working classes from the life of the church was perceived as being as much social and political as it was religious and moral. Chalmers certainly saw it in this light and in this was representative of his church. Chalmers was both an ardent exponent of the

[4] Chalmers' role in the Disruption was vital because it was his stature, influence and organizational ability which ensured a high degree of Evangelical unity and determined the *scale* of the Disruption (S. Brown, 1982, p. 336). For a more detailed discussion of the Disruption and its significance, see *RVB*, II, 5.

laws of political economy and a passionate advocate of the ideal of the godly commonwealth. He thought trade unions and democracy futile, accepted the divine origins of a social hierarchy, believed individuals should accept their places in the hierarchy, that individuals were responsible for their own moral, spiritual and economic wellbeing, and that those who were wealthy were morally called to the practice of philanthropy, or, as he called it, 'an enlightened charity'. He also genuinely believed that the only remedy and hope for the labouring poor of Scotland's new industrial cities was to make the rural ideal of the godly commonwealth an urban reality. In the context of such social, economic and pastoral views, the remedy for poverty, irreligion and political radicalism was identical: namely, the effective extension of the church and its parochial structures.

Chalmers, therefore, campaigned for church extension and, thereby, for the effective urban operation of the traditional rural parochial structures of moral discipline and poor relief. If there were sufficient urban churches and parochial structures, then, Chalmers believed, by 'the principle of locality', the rural ideal of a small community (centred on church and day and sabbath schools, and with minister, elders and deacons to oversee both spiritual and temporal needs) might 'redeem' the emerging urban society of early Victorian Scotland. In Glasgow, first in his ministry at the Tron Church from 1815 to 1819, and then in the newly-created parish of St John's from 1819 onwards, Chalmers sought to put his principle into practice, the St John's experiment continuing after Chalmers' own departure from parochial ministry in Glasgow in 1823 to become Professor of Moral Philosophy at St Andrews. In St John's, Chalmers withdrew the parish from all public relief and sought to provide for the needy by private charity, thereby saving the public purse and (he maintained) fostering a morally beneficent spirit of charity which would otherwise have remained dormant. Even in the context of Chalmers' own pastoral idealism this resulted in a severe regime for the poor: once the ideas were popularized, as they were by his own prolific writings,[5] they provided less idealistic Victorians with a further rationale for the principles of self-help and laissez-faire economics (McCaffrey, 1981, p. 52).

Once the Evangelicals had gained the majority in the General Assembly in the early 1830s, an official church extension scheme was established with Chalmers as chairman of the Church Extension Committee. Between 1834 and 1838 it succeeded in raising £200,000 and building almost 200 churches. Chalmers also led the attempts to obtain funds from the government

[5] Most notably, *The Christian and Civic Economy of Large Towns* (1821–6) and *Lectures on the Establishment and Extension of National Churches* (1838). On Chalmers' social views see also *RVB*, II, 2.

for the effective development of the scheme on the scale required to make possible the national realisation of his 'principle of locality'.

Chalmers, however, was to face disappointment both in respect of his experiments in Glasgow and his efforts to secure government aid for urban church extension. The St John's experiment had to be wound up in 1837 (those operating it having become discouraged) and the government, after appointing a Royal Commission on Scottish church extension, finally refused in 1839 to make any grant for the towns, offering only some assistance for new parishes in the Highlands. Ironically for Chalmers, it was the Disruption with its 500 new Free Church buildings which eventually produced church extension on a scale approximating to that which he had hoped to secure from the government for the still united Church of Scotland. But the Disruption also meant the end of any possibility of Chalmers' system of parochial relief and social redemption being extended officially and nationally. The Disruption ended, in practice, the reality of a unified national parochial structure: the Free Church inevitably in practice became 'voluntary' and sectarian, and in 1845 the Scottish Poor Law Amendment Act took all official responsibility for the poor out of the church's hands.

The third challenge came from the area of worship and theology. In both, before 1830, themes were already emerging which were to become central to the transformation of Victorian Scottish Presbyterianism. In worship the desire for a more dignified and elegant style of worship found expression in the appearance of compilations of prayers and material for worship.[6] In theology the work of Thomas Erskine of Linlathen challenged the ethos and rigour of traditional Calvinist orthodoxy. Erskine was a layman and therefore able to publish his works without the fear of deposition from ministerial status and livelihood which faced ministers who tended towards theological unorthodoxy. He consistently appealed from the letter of doctrine to its spirit, and from dogmatic formulations about God to experience of God. In three important works, all published before 1830,[7] Erskine set out, rather as Coleridge did at roughly the same time in England, a theology which was subjective, experiential and personal: faith as the commitment of the heart, not assent to creeds based on 'evidences'. He also argued that God's forgiveness was declared for all, salvation being there for the acceptance, and that eternal life meant living in the love of God: hell meant living in self. It was an approach which was later to influence not only subsequent Scottish theologians but also F. D. Maurice in England and through him other Broad Church theologians. Last but not least, the growing influence of the Evangelical party in the first three de-

[6] For example, *Scotch Minister's Assistant* (1802) and *Prayers Adapted for Public Worship* (1829).

[7] *Remarks on the Internal Evidence for the Truth of Revealed Religion* (1820), *An Essay on Faith* (1822) and *The Unconditional Freeness of the Gospel* (1828).

cades of the century contributed a change of emphasis which affected both worship and theology. Although staunchly, even fiercely, orthodox in doctrine, the Evangelical emphasis upon the personal experience of conversion and salvation implicitly pressed both worship and theology in a more experiential and less didactic and intellectual direction.

The mounting challenge to strict Calvinist orthodoxy was focused dramatically in the General Assembly of 1831. First, one young minister, A. J. Scott, refused to sign the Westminster Confession because it taught a limited Atonement. (He was deposed from the ministry for heresy and moved to England, where he became a link between theological liberals in Scotland and England, an important influence upon leading Congregational liberals, and a co-founder of the Christian Socialist movement in 1848.) Also at the 1831 General Assembly, another minister, John McLeod Campbell, was deposed for heresy for arguing that a universal and moral (not substitutionary) doctrine of the Atonement was consistent with the Westminster Confession. (Campbell became minister of an independent congregation in Glasgow and published a classic and influential study of the Atonement in 1856.) Lastly, the Assembly began proceedings against another minister, Edward Irving, whose preaching was influenced by Campbell's ideas. (Irving was deposed in 1833 and duly founded the Catholic Apostolic Church. He died in 1834.)

What Scott, McLeod Campbell and Irving shared, despite other striking differences, was a determination to protest against both the over-intellectualized and abstract piety, and also against the overwhelming centrality of the doctrine of Atonement (indeed of limited Atonement), in traditional Scottish Presbyterianism. Atonement required, they argued, reinterpretation in the light of the doctrine of the Incarnation and a deeper appreciation of the love and Fatherhood of God. The moral critique of traditional evangelical teaching on Atonement was sharpened, in the Scottish context, by the additional moral objection to predestination. When Scottish Presbyterianism emerged, in the second half of the nineteenth century, from the turmoils of Disruption, the most notable feature of its mid and late Victorian history was the way in which all its branches were obliged in one way or another to come to terms with the theological and devotional issues raised by Scott, McLeod Campbell and Irving, and also to confront the further issues of biblical criticism, the continuing challenges of class and urbanization, and the changing social attitudes and lifestyles to which they gave rise.

II THE TRANSFORMATION OF SCOTTISH PRESBYTERIANISM 1850–1900

In 1850 the doctrinal orthodoxy of Scottish Presbyterianism and the status of the Westminster Confession apparently remained secure — or at least outwardly so. The heresy cases of the early 1830s resulted in a re-assertion of strict confessional orthodoxy. The re-assertion was particularly evident in the Free Church, but in 1841 James Morison had also been condemned and expelled from the ministry of the United Secession Church (which was to become part of the United Presbyterian Church in 1847) for questioning the doctrine of limited Atonement. Significantly, Morison placed the issue in an evangelical and missionary context as well as a moral one: if Christ did not die for all, he asked, what gospel is the missionary to preach in a foreign land? A missionary preacher with a gospel of limited Atonement must, he suggested, in practice hide the doctrine and *de facto* preach in a manner contradictory to it. The logic of the point was undeniable: even if subtle theological distinctions could reconcile election and mission, the practice of active evangelism could not, but in 1841 this remained sufficiently unorthodox to earn expulsion from his church.

Even in the 1860s and 1870s the majority in each Presbyterian church probably remained conservative in its interpretation of the Westminster Confession and its status (or at least the majority of ministers and certainly the majority of leading ministers — the precise attitudes of the laity are, as in most denominations and traditions, harder to gauge with accuracy). Yet within and beneath such continuing conservatism there were also indications that a more flexible and liberal understanding of the doctrinal standards of Scottish Presbyterianism was emerging alongside the traditional view, even if it could not yet replace it.

There was, on the one hand, the continuing influence of individuals such as McLeod Campbell and Morison. McLeod Campbell developed his position impressively in *The Nature of the Atonement*, published in 1856, and Morison founded the Evangelical Union, which espoused a warmly Arminian evangelical piety. The removal of such men from the ministries of the Presbyterian churches did not end their influence: their ideas worked, it has been observed, like leaven even on those who expelled them (Smout, 1986, p. 193).

There were also subtle changes within the various branches of Scottish Presbyterianism, however. In the aftermath of Morison's expulsion, the United Secession Church also investigated two of his theological teachers, Robert Balmer and John Brown. Balmer died before judgement was made on his case. Brown, however, successfully argued that there had always been a duality in Reformed theology whereby support could be found within the tradition for both the view that Christ died for all and for the view that he died only for the elect. The Synod of the United Secession Church resolved that Brown's views were consistent with the teaching of scripture and of the Westminster Confession. Officially there was no change: but the direction of the decision in Brown's case was significant, for it affirmed a greater breadth of interpretation than was usual. One of Brown's professorial successors in the United Secession Church, James Cairns, observed that the result of the controversy brought relief to minds exercised by the apparent inconsistency between strict doctrine and evangelical practice: he also remarked, significantly, that by its impression it helped to liberalize the tone of Scottish theology. James Buchanan of the Free Church, meanwhile, observed at the inauguration of New College, Edinburgh, in 1850, that numbers of people were becoming uneasy with dogmatic and confessional statements in general, and were tending to contrast the witness of the scriptures with the subtleties of systematic theology to the disadvantage of the latter.

In the Church of Scotland the Moderate tradition of a generally more relaxed attitude to subscription to the Westminster Confession had reasserted itself after the departure of so many of the conservatives into the Free Church. In the 1850s and early 60s Robert Lee, minister of Greyfriars', Edinburgh, was an outspoken critic of strict application of the Confession (speaking, for example, of the inadequacy of a seventeenth-century document in the nineteenth century), and in 1862 the Moderator of the General Assembly urged revision of the formula of subscription to make it 'more simple and more comprehensive'. In the 1860s some elders and would-be elders protested against the enforced subscription to the Westminster Confession which their offices involved. They failed to secure the change they desired but indicated a changing context. In 1865 John Tulloch observed that the historical consciousness of the age would eventually oblige changes in the way Confessions and dogmas were perceived in Scotland just as it had in England (where the 1865 Clerical Subscription Act had relaxed the terms of assent for Anglican clergy). Tulloch was a prominent advocate of such historical consciousness within the Church of Scotland. He sought to impress upon contemporaries that all creeds and confessions were 'historical monuments', understandable only in the context of their times, neither more nor less than the best thoughts of those who framed them: as such they may err and are never infallible.

By the 1870s ministers with liberal views such as John Tulloch and Norman Macleod in the Church of Scotland and T. M. Lindsay and Alexander Whyte in the Free Church were occupying prominent posts and pulpits within their denominations, and both lay observers in Scotland and clerical observers in England remarked upon the range of opinions now existing within Scottish Presbyterianism. In 1867 the Scottish layman, A. T. Innes, author of a standard work on *The Law of Creeds in Scotland*, observed in a perceptive essay on 'The Theory of Church and Creed' that, *de facto*, even granting that all ministers of all the Presbyterian churches in fact held all the propositions of the Confession of Faith, yet it was also undoubtedly the case that the way they held those propositions was open to wide variation. From an English vantage point, A. M. Fairbairn, examining the relationship between the Westminster Confession and contemporary Scottish theology in 1872, asserted that the 'struggle ... to escape from the harsher points of the Confessional theology has been nowhere without result', and cited examples from the Secession Synod, Free Church, United Presbyterian Church and Church of Scotland to prove his point.[8]

Faced with an increasingly widespread change in actual perceptions of the status of the Westminster Confession, the various branches of Scottish Presbyterianism gradually took up the question of their official position concerning the Confession. In 1879 the United Presbyterians adopted a Declaratory Statement in the light of which the Westminster Confession was to be accepted. The Declaratory Statement rejected extreme interpretations of the Westminster Confession, affirmed that it was God's will that none should perish, and established the right of a limited liberty of opinion concerning matters in the Confession 'not entering into the substance of the faith'. The latter phrase was ambiguous and imprecise and was meant to be, but its tendency was clear. Between 1887 and 1892 the question of subscription came to the fore within the Free Church. The Gaelic-speaking and intensely conservative Highlands had long provided an opposition to any 'liberalization' which had been of sufficient strength to deter action by the more numerous and more liberal elements within the Free Church. Now the balance shifted and the majority proceeded to press the question to a conclusion. In 1892 the Free Church also adopted a Declaratory Statement on the Westminster Confession. It was more guarded than the United Presbyterian one but its direction was the same: rigid Calvinism and limited Atonement were eschewed. It was only in 1910 that the Church of Scotland formally adopted a form of subscription which required only acceptance of the Westminster Confession as the Church's Confession and belief in the fundamental doctrines in it. That it took so much longer reflected the less urgent situation: in the Church of Scotland the whole question was less pressing because the Confession had long been treated in a more casual way.

Thus by the 1890s theological precision (or at least the attempt to maintain theological precision) had given way to a licensed (if still cautious) breadth of interpretation and a less rigorous degree of uniformity. The reasons for such change were, not surprisingly, largely the same as those which prompted similar changes in other churches south of the border: growing awareness of the historical nature of Christian doctrine and belief, awareness of the growing diversity of opinion within the churches, and moral rejection of the stricter aspects of traditional orthodoxy (a moral

[8] For the sources and more detailed context of contemporary opinions and assessments referred to on pages 126–8 above, see Cheyne, 1983, pp. 63–72 and Drummond and Bulloch, 1975, pp. 302–5.

issue made even more pressing in Scotland by the doctrine of limited atonement).

In Scotland, however, there was a further crucial factor in the dissolution of traditional orthodoxy. The mid and late Victorian era saw an increasingly rapid and fundamental change in the Scottish Presbyterian approach to evangelism. We noted earlier the way in which, even in the early decades of the nineteenth century, and again in the Morison case, the rise of the Evangelical party and of an increasingly active and evangelical missionary strategy implicitly undermined the 'logic' of orthodox Confessional Calvinism. In the last quarter of the century that process of undermining was carried further — and, crucially, in a dramatically public way — by the rise of revivalism within Scottish Presbyterianism. In 1859 Scottish Presbyterianism had shared in the intense revival which had swept the north of Ireland. Less intense in Scotland than in Ireland itself, the 1859 revival nevertheless stimulated popular evangelism, lay participation and witness to personal experience, and the popularity of hymns and hymn singing. In 1873–5 a second major revival affected all the branches of Scottish Presbyterianism, but the Free Church especially, when the American revivalists Moody and Sankey toured Scotland. In the present context the significance of such revivalism, with its intensely personal and emotional call to individual decision, was its practical rejection of the doctrine of election and limited Atonement. Moreover, such practical rejection came from within the Evangelical wing of Scottish Presbyterianism. Although they were not staunchly conservative and traditional Calvinists (those who were, such as the Highlander John Kennedy, opposed revivalism) the Presbyterian supporters of Sankey and Moody and their approach to evangelism were conservative in the sense that they were evangelicals in theology, not liberals, they believed in heaven and hell and miracles and an inspired, infallible Bible, and even if, in practice, they rejected election and limited Atonement they also rejected biblical criticism, 'liberal theology' and the retreat from dogmatism.

In short, traditional Calvinist Confessionalism was, by the 1870s and 1880s, undermined from the conservative theological right as well as from the liberal theological left. Moreover, it is quite probable that, at the level of popular perceptions of Presbyterianism, the practical revivalist undermining was more significant than the articulate 'liberal' objections of a Scott, a McLeod Campbell or an Erskine.

A similar process of liberalization occurred in the attitudes of the Scottish Presbyterian churches to the interpretation of the Bible. Here the Free Church occupied the centre of the stage, by virtue of a series of heresy trials over the issue of biblical criticism. The Church of Scotland, in contrast, accommodated itself to the impact of biblical criticism with less trauma, but also with less by way of substantial contributions to critical scholarship.

In 1863 Andrew Bruce Davidson was appointed to teach Hebrew and Old Testament at the Free Church New College, Edinburgh. A great teacher and Hebrew scholar, he applied to the Old Testament the principles of historical and literary criticism. Over some thirty-seven years Davidson was a central figure in the training of Free Church ministers and was also the first to introduce Scotland to scholarly biblical criticism as it was practised in Germany. Davidson was, however, also a cautious and careful man, who not only believed that criticism was principally a tool in the service of religion, but, importantly, was widely known to be of that opinion.

It was one of Davidson's pupils, William Robertson Smith, who provided Victorian Scotland with its *cause célèbre* concerning biblical criticism. Smith, whose mind was as versatile as it was brilliant, entered New College in 1866. He became a research student in Old Testament under Davidson. He also studied in Germany with leading Old Testament scholars and liberal theologians. In 1870, still less than twenty-four years old, he was appointed Professor of Hebrew and Old Testament at the Free Church College in Aberdeen. From his inaugural lecture onwards, Smith presented the case for an historical and critical, not dogmatic, approach to scripture — believing all the while that this enhanced its religious value and invited a deeper, more profound, understanding of faith and revelation. He was personally remarkably unaware of the controversy such views might arouse; in fact, somewhat surprisingly, his views, though published, did not for some time excite controversy. He might even conceivably have avoided any furore had he not become involved in the discussion of biblical criticism beyond the confines of New College and scholarly journals. Inevitably, however, given his intellectual scope and ability, he entered wider arenas and, crucially for his relationship with the Free Church, he became a contributor to the ninth edition of the *Encyclopaedia Britannica*, writing on a number of Old Testament topics, but most importantly on the topic 'Bible'.

Smith presented the Bible as a collection of documents, all of them 'edited versions', not 'originals', of events and stages in the development of Israel's faith and in the emergence of Christianity. Along the way he rejected Mosaic authorship of the laws in Deuteronomy; he suggested that most of the psalms were not written by David; he denied the predictive role of the prophets; and he rejected the traditional authorship of the Gospels. None of this was particularly radical by the standards of the German biblical criticism with which Smith was familiar. It was, however, rather more radical in the Free Church, and much more radical when read by Free Church laity in the *Encyclopaedia Britannica*. That Smith also believed the Bible to be of unique religious value and (like Jowett in England) enhanced in value when studied critically, did not matter: for conservative members of the Free Church such views were 'of a dangerous and unsettling tendency'.

The Robertson Smith case lasted five years and ended in 1881 with Smith's dismissal from his chair at Aberdeen. Along the way the case revealed as much about the nature of ecclesiastical politics as it did about biblical criticism in the Free Church. The years between 1876 and 1880 were occupied with complaint, protest and condemnation on the one hand, response, defence and explanation on the other. Opponents sought to have Smith officially condemned; allies to prevent it. Eventually his case came before the 1880 General Assembly and (due not least to mismanagement of their forces by his opponents) Smith won by 299 votes to 292: Smith and all the Professors of the Free Church were merely called upon to remember their position as official church teachers.

But then another volume of the *Encyclopaedia Britannica* appeared. The fact that the items in it by Smith were written before the 1880 General Assembly did not prevent the issue being reopened. This time the vote went decisively against Smith and he was dismissed from his chair, though not deprived of ministerial status. Significantly, the Assembly dismissed Smith for 'insensitivity to his responsibilities as a theological professor and culpable lack of sympathy with the reasonable anxieties of the Church', but they did not even specify, let alone condemn, specific errors in his teaching. Smith was dismissed for style, not content, and because of that critical biblical scholarship was able to continue in the Free Church.

One of the key figures in the process which led to this result was Robert Rainy, principal of New College. Rainy's own view of biblical criticism was not very different from Smith's, hence his desire to see biblical criticism itself remain uncondemned; but Rainy was also an ecclesiastical diplomat who desired to maintain the unity of the Free Church, and he knew that in the end failure to dismiss Smith would lead to the secession of the conservative Gaelic-speaking Highland section of the Free Church, led by the arch-conservative James Begg. Depending on one's view of Rainy and Smith, Rainy diplomatically preserved the unity of the Free Church and avoided inflicting anything worse than the loss of his chair on a provocative and unrepentant Smith; or, alternatively, Rainy, despite being closer to Smith's views than those of his opponents, felt it expedient that one outspoken professor should be dismissed for the sake of the church. Recent commentators have tended towards the latter view.

Smith spent the rest of his career, until his death in 1894, in Edinburgh and Cambridge, working on the *Encyclopaedia Britannica* and as a Semitics scholar. Within the Free Church biblical criticism did indeed continue as Rainy intended, and conservative attempts to repeat the defeat of Smith all failed. In 1890 Marcus Dods of New College was before the General Assembly for his critical views (concerning, for example, the historicity of the resurrection, the existence of alternatives to substitutionary Atonement, 'mistakes and immoralities' in the Old Testament, and the doctrine of verbal inspiration as an offence and stumbling block to honest men), as was A. B. Bruce of Glasgow College (for questioning the historical accuracy of the Gospels and presenting Christ as mystical rather than divine). This time the Assembly decided there was no case to answer for either man, and Rainy opposed the conservatives in each case. Lastly, in 1902, in the new United Free Church, George Adam Smith of Glasgow College was attacked for asserting that the early chapters of Genesis were unhistorical, the lives of the patriarchs fanciful at points, and pre-eighth century Israelite religion polytheistic. The Assembly again took the view that no censure was necessary, along with issuing the by now ritual warning to scholars to be careful.

The question remains why it was in the Free Church that the battle over biblical criticism was fought, for in the Church of Scotland and the United Presbyterian Church it was accepted without such a furore: opinions differed, and men like John Tulloch were distrusted by conservatives for their advanced liberal and critical views, but they were not tried, condemned or deposed. R. A. Riesen has suggested that part of the answer may lie in the very conservatism of the Free Church, which provided a hard doctrine for later scholars to react against (Riesen, 1979, p. 120; 1985, ch. 5). It is a plausible suggestion, especially if it is also recalled that although strongly Evangelical, the Free Church was never completely without more liberal members. With the passing of the Disruption generation, the more liberal elements in the Free Church began to raise the critical issues which confronted all the branches of Presbyterianism in respect of the Bible. Crucially in the Free Church, however, there existed a conservative tradition of sufficient size and strength to render the confrontation dramatic.[9]

A third transformation within Scottish Presbyterianism in the second half of the nineteenth century occurred in its liturgical life and worship. The pre-Victorian initiatives in compiling material for use in worship were followed by further collections, such as those of William Liston in 1843 and Alexander Bruton in 1848, and were supplemented between 1840 and 1860 by the republication of important historical Reformed and Presbyterian liturgies together with scholarly introductions. There were also two critical surveys of the Church of Scotland, *Presbytery Examined* by the layman and elder the Duke of Argyll in 1848, and *The Reform of the Church of Scotland in Worship, Government and Doctrine: Part I Worship* by Robert Lee, the minister of Greyfriars, Edinburgh in 1864. Both Argyll and Lee argued that the revival of influence of the Scottish Episcopal Church in the years before and

[9] For the place of Scottish controversies over biblical criticism within the history of the rise of Victorian biblical criticism as a whole, see *RVB*, II, 11.

after the Disruption was in large part due to the quality of worship available there and the poor quality of worship in the Church of Scotland. By the early 1860s these various initiatives had created a context in which major changes could occur: that they did occur (and indeed did so on a scale which has caused historians to speak of a renascence in Scottish Presbyterian worship in this period) was due not only to the official responses of the three main Presbyterian churches, but also to the activities of various societies for the reform and revival of public worship, and the local initiatives (and on occasion controversialism) of individual ministers. Whereas it was the Free Church which provided the focus for developments in biblical criticism, in worship and liturgy it was the Church of Scotland which tended to set the pace.

At the official level, the Church of Scotland General Assembly formed an Aids to Devotion committee in mid-century and, in 1863, published *Prayers for Social and Family Worship*, a collection compiled by the committee. The other area of official action was that of hymns and hymn-singing. There was a widespread and increasing demand from ministers and laity for the use of hymns and for organs to provide accompaniment for the singing. The most consistent opposition to both hymns and organs came from the austere Highland area of the Free Church but it was an opposition which found itself steadily overcome by the prevailing trend. The United Presbyterian Church produced an official hymn book in 1851; the Church of Scotland sanctioned a book of hymns in 1866 and, since its first attempt proved unpopular, produced a new book, *The Scottish Hymnal*, in 1870. The Free Church produced its first collection in 1872 and a larger one, *The Free Church Hymn Book*, in 1881. In 1898 the three main branches of Scottish Presbyterianism published a joint hymnal, *The Church Hymnary*. Along with such collections there was the phenomenal popularity of Ira Sankey's *Sacred Songs and Solos* following the 1873–5 tour by Sankey and Moody. The growth in the demand for and popularity of hymns was another sign of the change within Victorian Scottish Presbyterianism away from the old tradition of objective and intellectual Calvinism and towards a subjective and emotional form of Christian faith. 'Where their grandparents had been concerned with the doctrines they believed', it has been observed, 'nineteenth century believers were concerned with what they experienced or felt' (Drummond and Bulloch, 1975, p. 184). The introduction of organs to accompany congregational hymn-singing took longer but was well established in all three branches of Scottish Presbyterianism by the mid 1880s. First the Church of Scotland (1865), then the United Presbyterians (1872), and finally the Free Church (1883) sanctioned their use subject to local agreement. From being prohibited, organs quickly became a central feature of much Scottish Presbyterian worship.

Alongside such official developments in worship, the initiatives and activities of various societies for liturgical reform provided a 'progressive' context for official developments to respond to. The Church of Scotland again led the way. The Church Service Society was founded in 1865 and explicitly disavowed any attempt to impose a fixed liturgy on the Church of Scotland. They sought, rather, to study liturgical history with a view to publishing forms of service, and to construct, as they put it 'a great magazine of prayers' on which ministers might draw. They also hoped thereby to broaden the range of worship and theological opinions catered for within the national church. By 1900 the Society numbered a third of the clergy of the Church of Scotland among its members and exercised an enduring influence through its publications and meetings. In 1867 the Society produced its most important publication, *Euchologion*. It contained forms of service for Baptism, Lord's Supper, Marriage and Burial, tables of psalms and lessons, and selections of prayers. Intended to provide models or aids for worship, but not to replace extempore prayer, the book went through seven editions in the next thirty years and had sold over 10,000 copies by 1900. Other ventures by the Society included the reprinting of historic liturgies, the presentation of collections of liturgical works to the General Assembly's library, and the provision of a focus for liturgical interests and scholarship. The other Scottish Presbyterian churches founded liturgical societies somewhat later. The United Presbyterian Devotional Service Association was founded in 1882 and published *Occasional Papers* with draft forms of service. These were collectively published in 1891 as *Presbyterian Forms of Service*. In the Free Church the Public Worship Association was founded in 1891 and from the private circulation of papers there emerged, in 1898, *A New Directory for Public Worship*. After the union between the Free Church and the United Presbyterians in 1900, a Church Worship Association of the United Free Church was formed.

The Aberdeen and Glasgow Ecclesiological Societies, meanwhile, founded in 1886 and 1893 respectively, were concerned with the architecture, furnishings and decoration of church buildings. Form, colour and symbolism; high quality of work in glass, stone and wood; and even an enthusiasm for chancels, choir stalls and stone communion tables were among the concerns of the Scottish Ecclesiologists. Much smaller than the Church Service Society, the two societies (which were interdenominational and united as the Scottish Ecclesiological Society in 1903), like their denominational English forerunner, exercised an influence on Scottish Presbyterian architecture which was out of all proportion to their size (Whyte, 1984, p. 148).

Last but not least, there were the contributions of notable individuals, either by setting a prominent example and thereby diffusing their liturgical ideas, or by pressing ahead with innovations despite controversy (including the bringing of cases before the General Assembly) and thereby extending the limits of the permissible within the Scottish Presbyterian tradition. The most famous case was that of Robert Lee, minister of Greyfriars, Edinburgh. The renovation of his church in 1857, after a fire, gave Lee the opportunity to introduce the architectural and liturgical changes he desired. He introduced coloured windows, a harmonium and then an organ, standing for hymns and psalms but kneeling for prayer, and responses from a printed service book. Lee was formally accused of introducing unlawful innovations although he maintained that the changes were either sanctioned or at least not forbidden by the Westminster Directory. Synod and presbytery ordered him to stop and he appealed to the General Assembly. The Assembly censured only the reading of prayers from a book. Opponents of Lee, however, passed an Act in the General Assembly in 1865, the Pirie Act, which declared the regulation of worship in each parish to be the responsibility of local presbyteries: a minister would have to persuade his fellow local ministers, not just his own congregation, of the rightness of proposed changes. Intended as a check upon reform, the Pirie Act proved in practice to be the opening for a more widespread moderate reform. One or two restrictive decisions apart, the trend was for presbyteries to reject complaints and thereby sanction change.

Other notable pioneers of liturgical change in the Church of Scotland were John Macleod (who urged more frequent communion, the observation of festivals such as Christmas Day, Good Friday, Ascension and Pentecost, and the use of symbols on font and table, as well as many of the things urged by Lee); James Cooper (who pioneered retreats, observance of Christmas and Holy Week, advocated frequent communion, daily services, private communion of the sick, and weddings in church); and James Cameron Lees (who introduced a service book and daily prayers during his ministry at St Giles, Edinburgh, thereby carrying liturgical renascence into one of the showpiece churches of the Church of Scotland).

The Church Service Society had originally sought to confine itself to liturgy and not involve itself in matters of doctrine. Inevitably in the long run, however, it proved impossible to separate liturgy and doctrine so neatly. By the late 1880s there was a clear division within the Society between a High Church and a Broad Church party. In 1888 the latter presented a 'Broad Church Manifesto', which suggested that the services in the *Euchologion* were too doctrinal in tone and that the church and the world were too markedly separated in these forms of service. The High Churchmen took the opposite view and sought to enhance the prominence of doctrine in worship and to press for more frequent, even weekly, communion services. In 1892 the High Churchmen formed the Scottish Church Society to advance the doctrinal principles within worship. There were parallels here with the English Anglican experience: the interrelationship between liturgy and doctrine gave rise not only to an internal diversity within the Church of

Scotland but to the formation of parties to advance the various versions of Church of Scotland Presbyterianism. The contrast with the Church of England, however, lay in the tone of such party relationships: in England they tended to mutual ferocity; in Scotland the High Churchmen remained members and office-holders of the Church Service Society even after the foundation of their own Scottish Church Society.

By 1900 Scottish Presbyterian worship had changed widely and markedly, but not uniformly, from what it had been in 1850. It was in general more musical and more liturgical — although the limits of liturgy varied widely and the use of organs was still not universally accepted. It was also more sacramental and communion was more frequent — although the frequency varied not only across but within branches of Presbyterianism and was still often no more than quarterly. Most of all, worship was more participatory and more experiential, less overwhelmingly didactic and intellectual.

In the pre-Disruption Church the laissez-faire individualism of Thomas Chalmers dominated Presbyterian social thought. Even in the pre-Disruption church such views were not unchallenged. Patrick Brewster, for example, called upon his fellow ministers to recognise the underlying cause of poverty to be the unequal distribution of wealth: sin, he argued, was corporate as well as individual, and justice was the primary requirement for social well-being. Brewster was sympathetic to moderate Chartism and preached at Chartist gatherings. Such protest was utterly atypical, however, and received official condemnation. The General Assembly suspended Brewster for a year because of his Chartist sermons. Until 1850 Chalmers' approach to social issues was overwhelmingly predominant within Scottish Presbyterianism.

By 1850, however, it was becoming increasingly self-evident that both laissez-faire individualism and the traditional Calvinist social ideal of the local 'godly community' centred on the moral, social and religious influence of the Kirk, were breaking down in the face of an increasingly urban and industrial society. The scale and complexity of the social crisis posed by industrialization defied the abilities and capacity of the best efforts of Chalmers and the old Calvinist social vision. The old rural parish ideal could not be stretched to accommodate the challenges of the new urban environment, church extension could not be sustained on a large enough scale to make the effort viable, and even Chalmers' own last and much vaunted attempt to make the old ideal concrete, the West Port venture of 1844–7,[10]

[10] In 1844 Chalmers launched the West Port venture in Edinburgh. By interdenominational effort sixty new churches were to be founded, each catering for an area of 2,000 people and providing the pastoral ideal of services, day and sabbath schools, voluntary visitors, moral oversight and private charity to overcome poverty. It was the old ideal in a post-Disruption, interdenominational context. Chalmers launched the first such new church in the West Port area. He achieved some success in this one area but not on a scale which could fire enthusiasm for the larger project, which never materialized.

failed. As Stewart Brown has shown, Chalmers' voluntary idealism was unable to overcome the sheer scale of urban poverty (S. Brown, 1978). In 1843 the Disruption put an end to any practical possibility of realizing the ideal of the traditional parish as the focus of social, moral and educational life as well as of religious life, and in 1845 the Poor Law Amendment Act gave political expression to that fact: regular social welfare provision was officially removed from the oversight of the Kirk.

Scottish Presbyterianism did not respond to the new situation by a sudden or vigorous re-alignment of its social thought. Individual ministers began tentatively to urge a different and more radical approach. William Blakie (later to become Professor of Pastoral Theology at New College from 1868 to 1897) provides an example of older and newer emphases co-existing within a single Free Church minister. His early writings retain the ideals of the old order: paternalism, social hierarchy, acceptance of one's place, preservation of the existing order, prudence, patience, hard work and simplicity of life-style as the means to working-class self-improvement. He also included in his writings, however, tentative and cautious questions about the limits of political economy and individualism: strikes might not be wholly wrong, all aspects of Chartism not wholly unacceptable, housing must be made more healthy — and in the latter Blakie took the lead in forming an Association for the building of improved dwellings for artisans (Cheyne, 1983, pp. 119–21). A more radical (and in some respects more surprising) example of changing social attitudes was that of James Begg. Begg is chiefly remembered for his intense anti-Roman Catholicism and staunch conservatism in the controversies over worship reform, theological liberalism and the defence of the rights of the conservative Gaelic north-west. Begg was also, however, something of a social radical, particularly in matters of housing and social conditions. From as early as 1849 he campaigned and wrote about poor housing conditions and began to create an awareness of such issues within the Free Church.

Following the lead of individuals such as Blakie and Begg, in the 1860s and 1870s the churches began to address the various social problems of mid-Victorian Scotland more directly. Questions of poverty, housing and social conditions, social justice, and morality received more public attention from the churches and began to become the subjects of committees, commissions and enquiries. The Free Church set up committees on Working Class Housing (1858), Social Evils (1859), and the State of Religion and Morals (1860). The Church of Scotland appointed a Christian Life and Work Committee in 1869, which during the 1870s gathered information on the relationship of church and society through a series of enquiries and questionnaires. Many of the Assembly debates on social issues were published separately and given wide circulation and, significantly, the traditional 'answers' to such social issues were themselves increasingly questioned.

In the 1880s and 1890s an even more significant shift was discernible. The importance of 'the environmental factor' came to be more widely recognized and accepted as an essential element in questions of poverty, morality and social conditions. Whilst the importance of individual effort was still stressed, there was a decisive recognition that this alone was insufficient in the worst of the slum conditions of Scotland's late Victorian cities. Thus, for example, the Glasgow presbytery of the Church of Scotland was prominent in the debate concerning the religious implications of bad housing, and argued in their 1888 petition to the General Assembly on *Non-Churchgoing and the Housing of the Poor* that in the worst housing then prevailing it was difficult if not impossible to live the Christian life. 'What the Church has primarily to do', the presbytery petition observed, 'is to create a right public opinion. It has to teach that it has more to do for these 'lapsed masses' than to assault them with armies of district visitors and to shower upon them tracts and good advices'. Such changing perspectives were a feature of the life of all three of the major Presbyterian Churches in the 1880s and 1890s, although the United Presbyterians were probably somewhat in advance of both the Free Church and the Church of Scotland in such matters (Withrington, 1977).

At the theological level the changed perspective manifested itself in a rediscovery of the ethical witness of the Hebrew Prophets and their emphasis upon communal righteousness, justice and the needs of the poor, as well as upon individual righteousness, and also in greater stress upon the historical Jesus and his preaching of the kingdom of God in a manner which clearly indicated that he perceived the kingdom to be a social as well as an individual phenomenon. At the political level the change in attitudes was reflected in a marked weakening of traditional Presbyterian opposition to socialism (from the earlier tradition of identifying socialism with atheism and blasphemy it became possible for ministers to see socialism and Christianity as compatible, socialism as a necessary corrective to undue individualism and even, though rarely, for ministers to be Christian Socialists), and a new sympathy for trade unions (in 1890–91 Rainy gave his active and public support to striking railwaymen, and from the United Presbyterian church John Cairns, though not supporting the strikers, urged arbitration and indicated sympathy with both sides in the dispute). In the decade after 1900 the changed attitude towards social issues became even clearer with the foundation, in 1901, of the Scottish Christian Social Union and a further succession of publications, committees and reports on social issues.

Alongside such changes in Presbyterian attitudes to social problems, poverty and the structures of society, there were also changes in attitudes to social activities and lifestyle — or at least, some Presbyterians changed in their attitude and because they changed, and because Scottish society as a whole became more secular, the influence of Presbyterianism as a whole over social *mores* was diminished, though not removed. The classic case was Sabbatarianism. In the 1840s the defenders of the traditional Calvinist sabbath had successfully defeated a number of attempts to run Sunday railway trains (Robertson, 1978). In the 1860s the North British Railway introduced first goods services and then passenger services on Sundays. Defenders of the Sabbath protested and the Glasgow presbytery of the Church of Scotland called on dutiful church members to resist such encroachments. One ministerial member of the presbytery, Norman McLeod, then made a telling speech against such Sabbatarianism. His presbytery admonished him but the General Assembly of 1866 refused to censure him and in 1869 he became Moderator. It was a small incident in one sense, but a major turning-point in another: it 'shook the foundations' of the traditional Presbyterian stance and opened the way for other breaches in traditional Sabbatarianism (Brackenridge, 1966). It was also a recognition that in life-styles, as in theology and in worship, there was now less precise regulation and more diversity in Scottish Presbyterianism than had previously been the norm. Cheyne maintains that it was a turning-point in Scottish religious life, partly because it marked the acceptance within Presbyterianism of the possibility of a more relaxed social morality, but also because many laymen and women found relief in the fact that a theologian justified on theological grounds a relaxation of sabbatarian behaviour which they had in practice already adopted out of self-interest or instinct (Cheyne, 1983, p. 162).

By 1900 Scottish Presbyterianism had indeed been transformed. Under the pressure of increasing industrialization and urbanization the old Calvinist ideal of the godly community centred on the Kirk had ceased to be a practical possibility. Equally telling for the dissolution of traditional Scots Calvinism, however, were the theological changes within Scottish Presbyterianism in the second half of the nineteenth century. Although the Disruption and the creation of an evangelical and conservative Free Church seemed to give new life to the traditional confessional ideal, after the first generation the Free Church, as well as the Church of Scotland and the United Presbyterians, found their traditional Calvinist orthodoxy challenged from within by increasing theological liberalism and internal diversity on the one hand, and by revivalism and an increasingly emotional and experiential style of piety on the other. The moral and missionary doubts over 'election' and 'limited Atonement', the rise of a critical approach to the Bible, and the adoption of broader and less precise forms of assent to the Westminster Confession all signalled the emergence of less monolithic and broader, internally diverse versions of Presbyterianism. The diversity was also reflected in worship, where liturgical and congregational developments both accommodated a wider range of churchmanship than was hitherto customary in Scottish Presbyterianism and also encouraged greater congregational participation, involvement and experience. The trend to more experiential worship also coincided with the impact on Scottish Presbyterianism of Sankey and Moody and the rise of a personalized, emotional revivalism in which the decision of the individual was central.

In England, it has been observed, the campaigns of Sankey and Moody were an incident in church life, but in Scotland they were more. They affected all the main branches of Presbyterianism and, by their impact on the Free Church especially, showed that the age of traditional Calvinism was past (Drummond and Bulloch, 1978, p. 13). For traditional Calvinism the implications of such revivalism were as severe as the implications of biblical criticism and relaxation of the status of the Westminster Confession: the latter undermined the logical, intellectual bases of Calvinist orthodoxy; the former replaced assent to God's will by decision and personal acceptance of God's offer; and in the background to such changes within there was the changed position of the Kirk in society, no longer, even theoretically, the centre and focus of the local community, but rather one local focus, one local option, among others. With the coming of internal diversity in theology and worship and the rise of revivalist theology, a religious individualism, it has been observed, replaced the strongly communal style of traditional Scottish Presbyterianism: 'as the disciplinary element in her life was abandoned the Church came to be seen as a friendly group which you joined if you felt so inclined' (Drummond and Bulloch, 1978, p. 80). The ideal of the godly community had become the reality of the gathered congregation: religion was chosen by some as their way of life (or a part of their way of life), but it was no longer credible to see it as part of a genuinely national way of life. Only in the intensely conservative Gaelic speaking north-west did the older tradition persist on any substantial or widespread scale: a fact reflected in the secessions of conservative Highlanders to form first the Free Presbyterian Church in 1892 and then the continuing Free Church in 1900.

Moreover, beyond the broadened and diversified Presbyterianisms of each of the major Scottish denominations there remained, it was increasingly recognized, the continuing and growing phenomenon of the absence from (or at best but lukewarm involvement in) the life of the church of many of the working classes, especially the urban working classes. The pre-Disruption era of Church Extension had, much like its English counterpart, assumed, or at least hoped, that if religious facilities were provided then the 'unchurched' would make use of them. The Disruption produced a further — and large scale — increase in the buildings and facilities available: but the unchurched did not fill the new space available. The 1851 Census revealed in Scotland (as it did in England) that the absence of the urban working classes was not merely a matter of the absence of opportunity for religious practice: there was a deeper alienation at work than mere lack of opportunity. Surveys in the 1870s and 1880s, and the six-year long Church of Scotland Commission on the Religious Condition of the People, which began work in 1890, confirmed the basic findings of 1851 in relation to the churchgoing (or non-churchgoing) habits of the Scottish people.

It was a familiar story. Rural attendance was much better than urban — though not always itself so uniform or consistent as to leave churchmen unworried; mining and fishing communities were the targets of much missionary endeavour — but with varying degrees of success and without the equivalent of, for example, Durham and Northumberland Primitive Methodism south of the border; and in the towns the lower down the social scale, the less likely and the less widespread was involvement with the churches. The reasons were various and, again, familiar: resentment of the political and social conservatism of the clergy; the middle-class ethos of the church; the practice of renting pews; the loss of a sense of parish and locality in which the structures of Kirk and community might retain some personal meaning, together with the rise of a new sense of class and class divisions in which the significance of the church and its theology was at best unclear, at worst opposed to the interests of the working classes or perceived to be irrelevant or incomprehensible; the rise of popular mass entertainment, sport and recreation. Sunday schools remained well attended,[11] the churches continued to present their witness and to do so with increasing social sensitivity, and Sankey and Moody were popular, but the level of religious commitment of those not formally within the regular life of the church was vague and lukewarm — even the much acclaimed impact of Sankey and Moody in Scotland had, in fact, far more effect on developments within the churches than on the 'unchurched'. Moreover, by the 1890s sources such as the reports of the Church of Scotland Commission on the Religious Condition of the People suggest that it was not just declining numbers which caused concern but also the decline of active enthusiasm among many who still attended: religious activity in general was apparently becoming a less passionate affair (Smout, 1986, p. 203).[12]

[11] It has been suggested that Sunday Schools reached their heyday in Scotland from about 1890 to 1914, enrolment *per capita* having reached its highest level c.1890. But, significantly, even the Sunday Schools were also becoming more congregational in character, addressed less to the whole community and more to the 'central voluntary organisation in the growing community of congregational agencies' (C. Brown, 1981, p. 21).

[12] Callum Brown has noted, for example, that in the 1880s and 1890s the Presbyterian middle class became less willing to engage in active evangelism among the working classes. There was growing embarrassment over traditional questions as to an individual's 'religious state'. Such work was increasingly left to full-time missionaries, not lay volunteers. And whilst many churches still deployed a network of religious, educational and recreational agencies as a means of mission, a growing number of middle-class congregations began to see such agencies less in missionary terms and more as expressions of their own congregational sub-culture (C. Brown, 1987, pp. 171–82).

As in England, however, although the level of working-class alienation from regular participation in church life was causing increasing concern in the last decades of the nineteenth century, it was not until the First World War that the full extent of the phenomenon was understood. In 1919 a report was published entitled *The Army and Religion*. Sponsored by the YMCA, it was based upon research and responses to questionnaires inquiring into the religious attitudes of the British Army in France. Among the more memorable remarks in the report was the observation that 'the working faith of perhaps the majority of the youth of our nation' amounted to no more than a 'dim and instinctive theism'. The report was the work of an interdenominational committee but was largely written by David Cairns, Principal of the United Free Church College, Aberdeen. The 'nation' referred to was Britain, not just Scotland — but the accumulating experience of both the United Free Church and the Church of Scotland suggested that such 'dim, instinctive theism' was as prevalent in Scotland as it was in the rest of Britain.

III ESTABLISHMENTS COMPARED

At the beginning of the Victorian era the predominant influence in Scottish religious life was a still united and firmly established Church of Scotland. It was an established church troubled by internal division between Moderates and Evangelicals, by developing conflict over patronage and church-state relations, and by incipient doctrinal controversy. But it was the undoubted national church nevertheless, a fact symbolized not only by its unity and size relative to any other denomination in Scotland, but also in its central role in the provision of education and poor relief. The worship and devotional life of the church remained essentially bare, even dull, and uniform. The social thought of the church was conservative and its moral ethos severe.

By 1900 the Church of Scotland was still established but was one of two major Scottish Presbyterian churches. The intervening years had seen the Evangelical revolt of the Disruption, the creation of the Free Church and, in the 1870s and 1880s, even the attempt to disestablish the Church of Scotland. The latter project had failed, but establishment itself had been transformed and reduced in stature. In 1845 the Poor Law Amendment Act ended the official responsibility of the church for poor relief. In 1872 the Education Act removed the official power of the church over education; henceforth School Boards would determine the form of religious education and parents might withdraw their children even from this. (The content in fact continued much as before, but the balance of power was quite different; henceforth the church's influence was limited to the running of training colleges and its ability to shape opinion — it had no statutory force.) In

1874 the Patronage Act abolished patronage and gave communicants and adherents the right to choose their own minister. As for the Free Church, after the passing of the generation of the Disruption itself, and outside of the Gaelic north-west, Evangelical conservatism had become milder even to the point of union with the United Presbyterians.

In all the branches of Scottish Presbyterianism there was a decline of the old Calvinist tradition. In theology and doctrine traditional uniformity and precision gave way to new breadth, variety and deliberate imprecision of definition: the old strict authority of Bible and Westminster Confession gave way to new looser versions of authority. In worship didactic severity was modified by liturgical renascence, congregational participation, hymns and organs: this, together with the impact of Sankey and Moody, made Scottish Presbyterianism in 1900 altogether less objective and intellectual, altogether more subjective and experiential than its predecessor of 1837. In social thought the limits of individualism were more clearly perceived and the significance of environment more clearly recognized. In matters of social morality and life-style Scottish Presbyterianism remained austere, but it was a lesser austerity than once had been and exercised less influence over society as a whole.

Comparison with the Church of England reveals more significant similarity than contrast. The Church of England did not split, as in the Disruption, and the Presbyterian Churches of Scotland did not diversify into internal pluralism as wide as that of the Church of England by 1900.[13] But both the Church of England and Scottish Presbyterianism experienced transformations and diversifications amounting to internal revolutions, and both began their process of transformation in crises which involved a clash of church and state (Oxford Movement and Disruption) and a reassertion of theological orthodoxy (Tractarian and Evangelical). Moreover, by 1900 the process of reunification within Scottish Presbyterianism was well under way — begun in the union of the Free Church and United Presbyterians, and to be completed in 1929 with reunion between them and the Church of Scotland.

Establishment survived in both Scotland and England, but in each case did so not least because it became more nominal and less practically powerful, and because it became broader and less precise as Evangelicals, Broad Churchmen and High Churchmen were obliged to learn to co-exist in both national churches. In Scotland the co-existence was more genuinely peaceful, whereas in England it was more akin to ongoing sectarian rivalry with-

[13] That the internal pluralism of Scottish Presbyterianism was less broad than that of the Church of England was not surprising: it did not start from a position of calculated ambiguity between Protestant and Catholic wings, and its most challenging denominational rival in Victorian Scotland was a vigorous and assertive Roman Catholicism.

in a single institution. Both churches also became more liturgical and congregational in worship and both evolved a basic style of worship (in each of which congregational hymnody was prominent) which remains familiar even to the present. Both also discovered the increasing tension between their traditional rural parochial ideals and the urban reality of much of Victorian life; the essential intractability of working-class alienation from the churches; and that by 1900 their chief competition came, on the one hand, from the growing pressure of mass secular entertainment culture competing for the leisure time of the people and, on the other hand, from a lively, confident and expanding Roman Catholicism.

Comparison of Scottish Presbyterianism with English Protestant Nonconformity is also revealing. Both possessed a Calvinist past and a Protestant identity, and in the nineteenth century both moved away from closely defined Calvinism into a but loosely defined evangelicalism, and both rediscovered the churchly, liturgical, even 'catholic' elements in their heritage.

There was, therefore, as Callum Brown has also noted (1987, p. 20), beyond the distinctiveness and particularity of Victorian Scottish Presbyterianism, a sense in which it shared markedly in a range of trends and changes characteristic of both established and Nonconformist religious life in general in Victorian Britain. It was thus appropriate that David Cairns' remarks in *The Army and Religion* should have referred to 'our nation' and meant by that Britain, not merely Scotland, for by 1900 the predominant challenges facing the Scottish churches were even less peculiarly Scottish than had been the case in 1837. They were, rather, part and parcel of a genuinely 'British' trend in which national religious life steadily became at once more varied and less intense, more optional and less obligatory, than had hitherto been the case.

BIBLIOGRAPHY

R. D. Brackenridge (1966) 'The "Sabbath War" of 1865–66: the shaking of the foundations', *Records of the Scottish Church History Society*, Vol. 16, pp. 23–34.

C. G. Brown (1981) 'The Sunday-School movement in Scotland, 1780–1914' *Records of the Scottish Church History Society*, Vol. 21, pp. 3–26.

*C. G. Brown (1987) *The Social History of Religion in Scotland since 1730*, Methuen.

S. J. Brown (1978) 'The Disruption and urban poverty: Thomas Chalmers and the West Port Operation in Edinburgh, 1844–47', *Records of the Scottish Church History Society*, Vol. 20, pp. 65–89.

*S. J. Brown (1982) *Thomas Chalmers and the Godly Commonwealth in Scotland*, Oxford, Oxford University Press.

A. C. Cheyne (1983) *The Transforming of the Kirk: Victorian Scotland's Religious Revolution*, Edinburgh, St. Andrew Press.

A. C. Cheyne (ed.) (1985) *The Practical and the Pious: Essays on Thomas Chalmers (1780–1847)*, Edinburgh, St. Andrew Press.

A. L. Drummond and J. Bulloch (1975) *The Church in Victorian Scotland 1843–1874*, Edinburgh, St. Andrew Press.

A. L. Drummond and J. Bulloch (1978) *The Church in Late Victorian Scotland 1874–1900*, Edinburgh, St. Andrew Press.

J. A. Lamb (1957–59) 'Aids to public worship in Scotland 1800–1850', *Records of the Scottish Church History Society*, Vol. 13, pp. 171–85.

J. F. McCaffrey (1981) 'Thomas Chalmers and social change' *The Scottish Historical Review*, Vol. 60, pp. 32–60.

D. M. Murray (1977) 'Doctrine and worship: controversy in the Church Service Society in the late nineteenth century', *Liturgical Review*, Vol. 7, pp. 25–34.

D. M. Murray (1977) 'James Cooper and the East Church case at Aberdeen, 1882–3: the High Church movement vindicated', *Records of the Scottish Church History Society*, Vol. 19, pp. 217–33.

D. M. Murray (1984) 'Disruption to Union' in D. Forrester and D. Murray (eds.) *Studies in the History of Worship in Scotland*, pp. 79–95, Edinburgh, T. & T. Clark.

R. A. Riesen (1979) '"Higher Criticism" in the Free Church Fathers', *Records of the Scottish Church History Society*, Vol. 20, pp. 119–42.

R. A. Riesen (1985) *Criticism and Faith in Late Victorian Scotland: A. B. Davidson, William Robertson Smith and George Adam Smith*, Lanham (MD), University Press of America.

C. J. A. Robertson (1978) 'Early Scottish railways and the observance of the sabbath', *The Scottish Historical Review*, Vol. 57, pp. 143–67.

*T. C. Smout (1986) *A Century of the Scottish People 1830–1950*, Collins.

J. Whyte (1984) 'The setting of worship' in D. Forrester and D. Murray (eds.) *Studies in the History of Worship in Scotland*, pp. 140–55, Edinburgh, T. & T. Clark.

D. J. Withrington (1977) 'The Church in Scotland, c.1870–c.1900: towards a new social conscience?' *Records of the Scottish Church History Society*, Vol. 19, pp. 155–68.

CHAPTER 4

CARDINAL WISEMAN'S "LAMBS."

VICTORIAN ROMAN CATHOLICISM: EMANCIPATION, EXPANSION AND ACHIEVEMENT

BETWEEN October 1850 and August 1851, public opinion in Britain was much absorbed in an outburst of intense anti-Catholic feeling. There were excited, outraged and angry letters in the press (including one from the Prime Minister, Lord John Russell), outraged editorials in *The Times*, outbursts of public disorder and 'no popery' mobs threatening Catholic priests and property, extended and exaggerated Guy Fawkes celebrations with effigies of the Pope and leading English Catholics burnt, and even parliamentary legislation forbidding Roman Catholics the use of certain episcopal titles. By the end of 1851 the whole controversy had subsided and no comparable anti-Roman Catholic outburst occurred in the rest of the Victorian period. It was a remarkable incident and it was an anachronism: it was also very revealing, both of the place of Roman Catholicism within the overall religious context in Britain in 1850, and of significant trends in the development of Roman Catholicism in Britain between Catholic Emancipation in 1829 and the close of the Victorian era in 1901. It therefore bears a closer examination.

I 'PAPAL AGGRESSION' AND ITS CONTEXT

In outline, the main stages of the controversy over what came to be called the 'Papal Aggression' of 1850 were quite straightforward. Since the seventeenth century the government of the Roman Catholic Church in England had been in the hands not of a local domestic hierarchy of bishops but of Vicars Apostolic of episcopal status under the direct authority of the Congregation of Propaganda in Rome. At various points during the seventeenth and eighteenth centuries English Catholics had appealed to Rome for the restoration of a local hierarchy of bishops, on each occasion failing in their request. In 1837 the Vicars Apostolic themselves approached the Pope, Gregory XVI, who was unwilling to establish a restored hierarchy but was prepared to double the number of Vicars Apostolic in order to increase administrative efficiency. Accordingly in 1840 the number of administrative districts and of Vicars Apostolic was doubled to eight. The Vicars Apostolic nevertheless maintained their pressure for a restoration and, in 1847, the new Pope, Pius IX, agreed to their request.

Revolution in Rome and the Papal States in 1848–9 resulted in the implementation of the scheme being delayed until 1850, when, in a brief dated September 29th, Pius IX announced the restoration of a hierarchy of bishops, headed by Nicholas Wiseman, newly created cardinal and made Archbishop of Westminster. The restoration was framed and timed with every intention of allaying English Protestant anxieties: Rome insisted that it be promulgated whilst a Whig Government was in power, whilst Parliament was not sitting, and with the titles of the new dioceses carefully chosen to avoid all titles used by bishops of the Church of England — thus keeping within the boundaries of the Roman Catholic Relief Act of 1829. Events conspired, however, to negate all such papal efforts at allaying English Protestant fears.

First *The Times*, on 14 October 1850, reacted to the announcement of the restored hierarchy with an intemperate display of 'no popery' rhetoric, asserting that Rome had mistaken English constitutional tolerance for indifference to 'papal designs'. *The Times* also associated the Oxford Movement with the whole issue by claiming that Rome had mistaken the High Church renewal within the Church of England for a Romeward move. Then, on the 17 October, controversy became furore when a Pastoral Letter from Wiseman, issued by him from Rome on the 7th, was duly read in the churches of his diocese. It was a singularly ill-judged document. Wiseman spoke of 'Catholic England . . . restored to its orbit in the ecclesiastical firmament from which its light had long vanished', and of it beginning 'anew its course of regularly adjusted motion round the centre of unity, the source of jurisdiction, of light and of vigour'. This was not the stuff to allay fears and reassure Protestant sensibilities. When Wiseman also spoke of 'governing' the counties of his diocese (albeit intending to refer only to the spiritual and religious life of Catholics therein) he reactivated traditional English fears of Romish plots, doubtful Catholic loyalties, and foreign influences.

The English press now attacked in greater numbers and with renewed vigour. *The Times*, on 22 October, described the appointment of Wiseman to an arch-diocese entitled 'Westminster' as a 'gross act of folly and impertinence'. Bishop Ullathorne, one of the Vicars Apostolic, now appointed Bishop of Birmingham, attempted to reassure *The Times* and its readers that the new hierarchy and its rule was entirely a matter of church government and the religious life of Roman Catholics, not of politics or national life. Unfortunately, however, at Ullathorne's own enthronement on 26 October, Newman, the most famous of recent Anglican converts to Rome, preached a sermon which seemed, in the highly-charged air, to celebrate the restoration of the English *people* to the Roman Church. In fact, Newman actually had misgivings over the restoration, but felt he must join in the defence: his status as leading convert from the Oxford Movement and his apparent recognition of a national dimension to the restoration fuelled the furore once more.

Many Anglican clergy — and also some Nonconformists — issued protests: Blomfield, Anglican Bishop of London, even urged his clergy to preach controversial sermons on the subject. Guy Fawkes' Night presented an opportunity for popular excess. In a number of places effigies of the Pope, Wiseman, and the other bishops were burnt. A number of priests were assaulted and Catholic properties damaged. Police were required in a number of places to maintain order and restrain Protestant mobs: the restraint, however, prevailed and violence was more verbal than physical.

Then, on the 7 November, *The Times* published, with permission, a letter from the Prime Minister, Lord John Russell, to his old friend, Bishop Maltby of Durham. Russell indicated that he agreed with Maltby in regarding the 'late aggression of the Pope upon our Protestantism' as 'insolent and insidious'. He also said that he found, in the various Catholic documents concerned, assumptions of power and pretensions of supremacy inconsistent with the royal supremacy and the rights of the established church. These, he promised, would be scrutinized along with the existing law with a view to possible action. He also suggested that the greatest danger came not from Roman claims but from Anglican clergymen who practised and advocated Catholic and Romanizing doctrines and devotions. Russell's letter heightened yet further the public outcry against the restored hierarchy.

Wiseman, when he reached England, at once began a reply to the outcry, which he published before the end of November. The reply set out again to allay fears and to point out that the restored hierarchy was no more or less a threat to the royal supremacy than the existence of a variety of Nonconformist bodies: it was a purely ecclesiastical affair without temporal claims. By then, however, the controversy was too advanced to be smoothed away by such reassurances. Russell, ironically a life-long supporter of religious toleration, found himself committed to some kind of penal legislation. In 1851 a bill, the Ecclesiastical Titles Bill, was introduced to the Commons and duly passed into law, but only after modification of some of its original and more extreme provisions. In the end it amounted to a reiteration of the provision, dating from 1829, concerning the assumption of territorial titles by Roman Catholic bishops: such territorial titles were forbidden. The Act was opposed in the Commons by Gladstone and in the Lords by Archbishop Whately; it was regarded, even by much of the Anglican press, as absurd and childish, but the level of public furore made its passage inevitable. The bill received the royal assent in August 1851. By the end of 1851 the whole controversy had subsided.

What, then, was this extraordinary episode really all about? Without doubt it was an anachronism. The Ecclesiastical Titles Act was a relic of an earlier age of penal legislation in matters of religion. It stood in stark and incongruous contrast to the steady constitutional trend towards a tolerant religious pluralism which characterized the period from 1828–29 onwards. Its oddity was apparent from the start and no prosecution was ever brought under it in the twenty years during which it remained on the statute book before Gladstone repealed it in 1871. At one level the whole furore was simply a product of popular and crude anti-Catholic prejudice, the immensely tactless and imprudent words of a newly appointed cardinal, and the careless public stance of a Prime Minister. But there was also a deeper significance to the incident. On the one hand it revealed a good deal about the place of Roman Catholicism within the overall pattern of religious life and controversy in mid-nineteenth century Britain. On the other hand it focused and symbolized a number of issues and trends central to the internal development of Victorian Roman Catholicism.

So far as the place of Roman Catholicism within the religious life of mid-nineteenth century Britain is concerned, Walter Ralls has argued that the controversy over 'Papal Aggression' was so intense, and the anti-Catholicism it aroused so hostile, because of four underlying circumstances, each of which caused a restored hierarchy of bishops to appear the symbol of a threatening Roman Catholicism. First, there was the fact that between 1800 and 1850 the number of Roman Catholics in England and Wales had increased dramatically from under 100,000 in 1800 to approximately 750,000 in 1850.[1] Most of this increase was due to Irish immigration, and most of that due to the hungry forties and the great famine. To native English Protestant suspicions of disloyal, 'alien' Roman Catholics was added the dislike and distaste — often amounting to racial prejudice — of a desperately poor and, given the slums in which they were obliged to live, inevitably squalid immigrant community. Native Protestant prejudice thus met popular anti-Irish, anti-immigrant prejudice: as Ralls observes, the merging of the Irish poor and the old stigma attaching to Roman Catholicism raised anti-Catholic feelings to new heights.

Alongside such anti-Irish immigrant feeling, however, there was, secondly, a lively continuing tradition that Catholicism was incompatible with the English constitution. From the conservative side it was still argued that Catholicism necessarily involved a dual allegiance and, ultimately, loyalty to a foreign power; from the liberal side it was urged that civil and religious liberty were essentially fruits of a Protestant ethos, whereas Catholicism was in essence based on arbitrary power. Third, quite apart from an immense numerical influx due to Irish immigration, English Catholicism in the 1830s and 1840s received a revitalizing input from the arrival of a number of prominent, able, intelligent and immensely enthusiastic converts. Already by 1845 the Oxford Movement and its turmoils had produced a significant crop of converts from the Church of England to Rome: Newman, Faber and Ward being the most famous and influential. As well as such Oxford converts there were also three important Cambridge converts — Ambrose Phillipps, George Spencer and Kenelm Henry Digby — who had converted between 1825 and 1830, and the architect A. W. Pugin, who converted in 1834.

The significance of these converts has frequently been both exaggerated and misunderstood. The impression has often been given that it was the

[1] Ralls actually says from approximately 30,000 in 1800, but John Bossy, in probably the most detailed analysis of Catholic demography in this period, puts it at 80,000. The basic point remains, however, even at the larger figure (Ralls, 1974, p. 244; Bossy, 1975, p. 298).

converts who, initially, brought new vitality and revival to an essentially staid English Catholicism. It is an impression encouraged by the notion of a 'Second Spring', an image used by Newman in a sermon preached at the First Provincial Synod of Westminster, in 1852, to characterize the revival of English Catholicism. It is, however, too simple a view. The outstanding revival and achievement of Victorian Roman Catholicism was, as we shall note shortly, based upon a number of trends and influences, of which the zeal of the converts was but one, and which included important and ongoing influences from within the old English Catholic tradition. The importance of the converts was, rather, their impact upon public perceptions of the state of Roman Catholicism in England. Although in fact part of a many-sided revival in English Catholicism, they appeared to many observers to be the chief source of the new vitality of the English Roman Catholic church. Moreover, in the majority of cases (Newman, with his essentially quiet, reflective style was the great exception) the converts were passionate and vociferous in their advocacy of their newly-embraced faith and encouraged a variety of dramatically public manifestations of Catholic revival. Pugin, a prolific and passionate exponent of Gothic architecture (and also Gothic vestments and liturgical chants), published his famous manifesto, *Contrasts*, on the moral and religious superiority of the Gothic style, in 1836. Between then and his death in 1852 he was responsible for a remarkable amount of Catholic architecture, ranging from churches, chapels and schools to the first cathedral and the first monastery to be built since the Reformation. The Cambridge converts were also vociferous exponents of a medieval Catholic ethos and both saw and proclaimed themselves missionaries on behalf of Catholicism to English Protestantism. Phillips and Spencer were also influential in fostering the expansion of the existing religious orders in England and the introduction of new orders: an enthusiasm which they shared with the Oxford convert Faber.

The importance of such developments in the context of the 'Papal Aggression' controversy and the anti-Catholicism behind it lay in their dramatic public impact and emotional effect. The numbers of converts may have been, in reality, small to the point of insignificance, and the various programmes of building and expansion of activity among religious orders no more than the Catholic expression of that passionate atmosphere of activity, revival and expansion which was to be found in all the denominations in Victorian Britain as they embarked upon schemes and founded societies for the furtherance of church extension, tract distribution, and the evangelization of the masses. But the Catholic version of this general religious revival appeared, to concerned Protestants, as a threat to English Protestant Christianity: the spectacular conversions were, after all, not conversions from unbelief to Christian belief, but from the established church to Rome; and the enthusiasm, especially of many converts, for monasteries, convents, monastic dress, public processions and many of the more dramatic manifestations of a continental Catholic devotional style (with its flamboyance, ceremony, emphasis upon the Virgin, the Immaculate Conception, the rosary and a whole range of Italian and Ultramontane devotional activities) was strikingly alien to the English *Catholic* tradition, let alone to English Protestantism. The appearance of such 'un-English' manifestations of Catholic revival, together with the British government's decision, in 1845, to increase its annual grant to Maynooth, the Irish college for training Catholic priests, produced an emotional reaction among Protestants, who responded with a highly defensive anti-Catholicism.[2]

Last but not least among the background causes of anti-Catholic feeling in 1850–51 there was, as Ralls points out, the disarray of English Protestantism and, especially, the crisis within the Church of England. By 1850 English Protestantism was experiencing crisis and disturbance on at least three fronts: all the denominations were becoming increasingly aware of the challenges of natural science, geology, historical criticism and — most of all — moral critiques of traditional evangelical Protestant doctrine; dissent and the established church were locked in conflict over their respective rights and privileges; and the Church of England was exercised by conflict between Tractarians and Evangelicals. Whilst Rome presented an appearance of vitality and revival, the Church of England was in turmoil as to the nature of its own identity, and one side in the conflict urged that its true identity was Catholic. By 1850 the conflict within the Church of England had moved beyond the *Tracts for the Times* and into the highly emotive question of Ritualism and its limits, and the Gorham Judgement had produced a new wave of conversions to Rome — the leading among them being that of Henry Manning, later to become Wiseman's successor at Westminster. From the initial reaction of *The Times* to the restoration of the hierarchy onwards, 'Papal Aggression' and Anglican Ritualism were linked together.

Thus a mixture of anti-Irish immigrant prejudice, traditional doubts about the compatibility of loyalty and Catholicism, the vitality of converts and the unfamiliarity of much of their devotional life, and the internal disarray of English Protestantism, made Wiseman's rhetoric over the restoration of the hierarchy the cause of a turbulent, if short-lived, outburst of anti-Catholicism. The restoration of the hierarchy was also significant, however, as a symbol of, and a turning point in, the internal development

[2] Such anti-Catholicism was itself diverse. It ranged from the relatively restrained, if passionately held, 'no popery' of the Evangelical Alliance (the need to confront 'the progress of popery' had been one of the motives for the foundation of the Alliance) to the intemperate campaigning of the Ulster-born and Liverpool-based Evangelical Hugh McNeile, to the cheaply available literature combining apocalyptic prophecy and 'shocking' stories of the confessional, self-mortification, and the alleged moral improprieties of monks and nuns. For detailed accounts of the phenomenon see Norman, 1968 and Arnstein, 1982.

of Victorian Roman Catholicism. The seventeenth and eighteenth-century attempts by the English Catholic community to secure from Rome the restoration of a local hierarchy of bishops had been intended as a means of securing greater local and national control over the English Roman Catholic church, as opposed to rule direct from Rome. They were also part of the effort by the English Catholic community to demonstrate their Englishness, their relative independence from Rome, and hence their loyalty to the English Crown. In the late eighteenth and early nineteenth centuries such 'independence' from Rome was part of the case made by English Catholics seeking Catholic emancipation, a campaign in which, prior to the early nineteenth century, lay Catholics took the leading role. When the restoration of the hierarchy finally came, however, it proved to be not a symbol of independence from Roman and papal control, but rather the seal upon the process by which English Catholicism steadily came to be dominated by the continental tradition of Roman and Ultramontane devotion, loyalty to the papacy, and centralized clerical control.

The increasing clerical control of English Catholic life greatly increased during the struggles for Catholic emancipation between 1808 and 1829 and as a result of urban Catholic expansion from the 1770s onwards. In the campaign for emancipation, from the setting up of the Catholic Board in 1808 onwards, the clergy steadily took over control of the various committees and bodies established to further the cause. The role of the older lay aristocratic and gentry leadership correspondingly declined. In the emergence and expansion of an urban Catholic community in England a similar process occurred. In the absence of a rural gentry to lead, the clergy took over the role of focus and leaders of the community.

In the next two decades came the rise to prominence of Nicholas Wiseman (a supreme Ultramontane and 'Roman'), the influx of a number of Anglican converts of decidedly Ultramontane and Roman sympathies, and the introduction to Britain of a number of key missionary orders — especially the Rosminians, the Passionists, the Redemptorists and the Oratorians. The missionary orders, in particular, with the two Italian missionaries Luigi Gentile and Dominic Barberi as the figureheads, began what was to prove a remarkably successful attempt to transform the devotional ethos of English Catholicism. As Edward Norman has observed, the efforts of Gentile, Barberi and the missionary orders stamped English Catholic worship with features such as devotion to the Sacred Heart, the use of the rosary, the Forty Hours Devotion, veneration of the Virgin and reverence for the Immaculate Conception, which later came to be popularly regarded as the very heart and essence of Catholicism (Norman, 1985, p. 74).

Moreover, the new missionary orders were particularly active in the ministry to the Irish immigrant communities and in this way the new

Ultramontane and clerical spirit found much of its most fertile soil precisely in the fastest growing (and by 1850 numerically strongest) section of Catholicism in England. It was also the section of English Catholicism which made the development of a well-controlled administrative system essential. If pastoral provision were to be effectively co-ordinated, resources raised, and then rationally deployed so as to ensure adequate churches and schools, then a proper diocesan structure and episcopal hierarchy was required. Thus the steady revival and expansion of English Catholic activity, of which Catholic emancipation was a part (but not the cause), and the pressures of providing spiritual, pastoral and educational care for the large influx of Irish immigrants, obliged English Roman Catholicism to establish a centralized and efficient administrative structure (just as problems of church extension, mission to the urban poor, and growth in numbers had obliged the Church of England and the Nonconformists either to reform or create central, denominational structures and bureaucracies). And the restored hierarchy was, from the outset, captured by the clergy, and especially the new style of Ultramontane clergy who proceeded to create in the second half of the nineteenth century a Roman Catholic Church which was highly centralized, highly disciplined, and thoroughly clericalized in ethos. It was also a church which, building upon a variety of strengths already present in the pre-1850 era, proved remarkably successful. It is to the examination of those pre-restoration strengths and their development in the post-1850 church that we must now turn.

II THE FOUNDATIONS OF ACHIEVEMENT

The expansion and achievements of Roman Catholicism in Victorian Britain rested upon a number of interacting, though not always readily compatible, foundations. In seeking to understand and account for the remarkable progress of the Roman Catholic church in Victorian Britain, at least six such foundations must be taken into account, namely: the vitality of the old established English Catholic tradition; the added enthusiasm, talent and vitality of converts from Anglicanism; the presence of a large Irish immigrant community in mainland Britain and the impact of the clergy's efforts to transform Irish Catholic perceptions of the faith, both in Ireland and mainland Britain; the administrative skill, organizational insight, and determination of the bishops and archbishops; the pastoral heroism and devotion of the local Catholic clergy; and the work of the new missionary orders in consolidating in Britain the devotional revolution characteristic of nineteenth-century Roman Catholicism as a whole. Moreover, although not all of these foundations were equally important in each of the national regions of Victorian Britain (some indeed were relevant only to England), it is essential to see the overall revival of Roman Catholicism in Victorian Britain as a genuinely British, not merely English, phenomenon.

Traditionally, the old English Catholic tradition has been portrayed as severely restricted by penal laws; predominantly rural and gentry dominated; retiring and low key in public presence; and austere and unemotional in spirituality: an on-going concern no doubt, but not the stuff of renewal, revival and expansion. Recent studies of the old English Catholic community have shown, however, the incompleteness and, in some respects, inaccuracy of this portrayal and have revealed instead an English Catholic community which possessed strength, vitality and the resources for expansion *before* the advent of early Victorian conversions, large-scale Irish immigration, or the restoration of the hierarchy.

Reviewing the state of English Catholicism in the eighteenth century Edward Norman has described it as 'discreet and carefully unobtrusive' but certainly not 'underground or hidden' (Norman, 1985, p. 51). He cites in support of this assessment the fact that places of worship were well known to the authorities, who chose to do nothing about them; the fact that Catholic gentry still received, in a deferential society, appropriate respect; the fact that Catholics engaged in public life despite the very real disadvantage of exclusion under the penal laws from the professions; the fact that education, though hindered, was able to expand and that Catholic books were published and Catholic booksellers able to function. Thus when Parliament passed a Relief Act in 1778 giving Catholics virtual exemption from the penalities of the penal code, it was, in effect, giving formal sanction to a state of affairs which had existed in practice for many years, and when a further Relief Act was passed in 1791 Catholics virtually possessed religious toleration, if not yet civil equality. The church thus placed was, Norman suggests, 'an emergent church, quietly recovering the confidence of a public presence'.

The tone and direction of that judgement are supported by recent studies of the English Catholic community in the latter part of the eighteenth and first half of the nineteenth centuries. Of particular note is the work of, respectively, John Bossy and Gerard Connolly. Bossy has analysed the history of the English Catholic community from 1570 to 1850 and protests that the image of pre-Victorian English Catholicism as a gently declining community, suddenly, and seemingly miraculously, revived — not least by Anglican converts — and then massively infused with Irish numbers in the 1840s owes more to the ecclesiastical propaganda of the likes of Newman and Wiseman than to the realities of English Catholic history and experience prior to 1850. For both Newman and Wiseman, in their different ways, it was desirable to see the progress of Victorian English Roman Catholicism in terms of a 'Second Spring' — desirable for Newman as a leading convert, for Wiseman as a passionate advocate of Roman, Ultramontane style —

reversing the process of gentle (and genteel) decline in English Catholicism. The reality was, rather, a story of patient, modest and careful progress, culminating in the early nineteenth century in a period of numerical expansion and maturity of judgement which enabled English Catholicism to exploit the opportunities offered to it (Bossy, 1975, p. 297).

Bossy demonstrates that between 1770 and 1850 the Catholic community in England experienced an approximately ten-fold expansion, from roughly 80,000 to roughly 750,000. He also shows that the expansion was not merely the product of Irish immigration. The large influxes of Irish immigrants (especially in 1790, 1820 and most of all in the 1840s) notwithstanding, the *English* Catholic community was itself showing steady growth throughout the period. This growth, Bossy argues, was the product of both general population growth and also of the efforts of the Catholic clergy in patient missionary and catechetical work during the eighteenth century and early nineteenth century. During this same period there was a widespread movement of English Catholics into the emerging towns of the industrial revolution: Catholics no less than Protestants migrated from the countryside to the towns in response to population growth in the countryside and the economic opportunities offered by the new towns. This process contributed to a major change in the occupational and power structure of English Catholicism: the new town communities gave new opportunities for missionary work by the clergy and new scope for clergy independence of the lay gentry. When Irish immigration dramatically increased the *rate* of urban Catholic growth it further swayed the balance of power within the English community away from the rural gentry and towards the urban clergy: but what Irish immigration did *not* do was *create* the urban communities or *initiate* the process of English Catholic expansion (Bossy, 1975, pp. 297–317).

Bossy's study addressed the English Catholic community as a whole. It has recently received striking confirmation from the immensely detailed local study of the Catholic communities in Manchester and Salford between 1770–1850 by Gerard Connolly. Connolly's meticulous examination reveals that in the eighteenth century English Catholicism in the twin towns was experiencing a modest but steady revival and was in process of being absorbed into English life as another variety of religious Nonconformity, somewhat akin to Protestant Dissent. The active role of Roman Catholics in the civic life of Manchester and Salford between 1770 and 1850 gives the lie to the notion that the penal laws were, by the close of the eighteenth century, a major cause of restriction. There was, Connolly shows, a small but steadily growing Catholic community, widely tolerated prior to official legislation, and based initially upon a steady English immigration from the surrounding countryside. In short, the local case of Manchester and Salford demonstrates very clearly that the revival of Roman Catholicism in England indeed began in the eighteenth century, not the second quarter of the nineteenth century; that it was, in origin, a product of the English Catholic community, not of Irish immigration; and that it was developing within rather than over against English society: it was also clearly an urban phenomenon (G. P. Connolly, 1984).

Bossy and Connolly also identify important changes within the devotional and theological life of English Catholicism *prior* to 1850. The essential devotional and theological style of pre-Victorian English Catholicism was inherited from the eighteenth century and characterized principally by Richard Challoner's spiritual manual, *Garden of the Soul*. The spiritual and devotional life nurtured by this text was characteristically meditative and reflective, non-polemical and emotionally restrained. An essentially sober piety, Challoner's *Garden* enjoined charity as a principal religious duty — including charity to non-Catholics. The spirituality thus fostered also sought to emphasize the morality common to Christians of all denominations and to eschew controversy. Bossy illustrates the latter points by reference to the sermons of James Archer (Archer was most active in the 1780s and 90s, but his sermons were popular texts until the 1840s). Connolly provides striking local confirmation of this ethos in his examination of interdenominational respect and co-operation between Catholics and Protestants in early nineteenth-century Manchester and Salford.

By 1850, however, this gentle and sober devotional tradition was in retreat and was increasingly (and increasingly emphatically) replaced by an aggressive, exclusive and triumphalist spiritual and devotional ethos. Bossy identifies 1830 as the point at which the older style began to crumble — not least because of the steady erosion of the influence of the *Garden*, as alternatives to it, or amended editions of it, were published. Connolly, however, identifies the 1820s as the decade when, in Manchester and Salford at least, the decisive assault on the *Garden of the Soul* tradition, via amendment or alternative, took place.

Working at the local level, Connolly identifies the new militancy of the Protestant denominations as a key factor in the change within Catholicism. Catholic clergy, faced with militantly evangelical Protestantism and the possibility that such Protestantism would seek to 'poach' an as yet unassimilated Irish community from their care, responded by asserting an equally militant Catholicism and adopting Catholic versions of the pastoral activity and agencies characteristic of evangelical Protestantism. Co-operation and charity were replaced by competition and confessionalism. Bossy also recognizes the emergence of a more militant English Protestantism as one cause of the change, but adds three further factors: many of the Irish immigrants may in any case have arrived with a more anti-Protestant outlook (the result of the attempts of Irish Protestants from the 1820s onwards to launch a 'Second Reformation', in which Irish Catholics were a major target for conversion); the zeal of the converts from Anglicanism, with their dreams of the conversion of England; and the rise of Wiseman, who found such militancy and triumphalism congenial and, through his own rise to power, made it a feature of post-1850 English Catholicism.

Among the converts, Bossy singles out Ambrose Phillips and George Spencer as leaders of a movement to make the conversion of England a central feature of Catholic public worship. Though resisted during the 1830s and 40s by many attached to the older ethos — including a number of the Vicars Apostolic: Baines, for example, arguing that more priests, more money and more work would do more for conversions than litanies, aggressive evangelism or more flamboyant devotions — the placing of Wiseman at the head of the restored hierarchy made the triumph of the new style certain. It was, as Connolly aptly puts it, a move from an emphasis on the role of the Catholic in the world to an emphasis on the place of the Catholic within the church (Bossy, 1975, pp. 382–90; G. P. Connolly, 1984, pp. 94–9).

Thus there was within English Catholicism, prior to the 1840s and the putative 'Second Spring', a growth of numbers (quite apart from Irish immigration), the development of a lively urban Catholic community (again, quite apart from the Irish contribution), and the development of a more aggressive, exclusive, self-consciously Roman Catholic and distinctly anti-Protestant theological and devotional ethos. And behind each of these lay a further important development, namely the rise of clerical leadership and control of the community. It was the clergy who were the driving force in the creation of the new urban Catholic communities out of the migration to the towns; it was the clergy who took the lead in the transition to a more aggressive, self-conscious Catholic ethos; and it was the clergy who emerged from the process of campaigning for Catholic emancipation as the new leaders of the community.

On the eve of the restoration of the hierarchy in 1850, therefore, English Catholicism was already moving towards an expansionist, conversionist, and more clerical, self-consciously and exclusively Roman Catholic ethos and identity. The zeal of the Anglican converts, the clericalism and Ultramontane devotionalism of Wiseman and the missionary orders, and the impact of Irish immigration were not revolutionary innovations and did not constitute a radical break with the immediate past of English Catholicism. What these phenomena did do was accelerate, accentuate and seal a process of change already at work within English Catholicism. It is to them that we must now turn.

We have already noted, in exploring the context of the controversy over Papal Aggression, that the series of conversions in the 1820s, 30s, 40s and 50s was in fact numerically small, much exaggerated by Newman and Wiseman in talk of a Second Spring and probably as important for the public image of a reviving Catholicism that it created and the exaggerated hopes of mass conversion to which it gave rise, as for any more specific contribution of the converts. Moreover, the converts were a decidedly disparate group. Some, such as Pugin, Phillipps and Digby, were essentially romantic medievalists; others, such as Spencer, Faber, Ward and Manning (and probably the majority of the Oxford converts), were more in sympathy with the rising Ultramontane ideas and devotionalism; and Newman, the most famous of all the converts and neither romantic medievalist nor Ultramontane, was probably closest to the old English Catholic tradition before its turn towards a more exclusive and aggressive Catholicism.

If the significance of the converts has traditionally been exaggerated, however, revisionism must avoid the trap of overreaction: the converts did, in various ways, make a number of lasting contributions to the overall achievement of Victorian Catholicism. Phillipps, Spencer and Faber, for example, played an important part in the revival of monasticism and the expansion of the work of the religious orders within English Roman Catholicism — a revival which was itself a significant sign of, and element in, the advance of Victorian Catholicism. Phillipps founded the first monastery to be built in post-Reformation England — a Cistercian house opened in 1837. He also offered early encouragement to both Luigi Gentile and Dominic Barberi in the years before their missionary endeavours met with success and the support of Wiseman. Phillipps' romantic medievalism also led him to work for the reform of church music. He published two liturgical works, the *Little Gradual* in 1847 and the *Supplementum ad Graduale* in 1862, and an edition of Gregorian Masses in 1868. Spencer, after resigning his Anglican parish, being ordained a Roman Catholic priest and serving as a mission priest in Walsall and West Bromwich, became a Passionist in 1847 and was the Provincial of the Order from 1849 until 1863. Frederick William Faber, while still an Anglican, had turned his rural parish of Elton into a kind of monastic community. When he converted in 1845 he formed the Community of St Wilfred and in 1848 he and his Order joined the Oratorian house, which had been established that year in Birmingham with Newman as Superior. Differences soon became apparent, however, and in 1849 Faber left to set up the London Oratory, which eventually settled, in 1852, at Brompton. The differences between Newman and Faber were not merely temperamental: they also revealed the different emphases within mid-century English Catholicism. The Birmingham house was dominated by concern for education, including higher education. The London house, especially at Brompton, became the great showpiece of Italian, Ultramontane devotionalism in England. Indeed, on account of his own devotional writings and influence, as well as his role at Brompton, Faber has been described as 'the guiding spirit of Victorian popular Catholicism' (Gilley, 1985, p. 257). Well known for his popular devotional works (which included one entitled *Devotion to the Pope*) and for his hymns (some of which became popular among Protestants as well as Catholics), Faber's piety was at once exaggerated, emotional, sentimental and disarmingly simple. The combination of intensity and straightforwardness in his veneration of the saints and devotion to Mary did much to advance such piety in England. His book *All for Jesus*, published in 1853, was not only remarkably popular, selling 100,000 copies by 1869, but also an acknowledged spiritual classic of its age.

Pugin, on the other hand, found himself on the losing side of the conflict between 'English' and 'Roman' styles. Responsible for numerous churches and the first new monastery and cathedral in England since the Reformation, Pugin, like Phillipps and Digby, was a passionate advocate of Gothic architecture, vestments and plainchant. He was equally passionately opposed to Roman and Ultramontane styles of vestments, architecture and devotion. In the circumstances of an expanding Catholicism, in which new buildings were a priority, conflicts inevitably arose between the advocates of Gothic or Roman style and ethos: both sides being convinced that the prospects for the conversion of England were at stake. It was the Roman and Ultramontane style which won: as early as 1839 the authorities in Rome attempted to prohibit Gothic vestments. It was ironic that Pugin — the Catholic convert who believed Gothic to be essential to English Catholicism — should have had more influence upon the architecture of Anglicans and Nonconformists than on that of English Catholics. Ironic also that one who, by achieving, as a Roman Catholic convert, a high degree of public recognition for his architecture, did much to enhance the respectability of Catholicism in English life, should have had his *English* style rejected by an increasingly *Roman* Catholic church. The very controversies, however, were, as Edward Norman points out, the products of new vitality: it was the opportunities and challenges of expansion which occasioned them (Norman, 1985, p. 76).

Manning, by contrast, provided the most outstanding example of the Ultramontane converts. After many years as an Anglican priest of increasingly Catholic opinions, Henry Edward Manning finally converted in 1851, the Gorham Judgement having proved for him the final confirmation of the compromised position of the Church of England amid the increasingly liberal religious pluralism of mid-nineteenth century Britain. Ordained almost immediately as a Roman Catholic priest, his rise to power within English Catholicism was rapid: in 1865 he succeeded Wiseman as Archbishop of Westminster, and in 1875 was made a Cardinal. He led English Catholicism until his death in 1892. Wiseman had already, by the time of his death in 1865, established the basis of an Ultramontane dominance of English Catholicism: Manning confidently consolidated that basis. Manning's Ultramontanism was thorough and consistent. It was characterized by intense papal loyalty and championed both the temporal and spiritual claims of the papacy. In 1870 Manning was highly influential in the management of the declaration of papal infallibility at the Vatican Council. He was also an enthusiastic supporter of the Syllabus of Errors, proclaimed by Pius IX in 1864, seeing it as a bulwark against the corrosive, disintegrating influences of modernity: modern civilization, he believed, required, if it was to survive, the unifying influence of a centralized Catholic church. In both his detailed administrative skills and his emphasis upon ecclesiastical authority — even authoritarianism — he embodied such centralized Catholicism in his own career.

Alongside such 'Roman' loyalty and authority, however, and in a manner no less paradoxical than Pugin's rejected 'Englishness', Manning the Ultramontane became a popular figure with many of the English public, and especially the English poor. This popularity he owed to his commitment to social reform, charitable work and temperance campaigns. He supported the Dissent-dominated United Kingdom Alliance temperance movement; he supported trade unionism; he mediated in the 1889 London Dock Strike, showing sympathy for the dockers; he served on committees for social and charitable work and on the 1884 Royal Commission on the housing of the poor; and he supported systematic emigration to relieve the position of the poor. By such activities, Manning, the Ultramontane Roman Cardinal, strikingly demonstrated the extent of Roman Catholic involvement in English public life by the last decade of the nineteenth century.

In the intellectual sphere the chief contribution of the converts was through the work of Ward and Newman. Both had converted from Anglicanism in 1845, after the condemnation of Ward's book *The Ideal of a Christian Church* and the near condemnation of Newman's Tract 90, by the Convocation of Oxford University. Both were able, brilliant men and skilled writers. Thereafter their similarities ended. Ward, as an Anglican, had dared, challenged and provoked with his overtly Roman sympathies. When the challenge was met with condemnation he converted and applied his intellectual and polemical skills to the defence of extreme Ultramontanism, centralized ecclesiastical authority, and absolute loyalty to the papacy: he defended papal infallibility and espoused a more extreme version of it than that of the Vatican Council; he defended the Syllabus of Errors; and he was a consistent and fierce opponent of the various English Liberal Catholic thinkers.

Newman, by contrast, agonized as an Anglican and continued to do so as a Catholic. He only finally converted when faced with both the hostile reaction to his writings, especially Tract 90, and his own growing conviction that it was Rome, not the Church of England, which was the authentic heir of the early Christian Church. Once a Catholic, he faced, on the one hand, a challenge to his integrity and standards of truthfulness from the

Anglican Charles Kingsley, and on the other a long and uneasy tension between his own reflective, intellectual and meticulous style of faith and the often brash, aggressive and sweeping ethos of Ultramontanism.

The clash with Kingsley produced, in 1864, Newman's *Apologia* — an account of the stages of his conversion, which was not only a classic of English prose but also did much, by its sensitivity and care, to restore Newman's reputation with non-Catholics. To the Ultramontane leadership of English Catholicism, however, and to Rome itself, Newman remained suspect. He was claimed as an ally both by supporters of the older English tradition and by Liberals (but in fact remained aloof from all parties). He believed strongly in authority, but thought the clerical Ultramontane view of authority too narrow and consistently urged the need for the laity to be involved in the life — including the theological life — of the church. He accepted papal infallibility, but gave it the most minimalist interpretation possible. He wrote for and even edited the liberal Catholic journal the *Rambler*. And in his classic essay *On the Development of Christian Doctrine* (written when he was an Anglican, but not published until he had become a Catholic) Newman defended the continuity of development and the legitimacy of Catholic doctrines not found in the ancient church, but did so in a way which also recognized the necessarily human and circumstantial element in such development, the relativity of human perceptions, and the corruptibility of institutions: such nuances in the defence of Roman Catholic doctrine were unpalatable to both English and Roman Ultramontanes. Newman duly experienced ongoing tension between himself and Manning, and was regarded as doctrinally suspect and even potentially heretical in Rome.

Assessment of Newman is difficult. His thought was markedly original and he was always a somewhat isolated figure: as Norman observes, he was central to outsiders' perceptions of English Catholicism, yet on the periphery of its institutional life (Norman, 1984, p. 313). Claimed as an ally by the more liberal thinking Catholics, he was in fact set apart from them by his consistent opposition to liberalism and his scepticism concerning the claims and values of 'modernity'. And yet, by virtue of his intellectual precision and conflicts with strict Ultramontanism, he continues to appear as a kind of liberal voice within Victorian Catholicism. Paradoxically, Newman appears as an extremist when an Anglican, but a moderate once a Catholic, whilst his thought in fact reveals remarkable consistency and continuity: the apparent paradox actually reveals more about the contrasting moods of Victorian Rome and Victorian Canterbury than about Newman himself.

Assessment of Newman is also hindered by the role assigned to him by the post-Victorian Catholic community. The desire to establish Newman as some kind of saint (literally and colloquially) does not aid accurate historical assessment: but at least three achievements must be noted. A great writer of prose, he contributed to Victorian spiritual and theological writing a number of major works and, in the *Apologia*, at least one classic. In his overall theological output, moreover, he left one of the (perhaps *the*) most formidable and comprehensive bodies of theological thought to emerge from Victorian Christianity. His stature as a theologian would have been assured had the *Essay on the Development of Doctrine* or his subsequent *Grammar of Assent* (1870) been his only significant works. In point of fact there remains also an impressive body of sermons, essays and historical studies. Last, but not least, he did as much as any individual to render Catholicism not merely an acceptable but a respectable and respected element in English intellectual life and society. By the time he was eventually, in 1879, made a cardinal, he had become a much-loved national figure.

The stature of even such individuals as Newman or Manning notwithstanding, the main significance of the English converts as a group remained, in the end, the *sense* of revival and the *hope* of further dramatic conversions to which they gave rise. The hope of mass conversions from the Church of England was always, in reality, an illusion, and not infrequently gave rise to tensions between the older English Catholic tradition and the self-confident ebullience of the converts. But it was an important illusion: a symbol of a self-confident English Catholicism, increasingly public in its confidence, optimistic about its prospects, and assertive of its claims.

If hopes of mass *conversion* in the 1840s and 1850s were an illusion, however, mass *expansion* of the Catholic community in England (and also in Wales and Scotland) was very much a reality. The key to the scale of the expansion was Irish immigration. As we have seen, Irish immigration did not *initiate* either the general expansion of English Catholicism or the specific growth of urban Catholicism — but it did account for the massive *scale* of expansion and urban growth, and it did create, uniquely among the Victorian denominations, a large, even predominant, working-class constituency within English Catholicism. As with all generalizations there are important exceptions. There were urban Catholic communities, such as Cardiff, which were almost wholly the product of Irish immigration, and others, such as Wigan, where expansion, though marked, owed little to Ireland. The more general pattern, however, was of small but expanding and energetic urban communities massively increased by Irish immigration.

This dramatic expansion of the urban Catholic communities presented both an opportunity and a challenge. The opportunity consisted of the chance to capitalize upon the general trend towards revival and expansion within early Victorian Catholicism: Irish immigration gave the opportunity to turn steady but small-scale expansion into a statistically impressive phenomenon. It was also an opportunity for Catholicism to expand its specifically urban strength and create a strong, and deeply-rooted, urban and working-class base. The more characteristic pattern among the Victorian churches was of alienation from the urban environment and the working classes: both the Church of England and the Nonconformists expended much energy in seeking to actually establish a hold within the working-class areas of Victorian towns and cities — and, for all their efforts, achieved in the end only modest returns (at least in terms of the successful establishment of thriving parishes and chapels: arguably they achieved a great deal by way of spreading a diffusive, popular Christianity, failing only in that they did not achieve the sweeping institutional successes for which they hoped).[3] Victorian Roman Catholicism also expended much energy, effort and resources on urban mission. But the crucial difference in the Catholic case was that the effort was directed to an existing community and its needs, and to building up that community from a solid base, not in seeking to establish working-class parishes and religious allegiance out of alienation, indifference or simple absence. Whereas for Anglicanism and Nonconformity the upheaval of industrialization and urbanization broke up established patterns and posed new problems, for Catholicism, as Bossy has observed, the coincidence of industrial revolution, urbanization, Irish immigration, emancipation, and an already expanding community gave a remarkable opportunity (Bossy, 1975, p. 316). The result was that by 1900 Catholicism, uniquely among the Victorian denominations, possessed a large working-class element — indeed the greater part of its strength lay there, numerically overwhelmingly so.

The challenge of Irish immigration, on the other hand, was two-fold. First, there was the sheer demand for resources: human and material. The massively increased number of urban Catholics required priests, churches, schools and other local Catholic facilities. Second, there was the nature of Irish Catholicism itself and hence of the Irish immigrant communities. It is clear from recent studies of Irish Catholicism, both in Ireland and in the immigrant communities of mainland Britain, that, prior to the traumatic impact of the Great Famine between 1846 and 1849, Irish Catholicism was prone to laxity in matters of ecclesiastical discipline, lacking in clergy of sufficient numbers and quality, and, at the popular level, much committed to rites of passage, pilgrimages and folk religion, but lukewarm in matters of regular religious practice, such as attendance at mass and confession. Thus, for example, it has been calculated that the ratio of priests to people was deteriorating steadily between 1800 and 1845, and that weekly mass attendance was as low as forty per cent of the baptized population in many parts of pre-famine Ireland. Irish Catholicism at this time also lacked an adequate quantity and quality of church accommodation. Its churches and

[3] On which see *RVB*, II, 3.

chapels were too few, in poor repair and of poor general appearance; the average standard of worship was somewhat drab; the newer devotions characteristic of Ultramontanism were, as yet, relatively rare. Last, but not least, the Catholic church in pre-famine Ireland not only faced a lively tradition of popular or folk religion, but did so with a clergy whose general level of zeal and pastoral diligence was limited: abuses ranged from neglect of pastoral duties or exploitation of parishioners to excessive involvement in the social life of the laity and disputatiousness.

Sean Connolly has suggested that, in the decades before the Famine, 'the religious practice of the great majority of Irish Catholics remained severely limited, in frequency of attendance, in the range of devotional observances, and in the degree of ceremony and external display with which public worship was conducted' (S. J. Connolly, 1975, p. 98). He concludes that although the clergy may have impressed upon their people the importance of baptism and extreme unction, the performance of other regular canonical duties such as attendance at mass, confession and communion was not only much less than the canonical minimum prescribed by the church, but probably no better than the attendance figures of the English and Welsh Protestant churches revealed by the Census of Religious Worship in 1851. Moreover, much of the religious practice may have been qualitatively as well as quantitatively weak, viewed from the standpoint of orthodox Catholic teaching: folk belief was widespread (intermingling with Catholic belief) and understandings of religious obligations were often crude and legalistic (S. J. Connolly, 1975 and 1985; Larkin 1972; Miller, 1975).

The implications of such a situation for the religious life of the Irish immigrant communities are well illustrated by Gerard Connolly's study of Manchester and Salford. In the late eighteenth century the ratio of regular practice to numbers of baptized was healthy — probably above fifty per cent. As Irish immigration increased the ratio deteriorated, and did so most strikingly among the Irish part of the local community. By the 1820s the level of practice may have dropped as low as between twelve and fifteen per cent (G. P. Connolly, 1984, p. 90).

Such evidence does not mean that the Irish and Irish immigrant communities were hostile or actively opposed to regular Catholic practice: still less were they alienated from or apathetic about the Catholic Church *per se*. They simply possessed a conception of Catholicism which was crucially different from that of both the bishops and clergy (and especially the Ultramontane bishops and clergy), and the English Catholic tradition. Faced with such a phenomenon, the clergy and bishops of the English and Irish churches set out to transform it into a regular and practising form: a mission to build churches and schools *for* the community was accompanied by a mission to transform the spiritual and religious life *of* the community.

In mainland Britain at least four important factors combined to transform such potentially critical circumstances into a situation in which, by 1900, the urban centres of Catholicism in England, Scotland and Wales were flourishing, tight-knit communities with an unusually high level of active allegiance and practice, at least when compared with their Protestant neighbours. First, there was simply immense investment of effort and resources in building sufficient churches and schools to minister to and educate the numbers involved. In a community which was relatively poor and included a large working class, both the sacrifice involved and the success achieved were the more impressive. Second, the number of priests was increased and their work supplemented by that of missionary orders such as the Rosminians, Redemptorists, Passionists and Oratorians. The pastoral devotion and, not infrequently in the worst slum conditions, the sheer heroism of local clergy and members of the orders was an essential element in the nurturing of urban Catholicism. Third, the clergy, and especially the missionary orders, brought to the Irish poor the Ultramontane devotionalism of processions, statues, ceremony, and emotional fervour. Rousing hymns of sentimental or militant variety; dramatic and colourful ritual and devotions such as Benediction; Confraternities, Sodalities and Guilds for devotion to the Blessed Sacrament, the Sacred Heart, the Virgin, the Rosary or the Immaculate Heart of Mary; such devotional innovations served to heighten the intensity and strengthen the commitment and distinctively Catholic identity and experience of the local communities. Finally there was a range of parochial social, educational and recreational activities, organizations and societies which, together with the distinctive devotional ethos noted above, helped to create, consolidate and sustain a 'cradle to grave' structure that amounted to an urban Catholic 'ghetto'. Whether in the form of charitable societies, self-help and benefit societies, youth clubs, sporting clubs, temperance societies or literary societies (all under strict clerical leadership), the Victorian Catholic church sought to maintain, and even enhance, the distinctiveness of the local Catholic community.[4]

One must beware of overstating the case. By the 1880s and 1890s there was renewed concern over 'leakage' — as the dropping away from regular practice and communal involvement was inelegantly termed. But even here the very terminology is significant in comparison with Anglican and Nonconformist experience. 'Leakage' at least pre-supposes lapse from an initial involvement and membership, rather than an original estrangement and unfamiliarity. Examining Roman Catholic practice and allegiance in London (which in any case never attained the levels of practice reached elsewhere) in the first decade of the twentieth century, Hugh McLeod observes that a figure of twenty to thirty per cent of Catholics attending in any given

[4] For recent and convincing analyses of the construction and nature of the 'Catholic ghetto', see McLeod, 1986 and Aspinwall, 1986.

week seems well supported. Moreover, he points out, even the non-devout Catholic retained a strong sense of being Catholic which the non-devout 'Protestant' rarely did, or at least only in a much attenuated form. Also there remained the fact that so many of the urban Catholic devout were from the working classes: in comparison with Protestant working-class church attendance, the Catholic figures were impressive (McLeod, 1974, pp. 34–5). Jennifer Supple's analysis of the work of the Catholic clergy in Yorkshire from 1850 to 1900 is even more optimistic: she suggests that the clergy in Yorkshire achieved a level of fifty per cent of nominal Catholics actually practising their faith, and Gerard Connolly suggests that the average rate of practice for the community as a whole by the 1870s and 1880s may have been as high as fifty to sixty per cent (Supple, 1985a, p. 233; G. P. Connolly, 1985, p. 231). There was, indeed, it would seem, as Connolly neatly observes, something of a mass-conversion to Catholicism in Victorian England, but it was a conversion of relatively non-practising Irish Catholics to a version of their faith which was both practising and Ultramontane in style (G. P. Connolly, 1984, p. 93).

If the changes wrought in Irish immigrant Catholicism between, roughly, 1840 and 1900, were impressive, those in Catholicism in Ireland itself were remarkable. The changes were not a complete break with the immediate past. During the first half of the nineteenth century — not least because of the relaxation of the penal laws and the appearance and early successes of militantly Protestant missionaries among the Irish Catholic communities — there were concerted attempts by the Irish bishops to reform the administration and discipline of the church. Significant progress was made, and by 1850 there was an emerging uniformity in Irish Catholic ecclesiastical law and discipline. Moreover, by the 1840s there was also significant progress in church building, in the introduction of parish missions, and in the introduction of the new devotions characteristic of Ultramontane piety (Kerr, 1981; Corish, 1983; 1985, ch. 6).[5] By mid-century, however, the achievements of such reform were not yet fully co-ordinated, remained successful predominantly among the already more 'orthodox' urban middle class, and were, as yet, limited mainly to matters of basic efficiency, not overall ethos. Two factors transformed this situation, changed initiative into achievement, and produced immense changes in the nature of Irish Catholicism in the second half of the century: the famine was the first; the co-ordinating influence of Cardinal Paul Cullen was the second.

[5] Kerr argues that the older 'folk' devotions were already under attack from 'orthodoxy' by 1829, and points out that by 1860 some 2,000 churches had already been built or rebuilt since 1800. Corish observes of the pre/post famine contrast that 'before the famine we have an old world admittedly under pressure but still very much alive, but afterwards this old world is in full flight before a new pattern of things' (1983, p. 26), but also, especially in his later work, stresses the pre-famine origins of the church's revival and reform.

The potato famine of 1846–9 was a catastrophe of appalling human proportions. The Irish poor were reduced to the level of starvation and the population was reduced, by death or emigration, by perhaps as much as two million, out of an original population of just over eight million. In terms of the development of Irish Catholicism, however, in a bitter irony, the famine also produced a situation of potential advance. The loss of some two million people at once made the ratio of priests and church accommodation to people more favourable. Moreover, it was precisely among the rural poor, over whom the pre-famine church had least hold and among whom 'regular practice' was least observed, that the ravages of the famine struck: the pre-famine reforms among middle-class Catholics became all the more statistically significant. The famine was also an immense social, emotional and psychological shock: post-famine Ireland was arguably peculiarly open to the appeal of religious revival.

It was in this context that Paul Cullen's contribution was so crucial. After a career of some brilliance in Rome (first as Rector of the Irish College, then Rector of Propaganda) he was appointed Bishop of Armagh in 1849, over the heads of three names recommended to Rome by the Irish Church. In 1852 he became Archbishop of Dublin. He arrived in Ireland with a specific mandate from Rome to bring administrative unity and coherence to the Irish Church. In the three decades from his appointment in 1850, until his death in 1878, Cullen achieved precisely that, and, alongside the new coherence, also facilitated the spread in Ireland of the 'devotional revolution' characteristic of nineteenth-century Catholicism as a whole.

Cullen began by calling the Synod of Thurles in 1850, the first national synod of the Irish church for almost 700 years. The synod was concerned with the reform of the administration and regulation of the church, and consolidated and unified the reforming initiatives of the preceding fifty years. The administration of the sacraments was made more efficient, clerical abuses were reformed, the rites of the church were to be administered with full ceremony (and not, as often in pre-famine Ireland, informally in the homes of the laity), and the authority of the bishops was made clearer. Twenty-five years later at the Synod of Maynooth the reforms were reiterated and the authority of the bishops increased still further.

Cullen's work was not unopposed. He faced opposition from some of his fellow bishops and archbishops. Here, however, his skill as an ecclesiastical politician and his close contacts with Rome were essential. He gradually secured the appointment of new bishops of appropriately Roman and reforming sympathies. The number of priests increased by almost twenty five per cent and the number of nuns by even more. Churches, schools, convents, seminaries and parochial houses were built in profusion. Nor was it merely their existence which was significant: their style also changed. The bishops observed in a joint pastoral letter in 1859 that, 'In every part of the country we see churches rising up that rival in beauty of design and elegance of execution the proudest monuments of the zeal, the piety, and the taste of our forefathers'. In contrast to the churches characteristic of pre-famine Ireland, the new buildings included all the trappings of Ultramontane devotionalism. They also thereby became, in a way which their predecessors were not, the centre of local devotional and spiritual life; the practice of reservation of the sacrament is symbolic of the change: in pre-famine Ireland it was not usual, in post-famine Ireland it became customary.

Reservation of the sacrament was, however, only one of a wide range of devotional practices which were fostered in the post-famine church. The regular practice of confession, communion and attendance at mass was encouraged, and the zeal of the laity consolidated, by a widespread programme of parish missions and the introduction of the full range of 'Roman' devotions. Emmet Larkin lists the devotions as including the rosary, forty hours, perpetual adoration, novenas, blessed altars, *Via Crucis*, benediction, vespers, devotion to the Sacred Heart and Immaculate Conception, jubilees, triduums, pilgrimages, shrines, processions and retreats — all communalized and regularized under spiritual directors or in confraternities and sodalities, and all supported by devotional aids such as rosary beads, scapulars, medals, missals, holy pictures, music, candles, statues, vestments and incense (Larkin, 1972, p. 645). Although known in Ireland before 1850, such devotionalism assumed new and transforming proportions after 1850, and together with the new administrative efficiency, episcopal and clerical authority, centralized control, and loyalty to the papacy, turned post-famine Ireland into one of the most remarkably observant of Catholic countries.[6]

The successful transformation of Irish Catholicism, and indeed the successful consolidation of Victorian Catholicism in general, owed much, as we have already begun to see, to the efforts and abilities of the clergy — both the parish clergy and the religious orders, and the bishops and archbishops. Gerard Connolly indeed suggests that the various elements in the trans-

[6] The remarkably high levels of Catholic practice in post-famine Ireland were also a reflection of the fact that Catholicism could, at times, act as one expression of Irish nationalism. The correlation was not simple or complete, however: Cullen, for example, opposed Irish nationalism, and there is evidence that clerical influence on politics, if potentially considerable, nevertheless fell well short of automatic dominance of political life. (For a review of recent discussion see S. J. Connolly, 1985, pp. 36–41. Corish, 1985, urges the importance of Catholicism within Irish nationalism. See also *RVB*, II, 6.) In England, Roman Catholicism and Irishness were, again, mutually reinforcing, not least as a result of persecution and anti-Irish/anti-Catholic prejudice: the key concept, however, was not 'nationalism' but a sense of 'identity' (Samuel, 1985, pp. 279 and 288).

formation of *English* Catholicism may be understood as factors unified by the rise of the Victorian Catholic clergy as a profession (G. P. Connolly, 1985). Certainly the clergy, as we have already noted, first took control, and then held onto the initiative in English Catholicism between 1800 and 1850. The contribution of the bishops and clergy was not merely a matter of dominance and control, however: it was also a matter of the quality of leadership and example which flowed from that control.

At the episcopal level the contributions in England of Wiseman, Manning and Vaughan as successive Archbishops of Westminster, and in Ireland of Cullen, would be hard to exaggerate. We have already noted the significance of Manning and Cullen in some detail. Wiseman, as well as featuring so prominently in the conflict over 'Papal Aggression', experienced repeated controversies with his fellow bishops in the restored hierarchy. It was hardly surprising: his aim was to use the restoration to establish Ultramontane devotion and assumptions as the norm of post-restoration English Catholicism, but the majority of his bishops in the early years were of an older English and more independent temper. Through a series of conflicts and controversies with his bishops he did succeed in establishing the basis of a centralized and Ultramontane church — which his successor, Manning, was able to consolidate. Not the least important of his contributions to English Catholicism was the strong encouragement he gave to the work of the missionary orders, who in turn were the key agents in the successful popular diffusion of Ultramontane devotionalism.

Vaughan, who succeeded Manning at Westminster in 1892, having previously been Bishop of Salford from 1872 onwards, continued both the skilled administration and the triumphalism of his predecessor. Early in his career he had helped the Ultramontanist cause in England by his purchase of the *Tablet*, a newspaper he used to forward Roman papal and episcopal authority. At Salford he had demonstrated his administrative efficiency in fund-raising, building, clergy training, and 'rescue work' among the lapsed — it was Vaughan above all who raised to prominence the issue of 'leakage'. In particular he encouraged Catholic social and charitable work to avert the prospect of Catholic children receiving Protestant philanthropy or workhouse relief. Once at Westminster he was particularly active not only in rescue work but in presenting the Catholic case for state aid in Catholic schools on a par with Anglican and Nonconformist schools: this he achieved in the 1902 Education Act. His triumphalism was symbolized in the building of Westminster Cathedral — in Byzantine style — and in his rigid opposition to those within his church who wished to discuss the possibility of reunion between the Roman and Anglican churches.

Wiseman, Manning, Vaughan and Cullen, together with many of their diocesan bishops, shared a number of qualities which not only transcended their personal differences and differing contexts, but also played a vital part in consolidating Victorian Catholicism. They shared a commitment to sound, detailed, centralized and efficient administration. They all recognized the importance of building — not only churches, but equally schools — and duly committed their churches to the task of funding Catholic education. They each saw the importance of clergy training and to that end sought to establish adequate numbers and quality of seminaries,[7] and they also recognized the essential role, in sustaining the Catholic communities, of the network of pastoral, educational and charitable agencies of the church.

Such episcopal and archiepiscopal recognition of the importance of pastoral, educational and charitable work would have been of little use, however, without local parish clergy able and willing to carry out the work. Victorian Catholicism was well served by its priests. Edward Norman begins his history of the English Catholic church in the nineteenth century — a history which he himself acknowledges concentrates on the official leadership of the church — with the observation that beneath the history of church leaders, bishops and scholars on which he chooses to focus, there was another sub-structure of 'rich spiritual enterprise and astonishing personal heroism' (Norman, 1984, p. 1). That sub-structure was to be found in the lives and work of the local clergy. Its physical manifestation was the creation of local communities, complete with schools, churches, orphanages, and a host of other local Catholic institutions. Equally important, however, was the priests' pastoral and spiritual ministry — in most cases in communities which were poor and socially deprived, in many cases to communities in the worst of the slums of Victorian Britain. The work was unglamorous and arduous — it was also dangerous in the disease-ridden and cholera-prone conditions of early and mid-Victorian slum life: ten priests died in the 1847 cholera epidemic in Liverpool alone. Connolly gives a number of examples of similar sacrifice among priests in Manchester and Salford, suggesting that as many as a quarter of the urban clergy in the northern district contracted typhus in 1846–50, and noting that in 1838 no less than twenty-six priests had died over an eighteen-month period in the same region. In her study of Catholic clergy in Yorkshire in the second half of the nineteenth century, Jennifer Supple observes that priests working in the large towns seldom survived to a great age. Such priests, Connolly suggests, were the martyrs of the Victorian Catholic Church (G. P. Connolly, 1983, pp. 8–9 and 1984, pp. 99–101; Supple, 1985a, p. 221).

Priests in the poor and slum districts were also the leaders and advisers

[7] At the third provincial synod of the restored English hierarchy in 1859, for example, the bishops agreed to establish seminaries in all dioceses which could afford to do so. They reaffirmed the commitment at the fourth synod in 1879. The success in the project was limited, but the direction of policy clear (Holmes, 1978, pp. 170–4).

of the community — in social, educational and communal matters as well as in the life of the church. In many of the worst slums the priest possessed an authority — often born of his devotion and self-sacrifice as much as his individual personality or clerical status — which enabled him to be a mediator in communal conflicts, act as a moral arbiter, and move freely in areas normally dangerous or violent (G. P. Connolly, 1984, pp. 101–3; Supple, 1985a; Samuel, 1985).

The work of the local clergy was supported by the regular use of parish missions conducted by members of the religious orders. The work of the missionary orders in such missions not only served to reinforce the efforts of the local clergy to increase the spiritual zeal of their parishioners, but also formed a (perhaps *the*) crucial medium for the popularization and establishment of the 'devotional revolution'. Intensely evangelistic and revivalist in style, the parish missions took Catholicism forcefully into the streets in an uncompromising, often spectacular and certainly flamboyant style.

After early attempts to establish the work of such orders in the 1830s met with little success, the Passionists, the Redemptorists, the Rosminians and the Oratorians became firmly established in the 1840s and 50s. From within the orders the influence of the Rosminian Fr. Luigi Gentile and the Passionist Fr. Dominic Barberi was particularly important in establishing their work in England. The other crucial factor in their establishment as part of the fabric of Victorian Catholicism was the enthusiastic support of Wiseman. Wiseman, in any case disposed to favour their overtly Ultramontane style, quickly saw their potential for evangelistic work among the poor. As early as 1840 Wiseman petitioned the Pope for the establishment of a missionary institute in England. Once the missionary orders were established, Wiseman encouraged them to conduct not only retreats and small-scale missions but also large and spectacular missions, with emotional street preaching, mass confirmations and processions culminating in crowded services featuring such events as Solemn Benediction, Papal Blessings and indulgences for acts of public veneration. The parish mission and the missionary orders were also central to the spread of the devotional revolution in Ireland, where they began to be used in the pre-famine era and became widespread after 1850, not least because of the enthusiastic support they received from Cullen.

Although uncompromisingly and indelibly Roman Catholic in its specifics, in overall tenor and appeal such evangelism and its characteristic devotional style shared much in common with Protestant Revivalism and Anglican Ritualism: it was emotional and experiential; it presented a version of Christianity which was hard-edged and exclusive in its claims; it was revivalist and popular in aims and intentions; and it tended to extremes, not moderation. It also shared with Revivalism the characteristic of tending to make more impact upon the dormant or lax within the community than on those outside. As to its overall impact, we have noted already Edward Norman's verdict that the devotional style of the missionary orders came to seem, in the popular Catholic mind, the very substance of the faith itself.[8]

In Victorian Scotland the history of Roman Catholicism was at once very similar to that of its English counterpart, yet also crucially different in important details. The similarities are easily stated and familiar territory. In 1800 Catholics in Scotland were relatively few in number (about 30,000), predominantly rural (apart from a significant presence in Edinburgh), and located mainly in the north-east, the western seaboard and the isles. By 1850 numbers had risen to about 150,000 and by 1900 the figure was approximately 433,000. The immense growth in numbers was the result of Irish immigration, especially after the famine. Moreover, since approximately two-thirds of the immigrants settled in the west of Scotland, in and around Glasgow, the numerical strength of Scottish Catholicism had shifted dramatically to the urban, industrial region of the country (McCaffrey, 1983, pp. 275–6).

The Roman Catholic church in Scotland was thus confronted with the need to provide a pastoral and devotional structure for the new, immigrant community where none, or virtually none, already existed. It also, of course, faced the challenge of the nature of the Catholicism of the Irish immigrants: as in England so in Scotland, levels of practice were low and conceptions of Catholicism essentially those characteristic of pre-famine Ireland. The response of the Scottish church was both resolute and typical of the strategy deployed by Victorian Catholicism as a whole. By a combination of community effort and impressive philanthropy on the part of the old aristocratic Scots Catholics and a number of new upper-middle class and aristocratic converts, churches and schools were built for the new Catholic community of Glasgow and the west of Scotland. The religious orders were drafted in (and new ones founded) to provide teachers for the Catholic school system which began to emerge. The religious orders were also introduced with the express purpose of conducting parish missions to consolidate the 'devotional revolution', the elements of which were in any case already present in Scottish Catholicism by the 1840s. The Rosminians were active in parish mission work by 1853, and by the 1860s had been joined by the Vincentians, Passionists, Redemptorists and Jesuits. The devotional revolution, here as elsewhere, established the experiential spirituality of the Rosary, Benediction, Way of the Cross, Sacred Heart, Forty Hours Devotion, processions, hymns, colour and ornateness as the parochial norm, which was then duly consolidated in Guilds and Confraternities.

[8] For a fuller discussion of the relationship between such Catholic initiatives and both Protestant and Anglo-Catholic revivalism, see *RVB*, I, 6.

Along with the devotional societies and confraternities, there came also the network of cultural, recreational and charitable societies and organizations, which, taken together, created and sustained the tight-knit 'cradle to grave' community of the late Victorian urban Catholic 'ghetto'. In Glasgow the Saint Vincent de Paul Society was so active that it has been described as a 'welfare state within the state'. Other prominent societies were the Catholic Young Men's Society and its temperance offshoot, the League of the Cross (Aspinwall, 1982 and 1986).

The network of Ultramontane devotionalism, parish organizations and missions in turn centred on the parish priest, who became *the* leader and authority in the community. Beyond the parish clergy were the bishops, who were duly constituted a national hierarchy in 1878. Among the bishops the key figure was Charles Eyre. Appointed to the Western District as Vicar Apostolic in 1868 (not least to resolve conflicts in Glasgow between native Scottish and immigrant Irish Catholics), he became the head of the restored hierarchy in 1878 and was, at the level of individual leadership, the key consolidator, stabilizer and Romanizer of Victorian Scottish Catholicism, especially in the newly-formed community in the west of Scotland.

The distinctiveness of Victorian Scottish Catholicism, however, is to be found in the crucial role played by the upper-middle class and aristocratic laity in the period prior to the restoration of the hierarchy. In a series of essays, Bernard Aspinwall has argued that a network of well-placed and wealthy laymen (some Catholic born and some converts, frequently romantic medievalists in their vision of Catholicism, and centred on the co-ordinating personality of the wealthy convert Robert Monteith) played a vital role in funding and enabling the devotional-organizational transformation of Scottish Catholicism. They did so, Aspinwall suggests, in the clear understanding that the condition of Catholicism in Victorian Scotland — sharply divided as it was between old Scots and new Irish communities, and between aristocratic and upper-middle class on the one hand, and Irish, urban working class on the other — required a unifying structure and identity. Both structure and identity were to hand in the Ultramontane tradition of devotion, hierarchy and authority, and the lay leaders of early Victorian Scottish Catholicism duly worked for the establishment of this tradition in their church. With the restoration of the hierarchy in 1878 they ensured the success of their efforts (Aspinwall, 1981 a and b; 1982).

III VICTORIAN CATHOLICISM: AN ASSESSMENT

As Edward Norman has recently observed, even allowing for the Victorian period being one of general religious vitality, the achievements of Victorian Roman Catholicism were extraordinary (Norman, 1985, p. 28). Norman's concern was English Catholicism, but the judgement is appropriate for

Roman Catholicism in Britain as a whole. From a position of official civil disability and overt suspicion and hostility from much of the non-Catholic population, and from a definitely marginal status within the overall religious life of England, Wales and Scotland, Roman Catholicism moved in the Victorian period to a position of civil equality and calm acceptance by the majority of the British people, and to a position within the religious life of the nation which — though it was not to become clear until the twentieth century — amounted to being the major alternative to the established churches of England, Wales and Scotland. (In Ireland such a status had always been implicit, given Roman Catholic numbers.)

It is in this sense that the furore over 'Papal Aggression' in mid-century was such a curious anachronism. There remained a tradition of staunch 'no-popery', and there remained occasional outbursts of anti-Catholic rioting and even more occasional protests against public demonstrations of Catholic devotion. But they were increasingly atypical and isolated, local, and not infrequently the result of the deliberate agitation of anti-Catholic preachers.[9] The greater part of militant Protestant energy and campaigning in the second half of the century, however, was devoted not to Roman Catholicism but to the harassment of Anglican Ritualist clergy. The *national* furore over Papal Aggression was never repeated after 1850–51.

Similarly, there continued to be moments of crisis over the compatibility of loyalty to Catholicism and loyalty to the British constitution and its values. The controversy over the Vatican Decrees was the most pressing of such moments of crisis. In 1870 the Vatican Council had defined the doctrine of papal infallibility. A minority of more liberal bishops at the Council succeeded in restraining the Ultramontanes from proclaiming papal infallibility in the most extreme way possible: but even the pronouncement which occurred aroused old fears about the intellectual integrity of Roman Catholics, and the extent of the Pope's claims and jurisdiction. Manning, moreover, was a leading advocate of the doctrine, and would have been happy to see it proclaimed in an even stronger version. In 1874 Gladstone published a pamphlet entitled 'The Vatican Decrees in their bearing on Civil Allegiance', in which he argued that after the definition of papal infallibility a logical Roman Catholic must be disloyal in civil allegiance. The pamphlet sold rapidly; replies, including one from Manning, were written; and in 1875 Gladstone published a further pamphlet on the

[9] At Wolverhampton in 1867–71, for example, there were riots sparked off by the presence of the virulently anti-Catholic preacher William Murphy (Swift, 1984). The experience of such anti-Irish/Catholic agitation produced a correspondingly defensive militancy from the Irish Catholic communities (Samuel, 1985). Similarly, in cities such as Liverpool and Glasgow, there continued to be a lively local tradition of sectarian rivalry, on occasion erupting into violence (Gallagher, 1985).

subject, entitled *Vaticanism*. The reply which counted for most, and which calmed the brief furore, was that of Newman. Newman was known to be uneasy about the wisdom of the definition of infallibility (whilst personally believing it to be true) and was also known to be consistently at odds with the Ultramontane Manning: Newman preferring a quieter, less triumphal and more reflective style of faith. In his open letter to the Duke of Norfolk in 1875, Newman displayed all his characteristic care and calmness whilst also remaining loyal to Rome, the Pope and the definition of infallibility. He urged the continuing priority of conscience and argued that the definition of 1870 did not in fact *increase* papal authority and that therefore nothing had changed: Gladstone had overreacted; Catholics were as capable of loyalty after 1870 as they were before.

Like the occasional outbursts of popular anti-Catholicism, the flurry over the Vatican Decrees was atypical. The clear trend was towards the acceptance of Catholicism and Catholics as firmly within the fabric of national life. Newman, as we have noted, was probably as important as anyone in securing the emergence of this state of affairs, but even the fiercely Ultramontane Manning was increasingly regarded with affection by large sections of the public, especially the poor and the working classes. Another, institutional, sign of the acceptance of Catholicism within national life was the appointment of Catholic chaplains in the armed services, workhouses and prisons. The press was no longer instinctively anti-Roman Catholic but, rather, treated Catholicism and Roman Catholics with respect. By the end of the century there had been a Catholic Viceroy of India (Lord Ripon), a Catholic Regius Professor of Modern History at Cambridge (Lord Acton), and a Catholic Home Secretary (Lord Llandaff).

What, then, were the essential characteristics of the Catholicism which had made such strides between 1829 and 1900? Four characteristics stand out: Victorian Catholicism was at once centralized and clerical, Ultramontane in ethos, highly disciplined in doctrine, and exclusive in its claims and life-style.

We have already noted the way in which the bishops and clergy increasingly took control and leadership of the community in the campaign for emancipation and in the emergence of urban Catholicism. The restoration of the hierarchy sealed the process. We have seen also the importance of the devotion and dedication of the parish clergy and their emergence as leaders and advisors of their urban working-class communities, and the determination of the bishops in consolidating the expansion of Roman Catholicism in Victorian Britain. Beyond this, however, there was also an emphasis upon ecclesiastical authority and a demand for obedience to the archbishops and bishops on the part of the clergy, and to the local clergy on the part of the laity. Archbishops and bishops *led* their churches and dioceses; parish clergy *led* their parishes, and did so in a manner and to a degree which amounted to clerical dominance of the laity.

Similarly, we have noted the triumph of the Ultramontane spirit and its devotional style. The two leading Anglican converts, Manning and Newman, reflected the changed ethos of Victorian Catholicism in 1890 compared with that of 1830: Newman, instinctively retiring, scholarly, full of belief in the rightness of Roman Catholicism and its bright future in Britain, yet also very English; Manning, also full of belief in Roman Catholicism and its prospects, but in an assertive, triumphalist, and essentially Roman, not English, manner. By the 1880s they were both, in very different ways, immensely popular, with non-Catholics as well as Catholics: but it was Manning who held the power in the English Catholic Church.

The contrast of personal styles and the location of the power serves to summarize the changes in Victorian Roman Catholicism as a whole. Nor was it merely in the personalities of the leadership that the victory of the Ultramontane spirit was to be found. Even more significantly the norms of Catholic devotion had been transformed: the deep but undemonstrative piety of *Garden of the Soul* Catholicism became replaced by the emotional and publicly highly demonstrative piety of the devotional revolution and its processions, ceremonies, solemnities and societies. As ever, one must beware of oversimplification and exaggeration. Ultramontanism and its devotional style were not unopposed. As Jennifer Supple has demonstrated from her study of Catholicism in Yorkshire between 1850 and 1900, even in a diocese with a determinedly Ultramontane bishop, there were protests against the more extreme forms of Ultramontane devotionalism and a continuation of an older alternative devotional tradition (Supple, 1985b). But, equally, Supple also acknowledges that although the older tradition retained its supporters, the newer devotional style became increasingly popular and introduced a new vigour and variety to Catholic spiritual life in Yorkshire. It has been said of Victorian Catholicism that, in its post-1850 turn to Ultramontanism, it became 'more Roman than Rome'. Certainly, even when far short of the most extreme versions of Ultramontanism, Catholic devotional life, both nationally and locally, was much more 'continental' and 'Roman' in 1900 than it was in 1829. 'More Roman than Rome' may be an exaggeration: more Roman than hitherto is not.

The third major characteristic of Victorian Catholicism was its theological and doctrinal discipline: not for Victorian Roman Catholicism the theological heart and soul-searching and shift into *de facto* internal pluralism which occurred, supremely in the Church of England, but generally in the other mainstream denominations — or at least, not institutionally. That did not mean that Victorian Catholicism lacked individual crises of faith and conscience, or even groups of 'liberal' theological thinkers: it had both. But institutionally its response was quite different from those of Victorian Anglicanism, Nonconformity and Presbyterianism. The reaction of the hierarchy to theological liberalism within Victorian Roman Catholicism was clear, disapproving, and more frequently than not decisive.

We have seen already that Newman remained theologically suspect in the eyes of Rome and of many English Ultramontanes. In Newman's case however, the penalties for theological independence of mind were relatively slight: a certain coolness or antipathy and consequent sense of isolation, and a long delay in receiving his cardinal's hat. In other cases official reaction was overt and thorough. In the middle decades of the century a group of Catholic intellectuals (of which Acton was a leading member) produced a journal entitled the *Rambler*. Characterized by liberal opinions and a spirit of free enquiry, it had a poor view of the educational level of traditional Catholicism and scant respect for ecclesiastical authority. The bishops disliked it and frequently complained to Rome about it. In 1862 the group changed its title to the *Home and Foreign Review*, official censure clearly being close. In the event, all but one of the English bishops issued Pastoral Letters in 1862 which strongly disapproved of the journal (in both its old and new guises) and warned the faithful against it. In 1864 it became clear that censures of Liberal Catholicism in Europe were equally applicable to the stance taken by the *Review*: rather than face formal ecclesiastical censure the journal ceased publication voluntarily. Acton, a thoroughly English liberal, remained a Roman Catholic whose theological opinions were unacceptable to Rome and to the English hierarchy: he avoided official censure, however, by immersing himself in his historical studies.

In the 1880s and 1890s a new generation of 'liberal' Catholics raised questions of a theologically critical kind, and became a part of the loose network of liberal thinkers in late nineteenth-century Catholicism known as Modernists. Of the three leading so-called English Modernists, one, George Tyrrell, was Irish, and another, Friedrich von Hügel, was the son of an Austrian diplomat and a converted Scots Presbyterian. Only one, St George Jackson Mivart, was actually English. Mivart was an accomplished zoologist. He rejected Darwin's particular theory of evolution and appeared for a time to be intellectually acceptable to the Church: he proposed to reconcile advanced science and orthodox Catholic Christianity. His commitment to intellectual freedom, however, led to conflict with his church, not primarily over science and belief, but over biblical criticism, hell and eternal punishment. Consistently opposed to biblical criticism and resolute in the matter of hell, the Holy Office condemned his work: he died in 1900 and was denied the sacraments and last rites, Cardinal Vaughan having taken the sternest of stances in the matter. Tyrrell first clearly indicated his heterodoxy with an attack on hell and eternal punishment in 1899. Other heterodox works followed and he too died without sacraments or last rites in 1909. Von Hügel developed a highly mystical approach to Christianity and consistently avoided commitments to official theological statements. (He refused, for example, in 1901, to serve on the Pontifical Biblical Commission.) He escaped official censure. The English Catholic church made its position on such 'Modernism' clear by means of a joint Pastoral Letter of 1900 from Vaughan and the English bishops. It upheld traditional teaching. Its stance was to become official Roman Catholic policy in 1907 when two Papal Encyclicals condemned Modernism. Unlike the other major denominations in Victorian Britain, Roman Catholicism did not enter the twentieth century with a *de facto* theological pluralism within its own bounds. On the contrary, it retained a position of doctrinal orthodoxy and theological unity which set it sharply apart from the other major denominations.

This distinctiveness was further emphasized by the exclusivity characteristic of Victorian Roman Catholicism. At the doctrinal and ecclesiastical level the exclusivity was nowhere shown more clearly than in the papal pronouncement of 1896 on the question of the validity of Anglican orders. Between 1894 and 1896 a small group of Anglicans, led by the Anglo-Catholic Lord Halifax, and a small group of Roman Catholics held discussions concerning the possibility of reunion between the two churches. The validity of Anglican priestly orders was soon recognized as a central issue and an international commission was set up by the Vatican to consider the matter. Manning had previously taken a strict line, and Vaughan also now used his influence against any concession to, or recognition of, Anglican orders. The commission agreed. In the papal bull *Apostolicae Curae* of 1896, Leo XIII declared Anglican orders null and void.

Equally importantly, however, Victorian Catholicism fostered an exclusiveness of life-style as well. The 'ghetto' was one of its most obvious manifestations. The urban Catholic community was not cut off from its surroundings in the sense of having no contact or involvement with them — Roman Catholics took an active part in local life, including local political life — but the local Catholic community did seek to provide specifically Catholic recreational and social, as well as educational, cultural and religious facilities. Policy on mixed marriages was another example of the stern, exclusive face of Victorian Catholicism. Both Manning and Vaughan took a strict line and maintained the prohibition of mixed marriage.

Catholic exclusiveness was also reflected in the church's policy on education. The church authorities regarded it as essential that Catholic children should be educated in Catholic schools. Inevitably this meant a massive investment of time, energy and money in the building and maintenance of such schools. The question of state aid first arose in 1839 when government funds became theoretically available, but only at the request of the church and at the price of government inspection. The bishops divided on the issue and, at this stage, did not accept state aid. Later they were to do so, but only with a continuing and careful watchfulness to monitor the limits of state intervention thereby incurred, and to ensure Catholic parity with the aid given to Anglicans and Nonconformists. A measure of the Catholic commitment to denominational education can be found in the Catholic response to the 1870 Education Act. While standards of education rose dramatically as a result of the Act, so did the cost of maintaining denominational schools. Between 1878 and 1886 the number of Nonconformist schools declined as a result; the number of Anglican schools increased, but only by nine per cent; the number of Catholic schools increased by twenty-two per cent — and this in a church which was predominantly a church of the poor. In higher education the Catholic church again sought to retain an independence, providing its own colleges for advanced study, including one, St Edmunds, affiliated to London University. Oxford and Cambridge were especially mistrusted for their highly Anglican ethos — only in the 1890s was it resolved to sanction the establishment of Catholic halls at both Universities, and even then the acceptance of such halls by the Catholic hierarchy came not least because lay Catholics chose to avail themselves of the opportunities made available by the mid-century reforms of Oxford and Cambridge and go there anyway, if necessary to non-Catholic colleges.

Such exclusiveness had its ironic aspects: as the Victorian period saw a steady increase in the basic acceptance of the Roman Catholic presence in Britain, the Roman Catholic response was to construct a community with hard edges and a markedly separate identity. But that irony was in turn part of a larger paradox. Victorian Roman Catholicism, as Edward Norman has observed, was remarkably astute in its seizure of the opportunity offered by the emergence of a liberal, pluralist state (Norman, 1986, p. 71), but it exploited the opportunity by virtue of its disciplined non-liberalism and non-pluralism. Victorian Roman Catholicism accepted the scope and freedom made available to it, built dramatically upon the already modestly expanding Catholic community of the pre-Victorian era, and did so, moreover, to such good effect that by the end of the nineteenth century Roman Catholicism was poised to become the principal religious alternative to the established church. That it was in fact so poised was not yet clear in 1900, when Nonconformity still seemed, on the whole, to be on the point of consolidating its claim to such a place and status. But with the dramatic decline of Nonconformity in the twentieth century, the scale of the Catholic achievement became clear. The highly clerical, centralized, disciplined and conservative community created by the Victorian Catholic Church and its leaders continued into the twentieth century and did not suffer the dramatic decline experienced by Nonconformity, or the less dramatic but still serious decline within Anglicanism. Indeed, until the middle decades of the twentieth century British Roman Catholicism continued to expand. Such success was, however, bought only at a price. That price included the domination of the laity by the clergy, the stifling of theological liberalism and, crucially, the isolation and insulation of British Catholicism from many of the predominant trends within British society in the first half of the twentieth century. As a result, when in the late 1950s and the 1960s the old style of Catholicism inherited from the Victorian period finally began to give way under the combined pressure of greater social mobility, the social upheaval of urban renewal (and consequent decline of the urban 'ghettos'), the coming of the welfare state, and the public diversification of Roman Catholicism during and after the Second Vatican Council, British Roman Catholicism suddenly experienced the twin crises of decline and internal pluralism with a suddenness and shock which was in no small part the result of having been so disciplined and conservative for so long.

That, however, is another story. The paradox of Victorian Roman Catholicism remains that, given the opportunities afforded by the emergence of a liberal, pluralist state, Catholicism, by a prodigious effort, achieved the status of principal religious alternative to the established church: but did so by the creation of a fiercely disciplined, highly conservative, markedly exclusive and decisively non-pluralist church.

BIBLIOGRAPHY

W. L. Arnstein (1982) *Protestant versus Catholic in Mid-Victorian England*, Columbia (MO), University of Missouri Press.

B. Aspinwall (1981a) 'The Second Spring in Scotland: I' *Clergy Review*, Vol. 66, pp. 281–90.

B. Aspinwall (1981b) 'The Second Spring in Scotland: II' *Clergy Review*, Vol. 66, pp. 312–19.

B. Aspinwall (1982) 'The formation of the Catholic community in the west of Scotland: some preliminary outlines', *Innes Review*, Vol. 33, pp. 44–57.

B. Aspinwall (1986) 'The Welfare State within the state: the Saint Vincent de Paul Society in Glasgow 1848–1920' in W. J. Sheils and D. Wood (eds.) *Voluntary Religion*, pp. 445–59, Oxford, Blackwell.

*J. Bossy (1975) *The English Catholic Community 1750–1850*, Darton Longman and Todd.

*G. P. Connolly (1983) '"With more than ordinary devotion to God": the secular missioner of the North in the Evangelical age of the English mission', *North West Catholic History*, Vol. 10, pp. 8–31.

G. P. Connolly (1984) 'The transubstantiation of myth: towards a new popular history of nineteenth-century Catholicism in England', *Journal of Ecclesiastical History*, Vol. 35, pp. 78–104.

G. P. Connolly (1985) 'Irish and Catholic: myth or reality? Another sort of Irish and the renewal of the clerical profession among Catholics in England 1791–1918' in R. Swift and S. Gilley (eds.) *The Irish in the Victorian City*, pp. 225–54, Croom Helm.

*S. J. Connolly (1982) *Priests and People in Pre-Famine Ireland 1780–1850*, Dublin, Gill and Macmillan.

S. J. Connolly (1985) *Religion and Society in Nineteenth Century Ireland*, Dundalk, Dundalgan Press.

P. Corish (1983) 'The Catholic community in the nineteenth century', *Archivium Hibernicum*, Vol. 38, pp. 26–33.

*P. Corish (1985) *The Irish Catholic Experience: A Historical Survey*, Dublin, Gill and Macmillan.

T. Gallagher (1985) 'A tale of two cities: communal strife in Glasgow and Liverpool before 1914' in R. Swift and S. Gilley (eds.) *The Irish in the Victorian City*, pp. 106–29, Croom Helm.

*S. Gilley (1985) 'Vulgar piety and the Brompton Oratory, 1850–1860' in R. Swift and S. Gilley (eds.) *The Irish in the Victorian City*, pp. 255–66, Croom Helm.

D. Holmes (1978) *More Roman than Rome*, Tunbridge Wells, Burns and Oates.

D. Kerr (1981) 'The early nineteenth century: patterns of change' in M. Maher (ed.) *Irish Spirituality*, pp. 135–44, Dublin, Veritas Publications.

*E. Larkin (1972) 'The devotional revolution in Ireland, 1850–1875', *The American Historical Review*, Vol. 77, pp. 625–52.

*J. McCaffrey (1983) 'Roman Catholics in Scotland in the 19th and 20th centuries', *Records of the Scottish Church History Society*, Vol. 21, pp. 275–300.

H. McLeod (1974) *Class and Religion in the Late Victorian City*, Croom Helm.

H. McLeod (1986) 'Building the Catholic ghetto: Catholic organizations 1870–1914' in W. J. Sheils and D. Wood *Voluntary Religion*, pp. 411–44, Oxford, Blackwell.

D. Miller (1975) 'Irish Catholicism and the Great Famine', *Journal of Social History*, Vol. 9, pp. 81–98.

E. Norman (1968) *Anti-Catholicism in Victorian England*, George Allen and Unwin.

E. Norman (1984) *The English Catholic Church in the Nineteenth Century*, Oxford, Oxford University Press.

E. Norman (1985) *Roman Catholicism in England from the Elizabethan Settlement to the Second Vatican Council*, Oxford, Oxford University Press.

*W. Ralls (1974) 'The Papal Aggression of 1850: a study in Victorian anti-Catholicism', *Church History*, Vol. 43, pp. 242–56.

*R. Samuel (1985) 'The Roman Catholic Church and the Irish poor' in R. Swift and S. Gilley (eds.) *The Irish in the Victorian City*, pp. 267–300, Croom Helm.

*J. Supple (1985a) 'The Catholic clergy of Yorkshire, 1850–1900: a profile', *Northern History*, Vol. 21, pp. 212–35.

J. Supple (1985b) 'Ultramontanism in Yorkshire, 1850–1900', *Recusant History*, Vol. 17, pp. 274–86.

R. Swift (1984) 'Anti-Catholicism and Irish disturbances: public order in mid-Victorian Wolverhampton', *Midland History*, Vol. 9, pp. 87–108.

CHAPTER 5

TRUE HUMILITY.

RIGHT REVEREND HOST. "I'M AFRAID YOU'VE GOT A BAD EGG, MR JONES!"
THE CURATE. "OH NO, MY LORD, I ASSURE YOU! PARTS OF IT ARE EXCELLENT!"

THE CLERICAL RENAISSANCE IN VICTORIAN ENGLAND AND WALES

It is a mistake to assume that the clergy became a profession only in the nineteenth century.* But it is a mistake very frequently made. Some historians have argued that the professions as a whole emerged in the industrial period, the clergy no less than the rest. For instance, Anthony Russell's *The Clerical Profession* begins with the statement that it is 'an account of the development of the clergyman's role during its formative period in the nineteenth century. In this period, the clergy took the emerging professions as their model and reference group, and the role of the clergyman came to be shaped in its recognizably modern form. Indeed this period may be regarded from the contemporary point of view as the crucial period of change since when there have been only minor modifications' (Russell, 1980, p. 6). Alan Haig in his *The Victorian Clergy* (Haig, 1984) accepts this view that the professions emerged in the nineteenth century even while he expresses reservations concerning the professional status of the clergy. A. D. Gilbert boldly asserts that the Reformation was deprofessionalizing (presumably because it expressed a belief in the priesthood of all believers) (Gilbert, 1976). Even two of the most intelligent contributions to the study of the clerical profession (Roberts, 1983; Heeney, 1976) seem unaware that the 'occupational profession' of the clergy had existed in the late sixteenth century. Far from it being the case that the clergy used the secular professions as their model, the reverse could plausibly be argued — that the new professions were using the clergy and the lawyers as their reference group. The development of the clerical profession should be seen as a continuum stretching from the middle ages, through the Reformation to the present. There is no disjuncture between the nineteenth-century profession and the clergy of preceding years.

One does not wish to deny that there were changes in organization nor that the clergy were in touch with developments in the new professions.

**Abstract*. This essay takes issue with the popular view that the nineteenth-century clergy of the Church of England consciously professionalized on the model of the contemporary secular professions. It suggests instead that the Victorian clergy revived an earlier tradition of occupational professionalism and moral earnestness (which had never entirely died away). It indicates that this tradition was revised in the context of the new demands of religious life in an urban, industrial environment. It demonstrates why the revival took place. It shows that clerical professionalization was bounded by doctrinal and ecclesiological issues, but that these were by no means the only important determinants of clerical behaviour.

The essay makes it clear that profession and vocation were not, as some historians and contemporaries believed, distinct and opposed characteristics. The professions had their origin in the profession of a vocation. No conflict was involved. The essay explores the parameters of the redefinition of the clerical role in nineteenth-century society. While the essay concentrates upon the Anglican experience it indicates marked parallels with the Wesleyan and Roman Catholic experiences.

Historians of the nineteenth-century clergy have described developments within the profession in the context of a nineteenth-century crisis with little or no reference to pre-existing conditions. This is unfortunate.

There is evidence that some of the clergy were jealous of the independence of the secular professions. At the same time, however, many Victorian clerics were themselves aware of their distinctiveness as a 'profession' and of their debt to tradition.

Why have most historians ignored this continuity? They have focussed entirely upon the points of comparison between the clergy and the new professions of the Victorian era. They have, in general, argued that the clergy learned these traits (listed below) from others (ignoring their presence in the early modern church). They have excluded from their area of inquiry these features of the clerical profession or, what is worse, they have argued that the existence of differences between the clergy and the new professions imply that the clergy were not a profession.

This has made for a blinkered, narrow study of the nature of the clergy. There is an almost complete ignorance of the development of the clergy and its relationship with the church prior to the industrial period. Even knowledge of the eighteenth century is drawn largely from hostile early nineteenth-century criticism. Yet the professions existed well before industrialization and we cannot hope to understand the development of the clergy as a profession without a thorough grasp of its history. Many of the traits which appear characteristic of the modern professions — 'altruism', 'sense of vocation', 'service', 'close relationship between professional and client', 'code of practice', 'absence of the cash nexus' — in fact evolved among the clergy of the early modern period. The early modern clergy had also been as keenly aware of the desirability of self-regulation and self-determination as their nineteenth-century successors. An emphasis upon the ethos and the organization of the profession was characteristic of both the Protestant and the Catholic Reformations, whether in Britain or in Europe. Early modern clergy organized, in so far as they were allowed, as an occupational profession. Rather than being characteristic of industrialization, then, the professions can be viewed more usefully as anachronistic phenomena existing in industrial, urban society, adapting to it and to some extent being modified by it.

If the nineteenth-century clergy began to re-emphasize the professional elements mentioned above then we should see this not as a new development but as a resurgence of older preoccupations. If these had gone out of fashion before the nineteenth century, they had not entirely faded. Rather they had in England been cast into the shadows by the dominant role of the state and the laity in church life. For some clergy the revival of interest was expressed in terms of clerical exclusiveness. Others sought improvements in professional standards within the existing partnerships between church and state and clergy and laity. Clergy of all persuasions, while certainly noting the existence of the secular professions with interest, built upon their own traditions of professionalism.

The precise development of the clerical profession depended upon the shaping of the church itself both as an institution and as a concept. It is crucial that we understand certain aspects of the Church of England's special relationship with the state as it had evolved since the Reformation. The clergy's professional awareness developed within that special relationship.

The emergence in England of the clergy as an 'occupational profession' occurred in the wake of the Reformation. Prior to that the clergy formed an estate rather than a profession. Membership of this clerical estate did not inevitably imply a career in the pastoral ministry of the church. Lay administrators, clerks, lawyers, teachers, scholars, members of the religious orders were all clergy yet they did not share the same *occupation* as the parish priest. After the Reformation the clergy formed a profession — a hierarchically organized but occupational group which claimed status in society based upon the expert services which it offered the commonwealth. Clerical status now coincided more or less exactly with the pastoral vocation and occupation and it was expected to do so: there were to be no priests without a parish. A professional 'professed' a 'vocation' in the service of God and the Commonwealth. The distinction later perceived between a 'profession' and a 'vocation' had no validity (O'Day, 1987, passim).

From the Reformation onwards, however, the relationship between clergy and laity was a vexed question. Was the relationship precisely equivalent to that of professional and client in, say, the legal profession? There was conflict and there was confusion concerning the clergyman's proper place. Mixed views of the nature of the ministry were held by the post-Reformation hierarchy: Crown, rank-and-file clergy and laity. As a result the re-organization of the clerical profession was complex and sometimes contradictory. Protestantism itself was a creed which called for a return to the primitive condition of the New Testament church, which insisted on a priesthood of all believers and which denied the necessity of a mediatory, separate priesthood between God and Man. But, unfortunately for its revivalist message, Protestantism's leaders were as much caught up in the world of institutionalized religion as were the church and churchmen they attacked. The resulting tension between revivalist and institutionalized faith is most important for any discussion of professionalization: it spelt the persistence of many pre-Reformation characteristics and tendencies which might otherwise have been swept away. The established clergy saw themselves as called by God and trained by men to teach and preach the Word of God, to administer the sacraments and to offer pastoral care to God's people. They were experts in this field (O'Day, 1979, passim; O'Day, 1982, pp. 132–50).

The Crown also had stated views on the relationship between the clergy and the state. The clergy were the agents of law and order: they were the voices of the state church. The Crown preferred a clear line of separation between the professionals (the clergy) and their clients (the laity). Yet it was unwilling to permit the clergy the independence and status which many coveted. The church's ability to legislate for itself was severely restricted. Gradually Convocation's position as the church's parliament withered away. Only nominally after 1717 was Convocation the mouthpiece and talking place of the clergy and the legislative body of the church (O'Day, 1987, pp. 37–40).

These parameters were those within which the clergy of the English church had to operate down to the nineteenth century. The clergy had organs of internal government (Convocation, synods) and of internal policing and discipline (the Courts Christian) which might have been expected to guarantee 'professional' independence. But the Crown, Parliament and individual laymen held their powers severely in check. A cursory glance might have suggested that the clergy of a state church had an enviable independence and status; a closer examination gave the lie — the supposed guarantees of freedom proved to be the fetters which bound the church's clerical leaders hand and foot. Radical clergy early realized this and sought to break the bondage and increase the clergy's true independence.

The clergy's position as an independent profession was financially as well as politically weak. He who pays the piper calls the tune. And he who gives the piper work and maintains him within it possesses considerable influence. One of the fundamental difficulties which the ecclesiastical hierarchy faced stemmed from the fact that it did not pay the piper or even select who was to be paid; it was not the piper's patron and it was often forced to listen to the strains of an unwelcome tune. This unpleasant truth was forced upon the hierarchy before the nineteenth century and it had already made attempts to correct the situation.

In the nineteenth century a section of the clergy revived this earlier awareness of the urgent need for reform. Their appreciation of the parameters of their independence became more acute. But when we speak of the clergy's conscious 'professionalization', we should be quite clear in our minds that such clergy were not motivated wholly or mainly by a desire for self-determination, better working conditions and more money. Far from it: they wanted control of the profession in the interests of the role which they thought the clergy ought to be playing in a Christian society. The proper fulfilment of pastoral responsibilities was being hampered by the moribund financial structure of the church and the ancient system of patronage; by the church's ambiguous relationship with the state; and by the general reluctance of laymen to acknowledge the true importance of the clergy within the church's life.

II

Why did this revival of the 'professional' spirit occur? The Church of England was in the throes of a major crisis of identity in the early nineteenth century. The church claimed comprehensiveness yet other religious organizations were formally tolerated and accorded civil rights. The temporal privileges of the Church of England were also under siege. The church was not reaching the rapidly expanding urban, industrial populations.

Members of the Church of England reacted to this general crisis by attempting to locate afresh the source of authority in the established church. There was no uniformity of response. Broadly speaking, evangelicals sought this authority within the Scriptures; Broad Churchmen in the individual conscience which interpreted the Word of God; and High Churchmen within the church itself (Crowther, 1970, p. 19). This search inevitably led to a rethinking of the relationship between church and state. This had seemed to achieve an uneasy equilibrium at the Restoration. Nothing had changed technically since then but the balance seems to have been destroyed during the eighteenth century. Then the state church was 'more obviously' established than ever before. In particular, the influence of the state and the ruling classes over the church was greater. (Evans, 1976, p. 2). But the nineteenth-century constitutional revolution (c. 1828–38) undermined the very basis of the establishment. The clergy were made to think very hard about the nature of their position in the church.

The state was unwilling to permit a reassertion of hierarchical control in the church. When in 1832 the power to judge ecclesiastical appeals was transferred from the Court of Delegates to a Privy Council Judicial Committee, which included lay membership and had no ecclesiastical legal representation, it appeared that the hierarchy would not even be permitted to keep its own doctrinal house in order. In the 1850s and 60s the worst fears of churchmen were realized: the Judicial Committee reversed a judgement of the church courts that Gorham's Calvinist views on baptism were contrary to the church's teaching and then, in 1864, reversed the sentence passed upon the two beneficed contributors to *Essays and Reviews* by the church courts. Intervention of this kind seemed to many to be intolerable. The Old High Churchmen — once the party of church and state — sought to counter it with a revival of the ancient instruments of church policy-making and the old forums of discussion — the Convocation and the diocesan synods. More radically, the Tractarians looked for disestablishment (Crowther, 1970, pp. 18–21).

In facing the problems before them, Churchmen became deeply absorbed with the history of the church and its ministry. The Tractarians traced a continuous Catholic heritage within the church and blackened the Reformation and the Reformers themselves as unprincipled creatures of the state. They sought historical support for their position (e.g. T. Lathbury, *History of Convocation*, 1840). Others — including the Evangelicals — sprang to the defence of the Reformation and its leading lights. To do so, they studied closely the writings of the Reformers and works of Reformation history. There were 7,500 subscribers to the Parker Society's fifty-three volumes of the writings of English Reformation divines. Readers could not fail to identify with the central problems preoccupying sixteenth-century churchmen: the location of authority in the church; the role of the clergy; the role of the laity (O'Day 1986, pp. 84–101).

Specific problems related to the church's ability to serve the spiritual needs of nineteenth-century Englishmen also heightened the sense of urgency among its clergy. There were now many populous areas inadequately served by the established church and some heavily over-served rural areas. The ancient parochial boundaries no longer coincided neatly with centres of population. There was a crying need for more parishes in urban areas and for more properly qualified urban clergy. Parochial clergy were faced with the problem of 'shifting populations': formerly middle-class parishes could rapidly become predominantly working class or even slum areas; the 'improved' members of a working-class area often moved on to better things, only to leave the minister to attempt to reach their replacements with his preaching. It also seemed that the clergy were too poorly remunerated to perform their pastoral duties satisfactorily. This applied particularly to the urban clergy and to the large band of assistant curates. And there was an increasing awareness of the prevalence of certain abuses — pluralism, absenteeism, nepotism, simony — which decreased pastoral effectiveness and which seemed inextricably linked to the system of mixed patronage of ecclesiastical benefices.

But the question remains: why did the clergy agitate for a reversal of this state of affairs? The period 1805–48 was one of weak church leadership: Archbishops of Canterbury, Charles Manners Sutton (1805–28) and William Howley (1828–48) and Archbishop of York, Edward Venables Vernon (1808–47) did not assert themselves. It is probable that the changing composition of the clergy had much to do with the increased concern about these problems. In the eighteenth century non-graduate clergy had been common, especially in poor parishes and curacies. For example, only 45 of the 762 men ordained at St David's between 1750 and 1800 were degreed. Chester ordinands between 1757 and 1760 contained a majority of non-graduates and even in 1800–2 non-graduates constituted nearly half the ordinands (Walker, 1966, p. 79). Obviously, we should not be carried away by this argument — Chester and St David's both represented ecclesiastical backwaters and had always had problems recruiting well-qualified ministers: they represent the low point rather than the average. Nevertheless, it is true that the eighteenth-century universities were too small to supply the church with graduate recruits. The first three decades of the nineteenth century, however, saw an enormous rise in the numbers at Oxford and Cambridge and a commensurate rise in the number of graduate clergy. In the year 1827–8, 91 per cent of clergy ordained were graduates. In the 1830s and 40s 80 per cent of new clergy were Oxford and Cambridge men. It seems that the church was also attracting a high proportion of the most able graduates. Total numbers of clergy also rose: by 1841 the clergy were 14,000–15,000 strong. In its turn this meant a younger profession: by the 1840s young men (forty-five or under) were in the majority for the first time in many years (Haig, 1984, pp. 2–29). It is plausible that the new young graduates, conscious of their qualifications and eager for a satisfying career, were keen to see changes in the structure of the profession in their favour. The graduate recruits of the early century were not, as a rule, well born, but they tended to be able. This combination probably increased their eagerness to enhance the occupational status of the clergy. Their remoteness in many cases from the wells of patronage perhaps encouraged them to emphasize and define the pastoral role of the cleric (especially in the urban context) and dwell on the importance of the parochial clergy. It probably heightened their desire to have a status and power which were not dependent upon the laity. Newman's words must have appeared words for the times: 'therefore, my dear brethren, act up to your professions . . . "Stir up the gift of god which is in you". Make much of it . . . Keep it before your minds as an honorable badge, far higher than that secular respectability, or cultivation, or polish, or learning, or rank, which gives you a hearing with the many. Tell them of your gift . . . But wait not for the times . . . A notion has gone abroad, that they can take it away . . . Enlighten them in this matter. Exalt our Holy Fathers the Bishops, as the Representatives of the Apostles, and the Angels of the Churches; and magnify your office, as being ordained by them to take part in their Ministry' (Newman, *Tracts for the Times*, I, p. 4).

III

What did the clergy wish to do? Let us be quite clear: no single voice spoke for the Church of England's clergy on such issues. Membership of a single profession did not prevent diversity of opinions. Different groups wanted different things.

Many Churchmen had no wish to redefine the church-state relationship itself. What they wanted was to take advantage of the special relationship to make the church apparatus work more efficiently. Conservative but active High Churchmen sought the support of the government to buttress the system with grants to Queen Anne's Bounty and the Church Building Commission. Some members of the hierarchy readily co-operated in the Ecclesiastical Commission set up by the Peelite government in 1835 (inspired by Lord Henley's *Plan of Church Reform* of 1832). This began as a commission of inquiry with both lay and ecclesiastical membership and, importantly, was under the joint leadership of Robert Peel and Bishop Charles James Blomfield of London. Blomfield wrote in his *On the Uses of an Established Church* that 'the strongest of arguments for an established church is this: that it is the only, or at any rate the most efficient, instrument of instructing the people in the doctrines of religion, and of habituating them to its decencies and restraints'. The establishment ensured the maintenance of social order and stability. The Commission was initiated as a means to forestall radical attack through a programme of constructive reform. Its reports led to legislation in various areas — the re-organization of diocesan and episcopal revenues; the removal of pluralism and non-residence; the reform of Cathedral Chapters; the correction of abuses such as nepotism, simony and sinecures. Some historians have seen this type of ecclesiastical reform by commission as evidence of Benthamite administrative centralization (Brose, 1959). But, if these churchmen spoke of efficiency and utility, they were not yet willing to sacrifice the traditional relationships between church and state and church and aristocracy in its interests. The system of patronage and church finance (the root cause of so many perceived abuses) was to remain inviolate. There was to be no root and branch reform. And some churchmen who favoured the church-state relationship nevertheless opposed centralization even of the kind represented by the Commission, because it denied the principles of localism, voluntarism and sacred property rights.

The Oxford Movement involved a more radical re-thinking of the position. An established church is unused to legitimating its form of organization by reference to theological principles: instead it appeals to tradition or to social utility. Once the establishment is questioned and the Church of England is conceived of as a sect among sects, there is a need to discover the source of authority in order to establish the church's autonomous identity. Newman's first tract — *Thoughts on the Ministerial Commission* — asked the crucial question, 'On what are we to rest our authority when the state deserts us?' His answer came loud and clear: 'Our apostolic descent . . . apostolic succession'. This radical reassessment of the church's position *vis-à-vis* the state in the long run would allow the Church of England to adapt to its changing position in society, but, in the short term, it meant that members of the Oxford Movement were unable to contribute to the immediate plans for piecemeal reform and it intensified internal strife. There was also division in the Movement itself. The older leaders gravitated towards conservatism. Some members — most notably Newman —

left the Church of England. Eventually the *Lux Mundi* group of the 1880s became involved in the instrumental reform of the Church of England. Others continued to demand much more radical change derived from their perception of the church as an autonomous institution. Such change would imply less circumscribed clerical control of the church's affairs (Thompson, 1970, pp. 36, 47).

The work of the Commission gave churchmen of all persuasions cause to realize the inadequacy of their representation in church government. Although there were bishops present on the Commission from the beginning, they felt lacking in *ex officio* influence: 'Till Blomfield comes, we all sit and mend our pens, and talk about the weather' said the Archbishop of York. And there were constant complaints that the Commission was really under the control of a permanent secretariat led by secretary Charles Knight Murray, a lawyer. Its decisions seemed out of tune with much clerical opinion: for example, the support of the lower clergy was lost by Peel's decision in 1843 to use the Common fund to endow *new* churches rather than to augment old. And, despite its bureaucracy (or perhaps because of it), it seemed inefficient. Worst of all, the Commission served two masters — Parliament and the church — and of these the church seemed to have no representative voice.

Clerical reactions varied. In general, the lower clergy appear to have favoured a return to localism. Certain of the bishops — most notably Samuel Wilberforce — advocated strengthening the diocesan machinery of church government. Others urged the revival of the church's own parliament, Convocation, which had been dormant since 1717. This proposal initially had the support of both Evangelicals and High Churchmen. Evangelical support dropped away when it was appreciated that what was being urged was a self-governing church, separated legislatively from the state and dominated by clergy and episcopate. In 1852 the militant Evangelical paper *The Record* declared that synods were 'but great machines for enforcing unity by expelling all opinions but one'. For Convocation was the mouthpiece of the clerical members of the church and not the lay. In theory, Parliament was the talking place of the lay membership of the comprehensive church. But, should churchmen succeed in excluding the parliamentary voice from the government of the church, the balance between clerical and lay influence in the church's affairs would be destroyed and clericalism would reign supreme. Lord Shaftesbury in 1852 argued that Convocation spelt priestly despotism. This feeling led some — Blomfield and Archbishop Whately, for example — at least briefly to recommend not the revival of Convocation but the creation of a mixed lay-clerical assembly. Opinion on the issue of representation was not divided according to strict party lines. Pusey, for instance, argued for representation of the laity and clergy upon a central Church Council that would be able to pressure the bench of bishops. Blomfield eventually changed his mind to support the revival of Convocation because of the evident opposition to a mixed clerical-lay assembly by both ritualists and Evangelicals.

Convocation was revived in 1852. And during the 1850s purely clerical diocesan synods were re-introduced (beginning with that of Exeter by Bishop Phillpotts in 1851). By 1881 only three dioceses — London, Llandaff and Worcester — had no such synod.

These developments were seen to form a movement to assert clerical control of church government and clerical affairs. They were generally welcomed by High Churchmen. But in the latter half of the century there were still many among the clergy and laity who saw exclusively clerical representation as undesirable and who could not see a clear line dividing clerical 'professional' concerns from those of the church as a whole.

> This is the great defect in the constitution of our Convocation; it represents the conscience and will, and expresses the voice, of the clergy, not of the Church. This was suited to its original function of imposing taxes on the clergy, but unfits it for being the legislative council of the whole church.
>
> (Archdeacon Hare, Charge, 1841, quoted in Rigg, 1897, p. 96)

Henry Hoare's ideas (expressed in his *Hints on Lay Co-operation* of 1850) continued to influence opinion. In 1859 the Church Institution ('An Association of Clergy and Laity for Defensive and General Purposes') was begun. In Ely diocese in 1864 Archdeacon Emery organized a system of ruridecanal, archidiaconal and diocesan conferences with both clerical and lay membership, which met with much more widespread support than the High Church's synods. Church congresses began in 1861. These attracted clergy and laity of all 'parties' in a defence of the Church of England against external attack. They were purposely held in a different urban centre on each occasion and, in their concentration upon practical matters, they seemed set to promote harmony instead of friction. There were considerable problems in developing any of these bodies as governing bodies of the church, however. For instance, the Church Congresses and Church Institution both lacked authority because they had no formal system of representation and no legal status within the church and state. The clergy's position as a distinct profession would have been strengthened had there been an organization for professional regulation and a separate organization for the government of the church comprising lay and clerical representation. In fact, the hierarchy was placed in the awkward position of trying somehow to reconcile the exclusive professional spirit among the clergy with the need to enlist the support and co-operation of lower clergy and middle-class laity in the government of the church. Moreover, they had to accomplish this on the basis of an inadequate traditional structure.

Government of the church by bodies representative of both clergy and laity would, by its nature, restrict the control which the profession itself might exert over recruitment, training, discipline, the nature of its services and internal standards. Professional interests might be seen by the laity and some clergy to be in direct conflict with the interests of the whole church. Certainly many of the parish clergy were unwilling to press professional claims too far. This placed ecclesiastics in a quandary. Even the Archbishops disagreed as to the best means of governing the church and her affairs. Archbishop Tait of Canterbury (1868–83) believed that the laity were best represented in Parliament but retarded the centralization of ecclesiastical representation and government. His successor, Archbishop Benson (1883–96), supported the growth of a centralized organization but wanted lay representation. This made it difficult to provide consistency and continuity in leadership.

The views of the hierarchy traditionally had differed from those of the lower clergy, many of whom found the oligarchic nature of church government intolerable, even when they wished to retain control of the church in the hands of the clergy. There was a move to provide greater representation of the parochial clergy in Convocation to balance the large number of *ex officio* members and, also, to set up a House of Laymen. In 1885 the clergy of the Lower House agreed to create a House of Laymen. Certain safeguards were provided: the laity were forbidden to discuss faith and doctrine. In February 1886 Archbishop Benson opened the first session of the Canterbury House of Laymen. In 1892 the first assembly of the York House of Laymen occurred. Then in 1898 provision was made for the voluntary joint meeting of the Canterbury and York Houses of Laymen. The Houses of Laymen had no legislative powers. In 1903 a deliberative body of the two Houses of Convocation and the Houses of Laymen sitting in joint session — as the Representative Church Council or RCC — was formed. The RCC recommended a Commission on church and state relations in 1913. This Commission in its turn suggested the creation of a Church Assembly, which was duly constituted in 1919.

In retaining the relationship between state and church the hierarchy made it impossible to assert clerical control. The church also continued to claim that it was the church for all Englishmen; in an age when Englishmen expected representation in civil life, representation was demanded also in religion. The laity had, of course, always participated in Anglican religious life both in an institutional and a spiritual sense but the nineteenth century saw intensified articulation of their desires, perhaps in reaction to revived clericalism. It is a moot point whether the laity would have been quite so successful had the hierarchy more readily given adequate representation to the lower clergy. This error of judgement provided the laity with an ally. The exclusive professional spirit among the clergy, if it had not been defeated, had at least been dampened and rendered ineffective by the outbreak of the First World War. Convocation — which was the nearest equivalent to a professional association of the whole clergy — was not allowed to become the sole governing body of the church.

IV

It is against this background of uncertain control over its own destiny that a more detailed treatment of the clergy's professional organization must be set. Most church historians have failed to make this link, preferring to concentrate upon the efforts of the hierarchy to improve recruitment, training and discipline within a framework of party faction. But the nineteenth century saw the revival of the issue of the location of sovereignty in the Church of England and the clericalists did not emerge the victors. Ironically, the control of the profession over its own affairs rose in inverse proportion to the declining interest of the state and the laity as a body in the church itself. A reverse development has occurred in the twentieth-century medical profession — as medicine has grown in importance in the popular mind and as a concern of the state, so lay attempts to influence medical organization and the practice of medicine have also increased.

The clergy revived their earlier occupational professionalism against this background of an uneasy lay-clerical partnership in church affairs. This revival almost inevitably led to further conflict with the laity: it was the existence of private lay patronage in the church which many clergy and laity saw as the root cause of abuses; as a consequence, reforming efforts were concentrated upon this system. As the clergy laid claim to exclusive expertise in given areas, the conflict with the laity was deepened.

The argument over the continuance of private patronage as the chief means of recruiting and placing clergymen exemplifies this tension. For some, private patronage seemed iniquitous; clergymen were given preferment in return for obedience. The clergy were the lapdogs of the aristocracy. Private patronage was seen as a form of simony because it involved a 'trade' in souls. For its defenders, however, it guaranteed a church in which lay opinion was effectively represented and in which clericalism was prevented. A mixed system of patronage safeguarded religious liberty and doctrinal diversity. There was, therefore, ample potential for conflict but there were limits to this potential. Within an established church as committed to a relatively high doctrine of the ministerial order as was the Church of England, laymen, patrons or not, were hard put to deny the clergyman's specific expertise or the necessity for his services within the Commonwealth. Those who energetically denied such tenets were forced into formal dissent. Anticlericalism was possible only within given limits *within* the Church of England.

The patronage system had certainly given rise to abuse — nepotism, simony, forced resignations, pluralism and non-residence were probably its best-known manifestations. Undoubtedly the exercise of private patronage met with renewed and considerable criticism in the Victorian age. But there is a distinction to be drawn between criticism directed at the abuse of the system and that aimed at the system itself. Much of the characteristic legislation of the century struck at the abuse. For example, the Clergy Resignations Bonds Act of 1828 ordered the registration of such bonds. The Solicitor General, in introducing the legislation, stated that its purpose was to 'enable the holders [the patrons] of benefices whether lay or clerical, to provide for their families as they are enabled to do with any other species of property' (Best, 1964, p. 59). Such bonds were not abolished until the Clerical Subscription Act of 1865. In 1870 a bill sponsored to make illegal the sale of presentations floundered in the Lords because it too blatantly infringed private property rights. Bishop Magee's bill of 1875 sought to curb 'trafficking' in patronage. It passed the Lords but had roused such opposition in the country that it was withdrawn before debate in the House of Commons. Even the important late Victorian legislation — the Benefices Act of 1898 — did not abolish private patronage.

Abolition of private patronage was neither achieved nor sought after. But there do seem to have been two striking changes in the attitude towards its exercise. Firstly, the bishops (as a matter of policy) more than doubled the number of presentations in their gift in the mid-century, so that by 1901 episcopal patronage accounted for twenty-two per cent of the whole. Samuel Wilberforce was a pioneer in this respect when, as Bishop of Oxford, he sought to raise clerical standards in his diocese (1845–69). Secondly, patron-incumbents, independent of lay pressure, became more common. A third of the advowsons sold by the Lord Chancellor between 1863 and 1872 were purchased by clergy. By 1878 one ninth of privately owned patronage was in the hands of patron-incumbents. The clergy appear to have preferred to purchase rural advowsons: this implies the rise of a substantial group of clergy independent of the squirearchy in the agricultural counties stretching from Lincolnshire and East Anglia to Devon. Probably the late Victorian clergy of rural England were far less beholden to the squirearchy than had been their Georgian predecessors (Roberts, 1983, pp. 204–8).

The clergy had conflicting views about the value of private patronage. The reforming bishops bought up advowsons and presentations so that they could exercise greater control over recruitment and placement. The patron-incumbent had the practical problems of securing a livelihood. This said, the patron-incumbent saw his exercise of patronage as a way of asserting professional independence against all-comers — bishops or laymen — and of protecting his relationship with his clients — individuals in the congregation.

It is all too easy to see the issue of private patronage simply as a battlefield upon which the age-old war between clergy and laity was fought, without considering why the clergy wanted to fight in the first instance. Many contemporaries were convinced that private patronage undermined the attempt of experts to offer appropriate pastoral care to the people. Evidence for this was sought in the recent past: clergy were too ill-paid to perform their pastoral duties well; clergy were poorly qualified; clergy were dependent; clergy were negligent. The historian today is left with the unenviable task of determining whether the evidence which nineteenth-century clergymen gleaned to support this case was both accurate and representative. The history of the eighteenth-century church, especially at diocesan level, is as yet relatively unfathomed. Sufficient has been accomplished, however, to suggest that nineteenth-century commentators unsurprisingly selected the worst aspects of the eighteenth-century ministry for discussion and that they gave the impression that their predecessors were being negligent when it was frequently the case rather that they had a different perception of the duties of a parochial priest.

Churchmen, both lay and clerical, were aware of the relationship between a clergyman's income and his pastoral performance. The question was whether the Church of England, a medieval institution, archaic and ramshackle, was able to guarantee a clergy well enough paid, educated and disciplined to fulfil the responsibilities of a pastor. The pastor's relationship with his flock was deepened by time. The rector or vicar had effective tenure (the parson's freehold). Except in times of extreme crisis, deprivations were rare. Even temporal suspensions were relatively uncommon. The parson was thereby enabled to put down roots in his parish which were 'deep and widespread', offering pastoral care based upon personal knowledge of parishioners and their circumstances. And clergymen, in practice as well as in theory, tended to be relatively immobile. But continuity of service was apparently in direct relation to the wealth or poverty of the living concerned: it was the poor who looked for further preferment. Poverty made the clergy unsettled, detracted from their performance and led to the twin evils of pluralism and non-residence. It was generally accepted also that a well-qualified, preaching ministry would be attracted only to well-endowed livings. Moreover, by the eighteenth century it was felt that only an appropriate income would guarantee the gentility in the clergy necessary if they were to have effective social and moral authority over their congregations (Pruett, 1978, pp. 74–5; Virgin, 1979, pp. 67–90).

Were the clergy financed in such a way as to offer appropriate pastoral care? The long-term trend in post-Restoration clerical incomes was clearly upwards. There were phenomenal improvements in the economic position of the clergy in Georgian times. The poorest clergy in particular benefited. Even after taking general inflation and higher taxation into account, an overall rise of 200% in the real incomes of the clergy between 1700 and 1830 seems plausible. But the median income in 1830 (of £275 for an English parochial clergyman and £172 for a cleric in Wales) was still considered deficient: the desirable minimum was said to be £400. In other words, contemporaries thought that the beneficed clergy needed upper middle-class incomes in order to do their work properly. Only a quarter of the clergy were thus comfortably financed in 1830 (in receipt of £500 per annum). The remainder were not, although most were still better off than a great majority of their parishioners (a typical lower-middle-class income range was £60 to £200 per annum). A tenth of late Georgian beneficed clergymen received less than £100 per annum (Virgin, 1979, pp. 87, 90).

Did this improvement lead Georgian clergy to do a better job? The clergy of the eighteenth century are, in the popular and academic mind, associated not with high standards of pastoral care, education and discipline but with the leisured life-style of a neo-gentry and a casual if not always negligent performance of pastoral duties. A quarter of the clergy were financially equipped to live as pseudo-gentry. Extraordinary sources of income, be they inherited or earned, meant that others joined this group. Clerical social status rose sharply between 1700 and 1840.

But to keep this in perspective is important: only about a fifth of the clergy active in the 1830s had links with either gentry or peerage; if they had another source of income it was generally not inherited wealth; and very few clergy farmed any land other than their glebe. Much more commonly, clergymen were deriving an income from occupations which had a traditional association with the church — teaching and occasionally medicine. The great majority of clergymen were neither wealthy nor occupied in work other than their pastoral duties (Virgin 1979, pp. 92, 97, 98).

Were eighteenth-century parishes poorly served? The answer seems to be that they were *differently* served than nineteenth-century clergymen would have wished. The picture varies from diocese to diocese and parish to parish but a study of Exeter diocese in Georgian times indicates an overwhelmingly graduate beneficed clergy adequate in number to serve the population. Nothing suggests that here was a parish clergy growing rich at the expense of pastoral care. It is clear that the canons of the church were widely disregarded with respect to the services. Weekday and Holyday services were largely neglected. By 1779 there was no mention of them in the Exeter Visitation Articles. By 1821 it was accepted that the normal practice was of one service with a sermon on a Sunday, except in the larger urban Devonshire parishes. Holy Communion was celebrated infrequently.

Catechizing often took place in Lent alone. But it is far from clear that such practices marked a sharp decline from the standards of the post-Reformation period (Warne, 1969, p. 44).

Nineteenth-century criticisms of pastoral care tell us more about the changing expectations of the critics than they do about the actual performance of the clergy criticized. The clergy performed their canonical duties in a manner which was generally acceptable to the church's lay membership before the Victorian period. Wesley's 'Holy Club' (1729–35) at Oxford found this performance as deplorable as did the later Oxford Movement. But we should be careful to avoid accepting their criticisms as the 'truth' — they represented an 'opinion' about what were good standards of pastoral care, about what a clergyman's duties were. We are on safer ground if we examine the actual ministry of given individuals for evidence of conscientiousness, compassion and caring. John Skinner (b. 1772), Rector of Camerton in Somerset, offers an admirable example of a cleric who shared gentle and academic interests and occupations and yet was absorbed in parochial concerns and felt a deep responsibility for his congregation. His unattractive personality should not detract from his real merits as a pastor (Skinner, 1984, *passim*).

V

What we are seeing in the Victorian period is *not* the emergence of a new profession, modelled on the contemporary secular professions, but rather a conscious revival of the occupational professionalism of the early modern period and an urge to organize and systematize this professionalism. This self-conscious 'professionalization' was made manifest in many ways: attempts to correct the abuses connected with private patronage and to circumvent as far as possible restrictions upon the independence of the clergy; to define the role and responsibilities of the clergy and to make clear to the laity why this role was important; to design and implement a curriculum for the education and training of ministerial recruits in accordance with this ideal; to make parish clergy aware of their role and to supply them with the necessary materials to equip themselves for the task; to recruit suitable candidates; to supply the parishes adequately and to ensure that populous places were well served with churches and missions; to make special provision for identifiable groups, e.g. the young, the mothers, the poor, the sick, the armed forces and their families, and the criminal.

In this desire to organize and systematize, to define an area of expertise and a field of work, it is easy to stress the way in which the Victorian clergy fit the 'professionalization' model. More probable is that the newer professions modelled themselves upon the existing learned professions. If we examine contemporary literature carefully we can see that Anglican clergymen owed as much if not more to an earlier tradition of professionalization, into which the barristers also fitted. There was little that was distinctively 'Victorian' about their response to the Victorian crisis. Both the clerical and the legal professions were committed to the idea that they professed a vocation. The clergy were called by God to perform a specific service to the commonwealth. This service was given freely and those who were the professional's clients and who presumably benefited from this service were not charged but, out of gratitude, offered a fee. (In the case of the clergy, the 'fee' was offered to God in the form of tithe, Easter offering, oblations. But clergymen, if they were to serve, had to live and benefices were endowed to support them. As time went on, fees, tithes and oblations began to look suspiciously like payment demanded for services rendered, but this alters neither their origin nor their justification.) Many Victorian clergy were insistent that the clergy did not resemble the modern professions in one key respect: clergy did not practise in order to advance themselves on a career ladder or to accumulate a nest-egg — they practised in order to fulfil a vocation to serve God by bringing individuals to Him. Incomes and conditions of service were important only in so far as they were enabling or disabling in this context.

In seeking to identify the cleric's proper role the Victorian clergy, like their forebears, looked not to contemporary models but to the Scriptures, to tradition and to extant writings on the doctrines of the ministerial order. (I think, for example, of Charles Gore's *The Church and the Ministry*; J. H. Newman's first Tract; Lathbury's *Convocation*.) Distinct approaches to the clergyman's role were apparent. Firstly, there was the Evangelical approach. Evangelicals were pietistic in emphasis. Broadly speaking, they saw the clergyman as the 'ambassador' of Christ, the mouthpiece of God, urged repentance, preached the word. There was less emphasis upon ministry to an established congregation. The Creed, the Church, the Communion were subordinated to the Cross. Secondly, the Oxford Movement had its own distinctive approach. This was moralistic, as it sought to show the people how they might achieve holiness. As such, the Movement was a continuation of a line in the English Church which ran through Lancelot Andrewes and William Laud and the younger John Wesley. Within this scheme, the clergyman had a key role. It was he who was charged not only with winning souls for God but also with showing these souls the way to holiness, via the Sacraments, the Creed, the Liturgy. Within each tradition there co-existed various positions on the nature of the minister's call — whether it came directly from God or through the agency of men. It is helpful to envisage thinking about the minister's role as ranged upon a chain strung between these two extreme emphases upon prophet and priest — not only Anglican but also Nonconformist and Catholic doctrines of the ministerial order. Within the Church of England there was an attempt to 'comprehend' the whole continuum. Clement F. Rogers, Lecturer in Pastoral Theology at King's College, London from 1908, was amongst those who strove to achieve balance in the perception of the minister's role: 'they unite in themselves the function of prophet and priest, though, as individuals, in different proportions'. Having said this, Rogers was clear that the emphasis in a settled church must be upon the minister's priestly function: 'in an organized and established Church, the administration of the Sacraments, the office of a priest comes first. The ideas are distinct; the agents, and to a great extent the methods, are one' (Rogers, 1912, pp. 69–70). A useful comparison can be drawn between the emphasis which Rogers lays upon the minister's priestly function and that which the Primitive Methodist W. Jones Davies placed upon the preaching of the minister in his book *The Minister at Work* (1910). Like Rogers, Jones Davies sees pastoral work as complementary to preaching and essential to the work of the minister but, unlike Rogers, he spends only 45 out of 299 pages discussing the administration of the sacraments and pastoral visitation and 156 pages discussing preaching responsibilities and technique.

If a clergyman was to fulfil his pastoral charge he had need of expertise. This was fully appreciated by the early modern church: the church's inadequate control over the curriculum offered at the universities was a source of frustration among the church's leaders. Recent work has suggested that it was in the Victorian period that the need for a specific body of theoretical and practical expertise was both appreciated and answered (Russell, 1980, passim). The growth of theological colleges, the introduction of a competitive examination system, the emphasis upon curriculum, the burgeoning of clerical associations (both official and informal), and the plethora of handbooks, journals and directories certainly suggest that the Victorian clergy were aware of their corporate identity and of their need to legitimate their professional role through possession of a common expertise. In the introduction to the account of the proceedings of the Alcester clerical meeting (1842–60) Richard Seymour underlined 'the importance of cherishing a proper professional feeling among the clergy. Other learned professions have their own opportunities for conference, have their own informal tribunals which determine the conduct and behaviour of their members. None stand so much aloof from one another as the clergy; though none perhaps needs, so much as they, the support of counsel and example in the details of their common work . . .' (Russell, 1980, p. 43). The common identity which these informal gatherings cemented was also reflected in and strengthened by the regular appearance of periodicals. (Examples were *The Ecclesiastical Gazette* (1839), the *Clerical Journal* (1853) and directories such as *The Clerical Guide* (1817), *The Clergy List* (1841) and *The Clerical Directory* (1853).) The preface to an annual directory such as

Crockford's, which succeeded *The Clerical Directory*, did much to enhance *esprit de corps* and to inform clergy of professional and church affairs.

It is precipitate, however, to claim that the Victorian clergy did much more than to revive their sense of common purpose and to appreciate the problems before them. Richard Seymour went on to add:

> Unprepared in general by distinct training for their office, stimulated by no hope of temporal regard to gain thorough mastery of all that belongs to their calling, the clergy are tempted to consider a decent performance of needful pastoral administration the beginning and end of their work.
>
> (Russell, 1980, p. 44)

What he and others looked for was a revival of the clerical associations of post-Reformation England which had lingered in the form of the Evangelical Clerical Societies of the eighteenth century. It was the intensification of an old movement. And, as with so many movements, by no means all clergy belonged to it or subscribed to its ideals.

There is every indication that a body of expertise for the parochial minister was not developed until the last years of the nineteenth century and that it was not systematically communicated to new clergymen until after the First World War. In his interesting study of the lower clergy, Alan Haig shows that the theological colleges were concerned primarily to provide ordinands with a general education and a knowledge of the Bible. Pastoral theology was not in evidence. The 'discipline' and 'system' which the Rev. S. Best called for in 1839 were not forthcoming until the twentieth century. If some clergymen longed to mimic the secular professions they did not find the means so to do. Although many theological colleges were founded in the Victorian era, it was not until after World War I that all ordinands (including graduates of Oxford and Cambridge) compulsorily undertook a preliminary training year in a residential theological college. Professional control over the colleges was also uncertain. It was not until the 1860s that even diocesan control became the norm. (Haig, 1984, pp. 147–54) When Rogers wrote his new *Pastoral Theology* in 1912, he bewailed the fact that the handbooks and guides for ministers were singularly contentless: they did not begin to specify 'what exactly is the work of an English Clergyman?' Herbert, Baxter, Burnet, the ordination addresses of the bishops, the handbooks for clergymen published in 1807 under the title *The Clergyman's Instructor*, even the modern manuals of the nineteenth century — all emphasized the importance of preaching, defined the role of the priest as either 'a moral policeman' or 'professional good man who is not to be too different from a layman', but neglected systematic, specific approaches. No-one since Richard Hooker had produced a detailed work of pastoral theology. Nineteenth-century handbooks assumed that the clergyman knew what his job was and provided him with a collection of suitable prayers, hymns and consolations to assist him in doing it. .There was no attempt to explore and define the pastoral role. Rogers set out to correct this deficiency by a 'scientific study' of the subject. Rogers' rigorous study of what precisely the clergyman was 'to do' in his pastoral capacity was matched by other twentieth-century works. Charles R. Forder's *The Parish Priest at Work: An Introduction to Systematic Pastoralia* of 1947 presents an exaggerated example of the systematic manual — he shows the priest how to organize his study and his parish with a vengeance.

VI

The clergy of the Church of England developed their ideas within the context of establishment. The other ministries did not have to contend with the added complexities of establishment as they sought to define their role and respond to the crisis in religion but they may have had more in common with the Anglican clergy than meets the eye. When Newman looked at the position of the Dissenters this is what he saw:

> We know how miserable is the state of religious bodies not supported by the State. Look at the Dissenters on all sides of you, and you will see at once that their Ministers, depending simply upon the people, become the creatures of the people. Are you content that this should be your case? Alas! can a greater evil befall Christians, than for their teachers to be guided by them instead of guiding? How can we 'hold fast the form of sound words' and 'keep that which is committed to our trust' if our influence is to depend simply on our popularity?

If Newman thought that the ministries of Protestant Nonconformity had to be popular to survive, they were certainly having their problems. Anglicans, like the BBC, in theory had to worry less about losing constituency than did the other churches. This did not prevent them worrying. The prospect of losing lay membership through clericalism and unaccustomed opposition to lay property rights in the church was not pleasant at a time when 'competition for souls' was rife. Disestablishment sometimes seemed just around the corner. Thoughts such as these effectively reined in much extreme professional feeling among the Anglicans. Nonconformists felt the problem yet more keenly. There was, for example, the conflict within English Methodism over the nature of church government and its ministry which produced secession after secession. Fear of exacerbating this conflict and adding to the flood of lost members deterred the Methodist Conference from introducing specialist ministerial education before 1834, despite a conviction on the part of many ministers that it was necessary.

(i) Methodism

Methodism provides an excellent example of a Christian society which was originally evangelical and revivalist and possessed of no need for a settled ministry. During the late eighteenth and nineteenth centuries this position changed and it was because of this change that a certain movement for the 'professionalization' of the ministry occurred. The early Methodist leaders regarded themselves as members of the Church of England who were expected to attend services. Controversy regarding both the relationship of Methodism to the established church and the structure of the Christian ministry was provoked early by members of the Methodist societies. As early as the 1730s Wesley found it necessary to allow lay preachers, who were quickly organized into 'a kind of supplementary ministry' (George, 1978, p. 144) based upon circuits regulated by an annual Conference. The preachers were divided into itinerant and local preachers. A lay preacher would begin with a period 'on trial' and then eventually be taken into 'full connexion'. Wesley, despite his enthusiastic use of these lay preachers, remained very firmly of the opinion that they were laymen who could not administer the Lord's Supper. But the Methodists wanted their own ministers. Wesley resisted pressure to ordain ministers, preferring to recommend Methodist ordinands to Anglican bishops. But in the 1770s the American Methodists were 'ordaining' ministers of their own. Wesley sought to persuade the Bishop of London to ordain men for America. When Bishop Lowth refused, Wesley and two other Anglican priests 'ordained' two men specifically for America and made Coke Superintendent. In subsequent years Wesley ordained a number of men both for Scotland and England.

After Wesley's death there was confusion. Should men continue to be 'ordained'? Was a minister 'in full connexion' allowed to administer the sacrament or was this the exclusive right of the ordained minister? In 1792 Conference forbade ordinations without its consent. In 1793 it dropped the distinction between ordained and unordained, ignoring attempts by Coke and Mather to preserve the succession. In 1795 the Plan of Pacification laid it down that the Lord's Supper might be administered by persons authorized by the Conference — that is, by itinerant preachers in full connexion. *De facto* the preachers had become ministers of established Christian congregations. The idea took root that they were 'virtually' ordained by reception into the full connexion. The ceremony of reception was made more impressive. In 1836 the Wesleyan Conference debated the question of ordination and passed a motion that preachers who were to be received into full connexion should be ordained by the imposition of hands. Later the two ceremonies were distinguished, but ordination closely followed upon the heels of reception (George, 1978, p. 154). When Wesley first decided to allow lay preachers and to ordain ministers himself, the breach between Methodism and the established church was widened and deepened. While ordination separated the ministry from the laity, many Methodists came to appreciate that it was not solely the laying on of hands which had this effect. The definition of a distinct pastoral office within an ecclesiastical structure could itself be divisive.

'... the religious potential of Wesleyan Methodism was greatly reduced by internal dissension about the nature of the church and by actual secession' (Kent, 1978, p. 213) and a great part of that dissension focussed upon the conflict between the ministry and the laity. During the crisis of 1795–7 constitutional limits were placed upon the power of the ministry and the laity were assured a role in the government of Connexion. But, as time went on, a variety of interpretations were put upon this 'constitution'. These ranged from the Reformers' view that the ministry had concurred in the grant of co-pastoral status to the laity, to a more moderate view that the constitution protected the laity against irresponsible government, to the view of Jabez Bunting that 'an inherent, divinely ordained ministerial authority could not be overridden by an appeal to Conference legislation or to Congregationalist theories of the relationship between the laity and the ministry' (Kent, 1978, pp. 214–5). The theologian Richard Watson agreed that the last word in disciplinary matters rested with the ministry and the legislative power rested with the ministry assembled in the annual conference. In truth, Wesleyan Methodist opinion on the desirable organization for the church and the place of the ministry within it ran the gamut from independency to presbytery.

Within Methodism we can see a prominent section of the ministers becoming professionally aware and seeking to develop a role and an expertise in performing that role which 'separated' them from the laity. Once this was formally apparent, fierce opposition among the laity was engendered. In writing about the Evangelical Revival, John Kent has observed that its tradition of irrationalism nurtured a demand for revivalist preachers — in sharp contradistinction to the institutionalized ministry for which Methodists such as Bunting saw a need. 'The eighteenth century conflict between professional, academically trained Anglican priests and untrained, though not necessarily uneducated but certainly unordained, Wesleyan itinerants was repeated within Wesleyanism itself in the nineteenth century in the form of a conflict between the Wesleyan ministry ... and the lay or local preacher' (Kent, 1978, p. 246). The lay preachers, thrust into a position of inferiority, often expressed themselves with great bitterness. Secession after secession within Methodism was sparked at least in part by fundamental disagreement concerning the place of the ministry in God's church and its distinctness from lay membership (Wilkinson, 1978, *passim*).

In all this there is no suggestion that the Methodists used as their reference point the nineteenth-century professions. Issues of faith, of salvation, affected the position taken by any religious denomination on the nature of the clerical profession. The core questions absorbing Methodists related to the specific vocation of the minister — was it or was it not distinct from that of the people? If so, how was this difference to be made manifest in the life of the church? The position of the lay preacher within the scheme of things became crucial. There was nothing specifically 'Victorian' about these questions. They represented a continuation of the earlier Methodist discontent with the Anglican resolution of such problems. Like the Anglicans, the Methodists were seeking to define what the 'profession' of the ministry was. In so doing, the Methodists were also trying to decide whether this 'profession' needed to be sharply differentiated from the laity and institutionalized. Upon this decision rested the need for certain types of organization — specific training, recruitment procedures, and so forth. Because there was a substantial number of full-time Methodist ministers by mid-century (some 2,000 by 1851), there was a large group of people with a keen and vested interest in the outcome of this debate.

In large part it was the changing context of Wesleyan Methodism which shaped the professionalization of its ministers. A need was perceived for a settled, pastoral ministry to serve a Methodist congregation. This ministry had to be well trained and able to cope with the problems of an increasingly well-educated and questioning congregation, familiar with, for example, the controversies surrounding the theory of evolution or the composition of the Old Testament. But this training had to be (and was) accommodated within the framework of the Wesleyan tradition. When the Theological Institution was created in 1834 for the education and training of Wesleyan ministers it was placed under the control of the Conference and safeguards were provided to ensure that every candidate for the ministry still provided ample evidence of conversion and calling. Some of the more forward tutors complained that the Institution did not prepare ministers to deal with contemporary issues — such as Darwinism or the new Biblical Criticism — concentrating instead on the issues which had preoccupied eighteenth-century Methodism. The Institution was accorded an essentially passive role — it trained the labourers which Christ had chosen to work in the vineyards. During the course of the century some of the teachers in the Institution would have liked a more active role — in recruitment and preparation for the work ahead — but they were not to achieve it. It was not until after the First World War that the theological curriculum was updated and the emphasis upon preaching was balanced by a new concentration on the pastoral duties of the minister. K. D. Brown argues that the principals of the Methodist colleges themselves lacked the theological learning and the experience of pastoral work necessary to cultivate these areas of expertise (Johnson, 1982, pp. 307–8, 317–8; Brown, 1984, pp. 100–1).

The crisis which occurred within the Primitive Methodist Connexion closely paralleled at a later date that which had occurred within Wesleyan Methodism. 'In both Connexions, as they reached a certain stage of development, expansion gave way to consolidation, and Connexional and ministerial interests became increasingly dominant over those which were local and lay. These processes generated a vigorous debate . . . and in both Connexions the debate centred round the ministry, since ministers were in many ways the focal points of the changes. Their role, their status, their influence, their relations with the laity, their intellectual requirements, their conditions of work, their salaries — all were developing in ways which some saw as a threat to old-style Methodist practices, and others as a proper and necessary response to changing cirumstances' (Milburn, 1981, p. 4).

Primitive Methodists were concerned not only that an emphasis on formal education for the ministry would lead to a substitution of humane learning for a direct call from God as the only necessary qualification for the ministry but also that it would mean a loss of the 'common touch'. But by the 1860s some members of the Primitive Methodist Connexion were arguing that the ministers had to be in command of the contemporary learning with which an ever-increasing number of working people were now acquainted. Conversionist preaching was not now sufficient; second generation Primitive Methodists looked to their ministers for intellectual stimulus and pastoral care — the same old sermons lost their charm. Changes in the organization of Primitive Methodism also meant that ministers had a more permanent, personal relationship with an individual congregation, which might bear fruit if the minister were properly prepared for the task. The question was how to educate and train the ministry while holding fast on to what was good — the evangelical fervour of the Connexion and the mission to Christianize and improve the working classes. Such preoccupations led to the development in the 1860s of Ministerial Associations and of tutorial schemes for Probationers. Then in 1868 the first college for the training of men for the Primitive Methodist Ministry was founded in Sunderland. It was followed in the 1870s by the Manchester Theological Institute.

(ii) *Catholicism*

Unlike the Methodists, there had always been a definite place for a settled ministry within Roman Catholicism. It was the anomalous position of Roman Catholicism within English and Welsh society and polity which shaped the development of the profession. As with the Methodists, earlier traditions influenced the development of the Catholic Clergy within English

Catholicism. There was a strong native Catholic tradition which often conflicted with Romanism. But English Catholicism changed as a result of an infusion of foreign blood: French refugees after the Revolution; monks, nuns, priests and seminary students from France and the Low Countries; and an influx of Irish Catholics. Monasticism was revived. There were more priests. Religious worship was less austere. An open enthusiasm for the Virgin Mary appeared. The English Vicars Apostolic began to work for the introduction of a normally constituted English hierarchy of bishops. This was achieved in 1850. For the remainder of the century the Catholic hierarchy worked to improve the numbers of trained priests. The number of Catholics had risen from 250,000 in 1829 to 1,300,000 in 1900 and the demand for a ministry to a new rural and urban proletariat (instead of the traditional gentry congregation) was particularly urgent. The chief problems to be resolved were whether seminaries should be centrally directed and organized or a matter for diocesan initiative; whether there should be native English seminaries; whether the clerical recruits should be kept separate from secular learning, experience and associates. From mid-century onwards there were attempts to Romanize the clergy. As Archbishop of Westminster, Manning, in response to papal directives, insisted on the use of Roman vestments, Roman dressing of the altar, the Italian pronunciation of Latin, the use of the Roman collar, the employment of the term 'Father' to address secular priests, the creation of seminaries according to Tridentine rules. Peter Doyle has demonstrated that clerical recruits were educated in quasimonastic institutions which were modelled on the seminary at Douai. 'The suitability of such a training for men who were not to live their priestly lives in community, with all the support which that offered, but in isolated one-man missions, was not questioned' (Doyle, 1984, p. 209). Separation and distinctness from the laity were the order of the day. But the bishops did recognize that Catholic clergy had now to meet new challenges in the parishes. They had to be able to meet Protestant and secularist objections. They had to be able to quiet the fears of the better-educated laity. In the seminaries, therefore, the entire emphasis was upon dogmatic and moral theology and professional studies. Secular education had no place. And in the parishes, the paternalistic, pastoral role of the priest was emphasized (as within Anglo-Catholicism). It was within the context of the new Irish Catholic immigrant congregations as well as a traditionally hostile English society that the Catholic clergy worked out their professional destinies.

VII

There can be no doubt that the nineteenth-century Christian churches were actively concerned to explore and define the vocation of the minister and the organization of a clerical profession to fulfil that vocation. To see this concern within the context of the growth of new professions in Victorian Britain is to narrow the perspective and to distort the reality. The problem was fundamental to Christianity, its organization and its institutionalization. The question which should command our attention is: was there anything distinctively Victorian about the approach to resolving such issues? Clearly the Christian churches *were* responding to a specific set of problems (urban, industrial populations; the development of professional medicine; social work which encroached on traditional roles of the ministers; new scientific and theological issues). The manner in which these were faced, however, suggests a traditional exploration of the role of the minister and the institutionalization of that role. We should not be misled by the fact that the various ministries emphasized the importance of education and training, the need for a competent livelihood and incentives, and the desirability of professional awareness, into thinking that these were new emphases. Pastoral theologians looked back to the Scriptures, to the Reformation, to Trent, to John Wesley and not sideways to the teachers, the solicitors and the accountants when they sought definition of their vocation and guidance as to its profession or 'acting out'. The professionalization of all the Christian ministries — be they Anglican, Roman Catholic, Methodist or Congregationalist — took place within a *conservative* context. The ministers concerned did not wish to deny their deep-felt religious beliefs, to risk losing the congregations they served or the souls they had brought to Christ in the interests of 'professionalization' and improved conditions for themselves. Belief that there must be a ministry was a matter of faith in a way that belief that there must be secular teachers or doctors or lawyers was not. To carry this 'professionalization' too far would negate the true 'vocation' of the minister.

Recent work on the secular professions and on the various ministries has provided little reason for scholars to doubt the view that the newer professions of teaching, nursing and social work owed a debt to the older professions of the church, law and medicine. There is no reason to substitute a new thesis that the clergy began to model itself on the fledgling professions. What recent work has done is suggest that the professionalization of the clergy or the ministry was closely bounded by an understanding of the vocation of the Christian minister. One cannot, therefore, successfully study the Victorian clergy without a sound and deep knowledge of the *history* of the Christian ministry or a recognition that the commitment of this ministry was always to a 'religious vocation', no matter what its institutional framework.

BIBLIOGRAPHY

In compiling this essay a good many works were used, including basic texts such as Owen Chadwick (1966 & 1970) *The Victorian Church*, 2 Vols., A. and C. Black. I have footnoted only potentially contentious points. The following books and articles will prove useful to readers wishing to delve further into the subject.

G. Best (1964) *Temporal Pillars*, Cambridge, Cambridge University Press.

O. Brose (1959) *Church and Parliament: The Reshaping of the Church of England, 1828–1860*, London, Oxford University Press.

C. K. F. Brown (1953) *A History of the English Clergy, 1800–1900*, Faith Press.

K. D. Brown (1984) 'Nineteenth-century Methodist theological college principals', *Proceedings of the Wesley Historical Society*, Vol. 44, pp. 93–102.

K. D. Brown (1987) 'Ministerial recruitment and training: an aspect of the crisis of Victorian Nonconformity', *Victorian Studies*, Vol. 30, pp. 365–83.

K. D. Brown (1987) 'College principals — a cause of Nonconformist decay', *Journal of Ecclesiastical History*, Vol. 38, pp. 236–53.

K. D. Brown (1988) *A Social History of the Nonconformist Ministry in England and Wales, 1800–1930*, Oxford, Oxford University Press.

F. W. B. Bullock (1955) *A History of Training for the Ministry of the Church of England and Wales, from 1800–1874*, St Leonards on Sea, Budd and Gillat.

M. A. Crowther (1970) *Church Embattled: Religious Controversy in Mid-Victorian England*, Newton Abbot, David and Charles.

*R. E. Davies, A. R. George and E. G. Rupp (eds.) (1965–1978), *History of the Methodist Church in Great Britain*, 3 Vols., Epworth.

W. J. Davies (1910), *The Minister at Work*, Charles Kelly.

P. Doyle (1984) 'The education and training of Roman Catholic priests in nineteenth-century England', *Journal of Ecclesiastical History*, Vol. 35, pp. 208–19.

E. J. Evans (1976) *The Contentious Tithe: The Tithe Problem and English Agriculture, 1750–1850*, Routledge and Kegan Paul.

K. B. Garlick (1985) 'Ministerial training in Methodism and our colleges, 1834–1984', *Friends of Wesley's Chapel Annual Lecture*, published privately.

A. D. Gilbert (1976) *Religion and Society in Industrial England: Church, Chapel and Social Change, 1740–1914*, Longman.

C. Gore (1899) *The Church and the Ministry*, 4th edn., Longman.

A. Haig (1984) *The Victorian Clergy*, Croom Helm.

A. T. Hart (1970) *The Curate's Lot: The Story of the Unbeneficed English Clergy*, J. Baker.

B. Heeney (1974) 'The theory of pastoral ministry in the mid-Victorian Church of England', *Historical Magazine of the Protestant Episcopal Church*, Vol. 42, pp. 215–30.

B. Heeney (1976) *A Different Kind of Gentleman*, Connecticut, Yale University Press.

D. A. Jennings (1975) *The Revival of the Convocation of York, 1837–1861*, Borthwick Papers, No. 47, York, University of York.

D. A. Johnson (1982) 'The Methodist quest for an educated ministry', *Church History*, Vol. 51, pp. 304–20.

T. Lathbury (1840) *A History of the Convocation of the Church of England*, London.

D. McClatchey (1960) *Oxfordshire Clergy, 1777–1869*, Oxford, Oxford University Press.

G. E. Milburn (1981) *A School for the Prophets: The Origins of Ministerial Education in the Primitive Methodist Church*, Manchester, Hartley Victoria College.

J. H. Newman (1833–4) *Tracts for the Times*, Vol. 1, Rivington, London.

R. O'Day (1979) *The English Clergy: The Emergence and Consolidation of a Profession, 1558–1642*, Leicester, Leicester University Press.

R. O'Day (1983) *Education and Society, 1500–1800*, Longman.

*R. O'Day (1986) *The Debate on the English Reformation*, Methuen.

*R. O'Day (1987) 'The anatomy of a profession: the clergy of the Church of England' in W. Prest (ed.) *The Professions in Early Modern England*, Croom Helm.

J. Pruitt (1978) *The Parish Clergy Under the Later Stuarts*, Illinois, University of Illinois Press.

J. H. Rigg (1897) *A Comparative View of Church Organizations*, third edition, C. H. Kelly.

*M. J. D. Roberts (1981) 'Private patronage and the Church of England 1800–1900', *Journal of Ecclesiastical History*, Vol. 32, pp. 199–223.

C. F. Rogers (1912) *Pastoral Theology*, Oxford, Oxford University Press.

*A. J. Russell (1980) *The Clerical Profession*, S.P.C.K.

*K. A. Thompson (1970) *Bureaucracy and Church Reform: The Organizational Response of the Church of England to Social Change, 1800–1965*, Oxford, Oxford University Press.

P. N. Virgin (1979) 'Church and State in Late Georgian England, 1800–1840', unpublished Cambridge University Ph.D. thesis.

R. B. Walker (1966) 'Religious changes in Cheshire, 1750–1850', *Journal of Ecclesiastical History*, Vol. 17, pp. 77–94.

A. Warne (1969) *Church and Society in Eighteenth Century Devon*, Newton Abbot, David and Charles.

CHAPTER 6

THE CHICHESTER EXTINGUISHER.

Bishop of Chichester. "GO! GO! YOU INSOLENT, REBELLIOUS BOY.—WHAT, WITH YOUR NONSENSE AND INCENSE AND CANDLES YOU'LL BE SETTING THE CHURCH ON FIRE."

Master P-ch-s. "JUST WHAT I'D LIKE TO DO. THERE!"

EMOTION AND PIETY: REVIVALISM AND RITUALISM IN VICTORIAN CHRISTIANITY

Not a little of the fascination of Victorian religion derives from the co-existence within it of an urgent sense of intermingled crisis and confidence, revival and decline. On the one hand expansion, vitality, growth: more churches, more chapels, more clergy, more lay agencies; missionary activity at home and abroad; numerous and large-scale ventures in religious publishing (in the 1860s the Religious Tract Society produced and distributed as many as 33 million tracts in a single year); often a sense of vitality after eighteenth-century docility; and large-scale growth, in absolute terms, in the numbers of people attending religious worship and becoming active in religious life. On the other hand recurrent crises in belief — was Christian orthodoxy true? was it moral? was the Christian identity of society being threatened and eroded by secularizing trends in national life? And, added to this, the ever-present fear of the unchurched, especially the urban unchurched, working classes who, as a group, remained so markedly indifferent to the urban missions of the Victorian churches and thereby ensured that, whatever the absolute growth in religious practice and adherence, relative to the growth in population there was an overall decline in the numerical strength of the churches in society by 1900.

The paradox of co-existent revival and decline is the more fascinating because it was also self-conscious: Victorian churchmen and women *sensed* that they were involved simultaneously in both crisis and opportunity. Often the sense of crisis and the expression of vitality were the opposite sides of the same phenomenon: the vitality and commitment of urban mission was the obverse of anxiety and fear at urban irreligion and its presumed social consequences; the reassertion of theological conservatism was often the product of a more open expression of theological liberalism. One of the most self-conscious aspects of the expansive, assertive side of Victorian Christianity was the phenomenon of revivalism and the attempt to sustain, enthuse and invigorate the churches through the promotion of a variety of rituals and ritualized activities and devotional styles. It is the aim of the present essay to focus on such self-conscious revivalism and ritualism as they affected each of the major traditions of Victorian Christianity — Protestant, Anglican and Catholic — and to attempt to assess the significance of the phenomenon within Victorian Christianity as a whole.

I PROTESTANT REVIVALISM BEFORE SANKEY AND MOODY

Traditionally the religious revival in the British Protestant and Nonconformist traditions was a spontaneous and unstructured affair — an outpouring of God's spirit upon a community whose only preparation was a period of intense and deeply persistent prayer asking for a 'shower of blessing' from God, but not actually seeking to orchestrate or organize it. Such had been the Methodist revival of the eighteenth century, and such also was the revivalism of Primitive Methodism in the opening decades of the nineteenth century. The origins of Primitive Methodism lay in a combination of local assertions of working-class communal identity and the desire for a return to the more emotionally intense spirituality of early Methodism, which, by the early nineteenth century, had become muted as Wesleyan Methodism became increasingly structured, ministerial, urban and middle class. In the large open-air camp meetings of early Primitive Methodism (some of them lasting several days) in the first two decades of the nineteenth century, local communities shared religious experiences of great intensity: a mixture of sermons, testimonies, prayer and hymn-singing; often ecstatic, 'dissociative' phenomena such as sensations of burning, weeping, shouting and fainting; and underpinning it all a reiterated theme of guilt and despair turning to forgiveness and the experience of salvation, with heaven and hell always the stark eternal choice. The membership of such gatherings was characteristically working class and from a local and non-urban community: agricultural communities and mining and fishing villages were the customary strongholds of Primitive Methodism.

By 1850, however, even Primitive Methodism was well on the way to becoming an established denomination — still more intense and revivalist than Wesleyan Methodism, but also much less emotional than in its own early days — and the older tradition of spontaneous, unstructured revivalism was becoming an increasingly localized phenomenon. It survived, for example, in Cornwall, and also in Wales where it even achieved a final, remarkable outburst as late as 1904–5, but the distinctively local character of such revivals became increasingly evident.[1]

Such local revivalism aside, from the 1840s onwards Protestant revivalism in Britain began to take on a new appearance and character. Revivals were no longer, in general, spontaneous, unstructured affairs. By the 1840s revivals and revivalism were becoming organized, planned and arranged, and also much more urban in location. Halls were booked, posters printed, specific groups (Sunday school members for example, or members of other groups such as temperance societies, linked to the church but as yet only on the periphery of its life) were deliberately targeted, and prayer meetings

[1] See, for example, David Luker's discussion of the Cornish Methodist revival as a local popular 'indigenization' of Methodism, both reflecting and contributing to the relative isolation of nineteenth-century Cornwall, its strongly local communal identity, and the lay ethos of Cornish Methodism (Luker, 1986). On Welsh revivalism, see Turner's recent discussion of the relationships between the humble origins and inherent emotionalism of much Welsh Nonconformity; the significance of cholera, natural disaster and social dislocation; and the notable links between the rural origins of many immigrants to new industrial towns and their new environments, revivals characteristically beginning in such rural areas and then spreading to the towns (Turner, 1987).

were no longer 'that revival might come' but 'that the revival would be a success'. The nature of the revival meeting itself also changed — again away from spontaneity and towards organization. Revival campaigns were centred on 'protracted meetings' held at the beginning and end of each day, every day, perhaps for several weeks. The preacher characteristically ended an evening service with an appeal that those who felt concerned as to their spiritual state should come forward to 'the anxious seat' where, before the whole congregation, they might become the focus of the congregation's prayers in an exercise calculated to exert maximum emotional and psychological pressure. After the main meeting those who were considering conversion or decision might remain behind for a smaller 'inquiry meeting', where more personalized preaching or counselling was offered. In short, British Protestant revivalism was becoming professionalized and, following American precedents, notions of 'human instrumentality' and 'systematic effort' increasingly replaced dependence on God's intervention.

This change was in turn part of a broader series of transformations and trends. By the mid-1830s the various Protestant and Nonconformist denominations were becoming increasingly committed to, and organized in, their missionary endeavours — at home, as well as abroad. Developments in the Baptist Home Missionary Society in the 1830s were symptomatic of the trend. The Society not only increased its total activity and directed more of its efforts to the towns but also deliberately adopted the 'new' systematic revivalist techniques and approaches such as the local campaign over several weeks, the appeal, and the inquiry meeting. But such organized home missions inevitably undermined 'spontaneous' revivalism: once revivalism began to be institutionalized within a home missionary strategy, spontaneity itself began to be organized. No less significant was the general drift in British Protestantism and Nonconformity away from traditional Calvinism towards a generalized 'evangelicalism', which was calculatedly unspecific in many points of theological detail but inescapably Arminian in overall drift and import. Old-style revivalism, spontaneous and unstructured, was compatible with Calvinism: prayer and penitence might ask God for revival, but whether or not it came was God's choice and decision. Organized revivalism, however, was logically incompatible with strict Calvinism — as indeed was organized missionary endeavour in general. The organized revival set out to arouse the emotions and urge the hearer to decide to accept Christ: it was a warmer, more experiential business altogether, and had at its centre the conviction that all and any might be saved — if *they* so chose.

To such changes *within* British Protestant and Nonconformist life was added, from the 1830s onwards, a further external factor which pressed revivalism in a structured, organized direction. American revivalists had been a feature of British revivalism even in the period from 1800 to 1830:

Primitive Methodism, for example, had been influenced by the American revivalist Lorenzo Dow. In the 1830s, however, a new American contribution to British revivalism began to make a significant impact.

In 1832 there appeared *The History and Character of American Revivals of Religion* by a New England minister, Calvin Colton. Colton distinguished sharply between old-fashioned revivalism, which waited on God, and the new revivalism, which involved 'human instrumentality', 'systematic effort' and 'divine blessing upon measures concerted by men and executed by men, where the instruments are obvious'. Colton sought to promote the latter. In 1835 appeared Charles Grandison Finney's *Lectures on Revivals of Religion*, in which a revival was described as 'the right use of the appropriate means', and in England the Baptist Francis Cox published, shortly after his return from visiting American Baptist churches, *Suggestions Designed* [sic] *to Promote the Revival and Extension of Religion*. The 'new' revivalism advocated in such books began to set a new pattern for revivalism in Britain — the developments in the Baptist Home Missionary Society strategy, for example, were directly influenced by them (Carwardine, 1980). As well as the books, there was also the presence of visiting professional revivalists from America to provide personal demonstrations of the new approach. In the 1840s James Caughey led a number of successful revivals in the north of England and in so doing greatly contributed to the turmoil and schisms within Wesleyan Methodism during 1847–9: the 'reformers' who were eventually expelled or broke away having made acceptance of his style of revivalism an issue within the Wesleyan controversies over centralization, ministerial control and the role of Conference. In 1849–51 Finney was also present in Britain but made less impact than Caughey.

As well as the efforts of visiting Americans and of groups such as the Baptist Home Missionary Society, there was also an English revivalist network of both full-time revivalists, such as Reginald Radcliffe and Richard Weaver, and part-time revivalists, some of whom were of upper middle-class or even aristocratic background. Although loosely rather than formally connected, they sprang from a common evangelical sub-culture which, as John Kent has observed, emerged roughly between 1830 and 1850 and was characteristically lay (even anti-clerical), urban and undenominational, and which found much of its strength and its contacts through such institutions (also notably lay and undenominational) as the London City Mission (founded 1835), the Y.M.C.A. (founded 1844), and the temperance organization the United Kingdom Alliance (founded 1853) (Kent, 1978, pp. 101–4).

The American revivalism of the Caughey and Finney generation and the English network of Weaver, Radcliffe and the early Victorian lay evangelical sub-culture coincided (and also met with mutual disappointment) in the events of the so-called Second Evangelical Awakening, 1859–62. Between

1859 and 1862 a religious revival of remarkable intensity and emotion gripped Ulster. In terms of scale it has been suggested that the Protestant churches in Ulster gained as many as 100,000 additional church members as a result of it. As to the style of the revival, it was highly emotional and exuberant: open air meetings; widespread instances of dissociative behaviour such as shouting and fainting, speaking in tongues and prolonged weeping; and highly dramatic testimonies and conversions were common. From Ulster the revival spread to Scotland, where it affected all the main branches of Scottish Presbyterianism, although not on the same scale or with the same degree of accompanying ecstatic behaviour as in Ulster.

The English revivalist network and the American revivalists present in England in 1859, who included Caughey and Finney, hoped that the Ulster revival would also spread effectively to England and to that end sought to publicize and extend, and even co-ordinate, the various efforts of Finney, Caughey, Radcliffe, Weaver and others. They met with a number of local successes (Caughey, for example, had a considerable impact upon the Free Methodists of Rochdale and Bury), but the hoped for general revival did not materialize and even the English evangelical sub-culture was not generally united in enthusiasm for the project. Kent has indeed described 1859–62 as 'the failure of English revivalism' and suggests a number of reasons for the failure. There was still a crucial division within the Evangelical ranks in 1859–62 between those who supported the revivalists and those who found them altogether too dramatic and instantaneous in their appeal: Weaver especially stressed the possibility of salvation in an instant of decision whilst an older generation looked for a more prolonged experience of apprehension, conversion and then the sense of forgiveness. The basic difference of approach which this indicated was further exacerbated by the ecstatic and dissociative phenomena of the Ulster revival: the stories of seeming hysteria smacked of excess. A further problem was the acutely lay and even anti-clerical nature of much of the revivalist network: the support of the churches was inevitably far from united as a result. Lastly, despite the 'network' and the hope of nationwide revival, there was no genuinely national figure and no genuinely national structure to the events of 1859–62 (Kent, 1978, ch. 3).

A decade later it was to be different: Moody and Sankey were genuinely national figures and planned a campaign accordingly; they operated with a more subtle emotionalism and avoided hysteria; they soothed clerical sensibilities by claiming only to convert in order to hand on to the local churches; and by the 1870s the urban dilemma of the churches was even clearer than it had been in 1860, and the possibilities held out by Moody and Sankey could not be ignored — the evangelical sub-culture, lay and clerical, rallied round.

II MOODY AND SANKEY AND AFTER

Dwight L. Moody and Ira D. Sankey were both products of the early evangelical phase of the Y.M.C.A. in America. When they arrived in Britain in early 1873 to begin the tour which was to become the most famous single episode in Victorian revivalism, Moody was thirty-six and Sankey thirty-three. At first they made little impact, but after an immensely successful six months in Scotland (November 1873–May 1874), and a further period of success in Ireland, they returned to England, where their own advance publicity efforts and the dedicated preparations of the English evangelical subculture had ensured that they would find success there too. They held two successful series of meetings in Manchester and Birmingham, and finally moved to London and a series of meetings at the Agricultural Hall, Islington, from 9 March to 21 July 1875. The Manchester meetings were attended by crowds of up to 17,000 on Sundays and 12,000 on weekdays. In London the Agricultural Hall could hold over 21,000 and was regularly full. There were also other London meetings in the East End and it has been estimated that as many as one and a half million people attended the Moody and Sankey meetings in London in 1875. Moody and Sankey returned for further tours in 1881–3 and 1891–2, but these were much smaller affairs and of less enduring importance than that of 1873–5.

Moody and Sankey represented the triumph of the new professional version of revivalism. Both the advance preparations and the meetings themselves were professional, planned and performed in a way which severed any remaining link with the notion of spontaneity and the priority of divine initiative over human effort. They also operated on a national scale — as Kent has put it, it was a move from margin to centre, local chapel to metropolitan hall, religious press to *The Times* (Kent, 1978, p. 132).

The advance organization included the free distribution of 30,000 copies of the evangelical paper *The Christian*, in which Moody's success in Ireland was described, and the provision through a fund raised by Moody of a three-month subscription to *The Christian* for every minister in Britain. As for the meetings themselves, although Moody varied the precise content from meeting to meeting, the basic pattern was clear: mass audiences; homely, powerful preaching; by turns both rousing and sentimental singing from Sankey as a soloist and from a massed choir; repeated appeals to make a decision for conversion; the request that those who wished to do so should stand that the meeting might pray for them; and then the use of an inquiry room where official counsellors sought to consolidate the initial decision just made.

The message proclaimed at such meetings depended for its effect as much on Sankey's singing as on Moody's preaching. The preaching was relatively brief, vivid, powerful, sincere, and above all homely and commonsensical — full of anecdotes, many of which sought to convey a sense of the workings of providence and the hand of God in everyday life. As to content, the sermons used knock-down arguments to dispose of supposed difficulties with the Bible or disbelief and aimed to simplify the matter of conversion to a stark and simple decision: for God or against, black and white, yes or no. The individual was called (or cajoled) to an act of will, obedience and decision and the prevailing tone of the call was urgency passing over into fear: decide for God now or it might be too late, not only might death intervene but God might reject the individual even in this life if this opportunity were not taken. The God involved was severe, sovereign and tyrannical. The consequence of rejecting God was hell for eternity. The old lurid hell of devils, fire and torture had disappeared, but it had been replaced by a hell of eternal separation from God and from loved ones in heaven, an eternity of agonized and unending regret. It was, as John Kent has put it, a more subtle system of terror than lakes of fire — but it was terror nonetheless. The anecdotes which supported the arguments were characteristically about parent-child or husband-wife relationships — especially the former. Images of loss and return, last chances and missed-for-ever opportunities abounded.

The songs of Sankey's repertoire tended to the same ends. The original collection of songs used by Sankey in 1873–5 numbered only thirty, although the hymn-book which grew from it ran to 1200 items. The core of his message remained the thirty songs, however, and within their words was to be found a set of themes which repeated and supplemented those of Moody's preaching. Sankey's solos and the massed choirs presented a sentimental and emotional amalgam of the themes of sin, salvation, crude substitutionary atonement, fear of rejection, a siege mentality (the sense of a small embattled remnant of the faithful), and heaven as an eternal home and place of reunion. Children, the return of prodigal offspring and images of family grief and joy were central to the songs: the result was a curious blend of severity and reassurance.

Reactions to Moody and Sankey varied. Evangelicals (Anglican and Nonconformist — but especially the latter) were generally supportive, and in Scotland their impact upon all the branches of Presbyterianism (but especially the Free Church) was marked. The majority of Nonconformist ministers gave their support and many sat behind Moody at his meetings. Evangelical opposition when it occurred was concerned either with the familiar, even vulgar, tone of Moody and Sankey's preaching and singing as contrasted with an older and more austere evangelical ethos, or with their *de facto* abandonment of Calvinism. John Kennedy of the Scottish Free Church and J. K. Popham of the English Particular Baptists protested that in Moody human decision replaced divine action — they were right, but quite out of step with the general trend of Victorian evangelicalism, which was going in the same direction as Moody and Sankey. Not surprisingly, with theological liberals sensitive to the contemporary moral critiques of hell and substitutionary atonement, Moody and Sankey were unpopular. Anglicans, other than Evangelical ones, and Anglo-Catholics in particular, disliked their aggressively non-sacramental approach and the calculatedly lay orientation of the whole affair.

The later visits of Moody and Sankey to Britain in 1881–3 and 1891–2 were smaller affairs. The enduring legacy of their influence we shall consider in the final section of this essay. After the 1873–5 tour by Moody and Sankey the main developments in Victorian Protestant revivalism were to be found in the Salvation Army, in the Holiness Revivalism of the Keswick Conventions, and in the plethora of independent evangelical churches and mission halls which sprang up in virtually every urban centre.

In the Salvation Army revivalism was institutionalized. In 1861 the Methodist New Connexion refused to sanction one William Booth as a travelling evangelist. Booth became an independent evangelist anyway, founded the Christian Mission in the East End of London in 1865 and by 1868 ran thirteen preaching stations. Between 1870 and 1878 he experimented with a variety of constitutional arrangements for the expanding evangelical organization of which he was the leader. By 1878 Booth and his followers had settled on the military model as the basis of their movement. They were to be a Salvation Army with a General (Booth himself), officers, a publication called *The War Cry*, brass bands, flags and uniforms: recruits signed 'articles of war', and the Army's buildings were called 'citadels'.

The Army prided itself on being a working-class movement with an appeal to the very lowest social strata and capable of reaching people outside the range of contacts of the other churches. Up to a point the claims were justified. The Army probably did reach more of the lowest social groups than any other church (save for the Roman Catholics, whose working-class Irish constituency was very large, but also quite different from the group the Salvation Army was seeking to reach, being ethnically based and already at least culturally Catholic). The Army also sought to present itself in self-consciously proletarian terms: brass bands and popular music in which revivalist hymnody was central; citadels designed like music-halls; flags and uniforms reminiscent of the images of contemporary popular imperialism; and an organization which, although severely autocratic, was neither clerical nor churchly — the Salvation Army had neither clergy nor sacraments.

For all this, however, there remained definite limits to its claims of a working-class identity. The majority of members — certainly the majority of the officers — were of lower middle-class background, as also were the majority of Moody and Sankey's supporters (Robertson, 1967, pp. 96–102). Salvation Army processions, no less than some ritualist churches, were targets for riotous attacks,[2] and by 1890 even the Army's fundamental hope of making a significant impact upon the the conditions of working-class life simply by means of evangelism and the effect of individual conversions was supplemented by a commitment to social rescue work which Booth announced in his *In Darkest England and the Way out*. If they were less successful than they had hoped to be, however, the Salvation Army nevertheless achieved an impressive growth. By 1900 the Salvation Army had over 4,000 full-time officers and workers, over 1,300 buildings and centres, and a total membership approaching perhaps 100,000 — all achieved within twenty-five years.

Not the least part of their appeal was their provision of a spirituality which kindled memories of the early days of Methodism and Primitive Methodism. The Army provided not only a popular revivalist piety sustained by brass bands and chorus hymns, but also, 'Holiness meetings' and 'Holiness doctrine': the doctrine claimed that after conversion might come sanctification, a willingness and ability to give up all sinful things and as a consequence a spiritual joy of great depth; the meetings involved the old ecstatic features of revivalism, weeping, shouting, fainting, and also the public renunciation of pipes, snuff boxes, brooches and other symbols of sinful pleasures or ostentation.

Its holiness teaching linked the Salvation Army to a wider network of late Victorian holiness revivalism. Holiness teaching had been part of both early Methodism and Primitive Methodism, and had featured in Caughey's teaching and in the teaching of other American revivalist visitors to Britain such as Phoebe Palmer and Robert Pearsall-Smith. It reached its late Victorian peak in the Brighton Convention for the Promotion of Scriptural Holiness in 1875, and in the annual series of Keswick Conventions which issued from it. The Conventions, at first dominated by Anglican Evangelicals but subsequently also attended by many Nonconformists, promoted the ideal of personal holiness and urged its expression in missionary zeal and in a re-affirmation of the ideal of evangelical social concern expressed through personal philanthropy. Fundamentally middle class, the Conventions secured a place for holiness teaching, along with its deeply conservative understanding of the Bible, of theology and of personal and social morality,

[2] Between 1871 and 1891, Salvation Army riots occurred in sixty towns, forty of them small towns in the south and west of England. Partly a reaction to the Army's own 'warlike' approach and aggressive assertion of its presence, the riots were often led by a rival 'Skeleton Army'. Such Skeleton Armies were themselves also encouraged by, for example, local brewers and publicans angered by the Army's teetotalism and local councils' dislike of the Army's confrontation with the roughest and most dangerous social groups in their towns (Briggs, 1981; Bailey, 1977).

within both the Church of England and the main Nonconformist denominations.

The last of the strands of late Victorian Protestant revivalism was the amazingly diverse collection of local independent evangelical missions which sprang up in virtually every urban setting. Staunchly, even fiercely, evangelical and lay, they revealed a widespread dissatisfaction with the increasingly structured and centralized life of the main denominations and presented instead the option of a local evangelical community, puritan, revivalist, and both theologically and socially conservative in ethos. Although small in absolute terms their influence, especially through Sunday Schools and other ancillary organizations, was probably considerable, not least in providing the Protestant revivalist tradition with a presence in local, often working-class, communities and thereby diffusing the ethos and values of revivalism more widely than would otherwise have been the case.

III ROMAN CATHOLIC REVIVALISM

Revivalism was not an exclusively Protestant phenomenon in Victorian Britain. In 1840 Nicholas Wiseman, still ten years away from his appointment as first Archbishop of Westminster, petitioned Pope Gregory XVI for the foundation of an Institute of Missionary Priests in England who would visit areas where Catholicism was little known (or unknown); give missions to Catholic communities to arouse zeal and fervour; preach special Lent and Advent courses of sermons in cities, where overburdened parish clergy could not undertake such special measures; and conduct retreats and spiritual exercises for the clergy in colleges and convents. Such measures, Wiseman maintained, if energetically pursued, would secure a rapid expansion of Roman Catholicism in England.

Wiseman received only qualified support from the English Vicars Apostolic: only one, Walsh of the Midland District, was genuinely enthusiastic about the proposal. He did however, find support from the English Catholic converts George Spencer and Ambrose Phillipps and a willingness to undertake such missionary work on the part of the Passionist, the Redemptorist and Rosminian religious orders.

Between 1842 and 1844 all three orders began work in parish missions in the United Kingdom, and by 1850 each was firmly established. The Passionists, led by Fr. Dominic Barberi, arrived in England in 1842 and undertook their first parochial mission in 1844. The demand for their services quickly grew and they were soon committed to a whole series of week-long missions. At first, because of the lack of manpower available, the missions were generally conducted by one man, but from 1848–9 onwards the practice of two and three-man mission teams became more widespread. In 1849 the Passionists also held their first parish mission in Ireland.

The Redemptorists first arrived in England in 1843 and after a slow start to their work established themselves, in 1849, in London to minister to the needs of the rapidly growing Irish community. From 1850 onwards their activities expanded rapidly and in 1850–51 there were full-scale missions in London, Liverpool and Manchester. In 1851 they held their first mission in Ireland, met with even greater success than in England, and progressively concentrated the greater part of their British-based efforts there, playing a major part in the remarkable revival and development of Irish Catholic parochial life in the second half of the nineteenth century.

The Rosminians had first arrived in England as early as 1835 and, led by Fr. Luigi Gentile, had conducted missions from 1840 onwards at a small number of mission stations specifically assigned to them, only Gentile himself venturing further afield to lead retreats for clergy in London, Birmingham and York. From 1844 onwards, however, they began to conduct regular parish missions of up to two or three weeks' duration, travelling from parish to parish: the demand for such missions quickly grew.

It was with the appointment of Wiseman to Westminster, however, that the mission work of these orders (together with that of Frederick William Faber and the Oratorians at Brompton, and also the work of the Jesuits, the Marists and Capuchins), began to move from the periphery to the centre of the Roman Catholic revival in Victorian England. In the 1850s, under Wiseman's leadership and active encouragement, the missionary orders organized increasingly large-scale missions, such as that conducted by the Redemptorists in the East End of London in 1855, which began with the confirmation of 500 children and claimed over 10,000 communions, or that of the Jesuits in Southwark in 1859, which concluded with a congregation of 4,000 at a service to renew baptismal vows, or the one run by the Passionists at Rotherhithe in 1861, where the congregation on the final night overflowed the church amidst scenes of great emotion (Gilley, 1973, pp. 838–9). They also steadily increased and expanded their smaller-scale local parish mission work and their retreats for clergy — and they developed missions to specific groups, notably, for example, to children. By the 1860s and 1870s the parish mission was a central feature of Victorian Roman Catholic life and the recognized means of reviving and stimulating regular parochial experience. Just as in England the practice found a crucial sponsor and enthusiast in Wiseman, so in Ireland Cullen, although not the originator of the practice of regular parish missions led by visiting missionary priests (the Vincentians, for example, had been active since the 1840s), was central in the process of making such missions an integral feature of the Irish Catholic revival and expansion of the second half of the century. Similarly in Scotland (although less the result of any single bishop's initiative) by 1860s the Rosminians, Vincentians, Passionists, Redemptorists and Jesuits were all active in parish work.

What was the content and nature of these ventures in Catholic revivalism? At its centre lay the desire for the spread of the 'vital', 'ultramontane' piety and devotionalism that was so prominent in the history of Roman Catholicism in the nineteenth century, not only in Britain, but worldwide. The parish missions steadily introduced such practices as the Forty Hours devotion, processions of the Blessed Sacrament, renewal of Baptismal vows, Benediction, devotions to the Virgin, litanies and rosaries and the Way of the Cross. They also set out to consolidate the practice of the devotions thus introduced by the establishment of Confraternities, Sodalities and Guilds. At Clapham, in a new church established by the Redemptorists in 1852, there was a Confraternity of the Immaculate Heart of Mary and a Society of St Vincent de Paul; at Southwark in the 1850s there were societies for devotion to the Blessed Sacrament, Sacred Heart of Jesus, Passion of our Lord, and Immaculate Heart of Mary, and a Holy Guild of St George and the Blessed Virgin. The urban missions, and the sodalities and confraternities set up to consolidate them, deliberately fostered colourful, even gaudy, church furnishings — such as Stations of the Cross and statues of the Virgin, Joseph, or the Holy Family. They did so specifically because the clergy believed they were 'a source of devotion or enjoyment to the poor', who lived in such wretched conditions that the colour and brightness of such devotions were a welcome relief from everyday dirt and drabness. By the 1860s and 1870s such devotions and confraternities were becoming widespread among urban and working-class parishes generally (Gilley, 1973, pp. 846–7; Supple, 1985, pp. 229–31).

The large-scale missions, such as those in the East End, Southwark and Rotherhithe in 1855, 1859 and 1861, included such highly emotional devices as Italian-style street preaching (to arouse general interest and curiosity and to enthuse the faithful) and fiery preaching in crowded chapels and churches, in which the sermons characteristically concentrated upon sin, the agonized conscience, the threat of hell, and the need and possibility of redemption. One of the more famous, or perhaps infamous, missioners, the Redemptorist John Furniss, in fact specialized in such hell-focussed sermons, complete with descriptions of hell and its punishments, specifically for children. Between 1855 and 1862 he conducted over eighty such missions, often preaching to congregations numbering thousands. But in an age increasingly disturbed by the moral implications of hell in general, the idea of children going to hell caused particular moral offence, and by the 1870s this particular variety of Catholic revivalism began to decline. It was replaced by the practice of children's missions, with a rather less ferocious theology and as a direct preparation for an ensuing adult mission (Sharp, 1984). The ceremony and drama accompanying the large-scale missions might culminate in scenes like the climax of the 1861 mission in Rotherhithe, when, at the final overflowing meeting, the crowd was addressed in the open air and indulgences were offered for kissing a ten-foot cross on a high platform: a cross that bore a sacred monogram and a red thorn crown, and had scourges and a lance and sponge attached to it (Gilley, 1973, p. 839).

As Sheridan Gilley has observed, both the emotional appeal and the theological structure at work were at once crude and effective. The emotions were aroused by colourful, flamboyant and communal ceremonies, rituals and devotions; they were heightened by preaching which emphasized the proximity of death (which was indeed ever present in the conditions of Victorian urban slum life), the horror of hell and the need for repentance, confession and absolution. Gilley has described it as 'vulgar piety': heartily vulgar, and therefore unafraid of theological crudity and emotional excess, and therefore also peculiarly successful at reviving and sustaining the fortunes of Victorian Catholicism among the Irish poor (Gilley, 1985, p. 263). It was a measure of its success that, by 1900, Catholicism was the only denomination with a genuinely working-class base. This base, if not as strong as the church would have liked, was much stronger than ever appeared likely in the 1840s and 1850s, when the prospect of Irish immigrant communities without adequate pastoral provision or a regular practising version of the faith seemed to point to the inevitable loss of such Catholics in the coming decades.[3]

IV ANGLO-CATHOLIC REVIVALISM

Assessments of Victorian Anglo-Catholic revivalism have sometimes sought to explain it in terms of an adoption by mid-Victorian Anglo-Catholics of revivalist styles, techniques and convictions derived from Evangelical sources: the classic presentation of the view is indeed entitled 'Catholic Evangelicalism' (Voll, 1963). As John Kent has pointed out, however, such claims probably owe rather too much to twentieth-century needs to establish historical roots for contemporary ventures in ecumenism. 'It is curious,' Kent observes, 'how hard some writers ... find it to realize that both Roman and Anglo-Catholics could try to convert people without any 'Evangelical' inspiration' (Kent, 1978, p. 257).

In fact there is no need to search for 'evangelical' origins for the distinctive Anglo-Catholic revivalism of Victorian Britain. The origins are to be found, rather, in the experience of second-generation Anglo-Catholic priests ministering to the urban poor, and in the Anglo-Catholic 'rediscovery' of

[3] See *RVB* I, 4, for the location of Catholic revivalism and the role of the missionary orders within the consolidation of English, Scottish and Irish Catholicism in general during the Victorian period.

the seventeenth-century French Roman Catholic tradition of mission priests and parish missions inspired by St Vincent de Paul. In the 1850s and 1860s a number of Anglo-Catholic clergy ministering to urban parishes, and therefore confronted by the absence and alienation from organized religion of the majority of the working classes, concluded that a system of parochial missions was one means of contacting and converting the urban unchurched. In 1865, for example, G. H. Wilkinson published *Suggestions for a Mission Week* as a basis for a parish mission that he wished to hold in his parish of Bishop Auckland. The *Suggestions* were of a distinctively Anglo-Catholic kind: the clergy were to meet each morning for Communion, together with any parishioners who wished to attend; the morning was for Bible study and meditation; the evenings were for special services and 'after-meetings'; after which those who wished for further advice were to approach the clergy; and at the end of the mission a final meeting repeated the teaching of the week and asked those who wished for further advice to give their names that the clergy might contact them. Most significantly, the whole venture was to be called a 'mission' to distinguish it from a (Protestant) 'revival'. Other early experiments in parish missions by Anglo-Catholic clergy were undertaken by R. M. Benson at Bedminster, Bristol in 1862, by W. J. E. Bennett at Frome, Somerset in 1868, by W. D. Maclagan at Enfield in 1868, and by Charles Bodington at Willenhall, Staffordshire in 1869.

Of equal importance were the contributions of Charles Lowder and his foundation of the Society of the Holy Cross (1855) and R. M. Benson and his foundation of the Society of Saint John the Evangelist (1866). In 1854 Lowder had discovered the example of St Vincent de Paul and the order of mission priests founded by him in seventeenth-century France. In 1855 he duly founded the Society of the Holy Cross to strengthen the spiritual life of the church, defend its faith and carry on mission work — the latter by adapting Catholic practice to supplement the parochial structure. In 1856, at his parish of St George's in the East, he set up a mission station and lived in community with four other clergy and a small sisterhood. R. M. Benson meanwhile founded the Society of St John the Evangelist, based at Cowley, Oxford, with the explicit intention of supplying the Church of England with mission priests.[‡]

Such local experiments and would-be mission orders in turn gave rise to the two great ventures in Anglo-Catholic revivalism, the Twelve Days Mission to London of 1869 and the London Mission of 1874. The Twelve

[‡] For Lowder (and for an excellent study of the place of Anglo-Catholicism within mid-Victorian Anglicanism) see Ellsworth, 1982. For Benson, see Smith, 1980.

Days Mission of 1869 was not the exclusive product of the Anglo-Catholic tradition, but the predominant influences in its planning were London Anglo-Catholicism in general and the members of the Society of the Holy Cross and the Society of St John the Evangelist in particular. The result was a mission lasting from 14–25 November in 112 London parishes. The parochial focus was important, for although there were inevitably prominent centres in the mission — St Paul's, Knightsbridge, St Alban's, Holborn and All Saints, Margaret Street, for example — the aim was to locate the convert firmly within the structure of local parish life. The style of the mission was liturgical and sacramental. A day at St Paul's, Knightsbridge, for example, included Communion at 7 am, 8.30 am and 9.15 am; Matins at 8 am; Litany and Catechizing at 11 am; Evensong at 5 pm; and Mission Service and sermon at 8 pm. There were also instruction classes for men and for women and regular hours for confession. The preaching, as well as the liturgical structure, sought to stress an essentially sacramental religion centred on eucharist, baptism and confession. The renewal of baptismal vows was a feature of the mission and the practice of auricular confession and the acceptance of regular spiritual direction from a priest was a prominent theme of much of the mission preaching.

The emphasis upon confession provoked controversy — the Evangelical press inevitably brought charges of Romanism and priestcraft. Other reports on the mission were more balanced. *The Times*, for example, acknowledged that George Body, in his mission sermons at All Saints, Margaret Street, whilst urging the use of confession nevertheless stressed that the priest *of himself* had no power to forgive sins, and that if anyone came to him he would not press confession against that person's conscience.

The Twelve Days Mission was sufficiently successful (*The Times* reported mid-way through that the missioners claimed to be reaching 35,000 people a day) for a second experiment to be tried in 1874. The Bishops of London, Rochester and Winchester called for the mission in late 1873 and set out to make it genuinely representative of the breadth within the Church of England, thereby hoping to stifle the impression of Anglo-Catholic dominance. They succeeded in making it broader than merely Anglo-Catholic, but they failed to prevent the Anglo-Catholics who participated from again making renewal of baptismal vows and confession central. For ten days in February 1874 London was again the focus of a parochially based mission and the more extreme of the Anglo-Catholics again urged the priority of sacramentally based religious life and spirituality in which confession, absolution and spiritual direction were integral parts of the whole.

Anglo-Catholic revivalism reached its peak in the London missions of 1869 and 1874. Subsequently there were a number of other episcopally sponsored missions in other cities, although generally somewhat toned down by a more successful episcopal stress on 'comprehensiveness' of theological opinion. Specifically Anglo-Catholic parochial missions continued, but on a more local and restricted scale.[5] But if the national peak of Anglo-Catholic revivalism was thus reached and passed quite quickly, the significance of it was more enduring. The advocacy of auricular confession and of a high doctrine of the sacraments, and the use of 'ritualist' styles and services in the Missions caused controversy — but they also quite simply gave a new prominence to, and familiarized people with, the Anglo-Catholic tradition within the Church of England. The missions helped to consolidate Anglo-Catholic identity. They demonstrated publicly and dramatically the self-conscious commitment of Anglo-Catholics and Ritualists to the mission to convert the urban poor (a commitment which already had a long pedigree in the parochial work of individual priests such as Charles Lowder, A. H. Mackonochie or A. H. Stanton, but which now received national publicity). They helped further to establish the reputation of leading Anglo-Catholic clergy such as Stanton, Body and Wilkinson as powerful preachers and evangelists as well as 'ritualists'. And they contributed to the general movement of Victorian Anglicanism towards a style of worship and spirituality which was more sacramental, more ritually and visually rich and more liturgical, than its predecessor. Perhaps most of all, however, they were themselves a symbol of the determination of second generation Anglo-Catholics to take the sacramentalism of the Oxford Movement — its emphasis on eucharistic presence and sacramental priesthood — into the urban, working-class environment. Colour, ritual, music, processions, eucharistic worship, the renewal of baptismal vows and the confessional were attempts to embody Tractarian *ideas* in forms and actions which were accessible to poor, uneducated and theologically unsophisticated people. Indeed, some Anglo-Catholics were quite explicit in arguing that whereas evangelical Protestantism offered the poor only subjective experience and sermons (which many Anglo-Catholics believed, rather patronizingly, to be beyond the comprehension of the uneducated poor), Anglo-Catholicism offered sacraments and symbols which provided an objective presence capable of being grasped by the poorest and least educated. The Eucharist offered the very *presence* of God; Confession offered the forgiveness of *particular* sins. The later Ritualist attempts to introduce the reservation and adoration of the sacrament were but a logical extension of such arguments (Kent, 1978, pp. 264–6).

[5] The restrictions, however, were only of scale: in style parochial missions were often aggressively Ritualist, as for example at St Bartholomew's, Brighton, where, between 1888 and 1908, there were four missions which included public processions headed by a crucifix and surpliced men carrying processional lamps (Hennock, 1981, p. 185).

V THE LEGACIES OF VICTORIAN REVIVALISM

Victorian revivalism was not monolithic. It came in distinctive Protestant, Catholic and Anglican varieties — and the Protestant variant was itself, especially by 1900, a decidedly fragmented affair. Attempts to force such competing revivalisms into a neatly unified structure or to devise unifying concepts, such as 'Catholic Evangelicalism,' break down. On the contrary, the varieties of Victorian revivalism were in fact competing: they offered sharply, hard-edgedly, Protestant, Roman Catholic or Anglo-Catholic versions of salvation. They espoused doctrines and practices which many of their revivalist rivals found not merely distasteful but pernicious, heretical, popish or idolatrous. Protestant revivalism actively sought conversions from Roman Catholicism; Roman Catholic missions sought and valued Protestant converts; Anglo-Catholicism deliberately repudiated the 'revival' in favour of the 'mission', and one of the reasons for the general rallying around Moody and Sankey in 1875 was the evangelical need to 'answer' the Anglo-Catholic missions to London of 1869 and 1874. At this level the competing revivalisms were symptoms of mutually aggressive Christian traditions, moving and defining themselves further apart as they engaged in rival missionary endeavours.

On the other hand, provided the temptation to portray illusory unity is resisted, there remain ways in which Victorian Protestant, Catholic and Anglo-Catholic revivalisms were similar, and also a sense in which, taken together, they constituted a common and cross-denominational trend in Victorian Christianity. They represented a cross-denominational turn to the subjective, the emotional, and the conservative. They were all theologically conservative and dogmatic, pre-critical in their use of the Bible, strong advocates of the existence of hell and eternal punishment. They were all avowedly supernaturalist and proclaimed a God who acted and intervened. They were all dramatic and ritualized, whether in liturgical ceremonies and processions, or in orchestrated meetings of preaching, singing, prayer and appeals. They were all emotional and experiential: each emphasized sin, guilt, the agonised conscience, the need for repentance, and each provided the means of spiritual release and relief in the moment of conversion or confession. Each worked over long periods of time — through protracted meeting, repeated services, missions over several days or weeks — to raise the pitch of congregational or communal feeling. Each used music, hymns, and preaching to arouse, and the images of children and of family and of last chances were common to the preachers and hymnody of different revivalist traditions. They each combined fear, severity and threat with reassurance and sentimentality. Perhaps above all, they each, to use Gilley's term, expressed a 'vulgar piety' designed to appeal to the poor and the uneducated, deliberately shorn of theological complexity and presented boldly and bluntly, with more concern for the effect on potential converts than for the preservation of doctrinal subtlety or ecclesiastical propriety.

In these ways, the varieties of revivalism were each expressions of a new, experientially and emotionally based religious conservatism: a reassertion of dramatic, passionate belief within a new urban industrial society that was challenging traditional dogma and faith with new ideas and new technologies. Thus the various revivalisms of Victorian Christianity had, for the most part, more to do with the revitalizing and reinvigorating of the churches themselves than with a genuine appeal to those outside. The Salvation Army and the Anglo-Catholic missions of 1869 and 1874 were exceptions to this, for they genuinely sought the conversion of the urban masses as a primary (if also somewhat unrealistic) aim. Roman Catholic revivalism, on the other hand, self-consciously aimed at the revitalizing of the parishes and the conversion of the nominal Catholic into the practising Catholic. Similarly, the classic Protestant revivalism of Sankey and Moody was geared, in practice, much more to the conversion of the peripheral adherent into the convinced believer than to the conversion of the wholly unchurched: as Kent has put it, Moody hoped to 'convert' into intensity the broad fringe of church and chapel members who possessed the vocabulary of sin, guilt, wrath, repentance and forgiveness, but who had never felt this as vivid experience (Kent, 1978, p. 283).[6]

Each of the major varieties of Victorian revivalism also left its mark upon the particular tradition from which it sprang. The most decisive and dramatic case was the Roman Catholic one: as Edward Norman has suggested, the achievement of Barberi, Gentile and the missionary orders was to make it *appear* to subsequent generations that the new, vital Ultramontane piety and devotionalism was the very substance of the faith (Norman, 1985, p. 74).

The legacy of Protestant Revivalism is less easy to describe, but arguably no less important. It did not make a breakthrough with the urban working classes. It was geared too much to the already peripheral believer for that, and therefore also took for granted at least the rudiments of a doctrinal system with which, by the second half of the nineteenth century, the majority of the working class had already lost touch and had no continuing point of contact. Kent has suggested that the bulk of the support for Sankey and Moody came not from the working class at all but from the expanding lower middle class, 'the draper's assistants of the world of the Y.M.C.A., the middle class students of the slowly expanding groups of new universities,

[6] Similarly, in Wales, in the revival of 1859, it has been noted that whilst in industrial areas the emphasis lay on the conversion of the 'unchurched', in rural areas the majority of the 'converted' were 'hearers' or peripheral members of the chapels, who had now become 'committed', fully involved participants (Turner, 1987, p. 320).

and from other social groups uncertain about their identity, caught between rich and poor, longing for upward social mobility' (Kent, p. 67).

To this constituency, and especially that part of it already within the orbit of Protestant Nonconformity, Protestant Revivalism in the Sankey and Moody mould brought a gospel which was by turns emotional and sentimental (heaven made home and reunion with those lost and gone before), yet also on the surface starkly, even brutally, clear and no-nonsense (hell, even if transmuted from lakes of fire to eternal homelessness, was still remarkably definite in its reality and consequences). Examined more closely the message was less clear — indeed decidedly vague. Moody declined to define his theological concepts at all closely — indeed arguably he did not 'define' them at all. 'He had,' it has been observed, 'a strong, clear mind, resolute, direct and unhindered by qualifications ... any theology he had was implicit' (Drummond and Bulloch, 1978, p. 11). Coming as it did, however, at the point at which Nonconformist theology was in any case becoming less precise and less specific, the mixture of pathos and sentiment with (apparently) clear certainties requiring assent to starkly stated alternatives (not reflection on theological ambiguity), struck a chord in many late Victorian Nonconformist hearts and minds. Ian Sellers goes so far as to suggest that 'none of the great names in late nineteenth century Nonconformity, Congregational, Baptist or Presbyterian ... escaped the inspiration of the Moody-Sankey revival' (Sellers, 1977, p. 75). Moreover, they spread their version of Protestantism with remarkable success through popular publications and literature, most especially perhaps through *Sacred Songs and Solos*, which enjoyed phenomenal success and continued spreading the Moody-Sankey ethos long after Moody's sermons were no longer read. As the theological leaders of late Victorian Nonconformity articulated increasingly contrasting liberal and conservative theologies (opposed to each other but united in supposing theological detail to matter), a considerable part of the laity absorbed from the revivalist legacy a theology which was avowedly conservative in its assertions and assumptions, but decidedly imprecise in its details, and in which conviction was certainly more a matter of emotion and experience than of intellectual decision.

The legacy of Anglo-Catholic revivalism was more precise. On the one hand the missions of 1869 and 1874 and the specifically urban, working-class aims of Anglo-Catholic revivalism genuinely helped to foster the parochial spread of Anglo-Catholicism. On the other hand it also helped to foster the myths of the special appeal of Anglo-Catholic colour and ritual in the drab conditions of urban working-class life and of the centrality of the urban working-class mission within Anglo-Catholicism. Neither myth was quite justified. The pastoral sacrifice and devotion of 'slum-ritualists' such as Lowder, Mackonochie and Stanton in London, Dolling in Portsmouth, Prynne in Plymouth, or the Wagners in Brighton (as well as dozens of others equally devoted but less famous), was indeed a phenomenon to be admired, and the affection which such clergy frequently inspired in their communities was testimony to their achievements. But slum-ritualism was not the centre of Anglo-Catholicism: taken as a whole the movement was more rural than urban (hence late Victorian Nonconformist fears of popery in Anglican guise dominating English village life), and as much (probably more) middle class than working class. As to ritual and colour, as Yates has pointed out, it was the personality of the individual priest(s) which 'made' successful working-class Anglo-Catholic parishes, and the colour and ritual, if they were factors, were equally likely to be drawing a gathered congregation from nearby Anglican churches where such ritual was unavailable (Yates, 1978, pp. 410–11). Charles Booth had noticed the same thing as early as 1902 in his survey of the religious influences on the *Life and Labour of the People in London*: in the poorest parishes the Anglo-Catholics were more successful than others, largely because lives of voluntary poverty won confidence and appealed to the imagination — but even then their churches 'were largely filled by people from other districts and of higher class, attracted by the stir of religious life' (quoted in Rowell, 1983, p. 140).

But such 'myths', not just in the Anglo-Catholic case but in respect of revivalism as a whole, are in some respects as important as any other aspect of the legacy of Victorian revivalism. Quite apart from the specific legacies of the varieties of Victorian revivalism within their respective Protestant, Catholic and Anglo-Catholic sub-cultures, there was the diffused impression which, collectively, they left in the minds of the late Victorian population as a whole, and the lower middle and working-class population in particular. As the churches became, in practice, despite all their efforts to the contrary, more peripheral and more distant, the revivalist traditions were the more conspicuous precisely for their drama and deliberate prominence, aggressive self-publicizing, and widespread 'popular' literature. Even if *Sacred Songs and Solos*, high mass and benediction, or devotion to the Virgin were not really as central to and characteristic of their traditions as their enthusiasts would have liked them to be, in the minds of many whose contact with organized religion was *only* via such avenues, and even then only vaguely so, they must have *seemed to be* the substance of Nonconformity, of Anglicanism or of Catholicism. It is likely that in the popular mind the various versions of Victorian revivalism exercised (and perhaps still exercise) an influence on the *image* and public perceptions of the major traditions in Victorian Christianity out of all proportion to their actual size and role.

BIBLIOGRAPHY

V. Bailey (1977) 'Salvation Army riots, the "Skeleton Army" and legal authority in the provincial town' in A. P. Donajgrodzki (ed.) *Social Control in Nineteenth Century Britain*, pp. 231–53, Croom Helm.

A. Briggs (1981) 'The Salvation Army in Sussex 1883–1892' in M. J. Kitch (ed.) *Studies in Sussex Church History*, pp. 189–208, Leopard's Head Press.

R. Carwardine (1980) 'The evangelist system: Charles Roe, Thomas Pulford and the Baptist Home Missionary Society', *The Baptist Quarterly*, New Series, Vol. 28, pp. 209–25.

C. Charles (1964) 'The origins of the parish mission in England and the early Passionist apostolate, 1840–1850', *Journal of Ecclesiastical History*, Vol. 15, pp. 60–75.

A. L. Drummond and J. Bulloch (1978) *The Church in Late Victorian Scotland 1874–1900*, St Andrew Press.

*L. E. Ellsworth (1982) *Charles Lowder and the Ritualist Movement*, Darton, Longman and Todd.

*S. Gilley (1973) 'Catholic faith of the Irish slums: London, 1840–70' in H. J. Dyos and M. Woolf *The Victorian City*, Vol. 2, pp. 837–53, Routledge.

*S. Gilley (1985) 'Vulgar piety and the Brompton Oratory, 1850–1860' in R. Swift and S. Gilley (eds.) *The Irish in the Victorian City*, pp. 255–66, Croom Helm.

E. P. Hennock (1981) 'The Anglo-Catholics and Church Extension in Victorian Brighton' in M. J. Kitch (ed.) *Studies in Sussex Church History*, pp. 173–91, Leopard's Head Press.

*J. Kent (1978) *Holding the Fort: Studies in Victorian Revivalism*, Epworth.

D. Luker (1986) 'Revivalism in theory and practice: the case of Cornish Methodism', *Journal of Ecclesiastical History*, Vol. 37, pp. 603–19.

E. Norman (1985) *Roman Catholicism in England from the Elizabethan Settlement to the Second Vatican Council*, Oxford University Press.

R. Robertson (1967) 'The Salvation Army: the persistence of sectarianism' in B. R. Wilson (ed.) *Patterns of Sectarianism*, pp. 49–105, Heinemann.

G. Rowell (1983) *The Vision Glorious: Themes and Personalities of the Catholic Revival in Anglicanism*, Oxford University Press.

I. Sellers (1977) *Nineteenth-Century Nonconformity*, Arnold.

J. Sharp (1984) 'Juvenile holiness: Catholic Revivalism among children in Victorian Britain', *Journal of Ecclesiastical History*, Vol. 35, pp. 220–38.

M. L. Smith (ed.) (1980) *Benson of Cowley*, Oxford University Press.

J. Supple (1985) 'The Catholic clergy of Yorkshire, 1850–1900: a profile', *Northern History*, Vol. 21, pp. 212–35.

C. B. Turner (1987) 'Revivalism and Welsh society in the nineteenth century' in J. Obelkevich, L. Roper and R. Samuel (eds.) *Disciplines of Faith: Studies in Religion, Politics and Patriarchy*, pp. 311–23, Routledge.

D. Voll (1963) *Catholic Evangelicalism*, Faith Press.

W. N. Yates (1978) '"The only true friend": Ritualist concepts of priestly vocation' in D. Baker (ed.) *Religious Motivation: Biographical and Sociological Problems for the Church Historian*, pp. 407–15, Oxford, Blackwell.

CHAPTER 7

THE LATE DR. ADLER, CHIEF RABBI OF THE ENGLISH JEWISH CONGREGATIONS.

ANGLICIZED NOT ANGLICAN: JEWS AND JUDAISM IN VICTORIAN BRITAIN

THE CHAIRMAN [Dean Inge] What advice would you give to an epileptic who asked you whether he should marry? — *A. [The Chief Rabbi, Dr J. H. Hertz] I should strongly advise him not to marry.*

MR MARCHANT You would enforce the canon law of your Church? — *A. These laws have merely a moral sanction; Jewish Jews observe them.*

Q. If they disobey you have no disciplinary method of dealing with them? — *A. No; purely moral influence — moral suasion.*

(Hertz, 1916, p. 433)

The Chief Rabbi's evidence to the National Birth-Rate Commission (1914–16), as given above, not only indicates the absence of coercive power to prevent dysgenic unions, but also supplies one of the key questions to which this chapter is addressed: namely, how was religious conformity to be enforced within a liberal capitalist context? In terms of the historical experience of Jewry the problem was largely without precedent. Until the Resettlement of the Jews in Britain in the mid-seventeenth century and their subsequent dispersal throughout the English-speaking world, lay and spiritual leaders had relied upon the repressive apparatus of the state-supported self-governing communities, the *kehillot*, for the enforcement of social and religious discipline. The more tolerant environment that obtained in Britain and her colonies made the search for an alternative basis of Jewish communal organization obligatory. Religious pluralism and the withholding of state assistance meant that social and spiritual control would have to be re-set within a voluntary and associational framework. Renegotiation and relocation were not, however, uniform processes. One need only compare the subordinate status of Reform Judaism in Britain with its salience in the United States to appreciate the variant outcomes.[1]

Differences between Jewish communities — and not only in the Anglo-Saxon countries — are, indeed, marked. 'Operation Moses' (1982), the dramatic airlift of thousands of starving Falashas from the parched plains of Ethiopia for resettlement in Israel, provides striking evidence of the enormous variations — ethnic, cultural, social and economic — that co-exist in contemporary Judaism. Dissimilarities in religious practice and ritual forms, in this case, are so pronounced as to raise questions about the authenticity of Falashan Judaism and insistence by the Chief Rabbinate in Jerusalem that the Ethiopians submit to symbolic circumcision and undergo ritual conversion (*JC*, 21 December 1984). Nineteenth-century Jewry

[1] I am most grateful to Professor Bill Fishman of the University of London for his comments upon an earlier version of this chapter.

contained equal diversity. 'The difference between the Jews of one country and the Jews of another,' wrote one mid-Victorian commentator, 'is almost as great as that between one nation and another' (Anon, 1865, p. 532).

Variety in the religious experience of Jewry is, then, nothing new. The environment in which Jews have found themselves has, ever since Biblical times, influenced their spiritual and social development. A propensity to absorb the customs, tastes and religious outlook of the dominant or 'host' society is, indeed, the subject of much Old Testament comment. Two thousand years of exile and dispersion throughout the Diaspora has likewise registered an impact. The incorporation of Babylonian and other festivals into the Jewish calendar and the influence of the Zoroastrian system of angelology and demonology upon Jewish thought are but a few of the well-attested examples of the interaction of Jew and Gentile in times past (Philipson, 1907, pp. 3–4).

The extent of acculturation and assimilation, then as now, is determined not only by the internal composition and structure of the Jewish minority, but depends in no small part upon the character of the receiving society. Where legal, cultural, economic and political barriers are erected that serve to isolate Jewry from the course of mainstream social development, the tendency is to reinforce its cultural and religious distinctiveness. Where, however, the barriers are surmountable or non-existent, the impact of the non-Jewish environment upon the religious practices of the minority will be much greater (Sharot, 1976).

The lowering of the barriers between the faiths in early nineteenth-century Germany, for example, allowed for the penetration of Protestant practices into the architecture and service of the synagogue. Israel Jacobson's famous synagogue at Seesen, Westphalia (completed in 1810), possessed a bell tower with a full complement of bells. The interior, too, with its organ and raised pulpit in front of the ark and facing the congregation, evoked the contemporary church rather than the traditional synagogue. The relocated platform — it was customarily placed at the rear rather than the front of the synagogue — was for the occupation of a new-style incumbent. The occupant was not only required to be a man of learning and as capable of deciding ritual and religious issues as the rabbi of old; he was also expected to be a pastor and preacher patterned on the Christian clergy (Meyer 1971, pp. 289–303). In France, the first of the European nations to concede Jewish emancipation, the redefinition of the rabbinate and creation of a clerical hierarchy reflected the influence of the Catholic Church (Albert, 1977, pp. 169–72, 259–82). In Victorian Britain, with its low-profile state and non-monopolistic establishment, the Anglican Church supplied the major influence upon the minority religion. By contrast, the absence of an established church in the U.S.A. implied the adoption of an alternative referent. Congregationalism, the dominant form of American Protestant organization, exerted an influence upon the structure and ethos of American Jewry which was comparable with that of the Church of England upon Anglo-Jewry (Davis, 1963, pp. 7–8).

The interaction of church and synagogue, should not, then, be viewed in isolation. To understand the process of Anglicization we need to set the Anglo-Jewish experience within a comparative perspective. The disintegration of the autonomous corporate structure of traditional Jewry and the movement towards individual participation in state and society, which constitutes the dominant theme of Jewish history between 1700 and 1900, supplies a useful vantage point for our purposes; for it is only by examining the processes of acculturation and assimilation in relation to the wholesale transformation of European Jewry that we can hope to identify the peculiarities of Anglo-Jewry in Victorian Britain.

I

The voluntarist character of communal organization, lay and ecclesiastical, represents its most striking feature. Outside the United States it had no parallel. In Medieval and Early Modern Europe, Jews were assigned to one of several estates or self-governing corporations into which society was divided. Jewry of the European Diaspora possessed its own religion, language, civil administration, judicial institutions and educational system. Synagogues and cemeteries enjoyed special protection; judicial decisions were based on Talmudic law; authority to levy taxes, excommunicate sinners and, in some cases, to execute offenders devolved to the community. In Eastern Europe self-sufficient forms of communal organization persisted into the twentieth century; and even in the more advanced West, religious communities remained public corporations rather than private institutions. The replacement of the *kehillot* in the first half of the nineteenth century by the *Gemeinden* in Germany and the *consistoires* in France reduced but did not abolish communal control over the individual. Professing Jews in both countries were still required to belong to the local Jewish community and contribute through taxation to its upkeep. The contrast with the Jewish experience in the English-speaking world was extraordinary.

In Britain, where capitalism and the nation-state were both well developed, communal, corporate self-governing institutions of a kind common in many parts of Europe were already in an advanced state of decay by the time of the Resettlement (1656). Anglo-Jewry was, in consequence, spared the experience of state-enforced group autonomy. The re-admission of the Jews in the mid-seventeenth century was a remarkably informal affair. No official document defined the rights and duties of the newcomers; until the mid-Victorian years the status of Jewry was determined by the courts rather than the legislature. Anglo-Jewry, unlike its Continental counterpart, was not the object of discriminatory legislation. Until the middle of the nineteenth century Jews were excluded from Parliament and the universities because they were not Anglicans and not because they were Jews. Otherwise, native-born Jews enjoyed the same liberties and safeguards as other non-Anglican Englishmen. British Jews were not restricted to certain occupations; they were not required to wear distinctive clothing; nor were they condemned to enforced segregation in a ghetto. In all these respects the common lot of the British Jew differed markedly from that of his co-religionist in other lands.

In other respects, too, the position of the Jew was singular. Civil and political disabilities, though offensive, did not in practice impose a crushing burden upon the individual, who, since he did not in general aspire to a career in the learned professions, was not put out by exclusion from the ancient universities. Prohibitions on office-holding, in theory a formidable restriction, were not systematically enforced; Jews were not prevented from exercising the franchise nor from successfully pressing their candidatures at local elections. Emancipation was not, in consequence, a burning issue. 'I was told by a Hebrew gentleman', wrote Henry Mayhew, '. . . that so little did the Jews themselves care for "Jewish emancipation", that he questioned if one man in ten . . . would trouble himself to walk the length of the street in which he lived to secure Baron Rothschild's admission into the House of Commons' (Mayhew, 1861, II, p. 127). Opponents of Jewish emancipation never ceased to pinpoint the lukewarm support it received within the community. And they were right. Indifference to politics, a common feature of much mid-Victorian social observation, reflected the very considerable freedoms which the Jewish population already enjoyed (Endleman 1979, pp. 277–80).

Emancipation, in any case, did not mean acceptance, as the experience of the Catholic Irish immigrant was to show. Although Catholic emancipation preceded Jewish emancipation by thirty years, the relief of Catholic disabilities made little impression upon Protestant prejudice. The conjoint effect of religious rivalry and ethnic enmity in this case was such as to force the minority to withdraw into a self-enclosed ghetto. Anti-semitism in Victorian Britain, though hardly negligible, was not comparable in its intensity with anti-Catholicism. Whereas native hostility and Ultramontane belligerence reinforced Catholic insularity, self-segregation and the sectarian identity it engendered formed no part of the integrationist strategy pursued by the Anglo-Jewish élite. Anglicization and acceptance rather than separatism and self-sufficiency constituted its dominant concerns.

II

On the eve of the mass migration from Eastern Europe (1880) British Jewry comprised an estimated 60,000 persons. From less than two score families at the time of the Resettlement the community had grown prodigiously. In the two centuries that followed the Re-admission, growth was continuous and at times dramatic. The Anglo-Jewish population registered a twenty-five fold increase during the course of the eighteenth century and expanded at a steady, if less spectacular, rate thereafter. The 25,000 souls enumerated in 1800 had become 35,000 by 1850 and grew by a further 25,000 — an increase of 70 per cent — in the next three decades. The expansion of the population was not due to natural increase alone. Continuous immigration supplied a significant annual increment to the ever-growing proportion of native-born Jews.

The original Sephardi settlers from Spain and Portugal (1656) had long since been submerged beneath a ceaseless stream of Ashkenazi immigrants from Germany, Poland and Holland. At mid-century, the Sephardim comprised perhaps 13 per cent of the Jewish population of London. But by then the distinctions which once separated the two communities had lost much of their force. Intermarriage and business ties had transformed them into a socially homogeneous group. The Jews of Britain, indeed, represented an increasingly settled population. The sedimentation of Anglo-Jewry was well-advanced by 1850. At that point the majority of Jewish families had been settled for more than a half-century. Indeed, an estimated one in twelve families had been domiciled in England for more than one hundred and fifty years (Lipman, 1954, p. 9). Two more points must, however, be emphasized: first, that the arrival of newcomers from abroad was constant; and second, that from the 1840s onwards these newcomers were drawn increasingly from Eastern Europe.

Although Jews were not on the whole debarred from full participation in the economic life of the nation, the trades they entered owed more to custom than to calculation. The occupational structure of Anglo-Jewry long bore the imprint of previous experience. The absence of an industrial proletariat and a professional middle class were, until the third quarter of the nineteenth century, its most striking features.

In the genesis of Britain's industrial ascendancy Jews played no part. The expertise possessed by the well-to-do Marrano merchants of the Re-admission era secured them a comfortable niche in trade and commerce, which the élite of Anglo-Jewry continued to occupy; for the rest, Jewish industry of the eighteenth century was confined to the output of craftsmen shopkeepers. In London, where Jews were most numerous, some found employment in the luxury trades — as silversmiths, goldsmiths, diamond cutters and polishers, engravers, watchmakers and jewellers — supplying the wants of a rich and opulent clientele; others danced attendance on the privileged classes as barbers, wig-makers, tailors, footmen and domestic servants. These, though, attracted rather less attention than the more exotic and much-profiled street folk. Beneath the ranks of the self-employed craftsmen, journeymen, small dealers and menials, were the street traders and petty hucksters, the old clothes dealers and itinerant vendors who together with the floating population of vagrants, beggars and casual workers, the destitute and aged, made up the Jewish labouring poor. That so many took to the road is not surprising. The eighteenth century immigrant possessed of little money, few skills and an uncertain grasp of the vernacular, had no real choice but to continue the peripatetic calling of his forebears. The Jewish pedlar thus became as familiar a figure on the highways and by-ways of Georgian Britain as his Continental cousins who roamed the countryside in Poland, Germany and Holland.

For some, peddling was preparatory to a more settled existence as a small proprietor. Travellers who acquired the wherewithal to set up shop constituted the nuclei of provincial Jewry. Its centre of gravity lay in the flourishing southern ports and market towns. At the close of the Napoleonic Wars there were ten thousand Jews in provincial England dispersed throughout some twenty-five communities. Significant settlement in the industrial centres of the North had to await the second half of the nineteenth century.

By 1880 the industrial orientation of provincial Jewry was firmly established. Outside the Metropolis the largest concentrations of Jews were to be found in Leeds, Liverpool, Birmingham, Manchester and industrial South Wales. The new pattern of settlement was both indicative of, and a contributory factor to, the modernization of Anglo-Jewry's occupational structure. The East European immigrants who, for example, came to Manchester in increasing numbers from the late 1840s, and who by 1875 accounted for between one-half and two-thirds of the city's estimated seven thousand Jews, were not solitary pedlars-cum-shopkeepers or master craftsmen grasping at a precarious independence. Anything but! The newcomers were primarily wage labourers, who were absorbed into the industrial workforce, principally in cabinet-making and the rag trade, working in domestic workshops with uniform conditions and uniform rates of pay.

In London, too, the development of a Jewish working class is observable. The decline of hawking and the displacement of the Jews by the Irish in the street-selling trades to which Mayhew drew attention in the 1850s, is confirmed by other sources. Registers of the Sephardi community which record the occupations of marriages solemnized in its synagogue show a marked fall in the proportion of grooms who were general dealers and hawkers: from more than twenty per cent in the 1840s to less than nine per cent in the 1870s. Other contemporary analyses also point towards the growth of paid employment in clothing, tobacco, furniture and footwear as the characteristic occupations of Metropolitan Jewry.

Between 1840 and 1880 class divisions within the community became more pronounced. The concurrent shrinkage of the labouring poor and the multiplication of the middle classes was the outstanding development. The process of *embourgeoisement*, already well advanced by the time of Victoria's accession, continued without abatement in the second half of the nineteenth century. The period which saw the proliferation of bankers, brokers, overseas traders and wealthy merchants, also witnessed the penetration of the professions, albeit in a small way. 'My son, the lawyer!' or 'My son, the doctor!' was not at this juncture the anxious dream of every ambitious mother. The Jewish middle classes were, in the main, made up of shopkeepers and petty traders with a family income of £100 to £1,000 per annum. Their numbers, however, were exceedingly large. Half of London Jewry, according to the calculations of Joseph Jacobs, the pioneer of Anglo-Jewish statistics, were of the middle classes; more reliable estimates, based on the Census of 1871, suggest that between a third and a quarter of Manchester Jewry can be so classified. Whatever the precise percentage, it is clear that Anglo-Jewry contained a larger proportion of middle-class people than the population at large. Middle-class Jews, who accounted for a third of the community at mid-century, formed about half by the beginning of the eighties. 'Whereas in 1850 the social structure had been, as it were, a pyramid', writes V. D. Lipman, 'it now, in 1880, began to look more diamond-shaped, with a mass in the centre and tapering ends above and below' (Lipman, 1954, pp. 78–9).

Although a diminishing proportion of the population, the Jewish poor remained numerous. Their absorption into the proletariat had, at best, been partial. The abandonment of street-trading and hawking had done little to alleviate the insecurities of everyday life. Tailors, for example, formed one in four of all applicants for relief to the Board of Guardians between 1878 and 1882; boot-makers, clickers and slipper-makers comprised almost one in ten; while the more affluent cabinet-makers and carpenters supplied two per cent of all such applications. What had changed, though, was a new and growing awareness of their subordinate status as wage-earners within a capitalist system of production. Of them we know little.[2] At present the historian can offer no more than a schematic characterization of the making of the Jewish working class. The process of class

[2] 'When a writer sets about giving the history of a people', wrote one Victorian scholar, 'his attention is chiefly confined to the upper and middle classes of those he treats of, as it must be admitted that the history of the lower classes is generally shrouded in obscurity, and such is particularly the case with the Anglo-Hebrew poor' (Margoliouth, 1851, III, p. 156). In the one hundred and thirty-seven years since these words were written little has been published to invalidate the observation.

formation, signified by increased occupational mobility and the substitution of workshop-based employment for the nomadic life of the street traders and itinerant vendors, however, had advanced sufficiently to permit of shopfloor organization and the foundation of benefit societies and mutual aid associations. Progress was uneven. Those in the tobacco trades were amongst the most militant. In 1858 there occurred the first ever strike between Jewish workers and Jewish employers, when the Cigar Manufacturers' Association sought to resist the 'unnatural rise' demanded by the union. In these years, too, 'very large meetings' of operatives were reported to have been held to protest against infringements of the Factory Acts (Pollins, 1982, pp. 123–6).

It was this consciousness of class oppression which separated the mass of Jewish workers from their pedlar predecessors. The latter, without work discipline or craft pride, possessed neither time, inclination nor income to participate in the activities of the labour movement. Politics interested them little. 'I found among the Jewish street-sellers and old clothes men with whom I talked on the subject', wrote Henry Mayhew, 'a perfect indifference to, and nearly as perfect an ignorance of, politics' (Mayhew, 1861, II, p. 126).

Getting a living absorbed all energies. For the rest, sporadic rioting and casual criminality defined Jewish attitudes towards authority. In this they differed little from the non-Jewish poor, whose rough and dissolute habits, coarse conduct and pugilistic pleasures they shared. Tumult and disorder were by no means peculiarities of the English. The unruliness of the Jewish lower orders was as notorious as that of the Irish, and in the absence of restraint they were comparable to the English labouring classes with whom they lived. Their volatility made broil and disturbance a regular occurrence in the crowded quarters of metropolitan Jewry. On the streets of East London, in West End theatres, outside the *shul* (synagogue), wherever Jews foregathered, an unguarded comment could provoke disorder. Among the pauper-pedlars and ragged elements who comprised the Jewish lower orders, cheeks were not turned in a dignified and reserved manner. Verbal abuse and physical violence were readily heaped upon anti-semites and other critics of the community. These Cockney Jews, as one of them recalled, were 'a rough lot' (*JC*, 29 July 1898). To the anxious leaders of Anglo-Jewry the degraded condition and rumbustious life-style of the Jewish populace represented more than an embarrassment; it was also perceived as a major obstacle to their successful integration into British society.

From such concerns there sprang multiple proposals and projects to domesticate the Jewish poor and transform them into respectable citizens. Attempts to reform their manners and morals led to the proliferation of schools, hospitals and philanthropic agencies of all sorts. Common to all such interventions was the desire to re-fashion the character of the poor in accordance with the precepts of bourgeois respectability. To this end the various charitable institutions that were established pursued a common curriculum. The aim in all cases was, first, to remove the disreputable urchin from street life and, then, to supply suitable instruction and industrial training so that the pupil graduated with marketable skills and a character for thrift, industry, sobriety, obedience and honesty.

Preoccupation with discipline was not, of course, a unique feature of Jewish philanthropy, which, in many respects, mirrored the theory, practice and discourse of the Evangelical Movement. In one respect, however, they differed. Unlike its Christian counterpart, the Anglo-Jewish élite was not haunted by the spectre of class conflagration. The Jewish poor, inarticulate and unorganized, posed a threat to its position rather than its persons or property. The preservation of the *status quo*, in consequence, was not the object of Jewish philanthropy. Most definitely not! Integration and acceptance demanded the destruction of the street trades and the transfer of the hawkers and hucksters to workshop, warehouse and counting house. To the Jewish patriciate the incorporation of the poor into an enlarged and prosperous middle class represented its ticket of admission into British society.

The emergence of a more differentiated occupational structure in the mid-Victorian period did not, however, bring the Jewish patriciate peace of mind. The nascent proletariat, so far from adopting bourgeois norms, seemed determined to reject the roles prescribed for them by their 'betters'. Indeed, the perverse disposition of the workers underscored the pressing need for additional educational facilities, such as those provided at Sussex Hall, the Jews' Literary and Philosophical Institute. 'There cannot be a more efficient antidote to the poisonous doctrines of socialism, communism, chartism and other utopian solutions lauded by designing demagogues or shortsighted philanthropists than this frequent intercourse between the higher and the humbler classes on the common ground afforded by the platform of the . . . Institution', said the *Hebrew Observer* in 1854. The following year a correspondent to the *Jewish Chronicle* described the 'everywhere-to-be-found class distinction' as 'the canker which rankles in the heart of our community' (Finestein, 1959–61, pp. 128–9).

The formation of the Hebrew Socialist Union in 1875 seemed to confirm that analysis. Founded by Aron Lieberman and other Russo-Jewish exiles, all of them veterans of the Social Revolutionary movement, the new Union sought to organize the down-trodden workers of the East End in preparation for the instauration of the Socialist Commonwealth. The leaders of Anglo-Jewry, conscious of their problematic position within English society, viewed all departures from the standards of bourgeois respectablitity with concern. Agitation, atheism and communism, as practised by Lieberman and his associates, were, in their view, calculated to have a prejudicial effect upon English opinion. In politics and personnel, the Hebrew Socialist Union appeared to project the alien properties of Jewry and thereby to jeopardize the social standing of the élite, if only by association. Press and pulpit were thus united in their condemnation. The *Jewish Chronicle* wilfully confused socialism with conversionism; the Chief Rabbi equated socialism with sin (Fishman, 1975, pp. 103–21).

Politics, though, was not the sole source of discord. No less disturbing was the spontaneous growth of religious confraternities, or *chevroth*, which sprang up to meet the requirements of the East European Jews who settled in England in increasing numbers from the 1840s onwards. The *chevra* provided for the social and spiritual needs of the newcomers. For the pious and homeless, often one and the same person, it was both a sanctuary and tabernacle. Here a man could pray and study and pass the time of day. Here, too, a man might find comfort and support: for charity was a *mitzvah* (good deed) to be dispensed with kindness and consideration so that the recipient felt no shame. Simon Cohen's *chevra*, for example, held in his home in London at 32, Church Lane, was open daily from six in the morning until midnight and was a haven for destitute co-religionists: 'if strangers stayed the night and slept on the benches', he remarked, 'what was the sin in turning a blind eye to this instead of casting them out into the wintry streets when they had no shelter?' For such people, even when able to retain a roof over their head, a seat in the synagogue was unattainable. Small groups of 'poor foreigners' thus found it convenient to pool their resources and form a *minyan* (congregational quorum of ten men). 'They subscribe twopence a week and pay the occupier of the house in Hanbury Street where I was visiting two shillings a week for the use of his kitchen as a "Shul" [synagogue]', wrote an East End medical practitioner of one such group. The good doctor thought it curious that people should choose to worship in such a humble apartment. He continued, 'I put the question to my "Baal Boes" [host]: "Princelet Street Shul is within a stone's throw, why not go there?" "Oh, that's only for the rich people", was the reply, "and we are poor; if you go there you have to *schnoder* [offer a donation] half-a-crown, and a poor man has to wait ever so long before he can get a *leah* [opportunity to participate in the service]. But here almost everyone can get a *leah* every Sabbath for nothing. That's why we founded this Hebra. For twopence a week we can have as many *mitzvahs* [synagogue duties] as we want"'. Was there a regular Reader, the good doctor enquired. '"No", mine host replied, "anyone can read who likes. If you come here one day, we might ask you".'

The numbers enrolled in the *chevroth* were considerable. One enumeration, published in 1870, identified upwards of twenty metropolitan *chevroth* with a combined membership of close on 2,500; mid-Victorian Manchester boasted fifteen such associations with a membership that was, in the words of an anxious synagogue official, 'alarmingly large'. The Anglo-Jewish élite could not but view them with disdain; for unlike the Catholic confraternities that served the immigrant Irish, the self-generated *chevroth* were not a creature of the hierarchy but an alternative to it. Fiercely independent, these insanitary back-street bethels kept alive the spirit and strict religious standards of the Russo-Polish ghetto. 'In this way', writes one scholar, 'the ... Ashkenazim were split up into fragments not only horizontally by virtue of slight differences of observances but also stratified vertically because the poorer Jews broke away to establish humbler congregations in which they could give full vent to their genius for organization in *Rachmanot* [brotherhood]' (Quinn, 1958, II, pp. 485–91; Williams, 1976, pp. 271–2, 325, 333).

III

Coercion and control in a liberal setting represented something new in the annals of Jewry. Never before had the community been left to shift for itself. Enforcement of social and religious discipline within the *kehilla* had relied upon state support. Its absence left the Anglo-Jewish élite naked and defenceless before their unruly and depraved brethren. At the beginning of the nineteenth century, when the perception of criminality in general, and of Jewish criminality in particular, excited something of a moral panic among men of property, the leaders of the Ashkenazi synagogues petitioned Parliament for the restoration of communal self-government in order to suppress the dangerous and refractory elements who so besmirched their good name and reputation. Approval was sought for the formation of a Jewish poor relief board that was empowered to deport 'undesirable' alien Jews and imprison 'disorderly' native Jews and also authorized to tax the whole of the Jewish community for the relief of distress and prevention of pauperism. By such means the notables hoped to regulate the economy of the poor so as to abolish indiscriminate alms-giving, promote useful knowledge and productive labour, and thereby check the tide of demoralization that threatened to engulf rich and poor alike. 'Had the attempt proved successful', writes one scholar, 'it is more than likely that the whole course of Anglo-Jewry's social and economic development would have been profoundly altered, for the proposed reform would have instituted the Jewish community into an autonomous body, civilly, politically and legally' (Rumney, 1933, p. 87). Parliament, however, refused to cede such extraordinary powers to a private body. The *kehilla* was not to be rebuilt in England's green and pleasant land. The notables were forced back on their own resources.

Class separation and the want of central direction in ecclesiastical and charitable provision represented major obstacles to more effective communal control. Structural reforms designed to reduce resistance began in 1844–5 with the election of Nathan Marcus Adler to the Office of Chief Rabbi of the United Hebrew Congregations of the British Empire. N. M. Adler, who came from a long line of scholars and teachers, died in 1890 and was succeeded by his son Hermann in the following year. The Adlers, father and son, together occupied the Chief Rabbinate for a period of sixty-six years. In that time 'Adlerism' came to signify a preference for strong centralized religious government that was (and remains) a distinctive feature of Judaism in Britain.

The traditional rabbinate, which was neither centralized nor hierarchical, was replaced during the Adler years by an ecclesiastical establishment under the supervision of a primate in whose hands all powers were concentrated. The *Laws and Regulations for all the Synagogues of the British Empire*, issued by Adler senior in 1847, laid claim to complete control of religious and cognate matters. The conduct of services, appointment of officiants, formation of congregations, erection of synagogues — all henceforth required his approval. The Chief Rabbi also adjudicated in religious disputes, made pronouncements upon religious questions submitted to his office, authorized marriages, licensed slaughterers of meat and poultry and determined all other matters pertaining to the service of the synagogue. The lower clergy were mere functionaries restricted to non-rabbinical roles as preachers, pastors and synagogal administrators.

The emergence of the Office of the Chief Rabbi did not, however, exhaust the process of institutional innovation. The formation of the Jewish Board of Guardians in 1858 addressed the social condition of the community in much the same way as the Office of the Chief Rabbi addressed its spiritual condition. So far from reducing the Jewish poor, the proliferation of charities and unrestricted giving of doles seemed calculated to increase its *schnorrerdic* (beggarly) tendencies. The Jewish Board of Guardians sought to eliminate extravagance and restore order to the provision of eleemosynary assistance. It was nothing less than an attempt to Anglicize *Rachmanot* in line with the principles of 1834 (Lipman 1959, pp. 28–31). The Jewish Board of Guardians, in short, tried to do for charitable assistance what the Chief Rabbinate had done for the communal supervision of religion.

Co-operation in the field of relief work also provided the basis for the integration of the autonomous Ashkenazi congregations within a unitary structure. The difficulties posed by the uncoordinated character of communal provision, particularly in relation to the cost of pauper burials, had first received dramatic expression in 1790 when, contrary to custom and practice, a corpse had been deposited in the foyer of the Great Synagogue and left there for two days during an inter-synagogal dispute to establish responsibility for its interment. Such unseemly and damaging disputation had a sobering effect. Shamefaced communal leaders embarked upon intensive diplomatic activity in order to prevent its recurrence. A series of treaties, designed to pool resources, protect memberships and distribute the burden of relief more equitably, were concluded by the leading London synagogues and periodically renegotiated during the first half of the nineteenth century. With the rise of suburban Jewry and the growing imbalance between population and resources, however, these problems became more acute. Downtown synagogues, weakened financially by the loss of their wealthier members and largest subscribers, were even less well-placed than before to minister to the needs of the indigent poor. Self-defeating resistance to the construction of places of worship in the new centres of population was temporarily resolved by the building of branch synagogues under the supervision of anxious parents situated in the eastern boundary of the City. Ultimately, though, fusion was recognised as better calculated to promote the general interests of Jewish worship and religion. Amalgamation promised to secure the resources that would enable the synagogues — metropolitan and provincial, suburban and central — to address community-wide needs in a more satisfactory manner. Such recognition received institutional embodiment in the United Synagogue, which was first proposed in 1867 and endorsed by Parliament three years later (Newman, 1976).

The process of centralization, completed with the creation of the United Synagogue in 1870, was essentially the work of the aristocracy of finance who dominated the life of the community. This élite comprised a cousinhood of well-established merchant princes, bankers and professional persons — some Liberal, some Conservative — but all possessed of a common commitment to the social advancement of Jewry and protection of its recently-acquired civil and political rights. To their wishes the mass of Jews were expected to conform. Congregational participation was restricted. Government within the United Synagogue has, for example, been likened to a 'benevolent despotism . . . tempered by democratic forms and a patrician sense of obligation' (Finestein, 1971, p. 33). The Rothschilds, Goldsmids, Mocattas, Montefiores and other select families supplied the leadership of the Board of Deputies and Board of Guardians as well as the United Synagogue and also gave support and direction to the Office of the Chief Rabbi. The Chief Rabbinate and the notability were, indeed, mutually dependent. Uniformity within the United Synagogue was in no small measure secured by the provisions whereby the Chief Rabbi assumed sole responsibility for the form of worship and all matters connected with the religious administration of that body and its subsidiary charities. The end product of these centralizing measures has, rightly, been described as a 'regime of ecclesiastical papacy with its companion lay-rule of a benevolent grand-dukedom' (Barnett, 1961, p. 70). Without divisions of his own, the Yiddishe Pope, like his Catholic counterpart, leaned heavily upon the powers-that-be who largely determined his selection and salary as well as the enforcement of his decisions within the synagogues. As Bill Williams put it: 'The Chief Rabbinate was as much the ecclesiastical arm of the plutocracy, as the President of the Board of Deputies was its secular representative' (Williams, 1976, p. 193).

IV

No account of Jewry during the Queen's reign can fail to note the massive impact of the English establishment upon the Anglo-Jewish establishment. The Church of England supplied a model of authority and respectability which the leaders of Anglo-Jewry, lay and ecclesiastical, sought to emulate — even to the extent of seeking State recognition of the United Synagogue.[3] To raise the standing of the Anglo-Jewish ministry and obtain for the Chief Rabbi a position comparable with that of the Archbishop of Canterbury was a primary consideration. The status of Jewry as a whole, it was argued, would be considerably enhanced were its spiritual head to enjoy parity of esteem with his Anglican counterpart; for, his religious duties aside, the main function of the Chief Prelate was to represent the Jewish community to the Christian Commonwealth. How to dignify his office and invest it with the authority and influence which its religious and ambassadorial roles required was a constant preoccupation of the Adlers and their supporters. Hermann Adler, Chief Rabbi from 1891–1911, who did a good deal of hob-nobbing with the Anglican episcopate, was so taken with his associates that he not only adopted canonical garb but also assumed the title, 'The Very Reverend'. There was, in Cecil Roth's phrase, 'an inevitable tendency for him to interpret his position almost in Anglican terms' (Apple, 1971, p. 17).

The transformation of the Jewish ministry, and in particular the replacement of the traditional *chazan* (cantor), whose sole function was to read and intone the services, by a 'minister' who performed pastoral, preaching and teaching roles similar to those of the Anglican and Nonconformist clergy, also reflected the changing social composition of the Jewish population. Anglo-Jewry was increasingly middle class both in occupation and outlook. 'In my opinion' wrote the Rev. M. Hyamson of Dalston Synagogue, Canonbury, 'the Jewish Community has no Submerged Tenth' (Hyamson to Charles Booth, 1 November 1897, B179, p. 49; Sharot, 1973 pp. 57–63). To the acculturated bourgeois, who constituted the mainstay of the congregation, comparisons with the Church and its clergy appeared odious and

[3] Parliament, however, declined to create a Jewish version of the Church of England at the same time as disestablishing the Irish Church.

demeaning. Deficiencies in synagogue worship, it was felt, exposed all Jews to ridicule and calumny. The informality of the service of the synagogue gave a disorderly and chaotic appearance which non-Jews perceived as irreverent if not irreligious. Ashkenazic prayer, by comparison with Christian worship, seemed an ill-disciplined and anarchic affair with congregants responding to the cantor as the spirit moved them. Spontaneous outbursts of exuberance punctuated a service that was subject to constant disturbance by the comings and goings of the congregation, casual conversation and a general want of respect and restraint. Devotions were distracted by the swaying and sobbing and decency was offended by the sale of honours. The banging of the *bimah* (raised platform) and cries of 'Shah!' directed at the women's gallery by a distraught and long-suffering *shammas* (beadle), then as now, produced more noise than effect and served to confirm the unfavourable impression which had already been formed. Shorter services, the abolition of monetary offerings and introduction of choral singing had by the 1830s become part of a repertoire of reform that sought to beautify synagogue worship, curb congregational excess and generally render it more acceptable to an Anglican audience.

Nevertheless, the remedial measures introduced early in the nineteenth century required supplementation if the stamp of inferiority was to be erased. 'There is as yet a great deal to be done to secure that devotion without which prayer is an empty sound and an unmeaning form', observed the *Jewish Chronicle* at mid-century. 'The great length of the service on festivals, the hasty running through a cumbersome quantity of *Piyutim* [poetic additions to the prayers for the festivals], which but a few gabble over, whilst the majority are gaping, yawning or talking — and which even these few hardly understand — is a complete mockery, and loudly calls for abolition.'

The services of a preacher were no less pressing. Metropolitan and most provincial congregations were denied 'any of that pulpit instruction which, in the smallest congregation on the Continent, elevates the service, rouses the assembly to devotion within and without of the synagogue — instructs, informs, advises, and guides — which contributes so largely to that unity of purpose so much required, and to that fervent zeal we so much stand in need of'. The daughters of Zion, it concluded, 'who pant for religious instruction, would flock in numbers to the synagogue, if discourses were delivered there in the vernacular, at once entertaining and instructive, such as induce the ladies on the Continent . . . to attend the house of prayer' (*JC*, 11 October 1850). In short, Judaism was diminished and Jews humiliated, and all for the want of a preacher. 'We are anxious to obtain full emancipation', declared the *Chronicle* in 1849, 'and would it not be a disgrace if we were told by our Christian opponents, that the Jews of

England are so ignorant that they cannot find a lecturer in their community' (Harris, 1906, p. 6). What was required was a cultured and cultivated gentleman of a type thought to be common in the Church of England, who spoke with an engaging fluency and could deliver a learned, elegant and uplifting sermon with grace and refinement. These ambitions found institutional embodiment in Jews' College, a seminary founded in 1855 on the initiative of Nathan Adler, who, according to Cecil Roth, was 'the father of the Anglo-Jewish pulpit'. The Chief Rabbi's intention was to secure an adequate supply of clerical cadres to minister to the masses and service the synagogues with gentlemen preachers. These in due course came to grace the pulpits which many synagogues erected alongside the traditional reading-desks.

The manners of a gentleman, though necessary, were not a sufficient qualification for membership of the cloth. His oratorical skills notwithstanding, the Jewish minister was also expected to undertake the full range of duties performed by his peers in other denominations (see O'Day, *RVB*, I, 5). Visiting the sick at home; an enthusiasm for counselling the poor, comforting the bereaved and consoling the afflicted; charitable work and a willingness to undertake the extra-mural activities which such work entailed — these were increasingly identified as desirable qualities by synagogal appointment boards. Pastoral care, Hermann Adler insisted, was central to the reconstructed ministry. Its mission was defined and developed in a set of guidelines, issued to ministers in 1886, which underscored the significance of regular visitation conducted in a professional and business-like manner. The laity concurred. Lord Rothschild, who spoke for many, put it in a nutshell when expressing his desire for 'a minister living like a Christian clergyman in the midst of his flock' (Sharot, 1973, pp. 177–8).

Not only was the Jewish minister to perform like his Christian counterpart: he was also expected to look like him. A conference of ministers, convened in 1909, resolved to extend the term 'Reverend' to readers as well as to ministers. *Shohetim* (ritual slaughterers of meat and poultry), however, were excluded. Dog-collars and the outward habiliments of the Christian clergy, which Jewish pastors had taken to wearing, were meant to signify something more than an evident and decent distinction from the laity; as the Rev. A. A. Green, minister of the Hampstead Synagogue, put it:

> the clerical garb ... has shown the Christian world ... the foreign Jew ... [and] the English Jewish boy and girl that a Jewish minister had the bearing, the position and the educational standing of ministers of other denominations ... The foreign Jew has learnt that a Jewish minister can be an English gentleman, and the same revelation

> has been made to thousands upon thousands of Christian Englishmen whose idea of a Rabbi had been a man who cut the throats of bullocks for the Jews.
>
> (Sharot, 1973, p. 180)

The startled response of the newcomers from Eastern Europe strikingly revealed the extent of the Anglicization of the Jewish ministry. To the refugee fundamentalists, accustomed to non-uniformed rabbis and teachers, those who dominated the Anglo-Jewish ministry looked more like Jesuits than Jews.

Notwithstanding the strange apparel and adopted style, the Jewish minister remained an inferior sort of clergyman. The supremacy of the Chief Rabbi diminished his status in the eyes of 'foreign' Jews and undermined confidence in his calling. A prima donna-ish resistance to the extension of rabbinical status, on the part of the Chief Rabbi, deprived the lower clergy of the prestige attendant upon the exercise of scholarly and judicial authority. To Solomon Schechter, that penetrating and witty critic, the modern minister seemed little more than a drone. 'The Jewish clergy' he wrote in 1901, '... is rapidly losing touch with the venerable Rabbi of Jewish tradition, whose chief office was to teach and to learn *Torah* [the Mosaic or Jewish law]. With us the duty of learning (or study of the *Torah*) seems to be of the least moment in the life of the minister ... In his capacity as full Reverend, he is expected to divide his time between the offices of cantor, prayer, preacher, book-keeper, debt-collector, almoner and social agitator ... Occasionally rumour spreads anent some minister, that he neglects his duty to his congregation, through his being secretly addicted to Jewish learning. But such rumours often turn out to be sheer malice ...' (Schechter, 1908, p. 196). Grudging reforms, introduced in that year, enabled candidates to obtain the rabbinical diploma by examination at Jews' College under the presidency of the Chief Rabbi, but came too late to affect any significant improvement in the position of the ministry.

Ministers not only felt compromised in the eyes of East European immigrants; it is unlikely that their standing with native Jewish congregations bore comparison with that of parson and parishioner. Although ministers were better paid than their Christian counterparts, the distance between the minister and his congregation was, in social and material terms, often greater than that which separated priest and people. The Jewish clergy, recruited from the lower middle classes, ministered to an *haute bourgeoisie* in the synagogues compared to whom they felt like poor relations. The borrowed plumage of Anglicanism, moreover, provided little compensation or comfort. Its outward trappings represented the shadow and not the substance of a sacerdotalism that was foreign to post-biblical Judaism. Unable to appropriate its priestly role in its entirety, they fell back, without enthusiasm, upon pastoral duties which were themselves in process of devolution to secular welfare agencies. Truly, a minister's lot was not a happy one (Sharot, 1973, pp. 182–3; Newman, 1976, p. 55).

V

The Anglo-Jewish establishment during the Queen's reign faced two serious challenges. The most disturbing arose out of the unsettled condition of the Tsar's Jewish subjects at the beginning of the eighties. Between 1880 and 1914 the Jewish population rose from 60,000 to an estimated 300,000 souls. Immigrant and native Jews were sharply differentiated in level of income and depth of devotion. There was in fact an inverse relationship between the poverty and piety of the immigrant. As the Reverend Moses Abrahams of Leeds observed: '. . . it is the very poorest who keep the religious statutes strictest . . . the poorer the man the more strictly he adheres to those laws; it is a notorious fact' (PP 1889, X, QQ. 1217, 1221). The resultant strains — cultural, institutional, social and political — affected both the internal cohesion of the community and its standing in the nation at large. Mass migration from Eastern Europe, coinciding with renewed fears about national degeneration, gave rise to a 'Jewish Question' of a kind hitherto unknown on this side of the Channel (Feldman, 1986, pp. 183–242). The Reform Movement, by contrast, which had so disrupted German Jewry, registered a well-publicized but comparatively minor effect upon communal solidarity.

Anglo-Jewry was singularly free from the communal convulsions unleashed by the progress of Reform Judaism throughout Central Europe and the United States. Reform Judaism, a product of the *Haskalah* (Jewish Enlightenment) and French Revolution, represented an adjustment mechanism whereby the desire for social integration and acceptance could be satisfied without resort to the baptismal font. To this end the ancestral faith was to be modified.

In addition to sundry external reforms that aimed to bring order and solemnity to the public service and render it intelligible to the laity, Reform Judaism was distinguished by a discriminatory approach to the oral law. The distinction drawn between the prescriptions of the Pentateuch and the status of the rabbinical enlargements embodied in the Talmud, supplied a rationale for the modernization of Judaism. Rabbinical Judaism, with its emphasis upon election, exile, expiation and restoration, encased the faith within a nationalist framework which privileged Jews and served to perpetuate their social and cultural isolation. Reformers rejected it outright. The Chosen People, they insisted, were the bearers rather than the sole beneficiaries of God's grace. Judaism represented a mission to mankind; Jews constituted a religious community, not a nation. Equally important to their conception of Judaism as a universal rather than a national faith was the altered role of the Messiah. In place of the personal Messiah anticipated by Rabbinic Judaism, the reformers looked forward to a Messianic age of universal peace and goodwill initiated, not by an outstanding individual of the house of David, but by the priesthood of the whole people of Israel. Judaism, purged of its irrational rituals and divisive particularism, would serve to promote the reconciliation of Jew and Gentile. In short, the projection of Judaism as a universal faith was both rational and politic.

Anglo-Jewry, though cognizant of these controversies, was little affected by them. In Britain, where social acceptance preceded emancipation, pressures to modernize the faith were less urgent than elsewhere. The issues raised by Reform Judaism were in any case a minority concern. To the majority of Jews *Halacha* (Jewish law) signified little: *Haskalah* even less. Neither Orthodox nor Reform Judaism addressed their predominantly secular interests. A survey of the spiritual life of the community at mid-century was thus prefaced with the observation that there existed numerous Jews 'to whom . . . many of the facts recorded in the following pages are as strange as to the Christian reader' (Mills, 1853, p. iv). Support for Orthodoxy was strongest among the middle class of shopkeepers and small merchants; the upper class held itself aloof, while the working classes and labouring poor, with the exception of a fair-sized contingent of *Shulchan Aruch* Jews from Eastern Europe, were indifferent. The street Jews interviewed by Mayhew, for example, knew little of *Yiddishkeit* (Jewish way of life) and possessed but the haziest notions of the faith. Whether *trefa* (forbidden food) or *kosher* meat was consumed was to them immaterial (Mayhew, 1861, II, p. 124). Box office takings rose appreciably in East End theatres over the weekend, primarily owing to the profanation of the Jewish Sabbath; in pubs, clubs and establishments of low repute trade was equally as brisk, and for much the same reason. Weekdays were almost as bad: without paid *minyan*-men it was impossible to maintain the daily service of the synagogue.

The loss of faith, though, was not a product of the Victorian period. The autarchic character of traditional Jewish culture had, in fact, been abandoned well before the Queen's accession. Two factors were responsible. First, the absence of restraints that was a marked feature of state and society in the English-speaking world made for rapid acculturation; and second, the synagogue was not immune from the desacrilizing pressures visited upon church and chapel. By the close of the eighteenth century religion occupied but part of the life of the well-to-do Jew and a very small part of that of his poorest co-religionists (Endelman, 1979).

To the Jewish poor the interior of the synagogue was virtually *terra incognita*. And so it had always been. The absence of the lower orders was a significant feature of the earliest congregations. The Creechurch Lane Synagogue, the first to be consecrated after the Re-admission, was about as exclusive as a Pall Mall club. A non-Jewish correspondent, who attended the Sabbath service early in 1662, noted the 'comely, gallant, proper gentlemen' who comprised the one hundred-strong congregation, 'most of them rich in apparel, divers with jewels glittering'. 'I saw not one mechanic of them' (Hyamson, 1951, p. 19). Class exclusiveness was accentuated by the predominant form of synagogal organization. Taking as its model the closed municipal corporation of the eighteenth and early-nineteenth centuries, government within the London synagogues rapidly evolved into a self-recruiting and self-perpetuating oligarchy whose constitutional arrangements bore striking resemblance, in both name and practice, to the prevailing pattern of parish administration. Synagogues had their vestries, overseers and wardens; while privileged membership, like the freedom of a corporation, was a species of property to be bought for oneself and bequeathed to one's children (Lipman, 1959a, p. 85).

The distinction between those who paid and those who prayed was pronounced. Seating arrangements within the synagogue, based on the principle that wealthiness was next to Godliness, were an expression of communal hierarchy. The price of seats restricted membership to the privileged classes. Even the middling sort found the cost prohibitive. In 1847 the conjoint membership of the six London synagogues represented less than one tenth of metropolitan Jewry (Sharot, 1971, p. 131). Donations, too, served to advertise the wealth and relative standing of congregants. Gifts inscribed with the family name of the benefactor adorned the synagogue and reinforced distinctions between members. 'There is ... a great deal too much display of mundane influence in the house of God', declared the *Jewish Chronicle*, '... too much distinction between rich and poor in a place where all ought to appear alike humble' (*JC*, 11 October 1850).

The poor, though not debarred from worship, were given few inducements to attend. Not only in the Church of England was the working-class worshipper made to feel his place; the working man in the synagogue was about as welcome as a drunk at a funeral. As one of them put it: 'our poverty is thrown in our face at the synagogue; we are pushed and shoved about as soon as we go beyond the aristocratic bar, and more especially when the Chief Rabbi delivers his monthly lectures; we are all heaped together in a corner, whilst at the top the benches are empty, and present a most dismal appearance' (Sharot, 1979, p. 213). Prejudice of this sort was more than most Jews could bear. A comparison of the Sabbath attendance figures, as enumerated in the Religious Census of 1851, suggests a much lower level of observance among Jews than among Gentiles; 16 per cent of the Anglo-Jewish population as against 40.5 per cent of the Anglo-Christian population attended the service of the Sabbath (Sharot, 1971, p. 133). Only on High Holy Days was there a full turnout.

The missionary impulse was not, however, the defining feature of Reform Judaism in Britain, which was élitist rather than evangelical in character. The 'Great Secession', as the events which culminated in the formation of an independent reform congregation are inappropriately known, was the product of frustration and faction within Bevis Marks, the principal Sephardi synagogue (Hyamson, 1951, pp. 269–95). Doctrinal and theological issues were not involved. The 'length and imperfections of the order of service ... [and] ... the inconvenient hours at which it is appointed' supplied one of the twin foci of agitation; the refusal of the Sephardi authorities to sanction the formation of a western branch synagogue, supplied the other. Affluent members who had removed from the City, were in consequence unable to satisfy their spiritual needs unless willing to *schlepp* (traipse) to and from their Mayfair homes on the Sabbath. The want of dignity and decorum in the place of worship and the prospect of a footsore *Shabbos*, which underlay the rebellion of 1840, were not, however, unique to the Spanish and Portuguese community. The Sephardi schismatics were joined by a number of like-minded Ashkenazi dissidents who together formed the West London Reform Synagogue of British Jews in 1842.

The Reformers, recruited from among the most acculturated elements of the élite, were in most other respects indistinguishable as a group from the upper-class seatholders who comprised the Ashkenazi and Sephardi congregations. In neither sociological nor in spiritual terms was the distance between them great. Prayer-book reform in the West London Reform Synagogue amounted to little more than abbreviation and omission. No radical reconstruction of the liturgy was contemplated. References to the Resurrection, the personal Messiah, the Election of Israel, the return to Zion and the restoration of the sacrificial cult in the Temple of Jerusalem, were all retained. Revisions in ritual were equally undemanding. Changes in the hours of divine service, the introduction of choral singing and of preaching in the vernacular, were sufficient to satisfy the rebels. For seventeen years the sanctuary remained without an organ; while the separation of the sexes persisted until after the First World War.

Most of the amendments introduced into the service of the reform congregation were not different in kind from those which, with one exception, were subsequently incorporated into Orthodox practice. The exception concerned the status of the second days of the Festivals. The additional twenty-four hours was a post-biblical development, sanctioned by the rabbis in order to ensure the proper observance of the Festivals in the far-flung communities of the Diaspora. Improved transport and communications, it was argued, now made the abolition of the second days desirable. This apparently innocuous proposal struck at the vitals of Rabbinic Judaism and the Chief Rabbi, its principal guardian, struck back. The secessionists were promptly anathematized. The excommunication, issued by the Chief Rabbi and endorsed by the Sephardi authorities, served to render the split permanent.

The turmoil, however, was not protracted. Reform Judaism displayed little capacity for further growth. Independent congregations, established in Manchester and Bradford, proved short lived. The beleaguered West London Synagogue itself, having overcome the obstruction of the Board of Deputies and obtained permission to certify and register marriages, became as conservative an institution as the United Synagogue: in fact, wrote one observer, 'it has become quite as wedded to its traditions as are the orthodox congregations to theirs' (Philipson, 1907, pp. 144–5).

Continental contemporaries, viewing the development of Reform Judaism in these islands, would have been provoked by its particularism, puzzled by its Biblicism and perplexed by the rash and wrathful reception it encountered. Ludwig Philippson, the celebrated German reformer, for example, found the whole thing beyond his ken (Leigh, 1975, p. 22). Historians, too, have experienced some difficulty in developing an adequate characterization. Too often Reform Judaism in Britain has been presented as an echo effect of the German Reform Movement rather than an indigenous development that addressed the condition of Anglo-Jewry (Philipson, 1907, pp. 122–46; Lipman, 1961, pp. 82–4; Finestein, 1957, pp. 99, 126–8). The tendency has been to regard Reform Judaism as a minor variant within a uniform modernization process that was initiated with the Mendelssohnian Enlightenment and crossed the North Sea around the beginning of the Queen's reign. The comparison has not been to the advantage of the British. The want of insight and imagination have thus been identified as distinctive features. Michael Leigh, for example, concludes that, in theological terms, Reform Judaism in Britain was an invertebrate creature fitfully sustained by a negative anti-Talmudism that was inconsistent in application and political in inspiration (Leigh, 1975, p. 40).

A re-interpretation of the British Reform Movement in political terms has, indeed, been undertaken. Reform Judaism in Britain, it is suggested, represented something more than a response to an unsatisfied demand for greater order and solemnity within the Synagogue. The Great Secession, so the argument runs, provided a vehicle for dissident elements within the élite who were alienated by the moderation of the Board of Deputies in relation to the campaign for Jewish Emancipation. The creation of an independent reform congregation, on this reading, must be viewed as an attempt to construct 'an alternative political structure to the Board of Deputies' (Liberles, 1976, pp. 121–50). Political considerations, though doubtlessly important, do not, however, supply an adequate explanation for the curious combination of liturgical conservatism and militant anti-rabbinism that was without parallel in either Germany or the United States. It is the singularity of Anglo-Jewry that invites attention.

In Germany, Reform Judaism became the creed of the acculturated upper classes who wished to retain a Jewish identity but considered Jewish particularism an obstacle to their social acceptance and integration. Support for Orthodox Judaism was strongest among the rural poor, to whom upward mobility and advancement in Gentile society were irrelevant and immaterial. In liberal Britain, the pressures which compelled the wealthy to abjure their faith or dilute it were but feebly felt. The Anglo-Jewish élite, unlike its German analogue, was not persuaded of the need to abandon the ritual and nationalistic features of the faith as proof of its fitness for civil and political equality. On the contrary. Conversion was neither necessary nor desirable. 'To abandon one's faith is no longer regarded as a passport to good society, or as a preliminary entrance into public life', wrote James Picciotto in 1875. 'Apostasy is not considered by right-minded Christians as a title to their confidence, and a conscientious Jew may aspire to serve his country and to rise to high dignity, and still remain an open and zealous believer in the Lord of Israel' (Picciotto, 1875, p. 299). Among upper-class Jewry social rather than spiritual considerations were, indeed, uppermost. Their continued attachment to Orthodoxy owed more to religiosity than to religion, to what was prescribed by 'Society' than commanded by the Almighty. Sabbath observance, for example, remained *de rigeur* in the best social circles throughout the Queen's reign and beyond. No-one who was anyone worked on the Sabbath and few upper-class Jews did so. Public worship and family prayers were the 'done thing' and Jews were determined to do them. Conformity in religion, as in speech or dress, defined that gentility to which they aspired. In short, religion was respectable and for that reason alone it was worth the upkeep (Endelman, 1985, pp. 491–526). Orthodox ideas and observance thus continued to hold sway. 'It was this acceptance of Orthodoxy and the lack of desire for reform by the most acculturated and modernized class in the community', writes Steven Singer, 'which set London apart as a unique example of Jewish life in the nineteenth century' (Singer, 1981, p. 8).

Not only in its limited size and importance does Reform Judaism in Britain stand in marked contrast to its American and Continental contemporaries; its neo-Karaite character is no less singular (Petuchowski, 1960, pp. 223–48). Ironically, the same congenial climate that served to check the growth of Reform Judaism in these islands also exerted a profound influence upon its ideology and practice. Its neo-Karaite cast represented a form of scriptural Judaism which accepted the divinity of the Written Law but denied that of the Oral Law. In brief, the reformers maintained that the Mosaic Law was God given and its truths eternal; the Oral Law, by contrast, represented nothing but the opinions of men. The formidable body of interpretation and rabbinic tradition that was embodied in the Talmud remained worthy of respect but no longer shared an equal authority with the Bible.

This neo-Karaite critique of Rabbinical Judaism partly accounts for the comparative moderation of the secessionist congregation. British Reform Jews, unlike their German contemporaries, did not dispense with the ceremonial laws of the Bible. Phylacteries and prayer shawls continued to be worn and the dietary laws strictly observed. In its internal structure, too, the Reform Synagogue continued to conform to Orthodox practice. The *bimah* or reader's platform remained situated at the rear while the congregation continued to worship in Hebrew.

Indeed, the distance that separated Orthodox Judaism from Reform Judaism was not wide. The resistance encountered by the Chief Rabbi's antediluvian attempts to secure conformity were symptomatic of a general desire to avoid a division of the community into two armed camps. The notice of excommunication, which was to be proclaimed or posted in every synagogue in the land, was returned by Manchester, torn up by Liverpool and burnt by Plymouth. Metropolitan Jewry, too, withheld unanimous support. The Wardens of the Western Synagogue, in explaining their rejection, observed that 'it would be impossible to follow the spirit of the declaration without producing a schism in the congregation and disunion among the members, many of whom were entirely opposed to displaying any feeling of intolerance towards their brethren in faith' (Barnett, 1961, p. 181). Moderation was not merely politic, it also reflected the broad diffusion of reform ideas throughout the élite. Neo-Karaite ideas were not in fact the exclusive property of the secessionist congregation. The co-existence of a closet Karaism and a casual Karaism within the Orthodox community suggests that divisions among professing Jews are best represented by a traditional/progressive rather than an Orthodox/Reform dichotomy.

The neo-Karaite character of progressive opinion within Anglo-Jewry reflected the impact of the non-Jewish environment; for the Karaism that permeated the London community was without parallel in any other centre of Jewish settlement. Its roots, writes Dr Singer, '. . . must, therefore, be found within Gentile English society and the currents of thought present there, rather than be considered the local result of a philosophical movement agitating the entire Western Jewish world' (Singer, 1981, p. 74). Perceptive contemporaries were themselves conscious of the connection. Israel Zangwill, in a striking phrase, described the reformers as 'the Protestants of Judaism' (Zangwill, 1912, p. 390); and, as Dr Singer has shown, it was the pronounced Bibliocentrism of British Protestantism to which they and their sympathisers were most susceptible.

Jews occupied a unique place in English Protestant thought. The study of Scripture in general and the Prophets in particular focused attention upon the futurity of the Chosen People, arousing millenial expectations and a conversionist philosemitism which found forceful expression in seventeenth-century Puritanism and remained a vital influence upon Victorian Evangelicalism (Vreté, 1972, pp. 8–50; Katz, 1982). Indeed, Biblical awareness in Shaftesbury's England was comparable with that of Cromwellian England. Jews were not unaffected by the Bibliocentrism of the English. The progressives, drawn from the most acculturated elements of the élite, moved in the best circles and were not unmindful of the antagonism provoked by Rabbinical Judaism. Christian critics identified the Talmud as the principal obstacle to the integration of the Jews into the wider society. The Talmud and its teachings were condemned as a source of superstition, separatism, sterility and subversion. It was this attachment to rabbinicism which, in the eyes of the Evangelical Englishman, reduced Judaism to the same status as Catholicism, a religion which was also held to be deficient in its respect for the Word of God.

The Protestant environment not only supplied the sources of Victorian neo-Karaism; it also determined the prospects for reform within the minority religion. The moderating influence of the Church of England upon progressive opinion within the Anglo-Jewish élite in no small part accounts for the arrested development of Reform Judaism in this country. Opponents invariably argued that it would encourage the sectarian fragmentation of the community. Philipson, writing at the turn of the century, observed how in Britain the Anglican presence gave these arguments a special force: 'for there, as everywhere, the Jews are affected by their surroundings, and the doctrine of conformity to an established church which represents the prevailing religious attitude in England reacted and reacts without doubt upon the Jews, and for that reason it has been difficult for reform to gain a foothold in Anglo-Judaism' (Philipson, 1907, p. 128).

Conformity in religion also conferred social status; dissent, by contrast, had negative associations. The distinction was not lost upon upper-class Jewry. The progressive elements who perceived an analogy between Church and Chapel and Orthodox and Reform Judaism needed no reminding that gentlemen did not attend chapel. These, the most Anglicized elements in the community, also preferred evolution to revolution in religious reform and recoiled from the unseemly happenings which had produced a violent rupture within German Jewry. Equally consistent with their Anglican frame of reference was an unequivocal rejection of congregational control of doctrine and liturgy. It was this aspect of the reform movement which gave most cause for concern. The 'powers of making such important alterations assumed by a few unlearned men', declared the by no means unsympathetic *Jewish Chronicle*, 'is a usurpation forming a most dangerous precedent' (*JC*, 20 December 1844). Lay intervention not only smacked of American-style congregationalism; it was also perceived as disrespectful of tradition and therefore disturbing. 'I don't believe in reforms being brought about by merchants and city men', said Arthur Cohen in defence of the United Synagogue (Leigh, 1973, p. 31). Like-minded establishment figures of progressive outlook turned from the laity to an Anglicanized Chief Rabbi as the agent of improvement. 'Through their absorption of the concepts of Gentile society', writes Dr Singer, 'the progressives had come to look upon the Chief Rabbi, not as a traditional rabbinic scholar with the power to interpret the law, but rather as an Anglican bishop, possessing the right to grant dispensations from the observances required by *halacha* (Singer, 1981, p. 87).

Acceptance of Anglicanism touched externals rather than essentials. The Higher Criticism, as represented in Anglican theology, was, for example, unacceptable to traditionalist and progressive alike, though paradoxically it was the rabbinists who were least put out by it. Although no systematic study of Anglo-Jewish responses has as yet been published, it is clear that the community was by no means unaware of the religous rumpus occasioned by the advent of the Higher Criticism. One of the earliest replies, *Bishop Colenso's Objections to the Historical Character of the Pentateuch and the Book of Joshua . . . Critically Examined*, came from the pen of Dr Abraham Benisch, the progressive editor of the *Jewish Chronicle*. His book, published in 1863, was a vigorous defence of the Old Testament, the content of which was already familiar to *Chronicle* readers where it had previously appeared as the leading article for fourteen consecutive weeks! (Roth, 1949, p. 73). However, the heterogeneous composition of the Pentateuch, the comparatively late date of the Levitical Legislation and the post-exilic origins of certain Prophecies and Psalms, raised questions about the future of Judaism which Benisch's bravura did not begin to answer. In press and pulpit, wrote Solomon Schechter, the question was often asked: 'What now will become of Judaism when its last stronghold, the Law, is being shaken to its very foundations?' (Schechter, 1896, p. xiii).

'Catholic Judaism', his own reply, reflected the impact of the German 'Historical School' and its attempt to shift the centre of gravity in Judaism from Scripture to Tradition. Tradition, i.e. the Oral Law, as embodied in the Talmud and codified in the *Shulchan Aruch*, supplied the faith with a self-sustaining dynamism that enabled it to respond through changing circumstances. In short, the 'Historical School' was to Orthodox Jewry what *Essays and Reviews* and *Lux Mundi* were to Broad Church and High Church respectively. Krochmal, Rapoport and Zunz had, in the words of Schechter's biographer, 'called into being a new world of continuing development to redress the balance of the old world of literal inspiration' (Bentwich, 1938, p. 285). Tradition thus appeared in Schechter's conception of Catholic Judaism as a progressive force developing from age to age in the living body of the Jewish people as expressed in the Universal Synagogue. 'The Synagogue, with its long continuous cry after God for more than twenty-three centuries . . . the only true witness to the past, and forming in all ages the sublimest expression of Israel's religious life, must . . . retain its authority as the sole true guide for the present and the future. And being in communion with this Synagogue, we may also look hopefully for a sage and rational solution to our present theological troubles' (Schechter, 1896, pp. xxi-xxii). Implicit within his conception of Tradition was the superiority of custom over Scripture and primitive Judaism in forming the rule of practice. 'The norm as well as the sanction of Judaism is the practice actually in vogue. Its consecration is the consecration of general use, — or, in other words, of Catholic Israel' (Schechter, 1896, p. xxiii).

Schechter's influence was greatest in the United States where his brand of progressive conservatism accorded with the practice of observant Jews who found Reform and Orthodox Judaism unsatisfactory. (Davies, 1963). The Anglo-Jewish Establishment, though stung by his denunciations of its 'Flunkey Judaism', also found few grounds for dissent. Schechter's approach, though, was atypical. The Reader in Talmudic Studies at the University of Cambridge and a gifted practitioner of the Lower Criticism, Schechter was a passionate champion of Jewish tradition against the Pauline prejudice which enabled a Wellhausen to dismiss post-Pentateuchal Judaism as mere degradation. Such prejudice absolved the mass of Jews from any obligation to consider seriously the findings and implications of contemporary Christian scholarship. Schechter's damning phrase, 'the higher anti-Semitism', was symptomatic of the marginal position which the Higher Criticism occupied within the consciouness of Anglo-Jewry.

VI

Essays and Reviews and the reverberations set off by Colenso's assault upon the historical accuracy of the Pentateuch passed over the Jewish immigrant from Eastern Europe as the Angel of Death had once passed over his forebears. The newcomers, drawn from an environment that had been largely untouched by the rationalism and universalism of the *Haskalah* made no attempt to engage with the new school of textual and historical criticism. 'Scientific Judaism', as developed in Germany, left them cold. Nor were they moved by the denationalized spiritualism of Claude Montefiore and the Liberal separatists organised in the Jewish Religious Union (founded 1901). Trinitarian hymns and other alien practices incorporated into its liturgy made Liberal Judaism abhorrent to the pious people from the East. The Chief Rabbi, though unreserved in his condemnation of these 'un-Jewish' excesses, was not himself above suspicion. The Christian character of the Jewish ministry and the structure and spirit of the United Synagogue made native Orthodox Judaism scarcely less suspect. Immigrants accustomed to commune with unrestrained zeal and passionate self-abandonment found the sober service and board-room ethos of the United Synagogue singularly deficient. The proliferation of *chevroth*, where devotion took precedence over decorum, expressed their desire for a more satisfying form of worship.

These institutions, however, were something more than voluntary associations for devotional purposes. To thousands of newly-arrived Jews the *chevra* was, in Gartner's phrase, 'the primary cell of their social life' (Gartner, 1973, p. 187). Its role as a social, spiritual and cultural shock absorber was noted by contemporaries. The *chevroth*, wrote Beatrice Webb in 1889, combine the 'functions of a benefit club for death, sickness and mourning rites with that of public worship and the study of the Talmud. Thirty or forty of these *Chevras* [sic] are scattered throughout the Jewish quarters . . . Usually each *Chevra* is named after the town or district in Russia or Poland from which the majority of its members have emigrated: it is, in fact, from old associations — from ties of relationship or friendship, or, at least, from the memory of a common home — that the new association springs' (Booth, 1902, III, 1st series, p. 169). Disdaining the institutions of Anglo-Jewry, the immigrant communities established their own counterparts modelled on those left behind in the Russian Pale. Attached to the *chevra* was the *Beth Hamerdrash*, a study circle for adults, and a *cheder*, a class for the instruction of the young. Here, under the guidance of a *melammed* (teacher), the sons of the ghetto would learn Hebrew and the elements of Judaism. The daughters, though comparatively neglected, were not denied all opportunity to participate in prayer. The *chevra* usually possessed an adequate supply of the *Beis Rachel*, a popular prayer-book, written in Yiddish, with commentaries and legends, which enabled immigrant women, who did not as a rule read Hebrew, to follow the service.

The sparsely-furnished, foetid and somewhat insanitary dwelling in which the average *chevra* was located presented a striking contrast with the imposing and more salubrious settings of the United Synagogue or the Church of England. The appearance of the congregation and conduct of the service were no less curious. Israel Zangwill, the Jewish Dickens, commented on both. 'They dropped in, mostly in their workaday garments and grime, and rumbled and roared and chorused prayers with a zeal that shook the window-panes, and there was never lack of a *Minyan* . . .' The little synagogue was more than a place of worship, however, 'It was their salon and their lecture-hall. It supplied them not only with their religion, but with their art and letters, their politics, and their public amusements. It was *their* home as well as the Almighty's . . .' (Zangwill, 1914, pp. 154–5).

The enthusiasm and passion that characterized the proceedings were lost on the casual observer, who found the moaning and swaying, talking and praying, indecorous and unintelligible. Appearances, however, were deceptive. The commotion and crying, the singing and sighing, obscured a simple and sublime service which participants found meaningful and moving. 'It is indeed difficult to realise how strong is the affection which the Jewish liturgy excites amongst those who have grown up under its influence', wrote Harry S. Lewis at the turn of the century. A sensitive and perceptive critic who inclined to Liberal Judaism, Lewis nevertheless appreciated the poetry and the power contained in the Orthodox service. The *chevra*, he wrote, 'is the seat of deep devotion — a devotion full of self-abandonment, supplying the worshipper with an inspiration which transfigures his life and makes him feel that he too has a share in the traditions and hopes of the chosen race' (Russell and Lewis, 1900, pp. 206–7). And even where, as was so often the case, the service was but imperfectly understood, its musical portions provided an uplifting experience that served to confirm the unlettered Jew in his faith. Diffusive Judaism was no less potent than its Christian counterpart. An Anglican clergyman who, some years earlier, attended the Friday evening service at the Great Synagogue, Duke's Place, Aldgate, noted its force. 'I was amazed at the musical beauty of the service', he wrote. The choral work, sad and mournful, seemed 'as though it were really being sung by captive Jews beside the waters of Babylon' (Davies, 1876, p. 194).[4] Participation was what mattered. The chanting and the singing, even when the Hebrew words were unintelligible, registered an effect. The worshipper, as Lewis put it, 'feels a spiritual glow as he repeats the words which his father taught him, and which link him with so many past generations of Jewish worshippers'. Imagination, he added, would supply the hidden meaning (Russell and Lewis, 1900, p. 208).

The *chevroth* stirred the imagination of countless thousands. In the East End alone they provided the spiritual requirements of an estimated 15,000 souls (PP 1888, XI, Q. 2700). Extra-synagogal organization on this scale posed a threat to the unity of the community and the authority of its leaders. The *chevroth* were snubbed by the Chief Rabbi and deplored by the notables. To the Manchester Jewish Board of Guardians the *chevra* was a 'clandestine religious society' that impeded the process of Anglicization. Other critics were less restrained. 'The sooner the Hebra movement is crushed out of existence', wrote one Jewish clergyman, 'the sooner we will remove from our midst the only drawback to the advancement of Jews in this country' (Gartner, 1973, pp. 200–1).

Those without experience of the sobbing spirituality of the *chazenim* of old will find 'The Great Cantors', a recently released disc on the Pearl label, issued by Pavilion Records, instructive and moving.

The spectre of a separatist immigrant community, organized around an autonomous federation of small synagogues, was, however, sufficient to persuade Samuel Montagu, the observant bullion broker, to act. The Federation of Synagogues, formed on his initiative in 1887, was in large part a response to the spread of secessionist sentiment that had become apparent during the course of the decade. Unlike most communal magnates, who viewed the *chevra* movement as an embarrassment, Montagu, the Liberal Member for Whitechapel, recognized certain positive features. These, as Beatrice Webb observed, were easily obscured by the unwholesome environment: 'it is easy to overlook the unseen influence for good of self-creating, self-supporting, and self governing communities; small enough to generate public opinion and the practical supervision of private morals, and large enough to stimulate charity, worship, and study by communion and example' (Booth, 1902, III, 1st Series, p. 172). Montagu, who dominated the new body until his death in 1911, offered generous financial assistance for the improvement of synagogal facilities in East London and in general subtly sought to expose the 'foreign' Jew to the beneficent influence of the English. The Federation of Synagogues was more than an essay in containment, however. The integration of the *chevroth* with mainstream Jewry, it was hoped, might also serve to revitalize a somewhat somnolent Orthodox establishment. Montagu's attempts to incorporate the *chevroth* within established communal institutions were nevertheless insufficient to prevent schism.

Dissatisfaction with the compromised latitudinarian practices of the Anglo-Jewish establishment culminated in the formation of the *Machzigei HaDath* (Upholders of Religion), an ultra-orthodox association of German and East European Jews, that was founded in 1891–2. To be free of the Chief Rabbi, the 'West End *goy*', as Dr Adler was irreverently known, and his deficient supervision of the *shehitah* (slaughter of cattle and poultry according to Jewish law) system; to cast out the neo-Karaites and fortify themselves against Sabbath desecrators; to protect themselves from the spread of infidelity and to walk in the paths of righteousness required the creation of an independent synagogue-community in which traditional standards of piety would be maintained. Rabbi Werner, 'a Rabbi great in wisdom and religious fervour whose authority, competence and sanctity' had been attested by 'the great Rabbinical authorities of Russia and Poland' was chosen as its guide and teacher. The magnificent Huguenot church in Brick Lane that was acquired shortly afterwards, quickly became the most popular of East London synagogues. Ironically, it was the financial difficulties brought about by the cost of this centre for worship and study that finally forced the separatists to reach an accommodation with the Chief Rabbinate. *Machzigei HaDath*, though compelled to abandon its independence, did not surrender unconditionally. The authority of the Chief Rabbi was acknowledged 'provided that he acts in accordance with the Shulchan Aruch' (Gartner, 1973, pp. 209–14).

Failure to sustain a self-sufficient community did not, however, result in a rapprochement between immigrant and native Jews. 'There is a constant danger ... of a secession from the authority of the Chief Rabbi of the foreign element', said the Rev. J. P. Stern, the sole representative of the United Synagogue in Tower Hamlets. Dr Adler, he added, 'has to exercise all his powers of caution and diplomacy to avoid a rupture'. Stern spoke from experience. The introduction of a mixed choir, following the example of the Hammersmith and Hampstead Synagogues, led to a secession from his own congregation and the formation of an 'Orthodox Stepney Synagogue' close by (B197, pp. 89–91). Outside London, where the absence of the United Synagogue diminished further the authority of the Chief Rabbi, relations were no less tense. Not only were the tiny tabernacles equally as resistant, but provincial communities were often able to support a rabbi — some of considerable distinction — as their spiritual leader.

VII

Conflict between native and immigrant was not confined to the religious sphere. It was the political implications of mass immigration which agitated the native community and conditioned its responses to the newcomers. The rapid increase in the Jewish population between 1880 and 1905, its ghetto-like concentration in East London, Leeds and Manchester and the hostile response it engendered, alarmed the Anglo-Jewish élite. Overcrowded insanitary slums let at exorbitant rents were, it was claimed, the result of unrestricted alien immigration. Not only had the Englishman been ousted from his home, his job too had been seized by aliens who were willing to work without regard to hours, conditions or rates of pay. Public health and private employment were not the sole considerations; public morals were threatened by the alleged licentiousness of the immigrant and public order by his criminal and political subversion. These fears were central to the definition of the 'Aliens Question' and the growing clamour for the abolition of unrestricted immigration. Political anti-semitism, hitherto absent from these islands, now found institutionalized expression in proto-fascist bodies such as the British Brothers League, which stomped the streets of East London at the turn of the century (Garrard, 1971; Gainer, 1972; Fishman, 1975, pp. 245–6; Holmes, 1979).

The Anglo-Jewish Establishment, having anticipated popular reaction, went to extraordinary lengths to dissuade the victims of Tsarist persecution from seeking permanent residence in this country. The immigrants from the

East were perceived as a destabilizing element whose proposed resettlement imperilled both themselves and their hosts. To native Jewry the newcomers represented more than a threat to its position in the polity, however: the 'ghetto Jew' also posed a challenge to its self-image. Anglicized Jews, like their acculturated and assimilated co-religionists in France and Germany, carried with their critics much of the intellectual beggage of anti-semitism. Immigrants and their offspring were too easily thought of as less than human. Moses Angel, headmaster of the Jews' Free School, for example, considered his charges as worse than senseless things: 'until they have been Anglicised or humanized', he remarked 'it was difficult to tell what was their moral condition' (Gartner, 1973, p. 223). Only those deemed capable of cultural conversion received any assistance. 'In fact', said Hermann Landau of the Jewish Board of Guardians, 'if a man arrives here who, in our opinion, would not easily become Anglicised, we do our very best to return him to his own country' (PP 1888, XI, Q. 2456). He was not kidding. Between 1880 and 1914, 50,000 immigrants were repatriated or sent elsewhere by the Board and its associates (Lipman, 1959, p. 94).

Those who remained were confronted with a crash course in Anglicization prepared for them by the native community. Yiddish, the mother tongue of the East European Jew, was to the native Jewish clergy what Gaelic was to its Catholic counterpart and was discouraged. English language classes for the parents were supplemented by a multiplicity of clubs and societies — of which the Jewish Lads' Brigade was the most notable — that sought to transform their children into manly upright Englishmen. Portraits of the Queen and Mr Gladstone that adorned the walls of the various *chevroth*, alongside those of rabbinic luminaries from the Russian Pale, supplied a curious emblematic expression of their growing acculturation to Britain and the British (B197, pp. 93–4; Quinn, 1958, II, p. 489). Some, possibly encouraged by Tory jingoes like Hermann Adler, were even willing to sacrifice self and soul to Albion's greater glory. C. H. L. Emanuel, solicitor to the Jewish Board of Guardians and himself a strong advocate of muscular Judaism, proudly told the Royal Commission on Alien Immigration in 1903 that many immigrant offspring 'served with our Army in the late war, although their service necessitated the complete violation of their sacred dietary laws' (PP. 1903. IX. Q. 16632). Not only was Yiddish to be abandoned; the newcomer was also expected to foresake the congested quarters in Spitalfields and Mile End and remove to the outlying suburbs, or further afield — to small provincial communities like Chatham, Reading, Blackburn and Dover, where cultural resistance was more difficult to sustain. 'In the country', said the Chief Rabbi, 'foreign Jews become Anglicised much more rapidly than in London'. A Jewish Dispersion Committee, appointed in 1902, sought to organize their departure (B197, p. 9; PP. 1903, IX, QQ. 16776–16794, 16897).

As an Anglicizing agent, however, the school was considered pre-eminent. Although Anglo-Jewry made significant provision for its young — the Jews' Free School was the largest elementary school in England — its preoccupation with the acculturation of the immigrant meant that state involvement in education, particularly after 1870, was not experienced as a trauma comparable with that of Anglo-Christianity. Schooling, in so far as the Anglo-Jewish élite was concerned, came to be viewed increasingly in non-denominational terms — as an aid to Anglicization rather than a source of separatism.

The Jewish schooling systems comprised a complex of denominational day schools alongside the traditional *Talmudei Torahs* (schools for the study of Hebrew, Bible, Talmud and other classical texts) and *chedarim*. These latter institutions, concerned solely with religious education, represented the least acculturated forms of organized Judaism. The *chedarim* in particular were an affront to middle-class native Jewry. The long hours of after-school instruction given in these bastions of *Yiddishkeit* allegedly undermined the health of the student, diminished his academic performance and impeded his ability to adjust to the habits and customs of the host society. Neither the Catholic parochial school nor the Protestant Sunday School supplied an appropriate alternative, however. The former, it was feared, fostered a sectarian self-regarding outlook while the latter was inconsistent with the tradition of family-centred Sabbath worship. Both were rejected in favour of a supplementary system of weekday religious instruction, organized by the Jewish Religious Education Board, and given after hours in the secular state schools which the majority of immigrant children attended. The informal understanding with the local educational authority, whereby state schools in the East End 'were practically run by the Jewish community at the desire of the London School Board and its statutory successor', produced that unique hybrid, the 'Jewish Board School', and made it unnecessary to expand the voluntary sector or enter the political cockpit in its defence (Quinn, 1958, I, pp. 329–37, II, pp. 499–529; Gartner, 1973, p. 227). In short, Anglicization on the rates seemed more attractive than Anglicanism on the rates.

VIII

By the outbreak of the Great War the process of making immigrants into Englishmen was well advanced. No minority answered the call of King and Country with greater enthusiasm than Anglo-Jewry (Kosmin *et al.*, 1986, pp. 181–92). How far the over-representation of Jews in the British armed forces in the war of 1914–1918 was a reflection of the sorts of measures mentioned above, however, remains unclear. In this context, the historian is unable to separate the impact of specific initiatives from the general course of social development. The character of Anglicization, though, is not in doubt. Contemporary fears, that acculturation meant apostasy, were without foundation. That many forsook the faith is, of course, undeniable. In liberal capitalist democracies, where participation in organized religion was voluntary and Jews were not relegated to a position of statutory inferiority, lapses were numerous. Once moral suasion, family pressure or the influence of friends and neighbours had been rejected, there was nothing to restrain the individual from descent into infidelity and indifference. Such was the case in Victorian and Edwardian Britain. Jewish chaplains serving on the Western Front were distressed by the discovery that so many of the uniformed Cohens, Levys and other bearers of obviously-Jewish surnames were not in fact of the faith (Adler, 1920, p. 7). The losses, however, were never sufficient to endanger the community. The atrophy of Anglo-Judaism was not comparable in its severity with that which afflicted post-Revolutionary America or which in post-*Risorgimento* Italy brought the faith close to extinction (Jick, 1976, pp. 8–11; Roth, 1946, pp. 500–6).

Anglo-Jewry nevertheless bore the stamp of its environment. Among the acculturated upper classes the imprint was most apparent. Judaism as practised by the notables was an invertebrate religion — deficient in doctrine, without rigour in ritual and lacking spiritual warmth — that was much influenced by the prevalent pattern of religiosity within the best circles in which they moved. The intellectually undemanding and socially convenient forms of Orthodox Judaism to which the élite subscribed were as much conditioned by Anglican upper middle-class notions of decency and propriety as by religious conviction. For all that, the Anglo-Jewish élite felt neither the need nor the desire to renounce its faith. Its resolve to retain an unambiguous Jewish identity was, however, considerably strengthened by the continuous influx of immigrants from Eastern Europe from the 1840s onwards. As one perceptive observer noted in 1865: ‘this large admixture tends to keep up the distinction between Jews and Englishmen, which but for that circumstance would be hardly perceptible’ (Anon., 1865, p. 532). The immigrant poor were in spiritual terms made of much sterner stuff than their self-appointed native leaders. Their separatist tendencies, moreover, set narrow limits beyond which the Chief Rabbinate durst not go in trying to accommodate those who wished to modify the liturgy and forms of worship.

To the devitalized devotions of native middle-class Jewry the newcomers brought a new warmth and piety that touched the hearts of many. The consecration of the Spitalfields Great Synagogue in 1898, for example, gave an outward expression of the inner spirituality that animated the children of the ghetto. On that day, observed the *Jewish Chronicle* reporter, 'the East End was in a state of simmering excitement which grew to a deep enthusiasm as the day advanced'. As the procession approached the new synagogue, 'Gentiles looked on with reverence but the Jews were bubbling over with happiness. Men, women and children gave way to unrestrained joy, a few even broke into a dance. It seemed as if time had not moved on with them since the days when David danced with joy before the Ark of the Lord!' 'What a vast distance', he concluded, 'separated them from the stern austerity of the Gentile rites, and even from the solemn dignity of their more Anglicised brethren' (Homa, 1954, p. 56). Religion was for such people a central feature of their lives. When the *Kamenitzer Maggid*, Rabbi Hayim Zundel Maccoby, gave an oration police reinforcements were required to control the overflow crowds who flocked to hear the performance (White, 1981, p. 86). Similarly, the funeral of the beloved Rav Werner in 1912 was marked by what the *Manchester Guardian* described as 'unparalleled scenes'. A crowd, variously estimated between 20,000 and 30,000, accompanied the funeral procession through the streets of East London. 'The police, who must have numbered over 100, had great difficulty in restraining the people who, in their anxiety to touch the coffin, pushed and jostled one another to such an extent that the bearers could scarcely make any progress' (Homa, 1954, pp. 80–1). No rabbi before or since possessed such a following. The strictly observant immigrants whom Werner represented set a standard which Anglo-Jewry might not follow but could not ignore. In sum, the immigrant presence served to replenish the wells of orthodoxy and check the slide from latitudinarianism into licence. It is significant that Orthodox Judaism was decidedly stronger in Britain than in those countries, such as France or the United States, which had not been the beneficiaries of immigration from Eastern Europe before 1881, or afterwards, as in the case of Italy. Jews in Britain at the close of our period were not united people but their very divisions were indicative of Judaism's continued strength and vitality. Religion still mattered.

BIBLIOGRAPHY

The following abbreviations have been used in the text:

B — notebooks in the Booth Collection, British Library of Political and Economic Science, London School of Economics.

JC — *Jewish Chronicle*

PP — Parliamentary Papers

M. Adler (1920) *A Jewish Chaplain on the Western Front*, The Jewish Guardian.

P. Cohen Albert (1977) *The Modernization of French Jewry: Consistory and Community in the Nineteenth Century*, Hanover (NH), Brandeis University Press.

Anon. (1865) 'The Jewish Community in England', *Chambers's Journal of Popular Literature, Science and Arts*, pp. 532–6.

R. Apple (1971) 'United Synagogue, religious founders and leaders' in S. S. Levin (ed.) *A Century of Anglo-Jewish Life*, pp. 13–28, United Synagogue.

A. Barnett (1961) *The Western Synagogue Through Two Centuries (1761–1961)*, Valentine Mitchell.

N. Bentwich (1938) *Solomon Schechter: A Biography*, Cambridge, Cambridge University Press.

C. Booth (1889–1903) *Life and Labour of the People in London* (1st series 'Poverty'; 2nd Series 'Industry'; 3rd Series 'Religious Influences'), 17 Vols., Macmillan.

C. M. Davies (1876) *Unorthodox London: Or Phases of Religious Life in the Metropolis*, second edn., Tinsley Brothers.

M. Davis (1963) *The Emergence of Conservative Judaism: The Historical School in Nineteenth-Century America*, Philadelphia, Jewish Publication Society of America.

T. M. Endelman (1979) *The Jews of Georgian England 1714–1830: Tradition and Change in a Liberal Society*, Philadelphia, Jewish Publication Society of America.

*T. M. Endelman (1985) 'Communal solidarity among the Jewish élite of Victorian London', *Victorian Studies*, Vol. 28, pp. 491–526.

D. Feldman (1986) 'Immigrants and Workers, Englishmen and Jews: Jewish Immigration to the East End of London, 1880–1906', unpublished Ph.D. thesis, University of Cambridge.

I. Finestein (1957) *A Short History of Anglo-Jewry*, Lincolns-Prager.

I. Finestein (1959–1961) 'Anglo-Jewish opinion during the struggle for emancipation (1828–1858)', *Transactions of the Jewish Historical Society of England*, Vol. 20, pp. 113–43.

I. Finestein (1971) 'The lay leadership of the United Synagogue since 1870' in S. S. Levin (ed.) *A Century of Jewish Life*, pp. 29–42, United Synagogue.

*W. J. Fishman (1975) *East End Jewish Radicals, 1875–1914*, Duckworth.

B. Gainer (1972) *The Alien Invasion*, Heinemann.

J. A. Garrard (1971) *The English and Immigration: A Comparative Study of the Jewish Influx 1880–1910*, Oxford, Oxford University Press.

*L. P. Gartner (1973) *The Jewish Immigrant in England 1870–1914*, second edn., Simon Publications.

I. Harris (1906) *History of Jews' College*, Luzac and Co.

J. H. Hertz (1916) Evidence of the Very Rev. the Chief Rabbi, 10 February 1915, in *The Declining Birth-Rate, Its Causes and Effects, Being the Report of and the Chief Evidence Taken by the National Birth-Rate Commission, Instituted . . . by the National Council of Public Morals*, Chapman and Hall.

*C. Holmes (1979) *Anti-Semitism in British Society 1876–1939*, Arnold.

B. Homa (1954) *A Fortress in Anglo-Jewry: The Story of the Machzike Hadath*, Shapiro Vallentine & Co.

A. Hyamson (1951) *The Sephardim of England, A History of the Spanish and Portuguese Jewish Community 1492–1951*, Methuen.

L. A. Jick (1976) *The Americanization of the Synagogue 1820–1870*, Hanover (NH), University Press of New England.

D. Katz (1982) *Philo-semitism and the Re-admission of the Jews to England, 1603–1655*, Oxford, Oxford University Press.

B. A. Kosmin, S. Waterman and N. Grizzard (1986) 'The Jewish dead in the Great War as an indicator for the location, size and social structure of Anglo-Jewry in 1914', *Immigrants and Minorities*, Vol. 5, pp. 181–92.

M. Leigh (1975) 'Reform Judaism in Britain (1840–1970)' in D. Marmur (ed.) *Reform Judaism: Essays on Reform Judaism in Britain*, Oxford, Reform Synagogues of Great Britain.

R. Liberles (1976) 'The origins of the Jewish Reform Movement in England', *Association for Jewish Studies Review*, Vol. 1, pp. 121–50.

*V. D. Lipman (1954) *Social History of the Jews in England 1850–1950*, Watts & Co.

V. D. Lipman (1959) *A Century of Social Service 1859–1959: The Jewish Board of Guardians*, Routledge and Kegan Paul.

V. D. Lipman (1959a) 'Synagogal organisation in Anglo-Jewry', *Jewish Journal of Sociology*, Vol. 1, pp. 80–93.

V. D. Lipman (ed.) (1961) *Three Centuries of Anglo-Jewish History*, Cambridge, Jewish Historical Society of England.

M. Margoliouth (1851) *The History of the Jews of Great Britain*, 3 Vols., Richard Bentley.

H. Mayhew (1861) *London Labour and the London Poor*, 4 Vols., Griffin, Bohn & Co.

M. A. Meyer (1971) 'Christian influence on early Reform Judaism' in C. Berlin (ed.) *Studies in Jewish Bibliography, History and Literature in Honor of I. Edward Kiev*, New York, KTAV Publishing House.

J. Mills (1853) *The British Jews, Their Religious Ceremonies, Social Condition, Domestic Habits, Literature, Political Statistics*, Houlston and Wright.

*A. Newman (1976) *The United Synagogue 1870–1970*, Routledge and Kegan Paul.

Parliamentary Papers 1888, XI, PP 1889, X, Report of Select Committee on Emigration and Immigration (Foreigners) with Minutes of Evidence.

Parliamentary Papers 1903, IX, Royal Commission on Alien Immigration with Minutes of Evidence.

J. Petuchowski (1960) 'Karaite tendencies in an early Reform Haggadah', *Hebrew Union College Annual*, Vol. 31, pp. 223–48.

D. Philipson (1907) *The Reform Movement in Judaism*, New York, Macmillan.

J. Picciotto (1956) *Sketches of Anglo-Jewish History* (first published 1875), revised and edited by Israel Finestein, Soncino Press.

*H. Pollins (1982) *Economic History of the Jews in England*, New York, Associated University Press.

P. L. S. Quinn (1958) 'The Jewish schooling systems of London 1656–1956', 2 Vols., unpublished PhD. thesis, University of London.

C. Roth (1946) *The History of the Jews of Italy*, Philadelphia, Jewish Publication Society of America.

C. Roth (1949) *The Jewish Chronicle 1841–1941: A Century of Newspaper History*, The Jewish Chronicle.

J. Rumney (1933) 'The Economic and Social Development of the Jews in England 1730–1860', unpublished Ph.D. thesis, University of London.

C. Russell and H. S. Lewis (1900) *The Jew in London: A Study of Racial Character and Present-day Conditions*, T. Fisher Unwin.

S. Schechter (1896) *Studies in Judaism*, A. & C. Black.

S. Schechter (1908) *Studies in Judaism*, Second Series, Philadelphia, Jewish Publication Society of America.

S. Sharot (1971) 'Secularization, Judaism and Anglo-Jewry' in M. Hill (ed.) *A Sociological Yearbook of Religion in Britain — 4*, pp. 121–40, S.C.M. Press.

S. Sharot (1973) 'Religious change in native orthodoxy in London, 1870–1914: Rabbinate and clergy', *Jewish Journal of Sociology*, Vol. 15, pp. 167–87.

S. Sharot (1973a), 'Religious change in native orthodoxy in London, 1870–1914: the synagogue service' *Jewish Journal of Sociology*, Vol. 15, pp. 57–77.

*S. Sharot (1976) *Judaism: A Sociology*, Newton Abbot, David and Charles.

S. Sharot (1979) 'Reform and Liberal Judaism in London 1840–1940', *Jewish Social Studies*, Vol. 41, pp. 211–28.

S. Singer (1981) 'Orthodox Judaism in Early Victorian London 1840–1858', unpublished PhD. thesis, Yeshiva University, New York.

M. Vreté (1972) 'The Restoration of the Jews in English Protestant thought 1790–1840', *Middle Eastern Studies*, Vol. 8, pp. 8–50.

J. White (1980) *Rothschild Buildings: Life in an East End Tenement Block 1887–1920*, Routledge and Kegan Paul.

*W. Williams (1976) *The Making of Manchester Jewry 1740–1875*, Manchester, Manchester University Press.

I. Zangwill (1889) 'English Judaism, a criticism and a classification', *Jewish Quarterly Review*, Vol. 1, pp. 376–407.

*I. Zangwill (1914) *Children of the Ghetto*, Wayfarer's Library edn., J. M. Dent.

CHAPTER 8

"COMIC BIBLE" SKETCHES.—XXVIII.

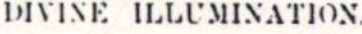

DIVINE ILLUMINATION.

"COMIC BIBLE" SKETCHES.—XXXIV.

THE LOAVES AND FISHES.

Bible history according to *The Freethinker.* The cartoon 'Divine Illumination' (see Genesis 1:3), together with an article entitled 'What Shall I Do to Be Damned', both published in the issue of 28 May 1882, formed the basis of the indictment brought in July 1882 against G. W. Foote, the editor, and Charles Bradlaugh, who was then wrongly supposed to be the proprietor. 'The Loaves and Fishes' (see Matthew 14:17–21) in the issue of 9 July was the last cartoon in the series to be published before the defendants appeared at the Old Bailey.

Charles Darwin, who died three months earlier but never supported secularists in his lifetime, frankly confided his own views on Bible history in his autobiography, which the family published with numerous deletions in 1887. By the late 1830s, he wrote, he had come to see that 'the Old Testament from its manifestly false history of the world, with the Tower of Babel, the rainbow as a sign, etc., etc., and from its attributing to God the feelings of a revengeful tyrant, was no more to be trusted than the sacred books of the Hindoos, or the beliefs of any barbarian'. 'By further reflecting', he added, 'that the clearest evidence would be requisite to make any sane man believe in the miracles by which Christianity is supported, . . . I gradually came to disbelieve in Christianity as a divine revelation'.

FREETHOUGHT, SECULARISM, AGNOSTICISM: THE CASE OF CHARLES DARWIN

IRRELIGION was never more variously religious than in Victorian Britain. A movement defined for the most part by negation inevitably took on the characteristics of what it opposed. There were infidel 'missionaries', secularist 'Sunday schools', agnostic 'catechisms', and freethinkers' 'hymns'. Indeed, the very inspiration of the movement depended on the robust well-being of the religion on which it was parasitic. Kill Christianity and with it went the life-blood of organized unbelief. When infidels were no longer prosecuted for blasphemy, when atheists could enter Parliament, while church attendance declined and orthodoxy disintegrated from within, militant irreligion lost its *raison d'être*. By the early decades of the twentieth century the National Secular Society and the inheritors of the British Secular Union were reduced to an impotent though vociferous rump in London. The movement could both credit itself and take comfort from the notion that it had been victimized by its own success (F. B. Smith, 1967).

But other forces were also at work in British society, and recent studies have shown the very considerable extent to which the fortunes of organized unbelief were tied to those of popular radicalism as espoused by the British working class, whose anti-clerical, republican, and democratic politics had been forged in the early struggles over industrialization. 'With the onset of a fully industrialised, mature capitalist economy', according to Edward Royle (1980, pp. 329–30), 'the structure of that class changed, and new social and political creeds became appropriate . . . Secularism was, therefore, the victim of circumstances beyond its control.' It is with this larger view of Victorian irreligion that I shall be concerned in the following pages, although the religious character of the movement will remain in view. I shall not explore in any depth the changing class structure or the 'new social and political creeds' that eventually supplanted the downright negations of traditional unbelief. Instead, I want to analyse a more general change of 'creed' among both working-class freethinkers and middle-class intellectuals, a change that accompanied the particular social and ideological developments of which Royle speaks. This change, leading to the evolutionary world-view that we take for granted today, occurred in British intellectual life during the middle decades of the nineteenth century. Why did it happen and who were the perpetrators? How did the new evolutionary creed serve to differentiate the interests and activities of Victorian unbelievers? What was the outcome for traditional forms of irreligion?

In order to answer these questions concretely I shall have recourse to numerous individual examples, but my prime illustration will be Charles Darwin, whose career as naturalist, evolutionist, and figurehead of science extended from the heroic era of radical freethought in the 1820s to the golden age of Secularism in the 1880s. Darwin, originally intended for the church, was a respectable bourgeois, never a militant unbeliever. But I shall argue that from his earliest career he was both aware of and troubled by beliefs that in early-Victorian Britain were condemned as 'materialistic and atheistic'. By the time he was buried in Westminster Abbey and the church reclaimed its own, as it were, Darwin had espoused these beliefs in a form that was both alien to militant unbelievers and serviceable to those who usurped their movement in pursuit of a liberal, industrialized and bourgeois social order. In Darwin's career, therefore, it may be observed that the fortunes of organized unbelief were tied not only to those of popular radicalism, but to the wider prospects for a culture dominated by scientific professionals and their class-allies among the clergy.

I A CHANGING CREED, 1830–80

In the half century between 1830 and 1880 there was a sweeping change in what a large and increasing number of educated British people believed, or found believable, about the world. It was a change in the most fundamental assumptions that gave their lives meaning and coherence, a change comparable to the collapse of bourgeois idealism and the belief in progress after the First World War. What it was that changed — the whole vast complex of what people believed, or found believable, at any time, about themselves, their society, and the natural world — I propose to call a 'creed'. This word, I realize, is rather imprecise. Endless distinctions could be made among the beliefs of individuals or groups. More sophisticated and possibly more problematic terms, such as 'cosmology' or 'world-view', might be used. But I think a simple generalization is instructive for a start, even if refinements have to be made later on. And the term 'creed' has the virtue of having been in common use at the time.

In Table 1 I have summarized as briefly as possible how the chief doctrines of the Victorian creed were modified. The table requires some explanation. First, the doctrinal changes should be seen as simultaneous and interlocking. They appear on the chart in a logical, not a chronological, order. Second, notice the elements of continuity over the period. People did not stop believing in nature as a law-bound system, in human nature as morally tainted, in a hierarchical society, in orderly progress spurred by natural evil, in a 'telos' — an end or purpose — of history, or in authorities who tell them what to believe. Third, notice, on the other hand, the main underlying changes. The rudiments of nature, including human nature and society, do not remain fixed but become indefinitely malleable through evolution. The material and moral realms do not remain separate, the latter known only by divine revelation or the intuitions of the mind; they become fused in one natural process which inevitably embodies ever higher states of objective Good. Society does not remain a hierarchy of individuals, ranked

Table 1

A CHANGING CREED

chief doctrine	1830	1880
nature	static material system	evolving material-moral system
human nature	morally improvable within limits	materially-morally improving
society	static hierarchical system of individuals, based on hereditary inequality	evolving hierarchical 'organism' based on natural inequality
natural order	God	law (God?)
natural law	God's will	Nature's (God's?) way
natural evil		
(origin)	God's providence, human sin	Nature (God's providence?), maladaptation
(purpose)	deterrent-discipline promoting moral progress & individual salvation	adaptation to environment & material-moral progress
progress		
(material)	contingent on moral progress	
(moral)	contingent on obedience & prudence	more or less inevitable
telos	otherworldly salvation of individuals	perfected material-moral world
authority	Bible & nature professional clergy	Nature (including Bible) scientific professionals

according to birth, but becomes an 'organism' whose parts — classes, races, nations, and so on — have a natural hierarchy of functions.

Finally, consider some of the changes that flow from these principal ones. Once the material and moral realms become fused in an evolving Nature, morality can be separated from theology. Morality can be judged by those who interpret Nature, or 'according to' Nature: namely, 'scientific' professionals. Formerly the material and moral realms were believed to be fused solely in the Bible (or perhaps also in Nature interpreted according to the Bible), where they had been fixed through divine inspiration. Clergymen and clerical exegetes had been the mediators of biblical morality to individuals and society. Now, however, if Nature furnishes the norms, these mediators can be displaced. Individuals and society can look to professional interpreters of Nature for guidance as to the meaning of law and order, the social structure that this implies, and the conditions of future progress. The Bible itself becomes the product of an evolving Nature, and its interpreters must be scientific as well, just like those of natural history. To be scientific does not preclude belief in God, for the natural order may be a divine order after all. But the God in whom it is not *un*scientific to believe does not intrude on the natural order. That God may be identified with the natural order or may stand beyond it altogether. He does not interfere, any more than clergymen, politicians, or other non-naturalistic interpreters of the world should interfere with the business of scientists.

Given this sweeping change in the Victorian intellectual outlook, the obvious question arises as to why it occurred. Was it an accident? Or did some brilliant discovery force the change on the collective mind? Or was it the cumulative effect of many such discoveries in the march of science? Perhaps the change was a consequence of all these things — a chain of accidental discoveries. How one answers this question depends on what one thinks moves people to believe the way they do. 'Accidents' cannot be ruled out, although in history they easily become the refuge of the perplexed. And certainly what people discovered through systematic investigation of the world — fossils of extinct animals, strata in the earth's crust, prehistoric human remains, 'primitive' tribes and civilizations — could be interpreted, and indeed were interpreted, as evidence of an evolving universe. But things can be interpreted in many ways. Why did people interpret the evidence the way they did? Why did they interpret some things as 'evidence' of anything at all? And why did one interpretation seem so authoritative and convincing in 1830, but so antiquated and naive in 1880? Does it boil down to the 'spirit of the times', a sort of cultural mania generated by enthusiastic researchers and their publicists, with no necessary relation to the 'real' world and the objective forces within it?

I do not think there is a simple answer. This means that accidents and discoveries, separately or in combination, cannot of themselves explain a changing creed. What needs looking at is, I believe, something far richer and more complex — something more concrete than the *Zeitgeist* — which takes account of the feelings and aspirations and everyday experiences of ordinary people in the mid-nineteenth century, perhaps especially of those who helped to forge the new creed and to convince the wider public that they should embrace it. For lack of a clearer, less ambiguous term, let me call that something 'the times'. No one supposes that a person's 'life and times' can be understood in isolation from each other. A person's ideas, beliefs, and feelings arise from and are imbedded in a social and historical environment. Similarly, I want to suggest that a changing creed in the mid-nineteenth century cannot be adequately understood, let alone explained, without reference to the changing times.

II CHANGING TIMES: EARLY VICTORIAN BRITAIN

Overproduction, speculation, recession, unemployment — the sequence is familiar. Add successive crop failures, a high tariff on wheat, extremes of wealth and poverty in over-crowded cities, and social 'services' that actually penalize people for being poor and without a livelihood, and it becomes a recipe for revolution. Such were the conditions, not in a Third World country of the mid-twentieth century, but in the world's first industrialized nation in the 1840s. A third of Britain's male population, half the women, were illiterate. Fewer than one man in five had the right to vote — there was no secret ballot — and a man's right to vote depended on the value of his property. In the industrial north of England the average life expectancy at birth of working people living in the cities was as little as twenty years. In the Wiltshire countryside this did not even double, although in London the mortality rate was twice as great in the East End as in the West. Within easy reach of opulence, in London, Manchester, and elsewhere, the masses lived out their ghastly lives, and died, in unimaginable squalor, their streets afloat with sewage, their drinking water brown with faecal particles, their foodstuffs paltry and expensive. They felt themselves 'hungry in a society reeking with wealth, enslaved in a country which prided itself on its freedom, seeking bread and hope, and receiving in return stones and despair' (G. M. Young, 1969, pp. 21–5; Hobsbawm, 1969, p. 95).

Most of all the people were hungry. The Corn Laws had made a loaf dear enough when times were good. One might merely resent the protection they gave the wealthy farmers and landowners, who could afford bread at any price. But when harvests failed in the late 1830s and the trade depression saw towns with ninety per cent unemployed, working people began to starve. Merchants lost their income to the farmers. Mill owners could not export to customers who had failed to sell Britain their grain. The Corn Laws, in short, began to look like the aristocrats' answer to proletarian fecundity and the rivalry of the middle classes. And in the spirit of class antagonism they were bitterly opposed. In January 1839 the Anti-Corn Law League was formed at Manchester to represent the commercial and manufacturing interests. It stood for standard liberal doctrines such as individualism, enterprise, and equality of opportunity, but most of all for the panacea of free trade. With support from working people who believed their interests were bound up with those of the middle classes, the League campaigned up and down the country with such effect that one historian has observed, 'The ideological foundations of Victorian England were laid by the battle for cheaper bread — and for higher profits' (Thomson, 1950,

p. 80). Finally in 1846 the Tory Prime Minister Robert Peel saw the national interest served by having the Corn Laws repealed. The potato crop in Ireland had failed the year before and it was pointless marketing expensive grain in that unbelievably pauperized nation. Still the repeal did not prevent upwards of a million Irish people from starving to death.

Peel became Prime Minister in 1841, and by then the poor were practically at the end of their tether. Charles Dickens had dramatized their plight, beginning with *Oliver Twist* in 1837. Thomas Carlyle was emerging as a prophetic advocate and would take up their cause in his *Past and Present* (1843). Similarly Edwin Chadwick in *The Sanitary Conditions of the Labouring Population* (1842) and Frederick Engels in *The Condition of the Working Class in England in 1844* (1845) would expose what it meant to live in society's dregs. These works stimulated middle-class sympathies, sometimes galvanized private philanthropy, and generally heralded gradual piecemeal reforms. But they were not the authentic voice of the disfranchized and oppressed. That was raised most conspicuously in a movement which ran parallel to the Anti-Corn Law League and by 1841 threatened outright revolution.

Its dreaded name was Chartism. In May 1838 a 'People's Charter' was drawn up in London by a handful of trade unionists and radical MPs. It called for electoral and parliamentary reforms that the vastly outnumbered upper and middle classes dared not concede — outrageous demands such as universal male suffrage, a secret ballot, and annual general elections. The Charter caught on quickly, especially in the cities, and by the end of the summer a national movement had formed. Crowds of desperate people, hungry, uneducated, overworked and unemployed, turned out to hear fiery arguments for social change through full political representation. They signed a national petition — over a million of them — and this was taken to a 'People's Parliament' at London in 1839. The motley band of activists met for several months. In July, when the House of Commons refused to consider the petition, they spent themselves arguing over what to do next. There were strikes and riots, the army was called in, and within a few weeks hundreds of Chartists had been imprisoned. But worse was to come. In 1842, in the miserable depths of the century's worst depression, the Commons again spurned the Charter, this time by an even greater majority, although its sponsors were now better organized. Again despair overflowed into insurrection, then Chartism began a slow decline. The Anti-Corn Law League was scooping the headlines, capital was finding an outlet in the railways, creating new jobs, and trade unions were on the rise. In 1848, as revolutions swept over Europe, Parliament dismissed the Charter a third time, effectively ending any threat of revolution in Britain (Briggs, 1960, pp. 294–312).

Another revolution, however, the authorities could not stop. It had gathered force since the late eighteenth century from protagonists of political revolution like Thomas Paine; it had sustained itself in the face of laws against blasphemy and sedition, and other constraints on freedom of the press. Most important, in changing times it passionately demanded a change of creed. This revolution was the maelstrom of radical freethought that both heralded and accompanied the Chartist movement, although remaining organizationally distinct; and it tore many of the more thoughtful working people from their Christian moorings during the 1830s and 1840s. The background of radical freethought is essential for understanding the manner in which Darwin contributed to the new Victorian creed as well as his perception of the religious bearings of his work.

III THE RADICAL CRITIQUE OF CHRISTIANITY

Working people wanted more than food and political representation. As they became better educated — usually self-educated — they demanded that society recognize beliefs which made sense of their just aspirations. Of necessity this required a critique of established Christian belief, which upheld the *status quo* by force of law. So radical religion — or irreligion — and radical politics went hand-in-hand (Royle, 1971, ch. 1). Frequently, however, among radical freethinkers the attack on Christianity took precedence over practical political concerns because Christian doctrines were held to be the root of all social evil. In the 1820s veteran infidels like Richard Carlile and the Reverend Robert Taylor, a lapsed clergyman, prefaced attempts at political reform with vindictive lectures and publications designed to undermine the Bible and its defenders, such as the Anglican apologist William Paley. Together in May 1829 they conducted a successful 'mission' in the north of England, stopping first at Cambridge, where they issued debating challenges to the heads of all the colleges and (like another reformer three centuries before) pinned copies written in Latin and Greek on the door of the University Library. But within two years Carlile was gaoled for sedition, Taylor for blasphemy. Their thunder had gone. Taylor subsequently retired to Jersey. Carlile grew increasingly out of touch with radical politics. He lived, however, to see his latter-day vision of the Church, regenerated as a 'School of the Moral Sciences', embodied in the communitarian socialism of Robert Owen (Royle, 1971, pp. 32–4; Royle, 1974, p. 39).

After a brief flirtation with co-operative and trades union movements in the early 1830s, Owen set his sights on nothing less than a 'new moral world'. He built on the foundations laid by Carlile and Taylor in the North, where the recession was biting deepest. Between 1837 and 1841 numerous local branches of Owen's 'Rational Society' sprang up there, many with educational buildings called 'Halls of Science'; and Owen began raising money for a grand socialist experiment which would demonstrate his deep conviction that human nature is not inherently corrupt, but improvable in an improved environment. The ethos of 'Owenism' was sectarian; its beliefs, though heterodox, were virtually religious. And the attempt to build socialism in one community at East Tytherly in Hampshire was hopelessly compromised by funding and leadership from wealthy capitalists. In an economic crisis, with the working classes united and socialism under fire from churchmen as never before, the experiment began to look wrong-headed. Owenites broke ranks and sought a more direct and effective way of attacking Christianity (Royle, 1971, ch. 4; Royle, 1974, pp. 43–72).

The new infidelity was at first violently atheistic in the tradition of Carlile. In November 1841 Charles Southwell, a disillusioned Owenite, began publishing the *Oracle of Reason* at Bristol with help from William Chilton, a self-educated compositor. Southwell was gaoled for blasphemy early in the new year and the editorship passed to George Jacob Holyoake, an Owenite but not yet an atheist. Holyoake set up an Anti-Persecution Union to help defend Southwell and other victims of the wave of prosecutions that followed in 1842. But in June, after suggesting publicly at Cheltenham that the people of Britain were too poor to have a God, he was summarily taken into custody. Released on bail, he went to London and his case became the *cause célèbre* of radicals during the summer. On 15 August he was tried at Gloucester and sentenced to six months' imprisonment. The experience confirmed his hatred of Christianity. In October when his elder daughter died, partly from malnutrition, Holyoake became an atheist. Immediately, while still in Gloucester gaol, he wrote *Paley Refuted in His Own Words* as a response to tactless correspondents who tried to convert him; and in 1845, after his release, his atheism emerged full-blown in *Rationalism: A Treatise for the Times*. The book was a vain though important attempt to consolidate the forces of freethought after the collapse of Owen's community experiment, and Holyoake got little farther after 1846 as editor of the *Reasoner and Herald of Progress* or through founding the 'Society for the Promulgation of Naturalism'. Success came only when he tempered his atheism, dropped overt attacks on Christianity, and allied himself with middle-class intellectuals in London. In 1851, the year of the Great Exhibition, radical freethought under Holyoake's leadership opted for a 'moderate, progressive, realistic, respectable future' with the launching of 'Secularism' (Royle, 1974, pp. 68–101, 162).

But to return to the immediate concerns of Holyoake and others in the 1830s and 1840s: Why did Christian doctrines appear to be the root of all social evil? What kind of objections were raised against them? And what beliefs did radical freethinkers profess instead?[1]

[1] The following paragraphs are largely indebted to Hart, 1977; Helmstadter, 1979, pp. 135–71; Royle, 1971, pp. 5–11; and Royle, 1974, ch. 3.

To begin with, Christian doctrines were what the churches believed, and the churches, according to radicals, held nothing for working people. The Church of England, or the clergy and aristocracy at any rate, formed the Tory party at prayer. Committed to a static traditional society based on hereditary privilege, it was anti-democratic by conviction. The Nonconformist churches — all the others except the Wesleyans (Tory), the Primitive Methodists (working class), and the Church of Scotland — were very largely bourgeois. Their religion was aggressive, independent, and individualistic, just like their members' business practices. Their politics were otherworldly and quietistic, except in so far as their members' interests were threatened — as by the Corn Laws. Radicals could ally with Nonconformists in opposing the Church of England, even to some extent in the Anti-Corn Law League. But on issues such as those that Chartism pressed, they divided sharply along class lines. Radical freethinkers were distinguished by their deep alienation from society as it was constituted and by their attack on all conventional forms of Christianity.

The attack, however, did not consist solely, or even mainly, of an exposé of the hypocrisy and oppression of the churches (although the practices of clerical magistrates and Christian mill owners added significantly to the ranks of freethought). It was above all what Christians believed, what sanctioned their practices, that called forth the freethinkers' wrath. Christian theology purported to make sense of the world: to explain and justify the course of nature, the structure of society, and the proportions of good and evil that people experienced in both. Christian doctrines, in other words, were supposed to give meaning and purpose to human existence and to serve as a basis of action and expectation in everyday life. But what hope or comfort could working people derive in the 'hungry forties' from believing in a God who ordains all things 'after the council of his own will', who providentially sustains the world as a system of rewards and punishments 'for our own good', and who sends people eternally to hell for their finite transgressions? Were these not the doctrines of those who forbad birth control among the working classes as an interference with divine law, who accepted poverty as a necessary evil consequent on overpopulation, and who feared lest the poor disbelieve in future punishment and (as a later writer warned) there be a 'bursting forth with savage yells of millions of ravening wolves, before whom the salt of the earth will be trodden underfoot, Church establishments dissolved, and baronial halls become piles of blackened ruin'? (quoted in Rowell, 1974, p. 83n).

Or, again, what sense did it make for hungry, powerless, despairing people to believe that they were innately and incurably sinful, that their only real hope of salvation lay in an innocent man whose blood God had seen fit to have shed on their behalf some two thousand years ago, and that this salvation would only be realized at the time of their death? Were these not the doctrines of those who defended the existing social order as the only one consistent with fallen human nature, who themselves persecuted and imprisoned innocent people, such as Chartists and freethinkers, and who counselled resignation and otherworldly hope in the face of mortal distress like the Irish potato famine and the cholera epidemic of 1849?

My point is simply this: in a time of unprecedented social and political crisis the radical critique of Christianity had an overwhelming *moral* tone (Royle, 1974, p. 108; Budd, 1977, ch. 5). Even the historical and scientific objections raised by freethinkers can be interpreted this way. The Bible, for example, was often attacked for its accounts of atrocities committed or commanded by God. Geology could be used to show that Genesis was no authority for believing in the sinfulness of human nature. It was not German historical scholarship or new researches in comparative religion that gave fresh impetus to radical freethought in early Victorian Britain. Nor was it geology and evolution that, as an English historian once remarked, 'changed us from a Christian to a pagan nation' (F. S. Taylor, 1949, p. 195). It was the everyday experience that the Christian creed had become a moral blight, a system of beliefs oppressively incongruous with the social realities of the time.

The changing times cried out for a changing creed. And a new creed first began to be popularized, at great risk, by radical freethinkers such as Southwell, Chilton, and Holyoake, some twenty years before Darwin brought out his *Origin of Species*. In 1842 Southwell argued in the *Oracle of Reason* for the material origin of the idea of God; at the same time his colleague Chilton was running a series, entitled 'The Theory of Regular Gradation', which undertook 'to prove the capabilities of unassisted, unacted upon, uncontrolled, undirected matter for the production of all the varied, complicated, and beautiful phenomena of the universe' (quoted in Royle, 1974, p. 124). Meanwhile Holyoake languished in Gloucester gaol, refuting Paley's argument from design and making plans to resurrect Owen's 'new moral world'. Rationalism, he wrote in his 'treatise for the times' in 1845, is 'the science of material circumstances ... It makes morality the sole business of life' and 'discovers in humanity the germs of indefinite moral progression'. Human nature is improvable 'under well-understood conditions' because, according to Holyoake's 'secular' principles, 'the methods of mind are as uniform and as calculable as the methods of nature'. Through 'the study of the laws or operations of Nature' science can effect conditions for the moral improvement of mind. Science thereby becomes 'the available providence of man' (quoted in Royle, 1971, pp. 117, 118).

Therefore, in place of a creed which legitimized a static hierarchical society, encouraged resignation to a temporal system of divine punishments and rewards, and diverted human hopes to a future life, radical freethinkers provided for a social transformation here and now, in mid-nineteenth century Britain. Moral progress, they believed, could be brought about without God's help through control of the social environment in accordance with the laws of an evolving nature (Desmond, 1987). This new heterodoxy was not, however, emerging just among working-class radicals in the early Victorian period. To situate Darwin and his work in relation to the new creed and its exponents, I must also indicate the extent to which similar convictions were held by contemporary middle-class reformers.

IV YOUNG REFORMERS

The crisis of the late 1830s and 1840s 'touched the mainsprings of human emotion and imagination', writes Asa Briggs (1960, p. 294). 'The discontens ... determined the way of thinking of a whole generation.' In 1842 Southwell, Chilton, and Holyoake — none of them yet thirty — were only among that generation's most notorious members. If a generation be measured as those born within a thirty-year span, there were many others who groped their way towards a new creed in these years. They were, however, very often quiet radicals, or reformers. They were more concerned to preserve and consolidate the new-won freedoms of the bourgeoisie than to fight for the extension of these freedoms to the workers. They experienced, accordingly, a crisis of conscience rather than the conflict of classes. They sought sanction for reforms that would promote both social stability and progress. They began to conceive Nature as the limiter, as well as the liberator, of human aspirations. They adumbrated a creed more conventional, less confronting, than the atheism of working-class radicals. But the inspiration of their changing creed was nevertheless a profound and varied sense of moral discontent arising from perilous times.[2]

Who then were these young middle-class reformers? In Table 2 I have named some of the better known individuals. Many reached their thirtieth year in this period, as indicated in the second column of the table; all belonged to the generation born in the first third of the century. The table also gives, in so far as possible, the approximate date and age at which each individual consciously withdrew from the Christian creed and began to embrace another. These dates fall almost entirely in the 1840s. The last column gives the titles of early publications that indicate the change of creed.

The young reformers were poets and lawyers, doctors and manufacturers, novelists and naturalists, engineers and politicians. If they had not

[2] The following paragraphs are inspired chiefly by Murphy, 1955. I have also been guided by Tulloch, 1885, p. 255; Himmelfarb, 1968, ch. 20; Paul, 1979; Jones, 1980, chs. 3–4; and Bell, 1981, pp. 280, 296–8.

Table 2

A CHANGING GENERATION

name	aged 30	date & age at change of creed	typical publications
Harriet Martineau	1832	1846 (44)	*Letters on the Laws of Man's Nature and Development*, 1851
R. W. Mackay	1833		*The Progress of the Intellect as Exemplified in the Religious Development of the Greeks and Hebrews*, 1850
F. W. Newman	1835	1842 (37)	*The Soul*, 1849; *Phases of Faith; or, Passages from the History of My Creed*, 1850
John Sterling	1836	1840 (34)	
Charles Hennell	1839	1837 (28)	*An Inquiry Concerning the Origin of Christianity*, 1838
Charles Darwin	1839	1838 (29)	*On the Origin of Species*, 1859
Alfred Tennyson	1839	1846 (37)	*In Memoriam*, 1850
W. R. Greg	1839		*The Creed of Christendom*, 1851
Charles Bray	1841	1837 (26)	*The Philosophy of Necessity; or, the Law of Consequences as Applicable to Mental, Moral, and Social Science*, 1841
G. H. Lewes	1847		*Biographical History of Philosophy*, 1845–6
J. A. Froude	1848	1848 (30)	*The Nemesis of Faith*, 1849
George Eliot	1849	1841 (22)	*Life of Jesus* by Strauss (trans. 1846); *Essence of Christianity* by Feuerbach (trans. 1854)
A. H. Clough	1849	1848 (29)	*The Bothie of Tober-na-Vuolich*, 1848
Herbert Spencer	1850	1842 (22)	*Social Statics; or, the Conditions Essential to Human Happiness Specified*, 1851
John Tyndall	1850	1842 (22)	
Frances Power Cobbe	1852	1843 (21)	*Broken Lights; or, an Inquiry into the Present Conditions and Future Prospects of Religious Faith*, 1864

A. R. Wallace	1852	1845 (18)	
Matthew Arnold	1852	1850 (28)	*Culture and Anarchy: An Essay in Political and Social Criticism*, 1869
Francis Galton	1852		
T. H. Huxley	1855	1843 (18)	*On Our Knowledge of the Causes of the Phenomena of Organic Nature*, 1863

already begun their careers in the 1840s they would do so soon. Some were independently wealthy. Others suffered financial straits and unemployment. All of them saw many less fortunate people suffer the same. They felt anxious in a society divided, as Disraeli put it, into 'two nations', one of which threatened revolution. They felt alienated from a society that excluded people with beliefs like theirs from positions of authority. They could thus affirm much of the radical critique of Christianity. After 1859 some of them would achieve fame and notoriety as 'honest doubters' by openly challenging established authority on the basis of what they had believed for many years, but which only embattled radicals had dared proclaim.

The impetus behind the changing creed of these young intellectuals was not so much the social conflict experienced by working-class radicals as a sense of intellectual crisis. For Francis Newman and James Anthony Froude it was revulsion at the moral implications of Christian doctrines such as the vicarious atonement and eternal damnation. For George Eliot it was the insights she owed to her friends, the brothers-in-law Charles Hennell and Charles Bray, that the Christian doctrines of salvation originated in natural human history and may be discarded in favour of higher moral principles. For Alfred Tennyson it was the tragic death of a friend coupled with the fear that nature reveals, not God's providential care, but the final mortality of all. For Arthur Hugh Clough it was not only the death of loved ones, but the turmoil of English politics, the Irish potato famine, and the European revolutions of 1848. For Frances Power Cobbe it was the 'moral earthquake' she underwent while ministering to her poor neighbours in County Dublin during the mid-1840s (Cobbe, 1904, pp. 85–100, ch. 6). For John Tyndall, an Irish Protestant, it was the starvation and distress he witnessed in England at about this time. For Thomas Henry Huxley, a medical student in London, it was all these things and more.

In a notebook he kept from 1840 to 1842 Huxley recorded moral objections to an established church and the compulsory payment of church rates. He reckoned that belief in the divine government had 'a very injurious effect on morals' and he speculated on the soul's relation to matter and on the possibility of morality without theology. Looking back on his medical work in London, he remembered 'Physical and Mental pain . . . Grief too — yet at the misfortunes of others'. He had seen grinding poverty and starvation at first hand while working as a medical assistant in the East End. But, he noted elsewhere, there were also 'wretched dens' full of drunken men and women, living amid a 'steam of filthy exhalations', almost 'within hearing of the traffic of the Strand, within easy reach of the wealth and plenty of the city' (Huxley, 1974, pp. 91–9). Such volatile situations would require that Huxley later take an active interest in educating working people about their environment.

Meanwhile, as Huxley and others sought to establish themselves in careers, their interests in reform took a more strictly intellectual turn. The generation of dissident thinkers set about systematizing their beliefs and cautiously committing them to print. A few were materialists and atheists. Most adhered to a heterodox doctrine of God and maintained tenuous links with the churches. But transcending all such diversity was an emerging consensus in favour of a creed that would underwrite a progressive, ameliorative social order. This can be gathered from some of the titles in Table 2. 'Law', 'Development', 'Progress', 'Origin', 'Necessity', 'Happiness', and the 'Future' — these were the key words of a creed that would encourage people to take hold of their circumstances, change them in accordance with natural laws, and hope for real improvements in their individual and social lives. The emerging consensus among the young reformers may also be judged from various intellectual interests they shared at the time. Phrenology, the science of predicting mental endowments and explaining the structure of society from the external form of the cranium, was the passion of Bray, Eliot, George Henry Lewes, Herbert Spencer, and Alfred Russel Wallace (as well as Holyoake). Thomas Carlyle, the prophet of 'natural supernaturalism', heroic hard work, and an aristocracy of merit, was the mentor of Froude, Clough, Tyndall, Huxley, and Francis Galton. Phrenologists and followers of Carlyle could readily agree that material and moral improvements were identical, that human nature was the product of natural laws, and that those who studied nature were the best qualified to administer society (Shapin, 1979; Turner, 1974–5; Jacyna, 1981; Cooter, 1984).

One other interest many of the young reformers had in common. They believed in evolution. For some the doctrine was virtually entailed by their materialistic and deterministic philosophy. Once abandon theism and how else can the world have assumed its present form? This was also the logic behind Chilton's 'theory of regular gradation' in 1842, but others at the time interpreted evolution differently. Tennyson, who remained a troubled theist, was composing the evolutionary stanzas of *In Memoriam*. And Robert

Chambers was writing the book that he saw published anonymously in 1844, *Vestiges of the Natural History of Creation.* Here was a sensational synthesis of the sciences, a vast panorama of unbroken progress according to a divine law, from inanimate matter to the farthest reaches of the mind. The vision of *Vestiges* came to Cobbe on the heels of her discovery that 'God's Goodness is what *I mean* by Goodness!' and she 'pinned her faith' on the book (Cobbe, 1904, pp. 95, 194). The same vision inspired Wallace's life-long hopes of social progress as well as his detailed researches in natural history. Darwin, on the other hand, read *Vestiges* and recoiled. He already believed in evolution; he feared the doctrine had been done a disservice. Amid troubled times, with his generation in search of a creed, this young reformer sought a safer and surer basis in nature for changing moral expectations.[3]

V THE YOUNG DARWIN AND RADICAL FREETHOUGHT

Charles Darwin (1809–1882) was a scion of middle-class Nonconformity in the West Midlands of Regency England. His grandfathers, Erasmus Darwin and Josiah Wedgwood I, were among the chief sponsors of nascent industrialism in the region, the one as its poet, the other as a manufacturer of pottery. Dr Robert Darwin, the son of Erasmus, was an eminent physician at Shrewsbury, and in the 1820s he sent both his own sons to Edinburgh to study medicine. Neither Charles nor Erasmus completed the course, but while Erasmus commenced a life of dyspeptic dilettantism, eventually settling in London to live off the family exchequer, his younger brother entered the University of Cambridge to prepare for the ministry. Charles had been baptized an Anglican, schooled in his mother's Unitarianism, and educated at Shrewsbury under a future bishop. A career in a country parish was not inconsonant with his upbringing, and Dr Darwin, a pragmatic freethinker, settled on it for his son as a respectable albeit second-best choice. Charles viewed the prospect with the reasoned reserve characteristic of so many ordinands before the Church reforms of mid-century. He would occupy a responsible station in life, affording him the freedom to do as he pleased in his considerable spare time. And at Edinburgh he had become passionately devoted to natural history.

Darwin entered Edinburgh University in October 1825 and remained there for two sessions. In that time it is likely that he learned through first-hand experience at least one lesson on the perils of freethought. He struck up a friendship with the physician and zoologist Robert Grant, who coached him on natural history expeditions and joined him and other

[3] The rest of the essay is generally informed by the extended studies of Darwin's religious life in Moore, 1985 and 1989. References to specific quotations in the text can be found there.

students in discussions at the Plinian Society. Grant was an evolutionist after the manner of the French *philosophe* J.-B. Lamarck; the Plinian Society served as a modest platform for his and other members' flagrantly materialist and reductionist views. At a meeting on 27 March 1827, where Darwin communicated a discovery about marine organisms and Grant enlarged on his finding, the president of the Society, a fervent phrenologist, read a paper arguing for the materiality of mind and consciousness. It was struck from the minutes (Gruber and Barrett, 1974, pp. 80–1, 478; Desmond, 1984). Darwin knew by then that Grant accepted a theory of evolution resting on the same dangerous premise. Although Grant had encouraged him to embark on a programme of research on marine invertebrates that would eventually bear fruit in his own evolutionary theorizing, he had also revealed enough of his underlying beliefs for Darwin to realize that these could jeopardize one's reputation, even if he were the president of a natural history society. In later life Darwin would, accordingly, remember his 'astonishment' at Grant's views; in the meantime their relationship deteriorated (Barlow, 1958, p. 49; Sloan, 1985).

Within a year of this episode Darwin had gone to Christ's College, Cambridge, where he studied in a desultory fashion and took an ordinary degree in 1831. He socialized now among clerical naturalists and wine-bibbing ordinands untainted by the radicalism of the French Enlightenment. But here as well we can be reasonably certain that he learned another salutary lesson on the perils of unbelief. It was on Thursday, 21 May 1829, that the veteran freethinkers Taylor and Carlile arrived in town at the start of their 'infidel home missionary tour'. Five days of moral mayhem ensued.[4] They went first to Trinity Church to brace themselves with a sermon from the evangelical incumbent, Charles Simeon, then they walked through several of the colleges, where they were recognized and greeted by undergraduates. Taylor had been at St John's before taking holy orders; he now exhibited himself in the customary full-sleeved gown and hat. The next morning the missionaries took lodgings at number 7 Rose Crescent with William Smith, a print-seller, and sent a formal challenge to the vice-chancellor, to the chief divines of the University, and to the heads of all the colleges, including Darwin's. A version of this was also fixed to the door of the University library.

[4] My authorities for the following paragraphs are the 'bulletins' issued by Taylor and Carlile during and immediately after the events. These were published at London in Carlile's unstamped paper, *The Lion*, 3 (29 May 1829), 673–92; (5 June 1829), 705–707. It is notable that these pages in the bound volume I inspected in the Cambridge University library were uncut.

CIRCULAR

> The Rev. Robert Taylor, A. B., of Carey-street, Lincoln's Inn, and Mr. Richard Carlile, of Fleet-street, London, present their compliments as Infidel missionaries, to (*as it may be*) and most respectfully and earnestly invite discussion on the merits of the Christian religion, which they argumentatively challenge, in the confidence of their competence to prove, that such a person as Jesus Christ, alleged to have been of Nazareth, never existed; and that the Christian religion had no such origin as has been pretended; neither is it in any way beneficial to mankind; but that it is nothing more than an emanation from the ancient Pagan religion. The researches of the Rev. Robert Taylor, on this subject, are embodied in his newly-published work, THE DIEGESIS, in which may be found the routine of their argument.
>
> They also impugn the honesty of a continued preaching, while discussion is challenged on the whole of the merits of the Christian religion.

Numerous copies of this circular were distributed among the collegians with the aim of gaining the support of those who avowed, or merely felt, infidelity; those who valued 'free discussion' and talked about 'philanthropy, benevolence, and humanity'; and those who favoured 'reform and patriotism'. Taylor and Carlile were not, however, merely seeking support; they were also courting persecution.

It began on Saturday. A messenger from the colleges, which regulated student lodging houses, called on Mr Smith, the print-seller, and demanded in the name of the vice-chancellor that he hand over his year-old licence. Smith refused, and immediately a bill was posted in the butteries of the colleges, notifying students that it had been revoked. No offence against the regulations had been committed. On Sunday Taylor and Carlile appealed to the vice-chancellor on Smith's behalf. The next day Smith himself did likewise, pleading also on behalf of his wife and six children. But all to no avail. The missionaries, interpreting stony silence to their challenge and the removal of an innocent man's livelihood as a moral victory, quit their self-styled 'infidel headquarters' on Tuesday, firm in their conviction that '*Christianity is indefensible*'. If learned Cambridge could offer them nothing better, no apologist for Church and state would henceforth be able to resist their radical demands.

Darwin was keeping term during Taylor and Carlile's visitation. He himself had occupied a lodging house in Sydney Street before obtaining rooms in Christ's College nearby, just a few hundred yards from Rose Crescent. He also had bought 'some very good prints' within the previous year (*Correspondence*, 1:71, 84–7). It seems probable that the outrageous posturings of the infidel missionaries would have caught the interest of a prospective parson at some stage during or after their five days in the small and tightly-knit collegiate community. Or if Darwin was insufficiently impressed by this episode, he might certainly have learned at second hand of the much greater notoriety achieved by Taylor and Carlile in London two years later.[5]

From early 1830 until his death in 1881, Darwin's elder brother was his fixed point of reference in the capital. Although Erasmus changed neighbourhoods several times, he remained in touch with intellectual and social developments in the nation's nerve-centre and reported these to his brother at intervals, chiefly, it would appear, in personal conversation. Like their father, Erasmus was a quiet freethinker, although there is no suggestion that he ever was an atheist; and with a medical education and a reformist outlook we may feel confident that he would have noted the progress or otherwise of lesser infidels who fell foul of the establishment. In November 1830 Carlile, doyen of London's illegal 'pauper press', did just that, and in January he was convicted on two counts of publishing a seditious libel — abetting the cause of agricultural incendiaries — which attracted a hefty fine and an exemplary sentence of two years' imprisonment. Taylor, now known by his traducers as the 'Devil's Chaplain', was targeted next. In March his discourses at Carlile's 'Rotunda', a radical venue on the south bank of the Thames, began to circulate under the title *The Devil's Pulpit*. These ludicrous charades of biblical preaching sold more than two thousand copies each week. They were seized on by a clerical front organization, the Vice Society, which in April hauled Taylor before the authorities. A month later he was taken into custody and released on bail to stand trial on seven counts of blasphemy. On 4 July — the anniversary of the American independence, it was pointed out ironically — the Devil's Chaplain also received a heavy fine and was sentenced to two years' imprisonment. The Whig government, solicitous for the Reform Bill introduced in March and the general election it provoked in May, had in the space of six months virtually 'destroyed the Rotunda as a center of theological and political radicalism' (Wiener, 1983, p. 180).

The travails of Carlile and Taylor were canvassed widely, if perversely, in the press. *The Times* not only carried verbatim reports of the parliamentary debates in June and July on blasphemous and seditious publications; it also gave a full account of Taylor's trial, including the origin of his nickname, and afterwards printed lengthy letters from him and Carlile; twice

[5] My chief sources for the subsequent paragraphs are issues of *The Times* for 1831 as follows: 31 May, p. 4, cols. 1–2; 29 June, pp. 1–2; 30 June, p. 4, col. 4; 2 July, p. 4, cols. 2–3; 5 July, p. 4, col. 3; 9 July, p. 3, col. 1; 21 July, pp. 4–5; 23 July p. 3, col. 5. Also employed are the 'Memoir' in R. Taylor, 1842; Aldred, 1942; Wiener, 1963; and Royle, 1979.

editorialized condescendingly on their plight; and transcribed the proceedings in the House of Commons when a petition was presented, calling attention to the cruelties deliberately inflicted on Taylor in Horsemonger Lane Gaol. By August 1831, in short, no freethinking member of the London intelligentsia could have been ignorant of the treatment meted out to those who publicized radical unbelief. Although Darwin visited his brother for a week in mid-April, about the time of Taylor's initial summons (*Correspondence*, 1:121), it seems likely that, if he did not read about the radicals for himself in the press, whatever he may have learned was communicated to him at a later date by Erasmus, perhaps in a letter that has not survived. That he was informed of Taylor, at least, there can be little doubt, as we shall see. But late in the summer of 1831 the example of a renegade parson would have held little interest for him. His path to a country parish was merely being diverted via a global voyage on the *Beagle*.

VI EVOLUTIONIST AMONG THE GENTRY

On debarking from the *Beagle* in October 1836, Darwin stepped into a new world. Or at least a new world awaited him the following March when he left his temporary accommodation in Cambridge to become Erasmus's neighbour in London. Five years at sea had insulated him from the crescendo of voices calling for reforms that exceeded anything envisaged by Darwin and Wedgwood Whigs. During the voyage, Captain FitzRoy had been a constant reminder of Tory-Anglican hostility to heterodox science; slave-owning Spanish Catholics had outraged his morality. The only protests to be heard had been the usual apolitical obscenities uttered by the tightly disciplined crew. Nothing more, save letters and the occasional newspaper, was to prepare him for the ferment of the capital in the period of Victoria's accession to the throne. The Reform Act and the New Poor Law, in force since Darwin had been half way round the world, were not reforms enough. Gentrified privileges remained intact in state, church, and science. The pauper press screamed for democratic concessions; Owenite unions attacked the religious establishment; Chartists rumbled ominously, from the publication of their demands in May 1838 until they had subdued the local Anti-Corn Law League and emerged full force in the mass meetings and 'riots' of August 1842 (Goodway, 1982, pp. 24–53). In scientific circles, where Darwin moved like a fish in water for the next five years, the lesson of his Edinburgh experience was recalled with particular force, for here the ferment touched importantly on evolution.

Before radical freethinkers such as Chilton and Southwell began to popularize a new evolutionary creed in the 1840s, the issue of evolution and its consequences was hotly debated for some years among naturalists, medics, and theologians. After exposure to Grant's views in Edinburgh,

Darwin had little more than Charles Lyell's imposing refutation of Lamarck in the second volume of his *Principles of Geology*, which he received at Montevideo in 1832, to apprise him of this controversy. In London, however, it hovered about the scientific societies and medical schools like the dingy fog Darwin found so detestable. Evolution had been embraced by a small number of rank-and-file scientific men and medical outsiders, not only as a true theory of life, but as an ideological weapon with which to beat the Oxbridge dons, Tory politicians, and wealthy placemen who controlled the corporations in the interests of a static Anglican science. Evolution to them was progressive, beneficent, and egalitarian. It was the natural legitimation of democratic political control in science and society. One of these reformers was Robert Grant, since 1827 the professor of zoology in the new, non-Anglican University of London. Having at first established his expert credentials among London's scientific élite, he became known as a Lamarckian leveller and was suspected of infidelity. In the mid-1830s he crossed his rival on the council of the Zoological Society, the Anglican anatomist Richard Owen, then in the pay of the élitist Royal College of Surgeons and soon to become its Hunterian Professor. Grant was ousted from the council in 1835. He quietly left the Society, thereby losing access to finance and research materials that might have supplemented his meagre means at the University. His career began a slow decline, and in 1849, though still lecturing, he was found living in a slum (Desmond, 1984).

If Darwin, on asking Grant to examine some coralline specimens from the *Beagle*, did not hear at first hand about his refined mode of persecution, the story was surely common coin at the Zoological Society, which Darwin visited and shunned for its 'mean quarrelsome spirit' (*Correspondence*, 1:512, 514), or even at the gentlemanly Geological Society, where Lyell introduced him to the Oxbridge savants. And within six months of settling in London, Darwin cut the image of a naturalist who could be told such a story with a nudge and a wink. He had obtained a £1000 government grant by courtesy of his clerical patrons at Cambridge to publish his *Beagle* researches; he had recruited Owen to the project to describe his specimens of fossil mammals. He had also read papers before the Geological Society and, in short, looked set to become the paragon of professional respectability. But the ambitious young man was not quite what he seemed. Known only to himself and probably his brother, kept quietly between the covers of a series of pocket notebooks, were the beginnings of a new theory of evolution, more acceptable than Lamarck's, that would explain the material origination of all plant and animal species, including human life, mind, and society, by means of a divinely ordained system of unvarying laws (Rudwick, 1982). Reformers such as Grant, not to mention radical freethinkers, had jeopardized their careers for lack of such discretion. One young man at least would not take the risk.

Darwin's views were materialistic and deterministic; they 'tended towards' atheism in the eyes of those he least wished to offend. Outside professional circles Darwin now socialized with a group of advanced thinkers to whom Erasmus had introduced him. None of them would have found his views offensive. To Harriet Martineau, a Unitarian, materialism and determinism were the basis of her creed. Thomas Carlyle shared her conviction that the universe obeys Eternal Law. Hensleigh Wedgwood, the Darwins' cousin, believed in the duality of body and soul, but Carlyle and Erasmus were competent to expound on ways in which matter could incorporate the spiritual through the categories of German idealism (Erskine, 1987). But, while Darwin no doubt felt supported by the like-mindedness of Erasmus's friends, he was still the aspiring professional naturalist who knew from past experience the perils of ill-concealed freethought. If none of his liberal companions was an atheist, this did not mean that he himself would be above reproach if the Oxbridge gentry or even the establishmentarian Lyell got wind of his speculations.

Therefore in his notebooks Darwin developed strategies for self-protection in the event that his theory should be exposed.[6] He would distinguish it categorically from Lamarck's; he would devise a manner of speaking to conceal his materialism. He would 'mention persecution of early astronomers, — then add chief good of individual scientific men is to push their science a few years in advance only of their age'. The word 'only' made a potentially radical statement into a reformist one. Darwin had learned his caution from the courtly Lyell. And in the same vein, he would stress the moral progressiveness of his theory in explaining, for example, how the present struggle for subsistence in Britain, owing to 'even a *few* years plenty' in the early 1830s, might lead in the long run to the elimination of 'evil passions', possibly through promoting the sort of religious education that had brought moral uplift to the natives of Tierra del Fuego and Tahiti whom he had encountered during the *Beagle* voyage. 'Educate all classes, avoid the contamination of castes. improve the women. (double influence) & mankind must improve —'.

Finally, in keeping with his moral and metaphysical moderation, Darwin would explain how his materialistic and deterministic scheme of evolution, far from overthrowing belief in God, entailed a far 'grander' theology than the one current among Oxbridge Anglican naturalists, who merely followed their predecessor, Paley, in conceiving the divine providence after the manner of their own creative interventions in science.

> What a magnificent view one can take of the world [.] Astronomical causes modified by unknown ones, cause changes in geography &

[6] The texts referred to below appear in Gruber and Barrett, 1974, pp. 278–9 (M 73–4), 289 (M 121–3), 389–90 (OUN 26–9), 450 (C 123), 453 (C 220), 456 (D 135e), 458 (E 47).

> changes of climate suspended to change of climate from physical causes, — then suspended changes of form in the organic world, as adaptation, & these changing affect each other, & their bodies by certain laws of harmony keep perfect in these themselves. — instincts alter, reason is formed & the world peopled with myriads of distinct forms from a period short of eternity to the present time, to the future. — How far grander than idea from cramped imagination that God created (warring against those very laws he established in all organic nature) the Rhinoceros of Java & Sumatra, that since the time of the Silurian he has made a long succession of vile molluscous animals. How beneath the dignity of him, who is supposed to have said let there be light and there was light.

'Bad taste', Darwin inserted at the end of the passage. He was worried that his theological one-upmanship might offend (Gruber and Barrett, 1974, pp. 454–5). But in 1842, the hungriest year of the hungry forties, he struck up the theme again in a private sketch of his theory, justifying the divine laws that led to 'death, famine, rapine, and the concealed war of nature' on the ground that they produce 'the highest good, which we can conceive, the creation of the higher animals'. 'The existence of such laws', he still believed, 'should exalt our notion of the power of the omniscient Creator' (De Beer, 1958, p. 87).

VII THE SECULAR VICAR

While Darwin was formulating his theory of evolution by natural selection and devising strategies to protect himself from the abuse it might incur, his clerical career died a 'natural death' (Barlow, 1958, p. 57). Urgent new preoccupations had edged out Dr Darwin's objective, which had remained his own even while on the *Beagle*. Geology had become the paramount thing, followed by the successful publication of his global researches. Privately, too, there was a change of emphasis. Darwin knew he was entertaining a creed profoundly at variance with established views in religion and science. When he wrote in a notebook that 'whole fabric totters & falls', he had precisely these views in mind. A young man thinking in this way was plainly ill-fitted to enter holy orders, even if he had no other pressing interests. He was flirting with unbelief, which had cost less discreet individuals dear, and this also created problems for his public career as a professional naturalist. His object in life must now be to find a low-profile livelihood to sustain a growing scientific reputation while at the same time freeing him privately to carry out a potentially dangerous enterprise.

In 1838 Darwin's desiderata were met. His father opened the family purse-strings to endow him as a gentleman naturalist, thereby enabling him to acquire a wife and other accountrements of leisured respectability. Within weeks Darwin was courting his cousin Emma Wedgwood, a fervent believer, who had known for many years that he had been intended for the Church. They married in January 1839, immediately started a family, and made plans to escape from London. In September 1842, just after the greatest Chartist uprising to be seen in the capital, a month to the day since *The Times* poured scorn on Holyoake's eloquent self-defence before his sentencing to Gloucester gaol, Darwin took up residence in the Kentish village of Down, sixteen miles from the metropolis. It seemed to him 'absolutely at the extreme verge of the world'. He settled his family in the old parsonage, which he had purchased from the late incumbent, and adopted the country clerical life-style that had long attracted him for the scope it gave to natural history.

Darwin remained a pillar of the parish for forty years. His infants were christened in the Church of St Mary the Virgin; the family attended there regularly, sitting in a pew of their own; and the ancient cycle of life was completed when Darwin after Darwin was laid to rest in the parish churchyard according to the rite of the Church of England. Although the head of the family finally ceased to attend public worship, he maintained his local reputation by undertaking a range of responsibilities characteristically assumed by the parish priest. His continuous financial support for the church could be taken for granted. He started a friendly club for the villagers about 1850; he became a local magistrate in 1857. In the 1860s, when his close friend the incumbent was compelled to leave the parish in the hands of curates, Darwin became treasurer of the Coal and Clothing Club and he took over the accounts of the National School. Even the Sunday School accounts came his way for a year or two before a High Church vicar, ordained by Bishop Samuel Wilberforce, arrived to wrest the parish administration from him and his friends. By this time, however, in the 1870s, Darwin's respectability could not be impugned.

Meanwhile the secret species research went on apace. Darwin's self-protective strategy did not entirely assuage his fears, and when forced to tip his hand in order to obtain information on the subject from fellow naturalists, he revealed a man under stress. To one he wrote in 1843 that his belief in evolution must appear 'absurdly presumptuous' and would open him to 'reproach'. To J. D. Hooker in 1844 he stated that declaring himself in favour of evolution was 'like confessing a murder', an offence for which men were imprisoned, tried, and executed. It was just six months later, after rewriting the sketch of his theory, that he gave his wife instructions for publishing it 'in case of my sudden death'. In 1845, when *Vestiges* had appealed over the heads of constituted authority to a popular audience and the Reverend Adam Sedgwick damned the book as subversive and unscientific, Darwin told Lyell that he had read his old geology professor's arguments with 'fear and trembling', although he thought he could answer them none the less. Subsequently he disclosed his secret to two further colleagues, so that by 1848 five select individuals outside his family knew that a potentially disreputable theory was in the making. At the same time, however, Darwin's need to conceal his views from the generality of naturalists and the wider public for fear of their perceived affinities gave rise to anger and frustration that could scarcely be expressed. These pent-up feelings about his work contributed more than any single factor to his subsequent ill-health (Colp, 1977, 1986; Yeo, 1984–5).

Events came to a head between 1848 and 1851, when Darwin experienced his first serious breakdown. While carrying on a voluminous correspondencc, extracting information from naturalists round the world, he remained cut off from his former allies — Erasmus's friends in London — as well as from younger reformers such as Spencer, Lewes, Eliot, and Francis Newman, who were discovering each other's commitment to an evolutionary creed. Holyoake had now joined them, and 'Secularism' as a moderate inclusive movement was launched in 1851 under their inspiration, particularly Newman's. Newman, whose elder brother had become notorious for his views on the 'development' of Christian doctrine and for becoming a Roman Catholic, was the chief link between Darwin and organized unbelief at this period. Both Holyoake and he underwent a metamorphosis, albeit in opposite directions. Holyoake, a militant atheist, learned from Newman personally and from his book *The Soul* (1848) the power of religious feelings, the universality of the moral sense, and the desirability of a reforming movement that, on these grounds, would unite people of diverse religious outlooks (Royle, 1974, pp. 157–8). Darwin, an increasingly nominal Christian, learned from Newman's spiritual autobiography, *Phases of Faith* (1850), which he thought 'excellent', that there was no resting-place *en route* from Anglicanism through Unitarianism to a purely theistic belief. So, while the radical freethinker with a criminal record discovered respectable support for Secularism in London, the respectable Cambridge naturalist living the parson's life in a secluded country parish discovered in himself a radical identity he had always shunned. Darwin gave up Christianity.

The circumstances were not unlike those in which other young reformers at the time were abandoning their inherited faith. While Newman consolidated the doubts that had festered in Darwin's mind for many years, two deaths rivetted his thoughts on the Christian doctrine of eternal retribution. The loss of Dr Darwin in 1848 at the age of eighty-two precipitated his physical breakdown. He despaired of his own life and became profoundly depressed. His father, whom he loved dearly, was not a Christian and therefore liable to be punished eternally for unbelief. If, however, this doctrine now began to seem 'damnable' to Darwin, as he would later call it

(Barlow, 1958, p. 87), what of the tragic death of his ten year-old daughter Annie in 1851, just a month after he had finished reading Newman's book? This was 'bitter & cruel', Darwin informed an Anglican clergyman; the next day he set down in a private memoir a stunning vindication of Annie's character in its moral sensitivity. 'She hardly ever required to be found fault with, & was never punished in any way whatever.' 'A single glance of my eye, not of displeasure (for I thank God I hardly ever cast one on her) but of want of sympathy would for some minutes alter her whole countenance.' For such a one there could be still less doubt than in Dr Darwin's case about the prospect of eternal retribution, and Darwin, now contemplating his own punishment both here and hereafter, as well as the cruel injustice of the struggle for existence, lost the will to believe. The present life was hell enough; Christianity was immoral. He would publish and be damned.

A few years later, after completing the onerous self-imposed task of dissecting and describing hundreds of barnacles — 'vile molluscous animals' — Darwin began to write up his theory for the press. He believed he had an 'instinct for truth . . . of the same nature as the instinct of virtue' (quoted in Colp, 1986, p. 31), and when commenting to Hooker on the 'indecency' of the method of fertilization in certain marine species, he evoked the danger of communicating truthfully to a mid-Victorian audience: 'What a book a Devil's Chaplain might write on the clumsy wasteful, blundering low & horribly cruel works of nature' (F. Darwin and Seward, 1903, I, p. 94). It was a book he himself might write if he were not careful. *On the Origin of Species* would not, accordingly, be like *The Devil's Pulpit*, although the fate of its author, another renegade ordinand, was well within recall.

VIII CREEDS IN COLLISION

What did Darwin accomplish? Everyone knows that by dint of massive researches, courageous insight, and heroic suffering he had pressed on where other naturalists feared to tread and singlehandedly solved that mystery of mysteries, 'the organic origins problem' (Ruse, 1979). And there can be no doubt that after 1859 Darwin made both evolution and an evolutionary account of human ancestry respectable by at least some contemporary standards of scientific explanation. But in the *Origin of Species*, a condensation of the larger work begun in the wake of Annie's death and the barnacles, he accomplished something more. This was less of a scientific 'revolution' than a revelation: a formidable disclosure of how minds had moved in the previous decades. In effect the moral crisis of the 1830s and 1840s was brought into the open; the creed towards which first radical freethinkers, then a generation of young reformers, had been groping was made both available and unavoidable as a serious alternative for those now finding their own reasons to dissent from the established Christian creed. The young reformers had grown into middle age; they had become authorities in their own right. Now the world would have to heed them as they competed to be heard.

No one saw the situation more clearly than Sedgwick, Darwin's old professor at Cambridge, a member of the inner élite of the Geological Society since the 1830s. Immediately after the *Origin of Species* was published in November 1859, he grieved over precisely its moral and social significance in a long and painful letter to his prodigal pupil, written, he said, in 'a spirit of brotherly love' (F. Darwin, 1887, II, pp. 249–50). He exemplified passages that 'greatly shocked' his 'moral taste', then delivered a parting rebuke:

> I greatly dislike the concluding chapter — not as a summary, for in that light it appears good — but I dislike it from the tone of triumphant confidence in which you appeal to the rising generation (in a tone I condemned in the author of the 'Vestiges') and prophesy of things not yet in the womb of time, nor (if we are to trust the accumulated experience of human sense and the inferences of its logic) ever likely to be found anywhere but in the fertile womb of man's imagination.

Creeds had collided. The 'rising generation' was at the gate.

By 1860 the rising generation and its leaders no longer faced the threat of outright persecution for publicizing their infidelities. Even working-class radicals could feel relatively safe. What stood in the way of dissident middle-class intellectuals as they pursued their careers and sought a voice in national affairs was still, however, what had confronted Darwin's teacher Robert Grant: namely, the likes of Sedgwick, a venerable old naturalist, an Anglican clergyman, and a professor in a university dominated by Anglicans. He typified the professional authority enjoyed uniquely by the clergy of the Established Church. It was their creed that defined the scope and bounds of legitimate knowledge; it was their power to propagate and impose this creed, from pulpits, universities, and the bench of bishops, that made their authority unrivalled. Those who sought professional recognition on the basis of another creed, who undertook, for example, to cross the frontiers of legitimate knowledge by enquiring into the origins of life, mind, and society, could be frustrated at every turn. Patronage might be withheld, careers obstructed, publications rejected, and reputations torn down. Only those who subscribed the established creed would certainly share the status and emoluments of established authority. Others who wished their due would have to tackle the system head on (Turner, 1978; Heyck, 1982).

This goes a long way towards explaining why there was a 'conflict' after the *Origin of Species* appeared. It was not simply a conflict between 'science' and 'religion' or a conflict over Darwin's book. It was a conflict between the adherents of differing creeds. What Grant and his handful of outsider-allies could not sustain thirty years earlier was now pursued by force of numbers and respectability. The conflict involved Darwin to such an extent because his book lent credibility to the new creed in terms that established authority could readily comprehend. Darwin possessed expert credentials, which he had gained while concealing his heretical ideas, and his arguments depended on assumptions that were widely held. Yet the conflict was not just over arguments or ideas either. It was at root a social phenomenon: a conflict that, from its inception in the 1830s and 1840s was primarily about the identity and character of moral authority in a changing society. Were the clergy to go on controlling people's lives through their bizarre and oppressive doctrines and their impotent incantations? Or would professional men of science now take the lead in reforming the social order on the basis of beliefs that had already underwritten impressive theoretical and technological achievements, from steam engines to public sanitation? This was how young reformers of the 1840s saw the conflict when once their emerging creed had received the powerful public backing of Darwin (Turner, 1974a, ch. 1; Turner, 1978, pp. 356–60). By the 'mingling' of moral and material realms, which Sedgwick so deplored, Darwin had brought moral questions within the jurisdiction of those who interpreted material nature. By naturalizing humankind, body and mind, through a credible theory of evolution, Darwin enabled the aspiring professional authorities to define social questions as 'scientific' questions, which were their competence alone (Jacyna, 1981).

For twenty years or more the professional élites — the spokesmen for the Christian and naturalistic creeds — struggled to establish themselves at the head of British society. This is the perspective in which the famous controversies of those years must be viewed. The notorious confrontation between Huxley and Wilberforce was in reality a thirty-five year old zoology instructor upbraiding a fifty-five year old bishop in his own diocese, the reactionary diocese of Oxford, after the bishop had patronizingly poked fun at the moral implications of Darwin's theory. The Metaphysical Society, an informal gathering of the intelligentsia that met regularly in London from 1869 to 1880, was an abortive attempt by liberal churchmen to maintain a cultural consensus — abortive because creeds ran very deep and no consensus could be achieved on a scale that included Roman Catholic archbishops, red republicans, evangelical clergy, agnostic naturalists, and High Church politicians. The 'prayer gauge debate' of the early 1870s, which played itself out in pamphlets and periodicals, was less about statistical tests of the physical efficacy of prayer than about whether bishops or scientific experts were more likely to prescribe effective measures for dealing with the natural disorders about which people prayed. The infamous presidential address to the British Association for the Advancement of Science in 1874 — the so-called 'Belfast Address' — was perhaps the most sensational pretence in the period to 'claim, and . . . wrest from theology', as its author John Tyndall put it, 'the entire domain of cosmological theory' (Lucas, 1979; R. M. Young, 1980; Turner, 1974b; Tyndall, 1899, II, p. 197).

The naturalistic creed was not, however, necessarily antitheistic, and so in time new alliances were formed between the clerical and the scientific professional élites. The Reverend Baden Powell, a reforming mathematics professor at Oxford, believed that science and theology had nothing to do with each other, and he gave Darwin's book a warm welcome in his contribution to *Essays and Reviews* (1860). F. D. Maurice and Charles Kingsley, both Christian socialists, were prepared to take scientific revelations as if from God — a flattering prospect for scientists like Huxley. Meanwhile Broad Churchmen like J. W. Colenso and A. P. Stanley helped put biblical interpretation on a naturalistic basis with historical studies based on German critical scholarship. Bishop Colenso was supported by Huxley on being deprived of his see; Dean Stanley enjoyed an intimate relationship with Tyndall for many years (Moore, 1979, pp. 88–97; Moore, 1986). When Tyndall wrote in 1863 of the clergy, that 'science does not need their protection, but it desires their friendship on honourable terms; it wishes to work with them towards the great end of all education, — the bettering of man's estate', he probably spoke for most of his professional allies (quoted in Turner, 1974b, p. 53). Huxley, at any rate, told Kingsley in 1860 that the Church of England was a 'great and powerful instrument for good or evil' and later described an 'Established Church which should be a blessing to the community'. Spencer agreed with the Reverend M. J. Savage, a Unitarian clergyman, that evolution did not simply negate people's 'precious ethical and religious beliefs' but placed them on 'a definite scientific and unshakeable foundation'. And Galton, Darwin's cousin, who above all looked for a new 'scientific priesthood' to usurp the clergy, nevertheless believed that the 'new moral duty' of furthering human evolution was 'to be exercised concurrently with, and not in opposition to the old ones upon which the social fabric depends' (L. Huxley, 1903, I, p. 320; T. H. Huxley, 1893, p. 284; Spencer, in Coley and Hall, 1980, pp. 27–8; Galton, n.d., p. 220).

IX BETWEEN CHRISTIANITY AND FREETHOUGHT

Darwin himself agreed. The orderly transfer of moral authority and spiritual power to an alliance of progressive-minded professionals in science and religion, among whom the scientists held the upper hand, was implicit in the conduct of his private and public life for the remainder of his career. From his work in the local parish to his burial in Westminster Abbey, it was obvious that the new creed of evolutionary naturalism need not be socially divisive. In the second edition of the *Origin of Species* Darwin inserted a commendatory remark from Kingsley; he lent his name to a letter from several naturalists supporting the authors of *Essays and Reviews*; he backed the clerical philologist F. W. Farrar for a Fellowship of the Royal Society; he became a trustee of the Sunday Lecture Society, which offered the London public uplifting discourses from clergymen and scientists. By the time his *Descent of Man* appeared in 1871, it was not unusual to find Darwin recalling there the historic debate between creationists and traducianists over the origin of the human soul in order to reassure his audience that his views on human origins need not offend (Moore, 1979, p. 347; Moore, 1986, pp. 340–3).

What Darwin's personal beliefs were was quite another matter. Although people continually looked to him for religious guidance, as if he had indeed become the father superior of Galton's new scientific priesthood, he was loath to speak out. This was partly because publicizing his religious views would expose him to persecution, which he had always feared, and this would injure his wife, with whom he differed grievously over Christianity. Partly it was because any controversy over his personal beliefs would also injure the cause of evolution, to which he had devoted his entire career. Partly, too, Darwin's reluctance to speak out on religion arose from growing uncertainty about whether he had any good grounds for still believing in God and personal immortality. It was altogether easier, and certainly much more respectable, to keep one's views to oneself and be judged by one's deeds as an eminent Christian gentleman.

Not all late Victorian freethinkers agreed (W. S. Smith, 1967). Efforts were made repeatedly to enlist Darwin's support for their causes. He was approached in the mid-1860s to give material and moral aid to Bishop Colenso; he was cultivated after 1869 by Charles Voysey, the Yorkshire vicar deposed for publishing heretical sermons, who in 1871 founded the Theistic Church in London; he was asked in 1878 by Moncure Conway, the American purveyor of spiritualized secularism at the South Place Chapel, to join the committee of the Association of Liberal Thinkers with Huxley, Tyndall, Holyoake, and himself. Darwin probably assisted Colenso, he sent Voysey a donation, and he may just once have attended Conway's chapel, even if he did not join his smorgasbord of religionists.[7] But ally himself

[7] For Colenso and Darwin, see Henrietta Powell to Charles Darwin, 11 Feb. 1863, and Erasmus Darwin to Charles Darwin, 1 Feb. [1864], in the Darwin Archive, Cambridge University Library, 105 (ser. 2): 23–4; 160. The Darwin-Voysey correspondence is also in the Darwin Archive, as are many of the letters pertaining to Conway, the rest being in Columbia University Library. On Darwin's relations with South Place Chapel and the Theistic Church, see the undocumented remarks in Kent, 1932, pp. 86–7, 106.

publicly with organized freethought he would not — not in Great Britain. Only in the United States did Darwin's name become identified with the movement, and even there it was abruptly withdrawn.

The Free Religious Association, founded at Boston in 1867 by an élite coterie of disaffected Unitarians and left-wing transcendentalists, aimed to demolish Christianity and erect in its place a universal rational religion, without priesthood or theology, based on evolutionary science. Among the organizers were Thomas Wentworth Higginson, Charles Eliot Norton, and Francis Ellingwood Abbot. Darwin met and corresponded with Higginson and Norton in the 1870s; the link with Norton was made permanent in 1877 when Darwin's eldest son, William, married his sister-in-law. Abbot and Darwin never met but they exchanged many letters. As editor of *The Index*, the Association's semi-official organ and voice of its more radical wing, Abbot was always on the look-out for contributors who would foster 'the spirit of reform' without 'deference to the authority of the Bible, the Church, or the Christ'. Conway and Voysey, as well as Newman, Cobbe, and Holyoake, appeared in his pages, and in 1871 Darwin was asked to contribute. He reluctantly declined, but he did subscribe to *The Index* immediately and thereafter until his death sent Abbot generous donations — as much as £25 one year, the same amount he subscribed in 1876 to the Down Vicarage Endowment Fund (Gohdes, 1931, ch. 11; Warren, 1943, ch. 4; Kuklick, 1977, pp. 92 ff.).[8]

Early in their correspondence, in a letter clearly marked 'Private', Darwin praised Abbot's evocation of the free religious spirit in a pamphlet he had sent him entitled *Truths for the Times* (1871): 'I admire them', Darwin wrote, referring to the 'truths', 'from my inmost heart, & I believe that I agree to every word'. Abbot, with scrupulous respect for Darwin's privacy, then asked whether he might reproduce the remark. Consent was granted, and for years afterward several thousand subscribers to the weekly periodical were exposed at intervals to Darwin's commendation as an advertisement for Abbot's tract. But in 1880 the advertisement was suddenly stopped. Writing on behalf of his forgetful father, William Darwin informed Abbot on 13 June that 'he had no intention that his words should be used for this purpose, and he wishes now that they should be omitted'. Darwin's flirtation with self-exposure as a freethinker was over, even in transatlantic safety.

Something had reined him in. It may have been Abbot's impending departure from the editorship of *The Index*, although this had no bearing on

[8] The Higginson correspondence and Abbot's letters are in the Darwin Archive. Darwin's letters to Norton and Abbot are at Harvard University, Norton's in the Houghton Library, Abbot's in the University Archives. On Darwin's support for the *The Index*, see the issue for 27 April 1882 and the recollections of Francis Darwin in the Darwin Archive; 140.3:23.

the misuse of Darwin's words. More likely, the cause of Darwin's renewed reticence lay nearer home. Radical freethinkers in Britain were now achieving notoriety they had not known since the trial of Holyoake and the incarceration of Taylor and Carlile. Since the late 1850s, when the staid diminutive Holyoake teamed up with Charles Bradlaugh, a big boisterous young man from London's East End, Secularism had changed its character. Bradlaugh was a fighter — he called himself 'Iconoclast'. Everywhere his voice boomed out he remade freethought in his indomitable image (Royle, 1974, pp. 211–12). In 1862 he wrested the editorship of the movement's mouthpiece, the *National Reformer*, from Holyoake and opened a breach that even the tightly organized National Secular Society, which Bradlaugh founded four years later, proved unable to contain. At issue was not only Bradlaugh's militant atheism and Liberal politics, but his advocacy of birth control. Respectable freethinkers, who had built alliances with liberal Christians, were chary of so-called 'neo-Malthusianism'. They thought it encouraged immorality, a point on which the Christians were pleased to agree. Bradlaugh, however, stuck to his guns and used the *National Reformer* to associate the Malthusian law of population with atheism and contraception (Royle, 1980, pp. 254 ff.).

When Darwin devised his theory of evolution in the late 1830s he made use of the same Malthusian law. The *Origin of Species* now advertised its creative and beneficent effects as seen in the struggle for existence. The permanent disparity, according to the Reverend Thomas Malthus, between available food and mouths to feed, meant, according to Darwin, that the congenitally less fitted to survive natural austerity and reproduce themselves must lose out in life's race. Those remaining must be in some sense improved. Tampering with this selective mechanism would, however, favour the losers. Tempering the struggle for existence would jeopardize human progress. In the *Descent of Man* Darwin therefore declared himself in favour of 'open competition' for all: 'the most able should not be prevented by laws or customs from succeeding best and rearing the largest number of offspring' (Darwin, 1874, p. 618). Among the 'laws or customs' he discouraged were those pertaining to the control of fertility. Big families among those 'most able' to feed themselves — Darwin sired ten children — had as its corollary small families among the less able, enforced through natural attrition. Birth control would mitigate the struggle for existence, reduce the disparity in family size, and make the less able relatively more numerous. By divorcing sexuality from its reproductive consequences, it would also loose on society a disruptive force inimical to bourgeois domesticity.

For these same reasons many radical freethinkers had long regarded themselves as neo-Malthusians: because, accepting the premise on which Darwin based his theory, the key to improving the lot of working people within a bourgeois social order lay, for them, in the control of human fertility. But the movement had never been united on the issue. Those, for example, who derived their evolutionary beliefs from Lamarck could argue that progress depended on individual striving, not on a slow, painful, and inevitable Malthusian struggle for existence. Bradlaugh, however, took his science from Malthus and his irreligion from the radical tradition. Having made the *National Reformer* scurrilous in the eyes of fellow Secularists for advocating birth control, he split the movement completely in 1877 by re-issuing an outdated booklet on the subject under the auspices of his Freethought Publishing Company. He and his co-publisher, Annie Besant, who had recently left her husband, an Anglican clergyman, were arrested on charges of obscenity, tried at the Old Bailey, and convicted. Only Bradlaugh's mastery of legal procedure prevented their imprisonment, and in February 1878 the judgement against them was set aside (Manvell, 1976).

Meanwhile, with Secularists divided and the public outraged by courtesy of *The Times* and other newspapers, Bradlaugh subpoenaed Darwin to testify for the defence, which he and Besant were to conduct themselves. Darwin's reply was swift and to the point.

June 6 [18]77

Sir

I am much obliged for your courteous notice. I have been for many years much out of health & have been forced to give up all society or public meetings, & it would be great suffering to me to be a witness in a court. — It is indeed not improbable that I might be unable to attend. Therefore I hope that if in your power you will excuse my attendance. I may add that I am not a medical man. I have not seen the book in question, but from notices in the newspapers, I suppose that it refers to means to prevent conception. If so I sh^{d} be forced to express in court a very decided opinion in opposition to you & Mrs Besant; though from all that I have heard I do not doubt that both of you are acting solely in accordance to what you believe best for mankind. — I have long held an opposite opinion, as you will see in the enclosed extract, & this I sh^{d} think it my duty to state in court, the words 'any means' of artificial means of preventing conception. But besides the evils here alluded to I believe that any such practices would in time spread to unmarried women & w^{d} destroy chastity on which the family bond depends; & the weakening of this bond would be the greatest of all possible evils to mankind; so that my judgment would be in the strongest opposition to yours. This Friday the 8th [blank] I leave home for a month & my address from the 8th to [blank] will be at my sisters home & from the 13th at my sons home

B[assett] S[outhampton]. If it is not asking too great a favour, I sh^{d} be greatly obliged if you w^{d} inform me what you decide; as apprehension of the coming exertion would prevent the rest which I require doing me much good. Apologizing for the length of this letter [3 words illegible]

C[harles] R[.] D[arwin]

Darwin's letter, full of dissent and apprehension, was painstakingly drafted.[9] He left no doubt in Bradlaugh's mind that his sympathies lay with the respectable Christian majority in Victorian Britain. The continued availability he proffered, which Bradlaugh did not acknowledge, was a measure of the ambiguity of his stance, even though he had no intention of testifying in defence of radical freethinkers.[10]

X THE IRRELIGION OF AN AGNOSTIC

The trial of Bradlaugh and Besant was only the sensational start of events that brought renewed notoriety to organized unbelief in late Victorian Britain, a notoriety from which respectable freethinkers such as Darwin instinctively recoiled. When Bradlaugh was elected a Liberal MP for Northampton in April 1880, the Christian nation faced the prospect of a convicted purveyor of obscenity swearing on the Bible in order to take his seat in the House of Commons. After an unsuccessful attempt to 'affirm' in the manner of Quakers, Bradlaugh determined to take the oath of allegiance. As an atheist he was prevented from doing so by every trick of the law and parliamentary procedure. His case became a *cause celèbre*, his name a household word. Fellow members tried to bankrupt him with fines, they connived to declare his seat vacant (which he promptly re-won), and on 3 August 1881, when Bradlaugh arrived at the Palace of Westminster with a young Secularist recruit named Edward Aveling and a vast crowd of supporters headed by Besant, he was forcibly prevented from taking his seat by the deputy Sergeant-at-Arms, then physically ejected from the Commons and flung into Palace Yard by a crowd of policemen, messengers, and Tory MPs (Tribe, 1971, pp. 209–11). Thereafter Bradlaugh's struggle for political existence went on year after year both within and outside Parliament.

[9] I have quoted the draft in the Darwin Archive, 202, with the kind assistance of Peter Gautrey and the archival staff. The version given in Bradlaugh's biography by his daughter (Bonner, 1895, I, p. 24) omits the central section of the letter, from 'Therefore I hope . . .' to the sentence beginning 'If it is not asking . . .', thereby deliberately conveying the false impression that Darwin would have been a favourable witness.

[10] For another view of Charles Darwin, see *RVB*, II, 8.

Only in 1886 was he permitted to swear on the Bible and take his seat unopposed (Arnstein, 1965).

By this time the split Bradlaugh had provoked among Secularists in 1877 had taken a permanent organizational and ideological form. If Holyoake and his moderate colleagues, who had broken away to form the British Secular Union, were embarrassed by the birth-control escapade with Besant, they were embittered by the spectacle of an atheist, whatever his political objectives, fighting cynically for the right to swear by the name of God and kiss the Bible. Being irreligious denominationalists, moreover, the public identification of Secularism with Bradlaugh's case and the phenomenal growth of the National Secular Society made them frankly jealous. None felt more strongly than those members of the British Secular Union who had begun to style themselves agnostics (Royle, 1980, pp. 31–2, 115 ff.).[11]

'Agnostic' was a respectable label to wear for working-class infidels bent on intellectual upward mobility. The word had been coined by Huxley in 1869 to mark himself as an orthodox opponent of latter-day 'gnosticism', an ancient Christian heresy, in the gentlemanly debates of the Metaphysical Society. An agnostic did not affront Christian gnostics by denying God's existence; nor could he agree with them in purporting to know what could not be known. His doctrine was ontologically neutral. It had a long and distinguished philosophic pedigree, from David Hume and Immanuel Kant through William Hamilton, the Scottish metaphysician, to the Oxford divine Henry Longueville Mansel, latterly Dean of St Paul's (Lightman, 1987). Mansel's 1858 Bampton Lectures, *The Limits of Religious Thought Examined* (1859) argued that human reason, unaided by revelation, could know nothing of God or ultimate reality. Spencer, who rejected revelation, used Mansel to baptize his ten-volume *System of Synthetic Philosophy*, which began to appear in 1860, the *Summa Theologica* of the new naturalistic creed. Huxley, in calling himself an agnostic, became something like Spencer's missionary, although the two apostles did not always see eye to eye. Agnosticism in his faith and practice became a scientific Broad Church, a basis for professional alliance, the bourgeois equivalent of Secularism twenty years before. Holyoake, never quite easy in his atheism, thanked Huxley for the term (McCabe, 1908, I, p. 201; II, p. 266).

Thirty years after Holyoake and Darwin had first approached each other like ships in the night, moving on opposite religious routes, they converged again. As the British Secular Union set itself against the bombastic blas-

[11] At its peak the British Secular Union probably had no more than twenty branches and only a few hundred members, compared to the hundred-odd branches and three to six thousand members and affiliates of the National Secular Society. The BSU featured 'quality, not quantity'; by 1884 it had all but 'faded away' (Royle, 1980, p. 32).

phemies of the National Secular Society under Bradlaugh, adopting agnosticism as the form in which the new creed that first emerged among their forebears could now most propitiously be held, Darwin saw that his own tenuous beliefs, which he had ever been reluctant to disclose, could now safely be characterized in a manner that would give minimal offence. 'Whether a man deserved to be called a Theist depends on the definition of the term', he told a correspondent in May 1879. '. . . In my most extreme fluctuations I have never been an atheist in denying the existence of a God[.] I think that generally (and more and more as I grow older), but not always, that an Agnostic would be the more correct description of my state of mind.' Darwin, like Holyoake, had recoiled from Bradlaugh's neo-Malthusianism. Now he would not mistakenly be associated with his atheism either, although he remained a dyed-in-the-wool Liberal.

The litmus test of Darwin's latter-day irreligion was Edward Aveling (Feuer, 1975; Colp, 1976). Before enlistment as Bradlaugh's henchman, Aveling, a medical doctor in his late twenties, lectured on comparative anatomy at the London Hospital. He was a brilliant teacher and a facile popularizer of science. In September 1878 he began to send Darwin a series of articles he was publishing on 'Darwin and His Work'. The series ran for a year and it is not known how many of the seven numbers Darwin received, but he sent Aveling encouragement at the start and asked to see future instalments. Meanwhile Aveling was introduced to Besant, with whom he became much involved, although both of them were still married, and Besant introduced him to Bradlaugh. In early 1879 Aveling wrote six articles on 'Darwin and His Views' for the *National Reformer*, using false initials; in November he began a new series over his own name, entitled 'Darwin and His Works', which by September 1880 had run to twenty-eight parts. While this series was advertising Aveling's new identity as a radical freethinker, he deployed his considerable talents on public platforms in London and round the country. By May 1880 he had delivered over one hundred lectures, drawing on his evolutionary expertise.

That month Bradlaugh's travails began. MPs raged, committees quarreled, and the papers were full of the controversy. Darwin, who had long been fascinated by 'any curious trial' and found the law report 'about the most interesting part of the paper', was reminded vividly of the support Bradlaugh had sought from him three years earlier. And if this, in turn, did not suffice to remind him of his continuing self-exposure in Abbot's *Index* as an ally of anti-Christian freethinkers, he had only to remember the encouragement he subsequently gave Aveling, who had now emerged as a Darwinian atheist. Whether Aveling's activities were familiar to Darwin is, however, unknown. What is certain is that by 11 June Darwin had instructed his son to have Abbot remove his name from *The Index*.

A few months later Aveling wrote to Darwin again, seeking approval for his plan to publish a collection of his articles from the *National Reformer*. He asked permission to dedicate the collection to him and offered to send the proof sheets. The volume, he said, was to appear in the 'International Library of Science and Freethought' under the editorship of 'my friends Mrs. Annie Besant and Charles Bradlaugh, M.P.' Enclosed in Aveling's letter was a pamphlet by the German materialist Ludwig Büchner, translated by Besant, with an advertisement explaining that the aim of the Library was to 'spread heresy' among the English 'reading masses'. Darwin replied by return of post:[12]

> Private
> Oct. 13, 1880
>
> Dear Sir
>
> I am obliged by your kind letter & the Enclosure. — the publication in any form of your remarks on my writings really requires no consent on my part, & it would be ridiculous in me to give consent to what requires none. I sh^{d}. prefer the Part or Volume not be dedicated to me (though I thank you for the intended honour) as this implies to a certain extent my approval of the general publication, about which I know nothing. — Moreover though I am a strong advocate for free thought on all subjects, yet it appears to me (whether rightly or wrongly) that direct arguments against christianity & theism produce hardly any effect on the public; & freedom of thought is best promoted by the gradual illumination of men's minds, which follow from the advance of science. It has, therefore, been always my object to avoid writing on religion, & I have confined myself to science. I may, however, have been unduly biassed by the pain which it would give some members of my family, if I aided in any way direct attacks on religion. — I am sorry to refuse you any request, but I am old & have very little strength, & looking over proof-sheets (as I know by present experience) fatigues me much. —
>
> I remain Dear Sir
> yours faithfully
> Ch. Darwin

There was nothing in Aveling's letter or its enclosure to indicate that the dedication Darwin politely refused would have appeared in a volume devoted to any more than the spread of 'heresy'. And Darwin's own books had done just that for many years. 'Direct arguments against christianity & theism' were not therefore at issue — unless one knew, as Darwin must

[12] I quote Darwin's letter as transcribed in Feuer, 1975. The letter had long been assumed to have been addressed to Karl Marx. See Colp, 1976, 1982.

have, that Aveling was a militant Secularist. Of Bradlaugh and Besant's 'International Library' Darwin may have known 'nothing', but Bradlaugh and Besant he knew full well. He would not now permit his name to be associated either with Abbot's publication or with theirs.

Ten months passed, and in August 1881, the week after Bradlaugh was thrown bodily from the Commons, the week Darwin returned from his final visit to Erasmus in London, Aveling sent his book, *The Student's Darwin*, begging forgiveness lest he had pressed the views of a great scientist farther than was permissible. Darwin replied coolly that he had no objection to people differing from him or carrying his arguments farther than he would consider 'safe'. Aveling felt emboldened. In September, during the Congress of the International Federation of Freethinkers in London, he telegraphed Darwin, requesting an interview for himself and Büchner, the congress president. This was granted, and the next day over lunch Darwin came face to face with his thirty year old *alter ego*, the freethinker he had long since feared others might mistake him for if they knew or suspected his thoughts.[13]

After the meal the two guests retired with their host and his son Francis to the study, where they lit cigarettes and fell to talking about religion. The subject, Aveling later insisted (1883, pp. 4–5), was chosen by Darwin.

> Almost the first thing he said was, 'Why do you call yourselves Atheists?' . . . Very respectfully the explanation was given, that we were Atheists because there was no evidence of deity, because the invention of a name was not an explanation of phaenomena, because the whole of man's knowledge was of a natural order, and only when ignorance closed in his onward path was the supernatural invoked. It was pointed out that the Greek *a* was privative, not negative; that whilst we did not commit the folly of god-denial, we avoided with equal care the folly of god-assertion: that as god was not proven, we were without god (*atheoi*) and by consequence were with hope in this world, and in this world alone. As we spoke, it was evident from the change of light in the eyes that always met ours so frankly, that a new conception was arising in his mind. He had imagined until then that we were deniers of god, and he found the order of thought that was ours differing in no essential from his own. For with point after point of our argument he agreed; statement on statement that was made he endorsed, saying finally: 'I am with you in thought, but I should prefer the word Agnostic to the word Atheist'.
>
> Upon this the suggestion was made that, after all, 'Agnostic' was

[13] The Darwin-Aveling correspondence of August 1881 is in the Darwin Archive, 202.

> but 'Atheist' writ respectable, and 'Atheist' was only 'Agnostic' writ aggressive. To say that one did not know was the verbal equivalent of saying that one was destitute of the god-idea, whilst at the same time a sop was thrown to the Cerberus of society by the adoption of a name less determined and uncompromising. At this he smiled and asked: 'Why should you be so aggressive? Is anything gained by trying to force these new ideas upon the mass of mankind? It is all very well for educated, cultured, thoughtful people; but are the masses yet ripe for it?' Then we asked him whether the same questions he now asked of us had not been addressed to him about the years 1859–60, when his immortal 'Origin of Species' first saw the light. Many at that time had thought a greater wisdom would have been shown in only enunciating the revolutionary truths of Natural and Sexual Selection to the judicious few. Many had, as of old, dreaded the open declaration of truth to the multitudes. New ideas are always at first regarded as only for the study. Danger is feared if they are proclaimed abroad on the house-tops, and discussed in market-place and home. But he, happily for humanity, had by the gentle, irresistible power of reason, forced his new ideas upon the mass of people. And the masses had been found ripe for it. Had he kept silence, the tremendous strides taken by human thought during the last twenty-one years would have been shorn of their fair proportions, perhaps had hardly been made at all. His own illustrious example was encouragement, was for a command to every thinker to make known to all his fellows that which he believed to be the truth.

Little did Aveling know of Darwin's protracted silence, for exactly twenty-one years, before the *Origin of Species* appeared, a period in which he shared his ideas only with the 'judicious few'. 'His own illustrious example' was in reality no encouragement at all to crude pugnacious Secularists, whose urge to move the masses arose from social and religious persecution rather than professional ambition. Darwin's happy family, his attentive servants, his imposing parson's-pile on the verge of a quiet country parish — all that met Aveling's eye that day in September 1881 disqualified his host as a beacon light to radicals. If Darwin was an agnostic primarily because he lacked aggression, he lacked aggression primarily because all his life he had got on comfortably, cushioned by hereditary wealth. The price he paid for freethought was an upset stomach, less by far in social terms than the losses sustained by any of Grant, Taylor, Carlile, Holyoake, Besant, or Bradlaugh.

On 19 April 1882 Darwin died peacefully at home. In London Bradlaugh was fighting Tory-Christian efforts to bankrupt him and pursuing the deputy sergeant-at-arms for assault. G. W. Foote, a recent convert from the British Secular Union, was trumpeting Bradlaugh's cause alongside blasphemous cartoons as editor of a new paper, *The Freethinker* (Herrick, 1982). And Galton, Darwin's cousin, was pulling the levers of power to commemorate good breeding and magnify his scientific priesthood: he had the President of the Royal Society ask the Darwin family if they would consent to a burial in Westminster Abbey. After some collective heart-searching they agreed; meanwhile Huxley and the president, with help from Canon Farrar, obtained the 'cordial acquiescence' of the dean. On Wednesday 26 April, at high noon, Darwin's body was borne mightily up the nave by Huxley, Wallace, and other dignitaries, through the Choir where Spencer sat, and finally to its resting place a few feet from the monument to Sir Isaac Newton. The procession was led by members of the family, including a son who had already been elected a Fellow of the Royal Society, two sons who would eventually receive that honour, and of course Galton, an F.R.S. Among the pall bearers were past, present, and future presidents of the Royal Society; in the procession followed an unprecedented assemblage of distinguished scientific men. It was their apotheosis as much as Darwin's. It was the rising generation reached full stature. It was the young reformers reached old age. It was the Trojan Horse of naturalism entering the fortress of the Church (Moore, 1982).

Papers and pulpits alike were full of Darwinian fervour, the very pens and mouths that railed at Bradlaugh and would soon pillory Foote for blasphemy. *The Freethinker* (7 May 1882, p. 148) characteristically found 'something almost ghoul-like in the twaddle of the clergy over Darwin's tomb . . . Now Darwin is dead the clergy put on a brazen look, and shout "He was with us all the while"'. Aveling in the *National Reformer* (30 April 1882, p. 339) reported the truth as he believed he had received it at first hand: 'All Freethinkers hail him as a brother and an ally. Not wholly consciously to himself he was, and will ever be, working with our cause'. Only after Foote had spent a year in prison, in 1883–4, and Darwin's three-volume *Life and Letters* had appeared in 1887, did the truth begin to dawn. The 'brother' and 'ally' faded. 'Had he gone more into the world', Foote complained in *Darwin on God* (1889, p. 64), '. . . he might have sympathised more with the aggressive attitude of those who challenge Theology *in toto* as the historic enemy of liberty and progress.'

Harsher but in many respects more accurate as an assessment of Darwin's cultured irreligion was the peroration in Oswald Dawson's *Indictment of Darwin* (1888, pp. 35–6), published by the Freethought Publishing Company almost as if it were Bradlaugh's personal revenge:

> Mr. Darwin was not purely and simply in religious matters a simpleton. He was a hypocrite and he knew it; he tried to smother his qualms . . . For he saw that the black beasts and their wood were no mere relics of the past. He feared, he propitiated, he won. And his

> body was placed within the four walls of Westminster Abbey in London — not scattered to the four winds of the Campo di Fiori in Rome. And the black beasts sang his praise.

'He feared, he propitiated, he won' — just so. But Darwin was no hypocrite. His attitude stood to reason; it made eminent common sense. Agnosticism was just the latest fashion in which he cloaked his lifelong religious reticence. To please his father, to shield his wife, to be well thought of by his peers, he could never become a radical. Nor, however, could his new creed, whether theistic or agnostic, countenance barefaced 'unbelief'. Like other scientific professionals, Darwin won out by fitting in. Agnosticism was the bulwark of the metaphysical 'neutrality' of science. Lower-class radicals bore the brunt of the attack on attitudes that Darwin and his allies were slower to espouse, quicker to conceal. It could hardly have been otherwise. The radicals had everything to gain; the scientists had much to lose. And in the end, when the radicals had done their work, silence was their thanks. To the strains of sacred anthems, Darwinian irreligion was swallowed up in respectability.

After Darwin's death — although, of course, not because of it — Secularism under Bradlaugh and Foote went into permanent decline. Bradlaugh's parliamentary struggle, punctuated by Foote's imprisonment, was the high-water mark of the movement. By 1884 the National Secular Society had about 100 branches nationwide. Then came victory and the membership began to fall. Bradlaugh died in 1891 at the age of fifty-eight; within ten years the number of branches had receded to half their peak. After Foote's death in 1915 only five branches remained, all of them in London (Royle, 1980, pp. 36–44, 132–6, 333–4). Secularism, like religious movements generally, depended inordinately for its success on thrusting leadership and persecution. Failing these factors, it was doomed.

Or so it would seem. For accompanying Foote's lacklustre presidency and the accession of public tolerance, the moral nerve of freethinking artisans and petit-bourgeois individualists was being co-opted by endeavours that stressed broadly social rather than narrowly irreligious objectives. By the 1890s the 'new Liberalism', the 'new unionism', and the Labour Party itself had recruited Nonconformist preachers and Secularist propagandists: Republican atheists were rubbing shoulders with radical Anglo-Catholics in public demonstrations of solidarity. The Broad Church of British socialism had grown to accommodate the interests of a multitude of sects. Secularism, therefore, like conventional religion, was secularized by something more than arguments and ideas. A new working class had emerged in an age of economic crisis. While the back-sliding majority, be they nominally atheist or nominally Christian, fell prey to new diversions — league football, the music hall, the *Daily Mail* — a dissident minority was reconstituted to challenge the ruling ideas by which the majority lived. Their challenge, like that of working-class radicals and their allies in the mid-nineteenth century, took on a distinctly moral tone. To many, however, the 'old creed' that *they* now confronted was called 'Social Darwinism'.

BIBLIOGRAPHY

G. A. Aldred (1942) *The Devil's Chaplain: The Story of the Rev. Robert Taylor, M.A., M.R.C.S. (1784–1844)*, Glasgow, Strickland Press.

*W. L. Arnstein (1965) *The Bradlaugh Case: A Study in Late Victorian Opinion and Politics*, Oxford, Clarendon Press.

E. B. Aveling (1883) *The Religious Views of Charles Darwin*, Freethought Publishing Co.

N. Barlow (ed.) (1958) *The Autobiography of Charles Darwin, with Original Omissions Restored*, New York, W. W. Norton & Co.

S. Bell (1981) 'George Henry Lewes: A Man of His Time', *Journal of the History of Biology*, Vol. 14, pp. 277–98.

H. B. Bonner (1895) *Charles Bradlaugh: A Record of His Life and Work*, 2 Vols., T. Fisher Unwin.

*A. Briggs (1960) *The Age of Improvement, 1783–1867*, Longman, Green & Co.

*S. Budd (1977) *Varieties of Unbelief: Atheists and Agnostics in English Society, 1850–1960*, Heinemann.

F. P. Cobbe (1904) *Life of Frances Power Cobbe As Told By Herself*, Swan Sonnenschein & Co.

N. G. Coley and V. M. D. Hall (eds.) (1980) *Darwin to Einstein: Primary Sources on Science and Belief*, Longman/Open University Press.

R. Colp Jr. (1976) 'The contacts of Charles Darwin with Edward Aveling and Karl Marx', *Annals of Science*, Vol. 33, pp. 387–94.

R. Colp Jr. (1977) *To Be an Invalid: The Illness of Charles Darwin*, Chicago, University of Chicago Press.

R. Colp Jr. (1982) 'The myth of the Darwin-Marx letter', *History of Political Economy*, Vol. 14, pp. 461–82.

R. Colp Jr. (1986) '"Confessing a Murder": Darwin's first revelations about transmutation', *Isis*, Vol. 77, pp. 9–32.

R. Cooter (1984) *The Cultural Meaning of Popular Science: Phrenology and the Organization of Consent in Nineteenth-Century Britain*, Cambridge, Cambridge University Press.

The Correspondence of Charles Darwin, F. Burkhardt and S. Smith (eds.), Vol 1, 1821–1836; Vol. 2, 1836–1843, Cambridge, Cambridge University Press, 1985/1986.

C. Darwin (1874) *The Descent of Man, and Selection in Relation to Sex*, second edn., John Murray.

F. Darwin (1887) *The Life and Letters of Charles Darwin, Including an Autobiographical Chapter*, 3 Vols., John Murray.

F. Darwin and A. C. Seward (1903) *More Letters of Charles Darwin: A Record of His Work in a Series of Hitherto Unpublished Letters*, 2 Vols., John Murray.

O. Dawson (1888) *An Indictment of Darwin*, Freethought Publishing Co.

G. De Beer (ed.) (1958) *Evolution by Natural Selection*, Cambridge, Cambridge University Press.

A. Desmond (1984) 'Robert E. Grant: the social predicament of a pre-Darwinian Transmutationist', *Journal of the History of Biology*, Vol. 17, pp. 189–223.

A. Desmond (1985) 'Darwin among the gentry', *London Review of Books*, 23 May, pp. 9–10.

*A. Desmond (1987) 'Artisan resistance and evolution in Britain, 1819–1848', *Osiris*, Vol. 3, pp. 77–110.

F. Erskine (1987) 'Darwin in Context: The London Years, 1837–1842', Ph.D. thesis, Open University.

L. S. Feuer (1975) 'Is the Darwin-Marx correspondence authentic?', *Annals of Science*, Vol. 32, pp. 1–12.

G. W. Foote (1889) *Darwin on God*, Progressive Publishing Co.

F. Galton (n.d.) *Inquiries into Human Faculty and Its Development*, J. M. Dent.

C. L. F. Gohdes (1931) *The Periodicals of American Transcendentalism*, Durham (NC), Duke University Press.

D. Goodway (1982) *London Chartism, 1838–1848*, Cambridge, Cambridge University Press.

H. E. Gruber and P. H. Barrett (1974) *Darwin on Man: A Psychological Study of Scientific Creativity*, Wildwood House.

J. Hart (1977) 'Religion and social control in the mid-nineteenth century' in A. P. Donajgrodzki (ed.) *Social Control in Nineteenth-Century Britain*, pp. 108–37, Croom Helm.

R. J. Helmstadter (1979) 'The Nonconformist conscience' in P. Marsh (ed.) *The Conscience of the Victorian State*, pp. 135–71, Syracuse (NY), Syracuse University Press.

J. Herrick (1982) *Vision and Realism: A Hundred Years of the 'Freethinker'*, G. W. Foote & Co.

*T. W. Heyck (1982) *The Transformation of Intellectual Life in Victorian England*, Croom Helm.

G. Himmelfarb (1968) *Darwin and the Darwinian Revolution*, revised edn., New York, W. W. Norton & Co.

*E. J. Hobsbawm (1969) *Industry and Empire*, Harmondsworth, Penguin Books.

L. Huxley (1903) *Life and Letters of Thomas Henry Huxley*, 3 Vols., Macmillan & Co.

T. H. Huxley (1893) *Method and Results*, Macmillan & Co.

T. H. Huxley (1974) 'Notebook: "Thoughts and Doings"' in G. De Beer (ed.) *Charles Darwin and T. H. Huxley: Autobiographies*, pp. 91–9, Oxford, Oxford University Press.

L. S. Jacyna (1981) 'The physiology of mind, the unity of nature, and the moral order in Victorian thought', *British Journal for the History of Science*, Vol. 14, pp. 109–32.

G. Jones (1980) *Social Darwinism and English Thought: The Interaction between Biological and Social Theory*, Brighton, Harvester Press.

W. Kent (1932) *London for Heretics*, Watts & Co.

B. Kuklick (1977) *The Rise of American Philosophy: Cambridge, Massachusetts, 1860–1930*, New Haven (CT), Yale University Press.

*B. Lightman (1987) *The Origins of Agnosticism: Victorian Unbelief and the Limits of Knowledge*, Baltimore (MD), Johns Hopkins University Press.

J. R. Lucas (1979) 'Wilberforce and Huxley: a legendary encounter', *Historical Journal*, Vol. 22, pp. 313–30.

*R. Manvell (1976) *The Trial of Annie Besant and Charles Bradlaugh*, Elek/Pemberton.

J. McCabe (1908) *Life and Letters of George Jacob Holyoake*, 2 Vols., Watts & Co.

J. R. Moore (1979) *The Post-Darwinian Controversies: A Study of the Protestant Struggle to Come to Terms with Darwin in Great Britain and America, 1870–1900*, Cambridge, Cambridge University Press.

J. R. Moore (1982) 'Charles Darwin lies in Westminster Abbey', *Biological Journal of the Linnean Society*, Vol. 17, pp. 97–113.

*J. R. Moore (1985) 'Darwin of Down: the evolutionist as squarson-naturalist' in D. Kohn (ed.) *The Darwinian Heritage*, pp. 435–81, Princeton (NJ), Princeton University Press.

J. R. Moore (1986) 'Geologists and interpreters of Genesis in the nineteenth century' in D. C. Lindberg and R. L. Numbers (eds.) *God and Nature: Historical Essays on the Encounter between Christianity and Science*, pp. 322–50, Berkeley, University of California Press.

*J. R. Moore (1989) 'Of love and death: why Darwin "gave up Christianity"' in J. R. Moore (ed.) *History, Humanity, and Evolution: Essays for John C. Greene*, New York, Cambridge University Press.

*H. R. Murphy (1955) 'The ethical revolt against Christian orthodoxy in early Victorian England', *American Historical Review*, Vol. 60, pp. 800–17.

E. F. Paul (1979) *Moral Revolution and Economic Science: The Demise of Laissez-faire in Nineteenth-Century British Political Economy*, Westport (CT), Greenwood Press.

G. Rowell (1974) *Hell and the Victorians: A Study of the Nineteenth-Century Theological Controversies Concerning Eternal Punishment and the Future Life*, Oxford, Clarendon Press.

E. Royle (1971) *Radical Politics, 1790–1900: Religion and Unbelief*, Longman.

*E. Royle (1974) *Victorian Infidels: The Origins of the British Secularist Movement, 1791–1866*, Manchester, Manchester University Press.

E. Royle (1979) 'Taylor, Robert (1784–1844)' in J. O. Baylen and N. J. Grossman (eds.) *Biographical Dictionary of Modern British Radicals*, Vol. 1, pp. 467–70, Brighton, Harvester Press.

*E. Royle (1980) *Radicals, Secularists, and Republicans: Popular Freethought in Britain, 1866–1915*, Manchester, Manchester University Press.

M. J. S. Rudwick (1982) 'Charles Darwin in London: the integration of public and private science', *Isis*, Vol. 73, pp. 186–206.

M. Ruse (1979) *The Darwinian Revolution: Science Red in Tooth and Claw*, Chicago, University of Chicago Press.

S. Shapin (1979) 'Homo Phrenologicus: anthropological perspectives on a historical problem' in B. Barnes and S. Shapin (eds.) *Natural Order: Historical Studies of Scientific Culture*, pp. 41–72, Beverly Hills (CA), Sage Publications.

P. R. Sloan (1985) 'Darwin's invertebrate program, 1826–1836: preconditions for transformism' in D. Kohn (ed.) *The Darwinian Heritage*, pp. 71–120, Princeton (NJ), Princeton University Press.

F. B. Smith (1967) 'The atheist mission, 1840–1900' in R. Robson (ed.) *Ideas and Institutions of Victorian Britain: Essays in Honour of George Kitson Clark*, pp. 205–35, G. Bell & Sons.

W. S. Smith (1967) *The London Heretics, 1870–1914*, Constable.

F. S. Taylor (1949) 'Geology changes the outlook' in *Ideas and Beliefs of the Victorians*, pp. 186–96, Sylvan Press.

R. Taylor (1842) *The Devil's Pulpit, Containing Twenty-three Astronomico-Theological Discourses . . . with a Sketch of His Life*, new edn., W. Dugdale.

D. Thomson (1950) *England in the Nineteenth Century (1815–1914)*, Harmondsworth, Penguin Books.

D. Tribe (1971) *President Charles Bradlaugh, M.P.*, Elek.

J. Tulloch (1885) *Movements of Religious Thought in Britain during the Nineteenth Century*, Longman, Green & Co.

F. M. Turner (1974a) *Between Science and Religion: The Reaction to Scientific Naturalism in Late Victorian England*, New Haven (CT), Yale University Press.

F. M. Turner (1974b) 'Rainfall, plagues, and the Prince of Wales: a chapter in the conflict of religion and science', *Journal of British Studies*, Vol. 13, pp. 46–65.

F. M. Turner (1974–5) 'Victorian scientific naturalism and Thomas Carlyle', *Victorian Studies*, Vol. 18, pp. 325–43.

F. M. Turner (1978) 'The Victorian conflict between science and religion: a professional dimension', *Isis*, Vol. 69, pp. 356–76.

J. Tyndall (1899) *Fragments of Science: A Series of Detached Essays, Addresses, and Reviews*, 2 Vols., New York, D. Appleton & Co.

S. Warren (1943) *American Freethought, 1860–1914*, New York, Columbia University Press.

*J. H. Wiener (1983) *Radicalism and Freethought in Nineteenth-Century Britain: The Life of Richard Carlile*, Westport (CT), Greenwood Press.

R. Yeo (1984–5) 'Science and intellectual authority in mid-nineteenth-century Britain: Robert Chambers and "Vestiges of the Natural History of Creation"', *Victorian Studies*, Vol. 28, pp. 5–31.

G. M. Young (1969) *Victorian England: Portrait of an Age*, London, Oxford Paperbacks.

R. M. Young (1980) 'Natural theology, Victorian periodicals, and the fragmentation of a common context' in C. Chant and J. Fauvel (eds.) *Darwin to Einstein: Historical Studies on Science and Belief*, pp. 69–107, Longman/Open University Press.

INDEX